Global problems and world order

Global problems and world order

R. D. McKinlay and R. Little

Frances Pinter (Publishers), London

© R. D. McKinlay and R. Little 1986

First published in Great Britain in 1986 by
Frances Pinter (Publishers) Limited
25 Floral Street, London WC2E 9DS

British Library Cataloguing in Publication Data
McKinlay, R. D.
   Global problems and world order.
   1. International organization
   I. Title   II. Little, R.
   341.2   JX1954

ISBN 0-903804-46-8

Typeset by Folio Photosetting, Bristol
Printed by SRP Ltd., Exeter

Contents

Preface   1

Part I: Introduction
1: A conceptualization of order   8

Part II: Models of world order
2: The liberal model   24
3: The socialist model   54
4: The realist model   71

Part III: Global economic problems and solutions
5: Liberal international economic problems and solutions   91
6: Socialist international economic problems and solutions   122
7: Realist international economic problems and solutions   147

Part IV: Global security problems and solutions
8: Liberal international security problems and solutions   172
9: Socialist international security problems and solutions   204
10: Realist international security problems and solutions   234

Part V: Conclusion
11: Reflections on world order   263

Index   275

Preface

Problems become global when their solutions cannot be achieved within the boundary of the state; with the growth of such problems, world order deteriorates.[1] When thinking about global problems, most people experience a profound sense of frustration because of the persistent failure to implement seemingly obvious solutions which would dramatically increase the level of world order. In an ordered world, for example, the superpowers would negotiate and bring the dangerous and counter-productive arms race to a halt; the rich nations would release their massive stocks of food to aid the starving populations in the poor nations; quotas would be introduced to prevent stocks of fish from being depleted; and tariffs would be eliminated to permit a free flow of trade. Since the solutions to so many global problems seem to bring mutual benefits to all the parties concerned, the failure to implement the necessary changes often seems inexplicable except in terms of the malevolence, vested interest or incompetence of world leaders.

In the academic literature on world order, the explanations for the failure to solve major global problems are generally less personalized. Instead, the failure is frequently attributed to the existing structure of the international arena. It is argued that many global problems cannot be solved until the present international arena has been transformed. The current conditions of disorder are contrasted with the world order which will materialize in the future once a new and preferred set of structures have been set in place.

These assessments are premised on the assumption that there is an agreed set of global problems and solutions and a common understanding of what constitutes world order. We hope to show that such an assumption seriously underestimates the contentious nature of world order and that it fails to come to terms with the host of divergent and conflicting assessments of global problems and solutions which consistently appear in popular and academic literature. The lack of consensus is impossible to ignore. In a discussion about how to deal with nuclear weapons, for example, one commentator concluded: 'Thoughtful people disagree about whether arms control is part of the solution or part of the problem.'[2] Such an assessment can be extended to virtually every aspect of international relations. Foreign aid, import quotas, military intervention, as well as arms control, are just a few illustrations of the many international activities which are viewed by some commentators as problems and by others as solutions. For some analysts, it is inconceivable that the donation of foreign aid could be criticized or that the resort to military intervention could be condoned: aid is a solution and intervention is a problem. Yet the fact remains that foreign aid is seen by other analysts to be a root cause of the poverty in many poor nations and military intervention is often considered to be the only effective means of promoting democracy: aid is a problem and intervention is a solution. The central purpose of this book is not to resolve such disputes but to account for why they arise and to explain why there is no way that such disputes can be resolved.

To accomplish these objectives a comparative approach to world order is developed in this book to examine and account for the existence of competing conceptions of global problems and solutions in the fields of international economics and security. Only by developing this comparative framework is it possible to make sense of the wide range of contending assessments of global problems and solutions. On the basis of our conception of order, we are able to link problems to solutions, examine the nature of their relationship, and distinguish one set of problems and solutions from another in a clear and logical manner.

There are three reasons why order seems to provide a relevant and economic organizational concept to account for the contending assessments of global problems and solutions. First, there is a conventional and well-established link. Order denotes an absence of problems. If a mechanic indicates, for example, that a car is in good working order, then it is assumed that the car is problem free. Second, it is also widely acknowledged that there can be mutually incompatible conceptions of order. Tucker argues, for example, that what may 'appear as order to one observer may appear as disorder to another' and Clark illustrates this point by indicating that 'what is order for the policeman may not be order for the anarchist'.[3] Finally, the conception of order constitutes a common denominator in the extensive literature on global problems. The competing conceptions of global problems and solutions can all be related to divergent conceptions of order.

There have, however, been some reservations expressed about using the concept of order as an organizational device. Although reference is frequently made to order in the study and practice of international relations, there have been few successful attempts to operationalize the concept. Indeed, for a variety of reasons, the concept has often been considered unsatisfactory. In the first place, order is seen to have acquired so many connotations that it becomes arbitrary to select a particular way of denoting order. Because of its multifarious meanings, order has been described as 'ambiguous',[4] 'dangerously simplistic',[5] and 'elusive'.[6]

In the second place, it has been argued that the concept of order has degenerated and its essential meaning has been irredeemably corrupted. The idea of order, it is argued, has become 'a disreputable one. At best it is taken to indicate a mindless adherence to the *status quo*'.[7] In the same vein, it has also been argued that because political leaders have so frequently used the idea to legitimize their policies 'paradoxically the success of world order language and imagery has been responsible for its growing disutility'.[8]

A third difficulty with using order to identify a problem-free world is that the concept is not always considered in a positive light. Situations which are highly distasteful may still be characterized in terms of order. It has been observed, for example, that

> the extermination of four million Jews and two million gypsies in the concentration camp gas chambers of Hitler's Germany was a highly ordered and structural business. Victims were not killed by frenzied and anarchic savages. They were slaughtered on a terrifying scale by ordinary members of a state machinery in a very rule-governed and structured manner.[9]

When reference is made to order, therefore, it is not possible to make any inferences about how it is being evaluated.

A final reservation about using order as an organizational concept is that, in the existing literature, it generally precipitates confusion when it is employed. It is far from obvious what is meant, for example, when one analyst asserts that world order is 'sustained by the co-operation of the superpowers'[10] while another indicates that the superpowers 'serve as sources, however unequally, of disorder'.[11] It is unclear whether these two analysts have different conceptions of order or different assessments of reality.

Such reservations about the concept of order, however, could easily be applied to any central concept in the social sciences which taps a fundamental and ubiquitous feature of the social world. Order represents a crucial dimension of any social setting and is too important to be ignored. It is, however, not only social scientists who are interested in the concept of order. The idea has also always played a vital role in the natural sciences and order is a concept which has been extensively drawn upon by natural scientists.[12] Moreover, in past centuries, scientists such as Boyle have made strenuous attempts to establish a common identity between order in the natural and social worlds.[13] For the natural scientists, order, in its most generic or nomothetic form, is associated with structure or pattern, and the level of order identified in any setting is determined by the endurance and complexity of the pattern. More complex and enduring patterns of behaviour denote a higher degree of order. So a crystal, for example, such as a diamond, displays a much greater level of order than laughing gas. The atoms of the diamond are bound together in three-dimensional lattices which severely limit their motion. The bonds can only be broken by the exertion of a considerable amount of energy. By contrast, the molecules which make up laughing gas can move in any direction with a wide variety of speeds, so that when exposed to the atmosphere, they immediately disperse. The molecular pattern of behaviour associated with laughing gas, therefore, is less patterned and less enduring than the diamond's atomic structure and, as a consequence, displays a lower degree of order.

Social scientists have also thought of order in terms of enduring patterns of behaviour, making it possible to compare levels of order in different social contexts.[14] For example, the players in a professional game of football can be considered to display a higher level of order than the crowd of spectators. The players' behaviour is more complex and enduring since their contact with each other persists before and after the game. But there is an additional dimension to social activity which extends beyond the conception of order as a pattern. Social behaviour is purposeful or goal-orientated and, as a consequence, it can be evaluated in terms of its goal. When a football match 'degenerates' into a brawl, for example, the result can be defined as disordered, not because there has been a disintegration of patterned behaviour — even a brawl reflects a distinctive pattern of behaviour — but because the new pattern of behaviour vitiates the established goal of playing football. Social order, therefore, needs to be considered in terms of both a pattern and a goal.

This formulation of order provides the basis for the comparative framework which is developed in this book. There are, we argue, divergent conceptions of world order which can be differentiated in terms of their goals. Problems arise when a goal is not being achieved and, as a consequence, proponents of different goals will identify different problems and advocate different solutions. The conceptual framework for this comparative approach to world order and global problems is elaborated in Part I of the book.

In the second part of the book, we provide the substantive bases for our analysis of global problems and solutions by developing three competing models of world order. The models are derived from the three most important ideologies to have emerged over the centuries in European social thought — liberalism, socialism and conservatism. Liberalism and socialism, however, need to be distinguished from conservatism. The first two ideologies directly provide very coherent and sophisticated accounts of how society can be structured and organized. Liberals argue that society should be structured so as to maximize freedom, while socialists are concerned to promote structures in society which will optimize the level of equality. Advocates of both these ideologies have always recognized that their ideas can only completely come to fruition when they have been adopted on a world-wide basis. As a consequence, just as liberals and socialists have very different and distinctive views of domestic order, so their views of world order also diverge sharply. Liberalisms and socialism, therefore, provide the substantive base for two of the models of world order developed in this study.

It is necessary, however, to distinguish conservatism from the other two ideologies because it cannot be associated with a distinctive set of structures and goals. Conservatives, in practice, are primarily interested in ensuring that the established structures and goals of an existing society are retained. As Seliger observes: 'the word conservatism does not convey how a society should be organized. Even though conservatism means "the articulated systematic, theoretical resistance to change", in different concrete cases, conservatism amounts to defending different political systems.'[15] In the context of international relations, realism can be considered to provide a 'concrete case' of conservatism because an essential element of realism is the need to maintain the existing society of states and realists are also prone to look back to earlier eras with a sense of nostalgia — another hallmark of conservatism. Although realism is an ideology that has purely international connotations, like liberalism and socialism, it too has a long and distinguished pedigree. Realism, therefore, provides the basis for the third substantive model of world order.

In Parts III and IV, these models are employed to identify competing sets of problems and solutions in the contemporary world. The analysis demonstrates that each model generates a distinctive set of problems and solutions and they account for the emergence of differences. Part III focuses on the world economy and Part IV focuses on international security. In Part V, the implications of this approach to world order are examined.

The overall objective of this book, therefore, is not to provide a profile of a preferred world order, nor to list the most pressing global problems in the world today, nor to provide an empirical analysis of the contemporary world order. There is already an extensive literature which performs these tasks. Instead, the intention is:

- to provide a nomothetic concept which permits a comparison of competing views of order;
- to establish, on the basis of this concept, three competing models of world order;
- to deploy these models of world order to identify and provide solutions to the major global economic and security problems.

The book, therefore, seeks to find a configuration which accounts for the existing contradictions and confusions surrounding the study of world order.

Although the authors accept joint responsibility for the structure and content of this book, the individual chapters were written largely independently. R.D. McKinlay formulated the concept of order in Chapter 1, along with the models of liberalism and socialism, developed in Chapters 2 and 3. He also wrote the chapters in Part III on international economics. R. Little originally conceived the three competing perspectives on world order and developed the model of realism in Chapter 4. In addition he wrote the Preface and the chapters in Part IV on international security. The conclusion was written jointly.

Notes

1. Throughout this book, 'global', 'world', and 'international' are used interchangeably. In each case, the word implies relations across state boundaries.
2. R.J. Worlsey, 'The Politics of Vulnerability: 1980-1983', *Foreign Affairs*, **62**, 1984, 805-19, p. 819.
3. R. Tucker, *The Inequality of Nations*, New York, Basic Books, 1977, p. 75; I. Clark, *Reform and Resistance in the International Order*, Cambridge, Cambridge University Press, 1980, p. 11.
4. C.S. Gray, *Strategic Studies: A Critical Assessment*, London, Aldwych Press, 1982, p. 75.
5. I. Pogany, 'The Legal Foundations of World Order', *Yearbook of World Affairs*, **37**, 1983, 277-91.
6. R.A. Falk, *This Endangered Planet*, New York, Vintage Books, 1971, p. 215.
7. R.J. Vincent, 'The idea of Concert and International Order', *Yearbook of World Afairs*, **29**, 1975, 34-55, p. 35.
8. F. Ajami, 'World Order: The Question of Ideology', *Alternatives*, **6**, 1980, 473-85, p. 476.
9. See P. Marsh et al., *The Rules of Disorder*, London, Routledge, 1978, p. 116.
10. H. Bull, 'World Order and the Super Powers' in C. Holbraad (ed.), *Superpowers and World Order*, Canberra, Australian National University Press, 1971, p. 142.
11. A.L. Burns, 'Introduction', to Holbraad, *Superpowers and World Order*, p. xxi.
12. J. Needham has discussed how natural scientists have developed two competing conceptions of natural order. According to the physicists, order is decreasing, while

according to biologists order is increasing. He argues that we need to assess this difference because 'our ideas on these questions have very marked and sometimes unrealized effects on our social behaviour' (*Moulds of Understanding: A Pattern of Natural Philosophy*, London, George Allen & Unwin, 1976, p. 182).

13. In the history of science, it is now being shown how scientists' views of the natural order are related to their view of the social order. See S. Shapin, 'Social Uses of Science' in G.S. Rousseau and Roy Porter, *The Ferment of Knowledge: Historiography of Eighteenth Century Science*, Cambridge, Cambridge University Press, 1980 and, in particular, J.R. Jacob, 'The Ideological Origins of Robert Boyle's Natural Philosophy', *Journal of European Studies*, **11**, 1972, 1–21.
14. See, for example, D.T. Campbell, 'Common Fate, Similarity and Other Indices of Aggregates of Persons as Social Entities', *Behavioural Science*, **3**, 1958, 14–25.
15. Seliger is quoting from S.P. Huntington, 'Conservatism as an Ideology', *American Political Science Review*, **51**, 1957, 454–73 in *Ideology and Politics*, London, George Allen & Unwin, 1976, p. 92.

PART I: INTRODUCTION

1   A conceptualization of order

A preoccupation with order is ubiquitous. Politicians often campaign for law and order; teachers ask for more order in students' essays; children are scolded for the absence of order in their rooms; revolutionaries fight against the ills of the existing social order. Although what is understood by order in each of these contexts is very different, we have little difficulty in comprehending what is meant. More importantly, it is not difficult to identify a number of common denominators running through this apparent diversity.

First, there seems to be a preconception of what order entails. To the politician, order is likely to be associated, in the law and order context, with a lower level of crime or violence. Parents are probably associating order with clothes or toys being in designated places. Teachers are likely to be thinking in terms of clear arguments. The revolutionary may be committed to the eradication of inequities in society.

A second common denominator is that the preconception of order appears to be used to identify disorder. There is a disorder in the child's room when toys are not in their prescribed place, and there is disorder in an essay when the discussion fails to correspond to an established line of argument. Disorder is revealed, therefore, when there is a mismatch between an existing state of affairs and a preconception of what ought to exist.

Third, order is presumed to be desirable and disorder to be undesirable. The politician considers disorder, reflected in violence, to be reprehensible; the revolutionary deplores the inequities in society; parents approve of the order in a room where everything is in its proper place; the teacher finds it satisfying to read a coherently argued essay.

Fourth, each of the examples suggests that where there is disorder a prescription for the restoration of order can also readily be identified. The politician may call for an increase in the size of the police force; the teacher may advise a rearrangement of the argument; parents may insist that toys be placed in their correct position; the revolutionary may demand the establishment of a new form of social organization to reduce inequities.

A final common denominator is that order is never uncontentious. Attempts by one party to achieve order or redress a disorder can often precipitate conflict and controversy with another. Students can argue that there has been a failure to appreciate their line of argument; children may insist that they have their own ideas about the appropriate place for their toys; an attempt by revolutionaries to achieve their conception of order might well precipitate the very actions that politicians, calling for law and order, are endeavouring to eliminate. Not only is the conception of order contentious, therefore, it is also the case that competing conceptions of order may prove to be mutually incompatible.

Despite the existence of these common denominators, it is often asserted that it is not possible to distil a common conception of order. One variant of this position is that nothing is added to the meaning of a statement when violence is referred to as disorder, or a tidy room is described in terms of order, or expanding a police force and tightening up an argument are seen as ways of generating order. Since comprehension is not aided, then the concept of order effectively becomes redundant. A second variant does attach more utility to the concept of order but characterizes order in relativistic or idiographic terms. Order and disorder are seen as essentially empty concepts until such time as they are given meaning by the specific circumstances in which the terms are applied. Order can indeed be associated with a tidy room or the absence of violence. The critical point, however, is that the meaning of the concept changes with the specific circumstances in which it is applied.

We hold the redundancy and idiographic objections to a common conceptualization of order to be quite unsatisfactory. Our principal objection to the redundancy position is that it totally ignores the type of common denominators to which we have pointed. These common denominators do not of course dispel the substantial diversity of settings in which order may be considered. What they do indicate is that we are dealing with a number of non-trivial properties which it may be desirable to accommodate in a common conceptualization. Additionally, the idiographic position inhibits any comparative analysis. As long as order is relativistically tied to particular settings, then it is impossible to identify order or compare order in two different situations. In practice, however, we regularly perform both these tasks and this ability not only indicates that the idea of order is firmly established in the way we analyse the world, but also that in so doing we draw upon a general or nomothetic conceptualization of order.

The combination of widely different settings in which order can be considered together with a number of non-trivial common denominators pushes us in the direction of believing that a common conceptualization of order can be developed. Such a nomothetic definition would, however, have to be expressed initially in abstract terms, so that we could maximize common properties and permit comparative evaluation. On the other hand, if this abstract conceptualization is to be at all useful, then it must be capable of being translated into substantive terms such that it can be applied across the diversity of settings in which one may care to analyse order.

With these prerequisites in mind, we turn now to develop a nomothetic conceptualization of order. This necessitates the establishment of two distinct, albeit related, conceptualizations: one relating order to pattern and the other to goal satisfaction.

Order as pattern

In the first instance, order can be identified by the existence of a pattern, with disorder being manifested in terms of deviation from that pattern. Order, as pattern, may be illustrated by considering an array of numbers such as (1, 1, 2, 3, 5, 8, 13, . . .). The order in this array is that any number (except the first two) is the sum of the two preceding numbers. Were any number to be changed, then we would have a disorder, or deviation from the pattern. The order or pattern would evidently be restored by changing the number back to its original form. From this simple example some important properties of order can be enumerated.

First, we cannot identify order until we know the rule which exposes its underlying pattern. In the example above, which is known as the Fibonacci sequence, the rule is that a number is the sum of the two preceding ones. In the array (2, 4, 8, 6, 8, 16, 14 . . .), the rule is add two, multiply by two, subtract two and then repeat the process; in the array (goat, carp, cat), the rule is that each element is a living creature. Identifying order then entails producing a rule which provides a structure or coherence to otherwise disparate elements.

Second, we must not assume that order is not present when a pattern is not immediately found. Take the array (3, 4.5, 10.125, 51.25781 . . .). Although there is no obvious pattern here, the sequence is, in fact, governed by a rule: each number is half the square of the preceding one. These elements, therefore, display an order just as clearly as the simple sequence (2, 4, 6, 8. . . .) because they are covered by a rule, albeit one more difficult to identify. Failure to find the 'half-the-square' rule could easily lead to the mistaken belief that the elements fail to constitute an order. Order, in other words, may often be masked by the inability to find the appropriate rule.

Third, we must avoid an obverse danger of assuming that any identified order is always obvious. Once a rule is known and understood then the order may well appear self-evident, but this is simply because we now have, thanks to the rule, a coherent pattern. The mistake that can easily be made here is that it is the identification of the rule that is the difficult task. To the average 13-year-old, the order in the Fibonacci sequence may be obvious but to the average 9-year-old this sequence would appear as a disordered set of figures.

Fourth, we need to acknowledge that a set of elements can display multiple orders. The elements of a sequence can, in other words, correspond to more than one rule. Consider the array (goat, carp, cat) and let us try to identify the odd one out. This is tantamount to creating an order defined by a rule which differentiates one element from the others in the array. We could select 'goat' since it does not begin with the letter 'c', or 'cat' because it does not contain four letters, or 'carp' because it is not a warm-blooded animal.

A final point is that, in searching for rules to define patterns, we are, albeit perhaps unwittingly, going through a form of hypothesis generation and testing. Assuming the correct rule does not strike us immediately, then we would start to produce rules, which can be thought of as hypotheses, testing each in turn until we get a satisfactory fit, that is to say, a rule that will provide coherence by fitting all the elements of the array. Thus in the array (goat, carp, cat), before hitting on the living creature hypothesis we might have tried out several others such as number of letters or number of vowels, which would not have fitted. Pursuing the testing idea, in the illustration where we were looking for the odd one out in the array (goat, carp, cat), we could ask for another element as a form of critical experiment to help us evaluate the rival multiple orders. Say we are given 'horse', then we could reject the not-beginning-with-'c' and the not-four-letter hypotheses, leaving us with the warm-blooded hypothesis as the correct one.

The search for order as pattern is extraordinarily extensive. Our remaining discussion of order as pattern is devoted to considering several illustrations that both document this pervasiveness and also amplify our general conceptualization.

The first of these illustrations concerns intelligence tests. Intelligence tests are primarily constructed of questions which involve sequences of numbers, shapes or words comparable to the examples given above. The task is invariably to find the rule which underpins the sequence and in this respect intelligence is being assessed in terms of capacity to identify patterns. Many criticisms have been levelled at intelligence testing and this is an area of controversy that we do not wish to enter except in so far as it helps us to amplify our conceptualization of order.

One problem is that if a test is made too easy for a particular age group, then brighter people may achieve only low scores. The reason for this is that they resist an easy pattern, which is in fact a correct answer, and search for more complex rules. Thus the less bright, who do not see beyond the easy pattern, perform as well if not better. A further problem is that intelligence-test scores can increase with the number of tests taken. This increase is not of course a function of any real increase in intelligence but rather of learning the type of pattern recognition demanded by intelligence tests. In other words, people can be trained in pattern recognition. It is this which underlies the cultural bias charge against standard intelligence tests. Some people, in other words, are better trained by their general education or socialization to identify more readily the type of pattern used in intelligence testing.

A second illustration of the pervasiveness of order as pattern concerns concept formation. Any concept is generally defined in terms of a series of properties or characteristics. The concept 'tree', for example, is defined by a set of characteristics that enables us to differentiate a tree from other objects such as flowers or bushes. As such, concepts are profiled by patterns of defining common properties. Thus we recognize something as a tree precisely because that object manifests that pattern of characteristics which we take to represent a tree. Furthermore, concepts are pattern creating. Thus once we have acquired a body of concepts, then to some extent they structure the way we see things and the way we think. Since concepts are one of the basic building blocks of language, it follows that communication is only possible among those that share a common body of concepts. In this respect we can see dictionaries as consensus-creating devices designed to facilitate communication.

A third area of illustration is that of detective novels. In these novels the reader is generally presented with a set of clues about a crime or series of crimes. The solution is achieved when these clues are pieced together in such a way as to form a pattern which identifies the person or persons who have committed the crime.

What we can see now is an important point that has not yet appeared in our previous illustrations. In a sense the numbers in the Fibonacci sequence can be likened to clues and the solution consists of finding the rule that enables us to extend the pattern. Thus, in the example above, the number 21 was the solution. In a detective story not only has this task to be satisfied but the clues have to be found in the first place. Thus, one of the main tasks of the detective or investigator is not simply to piece clues together but rather to distil from a massive body of information what are the relevant clues from which the final pattern will be formed.

The essential feature of a detective story, therefore, is the identification of a pattern. The process whereby the pattern is generated has been ingeniously and self-consciously explored in *The Name of the Rose* by Umberto Eco, a specialist in semiology. The book recounts the attempts by Henry Baskerville to uncover the pattern underlying a series of murders in a medieval monastery. Eco is trying to demonstrate in this novel how signs or clues can have more than one meaning. As a consequence Baskerville's clues form a variety of rival patterns. The irony revealed at the end of the book is that Baskerville correctly identifies the murderer but on the basis of an erroneous pattern, causing the hero to doubt the existence of order and the inductive process used to identify it. As Eco is well aware, non-trivial pattern identification requires a form of reasoning, and it is to this we turn in our final illustration, which concerns knowledge.

Knowledge can be defined as a body of agreed patterns. There is not simply one body of knowledge but rather a variety of different bodies of knowledge which are distinguished primarily by their epistemologies. By epistemology we understand that set of rules of inquiry which define what is acceptable knowledge, that is, what we will agree to stand as knowledge. For example, many people will accept that the earth is spherical and revolves around the sun but will not accept that the earth is flat or supported on the backs of elephants. The reason why some patterns are accepted as knowledge while others are rejected is that acceptable ones are the product of an accepted epistemology or set of rules of inquiry.

We can amplify this by considering the scientific method, a classic illustration of a particular epistemology, which consists essentially of a set of rules and procedures governing such factors as concept formation, measurement, hypothesis formation, controlled investigation and verification. The reason why such statements as the earth is spherical and revolves around the sun are accepted as agreed scientific knowledge is that the patterns contained in these statements conform to the rules of inquiry that make up the scientific method or the epistemology of science. The application of the scientific method produces patterns or scientific content. We turn now to consider some points on scientific knowledge that can amplify our understanding of order as pattern.

The main intellectual thrust of scientific inquiry is to produce corroborated laws and collections of such laws combined in theories. A law is nothing more than a stipulation of relationships between particular objects or events, that is to say, a stipulated pattern that has some form of empirical corroboration. In other words, the primary intellectual objective of scientific inquiry is to identify patterns or regularities usually with some explanatory content and to combine these explanatory patterns into theories. In so doing scientific inquiry is trying to integrate otherwise disparate events or objects into some coherent whole or pattern, and in this manner science is explicitly geared to the production of order.

We can give a concrete illustration of this by considering plate theory. Prior to this theory there was awareness of a whole range of observations such as: mountains had been laid down at very different times, the oceans were not uniform basins but had a topography similar to dry land, or volcanoes appeared to be non-randomly distributed in chains. With these observations came a series of puzzles, such as: why were volcanos to be found in chains, why were some rocks (such as limestone) that could only have been formed under the sea to be found on land, why did older rocks sometimes overlay younger ones, or why were radically different rock structures to be found next to each other. Plate theory suggests that the earth's crust is divided into several plates moving toward and away from each other and what we currently recognize as ocean and land have changed radically over the four and a half billion years of earth's history. Plate theory then starts to resolve these puzzles. The reason for the chain arrangement of volcanoes is that they mark plate boundaries; some rock that could only be formed under the sea had been pushed onto land by plate movement; the reason why the east coast of South America looks as though it would fit against the west coast of Africa is that it once did; the rock structure of Northern Scotland differs radically from that of Southern Scotland because they lie on different plates; the reason why we see the great mountain chains of the European Alps or the Himalayas is that these mountains were formed when the plates carrying Italy and India crashed into Europe and Asia. These illustrations, which could be multiplied manifold, demonstrate how one relatively simple theory is now able to unify a massive array of otherwise disparate information into coherent patterns which in this instance provides an order or understanding of the geological evolution of the earth's structure.

The scientific method does not, however, hold any monopoly on the production of knowledge. All the great religions of the world profile extremely elaborate patterns and explanations governing usually not only the natural but also the social world. Indeed in the history of civilized man, the use of science to produce patterns or knowledge is in fact very recent.

Furthermore an epistemology that underpins the creation of knowledge and which dictates what is acceptable knowledge is not novel. When Galileo was obliged to recant, it was not because an epistemology was coming up against previously non-existing epistemologies but rather because what we would now regard as a scientific epistemology clashed against another epistemology. What was acceptable knowledge under one epistemology was totally unacceptable under the other.

We can see epistemologies as collections of methodological rules containing postulates and rules of inquiry that are deployed so as to produce patterns of explanations. Such accumulated patterns constitute knowledge. It is clear that there is no one body of knowledge but as many bodies as there are epistemologies. These epistemologies differ not in that some produce patterns and others do not but rather in the particular patterns and explanations that are produced. The explanations of the development of life according to Darwinians and creationists have little in common in terms of substantive content but are identical in providing high levels of pattern. Since different patterns are a function of different epistemologies, there is little constructive debate that can take place between them. Patterns can only be evaluated in terms of a particular epistemology and any one epistemology can only be defended in terms of its own assumptions and objectives. There are then many orders, each dependent on its own epistemology, and since any epistemology can only be understood in terms of its own rules, then when bodies of knowledge, based on different epistemologies, come into conflict, that conflict must of necessity be irreconcilable.

Order as goal satisfaction

While the search for patterns can be undertaken in social as well as natural settings, the conceptualization of order purely as pattern is inadequate once we focus on systems involving human intervention. The reason is that humans endow their behaviour with purpose and meaning. Human behaviour is goal-orientated and it is necessary to incorporate goal orientation into a conceptualization of order. A simple example illustrates this point.

Consider a collection of books. If the books are grouped according to their size, from large to small, then the order will be immediately evident and a small book placed amongst the large ones will obviously reflect an element of disorder. In libraries, however, books are not arranged according to size, but rather by subject classification and then alphabetically by author. This dual pattern makes it easy to find any particular book. Ease of location, therefore, is the goal which underlies the arrangement of books in a library. Given this goal, it would be irrational to arrange books according to size, because this arrangement would unnecessarily complicate the task of finding a book. On the other hand, if the goal was to carry a set of books from one office to another, then it would be appropriate to stack the books according to size.

Put another way, if someone were asked to order a heap of books, then it is clear that a variety of patterns could govern the order. The books could be arranged according to the colour of the binding, the number of pages, the subject matter, and so on. Before ordering the books, therefore, it would be sensible to establish the purpose underlying the request, because what would appear to be order from the perspective of one goal would appear to be disorder from the perspective of another. It follows, therefore, that in any situation involving human intervention, the conceptualization of order must specify the underlying goal.

Our second conceptualization defines order in terms of goal satisfaction or goal attainment. In the book example, order is a function of locating books. Disorder or problems develop when a goal is not achieved. Thus, we would be experiencing problems in the book example if we could not locate books. The continuity from the first conceptualization of order is that any goal will be based, wittingly or unwittingly, on a structural arrangement or pattern deemed necessary to pursue the goal. The point to emphasize is that the structural arrangement becomes comprehensible only in the context of the goal. Thus, with a goal of ease of location we may well establish a structural arrangement or pattern based on a subject–author array. A size array, which is a perfectly coherent pattern, would be totally inadequate for the goal of location and would constitute a major problem or source of disorder. Were we to shift the goal, however, from finding a book to carrying books from one office to another, then a structural arrangement by size would immediately cease to be a problem.

Our objectives in the remaining part of this section are to amplify this conceptualization of order as goal attainment and to present a format for the analysis of order. This format entails the identification and explanation of problems and the presentation of solutions to these problems. We amplify the goal-satisfaction conceptualization and indicate the format of analysis of order by comparing and contrasting order in mechanical and social systems. Our interest lies with social rather than mechanical systems but we present this contrast partly because it is easier to see the format of analysis in the mechanical systems and partly because these systems can be used to point up some of the added difficulties in the analysis of order in social systems.

We take a car as our example of a mechanical system. If we set its major goal, at least initially, as the requirement of transporting people from A to B, then problems are identifiable in terms of the car failing to achieve this. Thus readily ascertainable problems would be the car failing to start or breaking down on a journey.

In addition to transportation, there are other more specific goals which, though common to all cars, may be specified variably. Thus, most modern cars would have specified an expected petrol consumption ratio (which we can express in miles per gallon), set at, say, 35 mpg for a saloon and 25 mpg for a sports-car. Or there might be an acceleration rate of 0–60 miles per hour in 15 seconds for the saloon and in 10 seconds for the sports-car. Now, if both cars actually achieved 25 mpg then only the saloon car would have a problem; or if both cars achieved acceleration rates of 0–60 mph in 15 seconds then it would be only the sports-car that had a problem. Since, other things being equal, there is an inverse relationship between petrol consumption and acceleration rates, we see here a classic illustration of goal incompatibility — petrol consumption can be enhanced but only at the expense of acceleration.

Goal specification, as well as being variable across types of car, may also be variable within a particular type of car. For example, we may well expect petrol consumption to reduce with variables such as the age of the car or winter driving. If the saloon car were to achieve only 25 pg during winter when it was ten years old, then this may well not be identified as a problem.

While problems are identified in terms of failure to satisfy goals, they are explained mainly, though not exclusively, in terms of some malfunctioning of the structural arrangement. For instance, the problem of a car failing to start may be explained by a faulty spark plug or lack of petrol. As with any explanation we can then enter into a causal regress by enquiring further why the plug was faulty or why the car was out of petrol. These further explanations may extend beyond the structural arrangement of the car itself — the plug may be faulty due to a lack of servicing or the petrol tank empty because someone failed to fill it (as opposed to a leakage). Furthermore, the explanation may be totally outside the system's structural arrangement. For example, assuming a car is not designed to drive through three feet of snow, then this amount of snow could well create a problem without necessarily implying any system malfunction.

Two features of problem explanation merit comment. First, we would normally require some considerable knowledge of the structural arrangement of a mechanical system before we could diagnose, that is, explain a problem, which is one of the reasons why there are mechanics.

Second, mechanical systems commonly possess problem-monitoring indicators, such as petrol and water-temperature gauges, designed specifically to forestall problem development.

The solution to problems is predicated in general on the explanation. Thus, if a car will not start and the explanation lies in a lack of petrol, then the solution in principle is straightforward. Knowledge of a solution does not of necessity mean the solution can be effected. Thus, a petrol station may be closed or a spare part may be unobtainable.

We can now, taking a business corporation as our example, illustrate the format for identifying, explaining and solving problems in the context of social systems. Problems are identified once again in terms of failure to achieve goals. Taking profit-making or the maintenance and expansion of market share as goals for a corporation, then a corporation's failure to achieve either would constitute problems. The identification and especially the measurement of problems in a social system can, however, be substantially more complex than in the case of mechanical systems, even though in principle we are following the same procedure.

First, while mechanical systems often have unambiguous goals, such as transportation, or precisely quantified goals, such as expected miles per gallon, goals in social systems are often difficult to specify with any precision. Consequently, the specification of problems is complicated. Thus, while we may readily take negative profits as symptomatic of a disorder, there is clearly no absolute or invariant profit level from which the intensity of problems can be assessed. On the other hand, it is likely that we can produce an expected profit level. For example, a corporation may use the behaviour of related corporations as a reference group and derive a market norm of, say, profits equal to 15 per cent of sales. In this instance an achieved profit of 15 per cent would not indicate a problem whereas a profit of 5 per cent would. Or again, a corporation may use its previous performance as a reference point. Thus, if a corporation has enjoyed a market share of 10 per cent but that share has been declining over a number of years, then this would indicate a problem.

A second difficulty is that social systems can modify their goals. In a recession a corporation may well expect lower profits without this being considered a major problem. In principle this is not a categoric difference from mechanical systems, where we have noted that, say, petrol consumption may increase with the age of a car or driving conditions. On the other hand, it is generally much easier in the case of the car to identify the variables that affect performance and specify in precise terms to what degree these variables will modify goals.

A third difficulty pertains to goal priorities. Both social and mechanical systems will generally manifest several goals which may entail some degree of incompatibility. A car does not, however, experience a problem in the incompatibility of say petrol consumption against acceleration rate. It is rather the potential purchaser who must make the choice of the relative merit of petrol consumption against acceleration. This difficulty will usually be surmounted by the purchaser establishing some set of goal priorities. Social systems can explicitly run into goal incompatibility. Thus, an expansion of market share may well conflict in the short term with volume of profit; or again, the size of a new investment programme may well conflict with dividend payments. Although goal priorities could again be invoked, a major difference would none the less remain in that different components of the social system may well have different priorities. Thus, different groups or components in a corporation, such as management or shareholders, may well have different priorities on market share and short-term volume of profit.

This leads to a final difficulty and an even more pronounced difference between mechanical and social systems. Different groups within any social system may often have not only different priorities but even different goals. Thus, while management may be committed to goals such as profits or market share, the work-force may be much more concerned with wage levels or job security. In such an instance, there would be systematic variation in the problems identified across these groups. It should be emphasized, however, that the method of problem identification, that is, failure to achieve goals, would be identical; it is the actual problems identified that vary.

There are unquestionably some major differences between mechanical and social systems which substantially complicate the issue of problem identification in social systems. Social systems do not have a single designer, their goals can evolve and adapt, they display a learning process and they can contain groups that hold competing goals. But while these difficulties complicate problem identification, they do not confound either the basic conceptualization or the general format of problem identification.

The search for explanations of problems in a social system is executed in principle in much the same way as in mechanical systems. Problems may therefore arise due to some malfunctioning within the system. A reduction in profits for a corporation may be due, for example, to halted production brought about by a strike, or to a decline in productivity brought about by inadequate innovation, or to lower sales due to poor promotional and marketing strategies. Problems may also be explained by changes in the corporation's external environment. Profits may reduce because of shortages of raw materials or a rise in corporation tax; productivity improvements may be thwarted by a rise in interest rates which damage a new investment programme; or sales may reduce due to a national or world recession.

The explanation of problems in social systems is substantially more complex than in mechanical systems. The specialized knowledge available to explain dislocation in mechanical systems is not nearly so refined or sophisticated in the case of social systems. Though structural arrangements can be identified, even the boundaries of social systems can be difficult to identify, and relationships are generally extremely complex. These relationships can change markedly as critical components adapt and modify their behaviour, and the issue of causal regress is more acute as levels of explanation are difficult to specify, or explanations are likely to entail more common recourse to an external environment, made up in turn of complex social systems. Once again, however, despite the additional difficulties, we would argue that in principle the format of the analysis, namely tracing problems to dislocations in the structural arrangement, is quite sound and viable.

As in the case of mechanical systems, problem solving is predicated upon the particular explanation of the problem. Problem solving therefore entails those readjustments to the malfunctioning of the structural arrangement or interaction with the environment such that goals can once again be satisfied.

In general, social systems are sufficiently adept at problem solving that they may often include specific problem-solving agencies. In a corporation, for example, extensive personnel departments have developed at least in part to resolve conflicts that might emerge between management and work-force. Or again, complex, institutionalized systems of negotiation or arbitration are often established to deal with different goal preferences among management, work-force and shareholders. Or again, large corporations contain strategic planning groups part of whose function is to adapt corporate behaviour in anticipation of problems. Or again, a whole industry of management consultancy has developed to assist corporations to increase productivity and efficiency so as to be better able to achieve their primary goals.

As the source of a problem extends beyond the confines of a system itself into the environment, a corporation is likely to experience greater difficulty in problem solving. Even in these areas, however, problem-solving strategies are available. Consider, for example, a corporation that is vulnerable to the input of some raw material whose supply may be disrupted by factors beyond its control. In response to such a situation a corporation may respond by stockpiling or by vertical or horizontal integration. A particularly interesting problem-solving strategy is goal modification. Thus, in the context of general disruptions such as high interest rates or recession, over which an individual corporation has no control, a corporation may well lower its profit expectations. Such a goal modification automatically reduces the problem, though the underlying structural source would of course remain unchanged.

Again there are several additional complexities to problem solving in social as opposed to mechanical systems. For example, the solution to one problem may often exacerbate another. Increasing inventories may be a useful solution to a restricted factor input but it also carries substantial opportunity costs. Capital tied up in stockpiles cannot be used for other purposes, such as new investment programmes, which in turn can damage the pursuit of expanded profits. A more acute variant of this difficulty is that it may not be practical to implement a particular solution because that solution would create an even greater problem. For instance, in a recession a corporation may wish to cut production. This would normally entail firing some of the work-force. If the work-force, however, threatens to strike if redundancies are made, then the solution of reduced production may effectively not be available. A further complication is that the consequences of a solution, particularly a novel one, may be extremely difficult to calculate. Whereas in a mechanical system the parameters of interaction are well known, meaning that solution impacts would be well understood, this is not necessarily the case in social systems. Partly through poorer knowledge and partly through a greater degree of complexity and change, it may be extraordinarily difficult to calculate the consequences of any solution, which in turn can result in substantial dispute over different solutions.

Although there are obvious and substantial differences between social and mechanical systems, we have tried to show in this section that the same format of analysis of order can be used. In the next section we indicate how the conceptualization of order and format of analysis can be applied to the main concern of this study in the examination of world order.

The analysis of world order

The central reason necessitating the conceptualization of order as goal attainment in addition to order as pattern is that humans endow their behaviour with meaning or purpose, which consequently has obliged us to incorporate a consideration of goals. In comparing and contrasting mechanical and social systems, we have not touched upon what is perhaps the single most important difference between them, which is that while mechanical systems have fixed and thereby agreed goals, social systems do not. In the context of social systems, there may be dispute as to what goals the system ought to be pursuing. Furthermore, variation in the perception of goals will also translate into systematic variation in the structural arrangement deemed necessary to pursue these goals. In other words, we are likely to find competing substantive conceptualizations of order.

In the rest of this study we focus on the area of world order, in which context there is undoubted dispute. To accommodate this dispute, we posit three models of world order. Each model has in common three dimensions: a goal, a structural arrangement and a belief system. These three dimensions can be thought of respectively in terms of what, how, and why: the 'what' is the goal or the prescription of what is to be pursued; the 'how' is the structural arrangement or organizational design which specifies how the goal is to be pursued; the 'why' is the belief system which justifies and rationalizes both the structural arrangement and particularly the goal and as such explicates why it is desirable to pursue the goal. Collectively these three dimensions constitute and define a model of order. Different or competing models vary then in the substantive content that is provided for these dimensions.

Part II of this book consists of three chapters which establish the liberal, socialist and realist models of world order. Each of these models can be represented in terms of a goal, structural arrangements and a belief system and in this respect each has an identical abstract conceptualization of order. Where they differ is in the substantive content of the dimensions.

In amplifying the conceptualization of order as goal satisfaction, we have introduced what we have termed a format of analysis defined in terms of the identification and explanation of problems and the profiling of solutions. In general, problems are identified in terms of deviations from or shortfalls in goal satisfaction; problems are explained in terms of dislocations within the structural arrangement or between the structural arrangement and its environment; solutions are profiled in terms of the readjustments in the structural arrangement required to restore goal satisfaction. As soon as we contemplate different models, then we will immediately expect to find different substantive problems, explanations and solutions. This substantive diversity is none the less identified and underwritten by a common format of analysis.

Having established the different substantive models, Parts III and IV confront international economic and security issues. The processes of problem identification and explanation are analytically distinct. For example, one may be able to identify a problem with a car but be obliged to turn to a mechanic to have it explained. In other words, knowledge of a structural arrangement is a prerequisite for explanation. In the case of the models presented in Part II, each has a very explicit arrangement and hence the basis of explanation. Since explanation subsumes identification, we fuse the processes of identification and explanation in the analysis of problems. When we profile the problems perceived by each model, we provide an identification of problems that has explanatory content. Thus, in each of the chapters constituting Parts III and IV, we present a particular model's perception of problems and its solutions to these problems in the international economic and security issue areas.

PART II: MODELS OF WORLD ORDER

2 The liberal model

In contrast to realism and socialism, liberalism is profiled in terms of two sub-models which we term pure and compensatory liberalism. The reason for profiling liberalism in this way is that there is sufficient systematic variation in problem identification and proposed solutions to merit an explicit distinction. On the other hand, there is sufficient affinity in goals, structural arrangement and belief systems that pure and compensatory liberalism cannot be regarded as separate models. As a brief, and far from comprehensive indication of the basis of the distinction, compensatory liberalism represents that development of liberal thought which has achieved some degree of fusion with socialism. As such compensatory liberalism, while still remaining in essence liberal, represents a partial transition to socialism.

Goal

The organizing goal for the pure liberal is the promotion and protection of negative freedom.[1] Freedom in this negative sense is defined as the absence of human interference.[2] The classic stipulation of negative freedom in contemporary liberal theory has been provided by Berlin:

> I am normally said to be free to the degree to which no man or body of men interferes with my activity. Political liberty in this sense is simply the area within which a man can act unobstructed by others. If I am prevented by others from doing what I would otherwise do I am to that degree unfree; and if this area is contracted by other men beyond a certain minimum, I can be described as being coerced... The wider the area of non-interference the wider my freedom.[3]

Much the same profile of negative freedom is given by Hayek, another major proponent of pure liberalism:

To regain certain fundamental truths which generations of demagoguery have obliterated, it is necessary to learn again to understand why the basic values of a great or open society must be negative, assuring the individual of the right within a known domain to pursue his own aims on the basis of his own knowledge. Only such negative rules make possible the formation of a self-generating order, utilizing the knowledge, and serving the desires, of the individuals.[4]

By way of initial expansion of this conceptualization of the goal of negative freedom, several points are worth emphasizing. First, while the expression 'negative freedom' is readily used by its advocates and indeed contrasted with 'positive freedom' which is thoroughly deplored, the adjective negative should not be taken to indicate any misgivings or any conviction that negative freedom is somehow second best.[5] Indeed not only is negative freedom held to be highly desirable but it is also considered to be very constructive. While this point will be elaborated in greater detail later (in the discussion on belief systems), we may note how Friedman, another major advocate of pure liberalism, in discussing the need for restraining government interference, emphasises both a negative and positive (positive as constructive) rationale:

The preservation of freedom is the protective reason for limiting and decentralizing government power. But there is also a constructive reason. The great advances of civilization whether in architecture or painting, in science or history, in industry or agriculture, have never come from centralized government. . . . Government can never duplicate the variety and diversity of individual action.[6]

A second point to emphasize is that negative freedom does not mean the total absence of interference, which would be taken by pure liberals to entail anarchism. Indeed unrestrained freedom, as for example in the freedom to commit murder, is taken by pure liberals to be absurd. In general, the guiding principle is that those freedoms that would be destructive of the freedoms of others must be curtailed. The critical issue is not whether freedom is unlimited (it assuredly is not) but rather that the necessary constraints on freedom need to be minimized to the point at which negative freedom can be enjoyed equally by all. Thus Hayek states:

The task of government is to create a framework within which individuals and groups can successfully pursue their respective aims, and sometimes to use its coercive powers of raising revenue to provide services which for one reason or other the market cannot supply. But coercion is justified only in order to provide such a framework within which all can use their abilities and knowledge for their own ends so long as they do not interfere with the equally protected individual domains of others.[7]

Illustrating a more specific form of interference or constraint, Machlup argues: 'Equality before the law involves enforcement of the law and enforcement involves the use of coercive power by the state.'[8] Or yet again Machlup, in attacking the popular and erroneous equation of liberalism with laissez-faire, argues: 'The preservation of a maximum of freedom may call for government measures to maintain competition, which private contracts might restrict, to provide services which private enterprise cannot supply, and to prevent misery which private charity cannot cope with.'[9]

We can turn now to consider how compensatory liberalism begins to deviate from the pure variant. In general compensatory liberals argue that the distinction between negative and positive freedom, as profiled by Berlin, is overdrawn and that an exclusive focus on negative freedom is too limited.[10]

Berlin is unequivocally clear in arguing that the pursuit of negative freedom entails some costs in that it precludes the pursuit of other goals or values. Thus:

> Everything is what it is: liberty is liberty, not equality or fairness or justice or culture, or human happiness or a quiet conscience. If the liberty of myself or my class or nation depends on the misery of a number of other human beings, the system which promotes this is unjust and immoral. But if I curtail or lose my freedom, in order to lessen the shame of such inequality, and do not thereby materially increase the individual liberty of others, an absolute loss of liberty occurs. This may be compensated for by a gain in justice or in happiness or in peace, but the loss remains . . .[11]

Compensatory liberals are willing to cede some partial loss for what they perceive to be a greater gain and that gain lies in the area of equality.

In objecting to the overly restrictive nature of freedom as absence of interference, compensatory liberals make two main charges: that Berlin fails to appreciate fully the distinction between freedom and conditions of freedom and the extent to which structural arrangements can coerce. An illustration from Crocker emphasizes this:

The positive libertarian is concerned that people are often prevented from doing things, not by laws or direct interference, but by matters whose roots lie deep in the institutional structure of the society. The welfare mother who is legally free to vacation on Corfu, but who barely has the wherewithal to get across town is a typical case . . . Similarly the blind man is not interfered with by those who could afford to pay for a sight-restoring operation. But because he goes without the operation, what he can do is significantly limited.[12]

Typically then we find compensatory liberals arguing 'that to know whether a man is free we must know what he is supposed to be free from, and what free to do'.[13] Or we find Crocker talking of freedom as 'a matter of the presence of options and opportunities'.

In emphasizing the range of opportunities and alternatives it may appear that the compensatory liberals are simply restating Berlin. Thus Berlin in his seminal paper argues: 'The sense of freedom in which I use this term, entails not simply the absence of frustration (which may be obtained by killing desires), but the absence of obstacles to possible choices and activities — absence of obstructions on roads along which a man can decide to walk.'[14] Where the compensatory liberals do begin to deviate is in their concern that these roads are distributed very unequally across individuals. The focus on equality is seen clearly in the work of Dworkin. Dworkin argues that it is necessary to distinguish liberty as licence (Berlin's negative freedom) and liberty as independence. The latter involves questions of equality of which two types are distinguished: the right to equal treatment and the right to treatment as an equal. It is the latter which needs to become the focus of attention.

The major divergence of the compensatory from the pure liberal is the contention by the former that the pure liberal devotes insufficient attention to the issue of the equality of the distribution of choice and opportunity. To anticipate briefly the next section, this leads the compensatory liberal to see a greater need for intervention so as to enlarge and equalize to some degree the range of choice. It is this perceived need for some degree of compensation which leads us to characterize this variant of liberalism as compensatory as opposed to the pure one, which in turn is the one exclusively devoted to negative freedom.

This position has not gone unchallenged by the pure liberals. Thus Machlup, in a more general attack on 'fuzzy liberalism', argues that some have confused 'I may' (what we call pure liberalism) and 'I can' (what we call compensatory liberalism):

> It bears again on the previously mentioned confusion between freedom as non-interference with an individual's actions and his effective power to act. Capacity to act, having the power and the means to do something, is surely not the same thing as having the freedom to do it ... I must admit that the freedom to buy a Rolls-Royce and a luxury yacht has little practical relevance to those who have no money to buy them. But this does not mean that we should expand the concept of 'freedom' to include 'capacity to buy'.[15]

This 'confusion', as we shall see later, becomes quite serious on occasion for the pure liberals as they see the compensatory liberals advocating an undesirable degree of intervention to try to secure greater equality in capacity to act and in so doing making serious inroads into negative freedom.

By way of conclusion to this section it may be useful to review the points of contact, as far as goals are concerned, between the two variants of liberalism and socialism. Pure liberalism, with its focus on negative freedom, and socialism, with its focus on equality, do not touch at all.[16] There is, however, some contact between compensatory liberalism and socialism, which is why compensatory liberalism represents something of a partial fusion of liberalism and socialism.[17] That contact is created by the partial preoccupation of compensatory liberalism with equality. It is, however, the case that the type of equality that concerns the compensatory liberal is quite different from that concerning the socialist and we shall see in the next section how derisory the socialists are of equality of opportunity, which they see as simply a prescription for maintaining inequality. Thus Dworkin, for example, in advocating the right to treatment as an equal very clearly distinguishes this from right to equal treatment: 'This is the right, not to an equal distribution of some good or opportunity, but the right to equal concern and respect in the political decision about how these goods and opportunities are to be distributed.'[18] Although the right to equal treatment is not exactly the socialist conception of equality, it is decidedly closer than the right to treatment as an equal.

The points of contact between pure and compensatory liberalism are substantially greater than the latter's contact with socialism. Thus compensatory liberals, while critical of an exclusive preoccupation with negative freedom, do not reject negative freedom as a major structuring goal, as would the socialists. Indeed, it is no coincidence that contemporary theorists of compensatory liberalism almost invariably use Berlin's formulation as a point of departure. Rather than abandoning negative freedom, however, they are more concerned to make some concessions in this area so as to achieve some supplement, which in turn explains why compensatory liberals are often inclined to see negative freedom as being contained within what they take to be their more comprehensive conceptualization.[19] The commitment to negative freedom unequivocally lands the compensatory liberal within the liberal model; it is only what the compensatory liberal takes to be the potential inequity of the intransigent and exclusive preoccupation of the pure liberal with negative freedom that distinguishes these two variants of liberalism.

Structural arrangement

Liberals of both the pure and compensatory variants posit a close connection between the political and economic dimensions of their desired structural arrangement and as such a viable liberal system requires both an appropriate political and economic arrangement. Having said this, the principal difference between the two variants is that the compensatory liberals give greater relative priority to the political arrangement. In the following presentation we focus primarily on the pure liberal arrangement after which we indicate the main points of divergence from the compensatory perspective.

While the pure liberals hold conceptions of both economic and political freedom, each is seen as but a dimension of more general freedom. As such economic freedom is necessary for political freedom and vice versa and full freedom cannot be enjoyed and sustained without this symbiotic relation.

The foundation of the pure liberal economic structural arrangement is the free market. In the absence of distorting constraints individuals will only engage in economic intercourse if it brings them benefit. The market then is simply a device through which individuals in their capacities as producers and consumers voluntarily interact to exchange goods and services. Price is the mechanism which transmits information to both consumers and producers and which enables them through demand and supply to determine exactly what is produced and in what quantity. For this arrangement to work efficiently interactions must be voluntary and informed, which in turn is achieved through competition. Hayek characterizes the free market thus:

> Competition, if not prevented, tends to bring about a state of affairs in which: first, everything will be produced which somebody knows how to produce and which he can sell profitably at a price at which buyers

will prefer it to alternatives; second, everything that is being produced is produced by persons who can do so at least as cheaply as anybody else who in fact is not producing it; and third, that everything will be sold at prices lower than, or at least as low as, those at which it could be sold by anybody who in fact does not do so.[20]

The genius of this incredibly simple arrangement, first recognized by Adam Smith, is that it manages to achieve so much. Thus, without any central direction (hence the invisible hand analogy) millions of individual economic decisions are coordinated to utilize resources in the most efficient manner possible to determine optimum production. That so much can be accomplished by so little together with the fact that the market simply emerged has led Hayek to declare: 'We have never designed our economic system. We were not intelligent enough for that. We have tumbled into it and it has carried us to unforeseen heights and given rise to ambitions which may yet destroy us.'[21]

The free market is seen as the structural embodiment of negative freedom in the economic arena. Thus, Friedman declares:

> So long as effective freedom of exchange is maintained, the central feature of the market organization of economic activity is that it prevents one person from interfering with another in respect of most of his activities. The consumer is protected from coercion by the seller because of the presence of other sellers with whom he can deal. The seller is protected from coercion by the consumer because of other consumers to whom he can sell. The employee is protected from coercion by the employer because of other employers for whom he can work, and so on. And the market does this impersonally and without centralized authority.[22]

We can amplify this conceptualization of the structural arrangement of the free market by considering what pure liberals hold to be two popular myths. The first of these concerns perfect competition. The idealized version of the free market is to be found in perfect competition which is that market arrangement whereby any one producer cannot affect price. This however is an explicit idealization of primary utility to economic theory. Actual markets can deviate substantially from perfect competition and still be very acceptable. The propensity of some to argue that since perfect competition does not exist then market ideas are worthless is an absurdity to pure liberals.

One common deviation from perfect competition is to be found in oligopolies. There has been an unquestioned growth in oligopolistic production and a substantial growth of vertical integration within oligopolies. While oligopolies can cause some problems (particularly with transfer pricing within vertical integrations), it is none the less the case that oligopolies are still obliged to set prices sufficiently low to attract and expand sales. Furthermore, as long as collusion among oligopolies in price fixing is prohibited, competition can still take place among them, thereby preserving incentives to the producers and providing security to employees and consumers.[23] Indeed even monopolies, a condition under which competition may appear to be reduced to zero, can be tolerated as long as any monopoly uses a smaller amount of resources than alternative production. What is critical is that competition is not prevented. Thus as long as other producers can enter the market, that is, competition is not prevented, then the monopoly would be obliged to perform as though there were competitors.[24] While, other things being equal, competition would be encouraged (it saves, for example, problems of collusion and price fixing), it is the prevention of competition which is crucial to the pure liberal. Consequently the observation that in reality perfect competition is not to be found is quite irrelevant.

A second myth concerns planning. While the invisible hand analogy is often used by liberals, this is not taken to mean that the market consists of automatons blindly responding to impersonal demand and supply forces. One of the main advantages of the free market, according to pure liberals, is that individual initiative and creativity are allowed to flourish and one of the major hallmarks of initiative and creativity is foresight. Foresight entails planning in the sense of anticipating or estimating changes in demand or production costs. Far from planning as foresight being anathema, it is not only desirable but is cleverly rewarded by the market in the form of expanded sales and larger profits. Hayek contrasts the liberal and non-liberal conceptions:

> it is not a dispute on whether we ought to employ foresight and systematic thinking in planning our common affairs. It is a dispute about what is the best way of so doing. The question is whether for this purpose it is better that the holder of coercive power should confine himself in general to creating conditions under which the knowledge and initiative of individuals is given the best scope so that *they* can plan most successfully; or whether a rational utilization of our resources requires *central* direction and organization of all our activities according to some consciously constructed 'blueprint'.[25]

32 *Models of world order*

The type of planning that is anathema to the pure liberal is centralized government planning, to which the objections are that it is divorced from market controls and entails a massive concentration of power.

The free market has its counterpart internationally in the open world economy. This economy is not seen as an arrangement that is in basic structure very different from a domestic free market but rather represents nothing more than the projection of the principles and logic of a domestic free market onto the international plane. The two principal components of an open world economy are comparative advantage and the free flow of goods, labour and capital.

Definitions of comparative advantage are legion throughout the liberal literature. One characterization by a leading advocate of pure liberalism is:

> According to that principle, freedom of trade permits each country to specialize on the production of those goods which it can produce most efficiently, and to avoid wasting resources on producing goods that it can produce only inefficiently, instead importing such goods from countries that produce them more efficiently and paying for them by exports of goods that it can produce efficiently.[26]

As originally espoused by Ricardo, the principle of comparative advantage focused only on variations in labour costs. Over time this has been seen to be insufficient and the underlying principle has been expanded, most notably by Heckscher and Ohlin, to include other variables. Hence we find the factor-endowment theories incorporating land, productivity, technology and natural resources in addition to labour. Despite limiting assumptions, for example factor prices around the world are not equal even adjusting for tariffs and transportation costs, on a policy level comparative advantage continues to be a keystone of liberalism. Thus there is a conviction that every country possesses a comparative advantage somewhere and that it is in the best interests of the liberal community as a whole that each country orientate its production to that advantage. Evidence, which there undoubtedly is, that trade patterns do not correlate perfectly with the dictates of comparative advantage does not daunt the liberal, who responds that production would be more efficient and welfare would be enhanced if trade did conform.

While comparative advantage has been discussed principally in the context of commercial trade policy, there is no reason why it should not be, and indeed it has been, generalized to cover the movement of capital. Thus if capital can achieve a higher rate of return in another geographic area of the liberal community then it should move there to enjoy that comparative advantage. Exactly the same argument is reiterated for technology or managerial expertise or productivity innovations. Of these factor movements unquestionably the free movement of labour is the most sticky as sudden mass migrations would clearly present intolerable burdens. None the less, within the limits of absorption, the free movement of labour is highly desirable.

The open world economy is then an international market in which capital, goods, technology and, albeit to a lesser extent, labour can flow without obstacle or hindrance and will do so in a pattern dictated by comparative advantage.

The structural arrangement of the political system can be summarized as limited constitutional government. While the ideal form of interaction is impersonally managed voluntary exchange, that is to say, market interaction, the pure liberal does not envisage that government is, or indeed will become, redundant — as might for example anarchists or socialists. While it is critically important for the pure liberal that government be limited, it is none the less the case that the limited role is an extremely important one — limited should not be taken to imply unimportant.

Government has several major duties to fulfil. These centre primarily on protecting the market, and thereby protecting economic freedom; on enhancing the market, by providing services that the market would not; and on providing a formal framework within which political freedom is assured. Friedman characterizes the role of government thus: 'Its major function must be to protect our freedom both from the enemies outside our gates and from our fellow citizens: to preserve law and order, to enforce private contracts, to foster competitive markets.'[27] This limited role leads liberal government to be characterized in such terms as 'umpire' or 'guardian' or 'housekeeper'. Thus, one critic of this limited liberal government defines the 'housekeeping' function as:

> (1) protecting liberty — which is to say, securing a safe and settled haven for individualized choice and the uninhibited exercise of that property power, (2) providing a rag bag of residual services that the market did not make available, and (3) dividing up whatever surpluses might appear in the public domain.[28]

The main preoccupation of the pure liberal is not with defending or justifying government but rather with ensuring that government remains limited. In much the same way that pure liberals have a horror of the concentration of economic power through market distortions, they have an even greater fear of the concentration of political power, where potentially the threat is greater. The task for the pure liberal then is to devise a series of measures that will simultaneously enable the critical governmental roles to be fulfilled while ensuring that government will continue to remain limited.

The principal measures include, first, the extensive use of the division of power. Classically this has entailed the separation of legislative, executive and judicial functions by prescribing specific spheres of competence for each, providing separate resource bases for each to protect autonomy, and instituting systems of checks and balances such that any one branch can be constrained by the others.[29] Second, there is a strong predilection for federalism and decentralization. This is in a sense merely an extension of the logic of separation of powers wherein the objective is once again to diffuse power and provide countervailing constraints. Third, there is a strong commitment to formal constitutional provisions. What is critical about these constitutional provisions is that they are dictated by the requirements of absence of interference enshrined in negative freedom. This not only requires the formal stipulation of individual rights such as freedom of speech or association but also formal constraints on areas of governmental legislation.[30] Finally there is the device of competitive and open elections whose main utility is to provide a means of recruiting and peacefully changing political personnel and making these personnel responsive to the electorate.[31]

Collectively these devices are intended to produce a type of governmental system which, though capable of executing a number of critically important tasks, is none the less explicitly circumscribed. In a comprehensive illustration of a 'blueprint' liberal government, Hayek presents a tiered structure of constitution, legislative assembly, governmental assembly and constitutional court.[32] In confronting the question of where sovereignty resides, Hayek responds: 'If it be asked where under such an arrangement "sovereignty" rests, the answer is nowhere . . . since constitutional government is limited government there can be no room in it for a sovereign body if sovereignty is defined as unlimited power.'[33] It is this limited capacity of liberal government that leads Macpherson to describe it as protective democracy: '. . . there is no enthusiasm for democracy, no idea that it could be a morally transformative force; it is nothing but a logical requirement for the governance of inherently self-interested conflicting individuals who are assumed to be infinite desirers of their own private benefits.'[34] Macpherson, who is very critical of this conception of democracy, suggests that though this characterisation is harsh it is also accurate. Pure liberals for the most part would agree entirely on the accuracy. Thus to the extent that they use the term democracy, democracy is taken to be primarily a set of procedures centering on electoral requirements. Democracy is not seen or defined as a particular desirable set of government outcomes let alone a particular form of society.[35] The main utility of democracy is, according to Hayek, simply as a 'sanitary precaution' and indeed one of the main fears of pure liberals is the development of democracy as popular sovereignty whereby government is perceived to be provided with a *carte blanche* for extensive intervention.[36]

The general rationale and form of domestic government is mirrored at the international level. As in the domestic case, pure liberals are adamant that some degree of government is essential, 'That there is little hope of international order or lasting peace so long as every country is free to employ whatever measures it thinks desirable in its own immediate interest, however damaging they may be to others, needs little emphasis now.'[37] Just as the free market is the basis of the domestic structural arrangement, the open world market is the core of the international arrangement. Pure liberals then require those constitutional arrangements that will enable the open world economy to function free from government interference. As Hirsch comments: 'The central political task, according to liberal thought, is thus essentially "constitutional" — it involves constructing an overarching framework for an international order as a way to make arbitrary day-to-day government intervention unnecessary.'[38]

Since the practical manifestations of an international structural arrangement will be dealt with in detail in later chapters, we will not develop them here. The main point to emphasize is rather the general principle or format of these arrangements, which is a minimal constitutional framework that will protect an open world economy and enable it to function efficiently.

In conclusion, the structural arrangement envisaged by the pure liberal is the combination of a free market with limited constitutional government. This arrangement furthermore is seen to be appropriate both at the domestic and international levels. While no liberal would deny that there currently is something of a hiatus between things national and international, the pure liberal is committed to a progressive blurring of the autonomy of national economies and their increasing integration into a world economy. The basic unit for the pure liberal is assuredly not the nation state, which is in fact viewed as increasingly archaic. The basic unit is furthermore not even individuals within nation states. Rather the ultimate constituency of the pure liberal is the global individual liberal consumer and producer located in an open world economy. It is then the twin components of a free market and limited constitutional government which, according to the pure liberal, provide the structural arrangement whereby the goal of negative freedom can be pursued.

While the compensatory liberal does not reject the goal of negative freedom, we have argued that such freedom is seen as requiring to be supplemented by some considerations of equality. Not surprisingly, therefore, compensatory liberals see the need for a number of structural modifications to the basic pure liberal design which in essence entail an increase in the salience of government and a concomitant diminution in the salience of the market.

Though it would be erroneous to suggest that compensatory liberals reject the market outright, as would the socialists for example, they do have substantial reservations about the market which moves their desired arrangement away from the free market to the so-called mixed market. The critique of the free market proceeds on two levels.

The first of these, working at an essentially empirical level, argues that the free market is massively removed from reality and as such provides an inadequate structural model. Thus Shonfield, in his analysis of modern capitalism, notes some developments (such as prolonged growth and the diffusion of benefits) and some characteristics of modern capitalism (such as the accelerated pace of technological development or the rapid expansion of internationsl trade) which are dear to the hearts of pure liberals.[39] Shonfield, however, also calls attention to some distinctive features which are decidedly unwelcome to pure liberals. Chief among these is economic planning. Indeed Shonfield refers to such increased planning as 'probably the most characteristic expression of new capitalism'. This in turn has led to the vastly increased influence of public authorities on the management of economic systems, a preoccupation with welfare, increased regulation of competition in the private sector and long-range national planning.[40] A similar form of critique of the free market is found in Galbraith.[41] The novelty with Galbraith is the emphasis placed on technology and the technostructure.[42] Certain technological imperatives are seen as having given rise to the development of large corporations which manage aggregate supply and in conjunction with governments manage aggregate demand.

The main point for our purposes is to emphasize that writers such as Shonfield and Galbraith see certain effectively inevitable transformations taking place within modern capitalism that render the free market model somewhat archaic. Thus, the requirements of modern capitalism are seen by Galbraith as producing certain critical common denominators leading to a process of convergence. 'Convergence begins with modern large-scale production, with heavy requirements of capital, sophisticated technology and, as a prime consequence, elaborate organization. These require control of prices and, so far as possible, of what is bought at those prices. This is to say that planning must replace the market.'[43] Having examined differences in planning and control in the United States and Soviet Union Galbraith states what to the pure liberal is tantamount to a heresy: 'But these, obviously, are differences in method rather than purpose. Large-scale industrialism requires, in both cases, that the market and consumer sovereignty be extensively superseded.'[44]

The suggestion here, it should be emphasized, is not that there is an ineluctable movement of free markets to command economies but that both free and command economies are converging to a common meeting ground in mixed markets.

The unreality of the free market is not confined purely to domestic economies but is applicable to the open world market also. Against comparative advantage it is argued that it does not predict trade. Apart from the fact that in extraordinarily complex production systems it is difficult even to identify where the comparative advantage would lie, it is also suggested that political factors or export credits, for example, distort trade or that comparative advantage cannot explain the high proportion of trade that takes place in like goods. On the free flow of goods, capital and labour, it is argued that labour, with small exceptions such as the brain-drain or *Gastarbeiter*, does not move at all. The more important charge is against the free flow of capital and goods where an increasing proportion of international production is dominated by multinationals. Thus:

> The fact that decisions as to the volume of production, the location of sales, direction of exports, prices, and qualities are made on the basis of inter-company relationships, and under a variety of governmental intervention, means that the flow to trade and payments is increasingly influenced by non-market forces.[45]

What we have termed the empirical critique essentially states that certain domestic and international developments have taken place that make a free market quite unrealistic. This attack is supplemented on a more normative level by the argument that not only is the free market unrealistic but it is also undesirable. The main contentions in this context are that a free market does not deliver all the benefits claimed by pure liberals and that it does not deliver at all on some desirable benefits (or alternatively that it delivers some undesirable benefits). Consequently, according to compensatory liberals, the free market or open world economy should not exercise the critical structuring role bestowed on it by pure liberals.

Central to this normative attack is the argument that an unrestrained market perpetuates unequal distributions and sacrifices justice and equality to efficiency. Thus Behrman argues: 'The self-regulating market of the neo-classical economy was, in fact, never permitted to work fully because of the quickly perceived injustices of poverty, ignorance, disease and squalor that resulted from unemployment, and because of the perceived ability of some to gain more for themselves by violating the rules.'[46] Or again: 'Nor is there a direct correlation between degrees of freedom in a market and economic justice; a free market may merely mean that existing power and injustices are perpetuated.'[47] Focusing on the international economy, Tinbergen argues for 'humanistic socialism' (what we would term compensatory liberalism) geared to 'equalizing opportunites within and among nations'. Such equalizing of opportunities cannot be achieved under the free market, which is seen as being responsible for many contemporary 'injustices'. Thus: 'If the inexorable workings of market forces have helped create the problems, it is clear that they, if left to their own devices, will not be able to solve them.'[48]

The crux of the matter concerns the invisible hand management system so beloved by the pure liberals. According to the compensatory liberals, the market is an inappropriate decision-maker. Decision-making involves, so it is argued, normative choices on the part of humans for which the impersonal market is quite unsuited. Since, in Behrman's words, the 'market is no more than a mechanism and, like a computer, cannot make decisions', then decision-making has to be transferred elsewhere. The right and proper place is

> in the political arena, through direct negotiation, for the free market will respond to what is (or what is thought to be) and not what ought to be. The market permits only those to participate who have 'earned' the income with which to participate; it will not redistribute benefits or opportunities to help change the system.[49]

This playing down of the salience of the free market of the pure liberals by the compensatory liberals has its counterpart in the increased emphasis placed by the latter on the role of government. While the pure liberals anticipate only limited government, primarily to protect or enhance the market, the compensatory liberals, because of their misgivings about the free market, envisage a much more active and extensive government.

The two most important general functions of government, over and above those envisaged by pure liberals, are taken to be aggregate management of the economy and the provision of collective welfare.

The main formal rationale of the aggregate management function came with the Keynesian revolution. The management function of the invisible hand of the pure liberals' free market was now to be replaced by governmental fiscal and monetary policies. It would, however, be erroneous to think that the market is defunct. Solo catches the difference well when he contrasts the 'housekeeping' function (pure liberalism) with the 'offset' function (compensatory liberalism):

> Keynes made no new discoveries, nor did he propose new policies . . . Keynes' accomplishment was of another order. What he and his followers did was to offer economic orthodoxy a schemata in which the realities of mass unemployment could at long last be recognized without rejecting the neoclassical faith. In the Keynesian conception of things the market system was taken without reserve as the proper, indeed as the only viable, allocator of resources, distributor of income, organizer of production and consumption — all was left as before except that it was now conceded that the aggregate of expenditures spontaneously generated in the private economy might be too little, producing unemployment, or too great, producing inflation . . . Hence, it becomes the task and responsibility of government to maintain the proper pressure by compensating for or offsetting deviations.[50]

Solo continues to argue that offsetting requires substantial public planning and hence the type of pictures drawn by Shonfield or Galbraith:

> It must respond to what happens in the market economy. It is a system of counter-punching. Effectiveness depends on a capacity to anticipate what is coming in a highly variable universe of private choice itself permeated with uncertainties, and as well on the capacity to foresee the response of the private economy to whatever the political authority attempts. Hence, offsets require forecasts.[51]

Structurally this is represented in the massive array of governmental monetary and fiscal measures and institutionalized in the use of budgets as a macro management device.

The collective welfare function is manifested in a large variety of ways including the provision of services (such as education and health), income redistribution (through transfer payments, progressive taxation or wealth taxes) or legislated welfare (as for example in minimum wages, job protection, health and safety standards). What is happening in this context is not any thorough-going commitment to equality, as would be found with the socialists, but a commitment to provide basic welfare to all members of the community and thereby to enhance the range of alternatives available to the populace. What is particularly significant is that such provision will often once again be 'offsetting' in the sense that it would involve some degree of positive discrimination, that is, explicit attempts to provide compensation to what are perceived to be less privileged groups. Thus we find the advocacy of mechanisms such as progressive taxation or regional development grants or job quotas to assist minority groups.

These two principal functions give government a much more active role than that of the pure liberal and lead compensatory liberals to grasp much more readily the notion and ethos of democracy. While it would be erroneous to see pure liberals as anti-democratic (though they certainly oppose certain forms of democracy), democracy does not figure prominently in pure liberalism except as a device primarily orientated to recruiting and changing governments. Compensatory liberals, by dint of seeing a more expansive role for government, see democracy as being substantially more central and important. Using Macpherson's terminology, the 'protective' conceptualization is traded for a 'developmental' one. A critical component of democracy is admittedly a mechanistic one whereby governments are elected by and subjected to popular demand, but another component is that whereby the government, calling on the legitimacy of popular sovereignty, plays an active and promotional role to produce a type of society, likely to be called even a democratic society, which affords increasing equality of opportunity or choice to its members.

Similarly at the international level, compensatory liberals anticipate the need for an active promotional role on the part of governments or intergovernmental organizations. Like the pure liberals, the compensatory liberals have not only a highly developed sense of world community but also one which reflects an extension of domestic values. Thus Tinbergen asserts:

> The fundamental aim of the world community should be formulated as: to achieve a life of dignity and well-being for all world citizens . . . The fundamental aim formulated above has its root in the conviction that all human beings have an equal right to a life of dignity and to satisfaction in their threefold capacities as citizens, producers and consumers.[52]

While the mangement and welfare functions of government have been well developed within the Western liberal democracies, the compensatory liberal holds that the international analogue is seriously underdeveloped. As such the compensatory liberal is generally committed to a substantial strengthening and extension of international governmental agencies well beyond the constitutionalism of the pure liberal so that international economic management and particularly welfare can be more actively promoted.

The desired continuity between domestic and international arrangements, common also to the pure liberal, does not however lead to the same blurring anticipated by the pure liberal. The more active role of government leads to a greater salience of the nation state and as such there is a greater hiatus for the compensatory liberal between national and international arrangements. While the pure liberal has a propensity to see the nation state as just about archaic and envisages a merging of domestic and international arrangements, the compensatory liberal sees nation states as more distinctive, and assuredly not archaic, and wishes to recreate internationally much of the same governmental machinery that has developed domestically within the Western liberal democracies.

Belief system

Although the term liberal only came to be employed, after having been imported from Spain, from the early nineteenth century, the liberal tradition is generally dated from the seventeenth century with the work particularly of Locke but also of Milton and Sidney. While there are undoubtedly certain pre-eminent liberal writers, there is certainly no single writer to whom one can turn for any core statement of the liberal credo.[53] The evolution of liberalism, though in some respects cumulative, is quite complex and tortuous. By dint of developing into a major tradition, liberalism is multi-faceted.[54] Furthermore, liberal writers have always, very understandably, been strongly influenced by the demands of their own particular times.[55] Our task, however, is not to trace the complex historical evolution but rather to indicate those core beliefs that provide a set of common denominators throughout this evolution.[56]

The cornerstone of the pure liberal belief system is an unwavering faith in and commitment to the individual. There are two sides to this commitment to the individual. The more negative is the abhorrence of coercion of one individual by another, in which respect coercion is the interference in one individual's wishes or desires by another. The more positive side is the conviction in individual initiative. In this respect liberals hold what is tantamount to an individual psychology in the belief that individual initiative is the main source of creativity and dynamism. Unfettered individuals constitute the main locus for change and innovation. These two sides are of course not discrete — creativity cannot be achieved except under the condition of absence of interference, while absence of interference, while desirable in its own right, is also deemed necessary for promoting creativity.

The emphasis on the individual should not however be taken to indicate that liberalism is an asocial doctrine. On the contrary, liberalism has a highly developed sense of community and indeed considers that substantial benefits can accrue from individuals forming themselves not only into societies but into ever larger societies. Indeed in this context the key liberal principles of the division of labour and comparative advantage are explicit manifestations of the gains from social intercourse. The critical point for the liberal is that the individual stands before society and that at no point must society take priority over the individual.

While liberalism values the individual above all else, liberalism is not a doctrine for the reification of individual autarchy. Conceptions of isolated or self-contained individualism are not germane to liberalism. In forming societies, however, individuals face very serious risks of having their individual wills compromised. The whole of the structural arrangement of the pure liberal is then a very explicit design, and the fact that it is minimalist does not stop it from being a design, to ensure the absence of interference and the associated spontaneous dynamism in a societal framework.

Thus, the appeal of the market is that it accommodates thousands or millions of economic decisions of individuals in their capacities as producers or consumers, which it achieves without employing coercion or interference. Furthermore it simultaneously not only allows but actually encourages spontaneous innovation. Producers are free to offer new products or invent ways of reducing costs on existing production. As such the market contains its own incentive or reward system in the form of enhanced profits. This logic of the market, moreover, is not confined simply to economic production but is generalizable to cultural or artistic or scientific or intellectual innovation and creativity. The appeal of limited constitutional government is that it permits those necessary restrictions of individual freedoms, that is, those that may be injurious to others, and simultaneously protects and enhances market intercourse.

It is from this perspective that the liberal abhorrence of planning in the form of centralized direction can be appreciated. Thus, it is absurd to the pure liberal that a small group of planners can anticipate the demands of a large and complex market. It is equally absurd to pretend, furthermore, that a small group could rival the innovatory potential of the market. Or again, the interventions of the centralized planning group are divorced from the type of built-in control that characterizes the market; there are, in other words, no criteria for evaluation save those created, or not created, by the planners themselves. Centralized planning, in short, totally destroys the spontaneous dynamism of individual initiative that constitutes the core of the liberal belief system.

We may turn now to examine very briefly some of the main corollaries of this conviction in individual initiative. One undoubted consequence is some ready acceptance of inequality. Pure liberals are not in the slightest committed to the institutionalization of inequality and indeed are strongly opposed to such institutionalizations on the grounds both of unacceptable interference and curtailment of innovation. On the other hand, pure liberals recognize very explicitly the variability in every form of human skill and talent. Furthermore, they wish to harness this variability, which explains why such store is set by the free market arrangement which allows such variability, that is, inequality, in skill and talent full rein. In this respect some degree of inequality actually becomes one of the main driving forces of pure liberalism.[57]

A second corollary is that the pure liberal does not see such inequality as immutable. Indeed not only is inequality a source of initiative but also a constant stimulus for change and adaptation. For example, if one producer happens to develop a more efficient means of production then this producer's competitors will quickly adopt that innovation, thereby ensuring a speedy diffusion. In this respect the pure liberal system anticipates a setting whereby the innovations of a few can be projected onto the many. Or again, if one region begins to lag behind others then wage rates or rental rates will fall, which in turn will make it attractive to future investment. What the pure liberal sees in this context are shifting centres of gravity. There will always be inequalities, and indeed these are necessary for dynamism, but there will also be built-in strains towards equalization. In this respect, the pure liberal envisages cycles of inequality–equalization–new inequalities and so on.

A third corollary pertains to efficiency. A free and competitive market ensures the most productive allocation of resources. Production only takes place in response to market demand and will increase or decrease in response to market changes. Furthermore the built-in incentive systems ensure constant pressure for productivity increases. In this way then the market provides the most productive allocation of resources and this is what defines efficiency.

A fourth corollary relates to progress. Liberalism is an optimistic doctrine not only in that it considers liberalism to be a viable but also highly desirable condition. More interestingly it also contains a built-in conceptualization of progress. Progress essentially is quite simply liberal change, which in turn is that change brought about by leaving undisturbed the spontaneous creativity of free individuals. In this respect then progress is not defined by particular substantive goals. Indeed trying to harness development to specified goals would be seen as a distortion. Thus progress for the liberal is not defined by approximation to particular substantive goals but rather by permitting the dynamic of liberalism free rein. It is in the very nature of spontaneous creativity that we would not know where it will lead.[58]

A fifth corollary concerns community welfare. As we have already emphasized, the liberal focus on the promotion of the individual does not detract at all from a highly developed sense of community. Community welfare is achieved in two rather different ways. First, the liberal structural arrangement of competition within a condition of the free market and limited government produces a system of cross-cutting diversity and pluralism. This complex diversity in turn is seen as providing security. Indeed with a high level of voluntary exchange and interdependence only minimal security is required — hence the limited role of government. Diffused competition is then a strategy for cooperation in which coercion is reduced to a minimum.

A second form of community welfare relates more specifically to economic concerns. The competitive market is seen as the most efficient means of production and the arrangement most conducive to general optimal growth. As long as the market is open then the benefits of growth will be diffused. For example, an improvement in production is likely to bring reduced prices which benefit consumers, or under certain conditions may lead to expanded production which means among other things an expansion of employment. Thus, there exist in the liberal schema a multiplicity of ways in which the benefits of growth, such as expanding production, are automatically diffused. This does not mean to say that inequalities will be eradicated (in fact they assuredly will not) but that some equalization will take place as benefits are diffused. In this respect liberal economic theory has a clear position on distribution, although its main focus lies on production.[59]

A final point, and one which has been mentioned already, concerns the universalizing tendency of liberalism. Other things being equal, liberalism considers that the larger a liberal community can become the better. Over and above the almost tautological point that liberals consider their system to be more desirable than any other, liberalism cannot interact easily with non-liberal systems. Furthermore the gains from the division of labour and comparative advantage are greater the larger the community. This means that pure liberalism is anational, or for that matter outside any other grouping, such as class or ethnic or religious group.

A very noteworthy facet of this universalizing tendency concerns what we might call the basic constituency of pure liberalism, which is located on the individual within the liberal community. While nation states may have proved useful and possibly may have been even inevitable historically, they are none the less a temporary and increasingly unnecessary form of organization. As such it is the individual liberal producer and consumer within an expanding liberal community that must take priority over individuals within nation states. Thus, let us assume, for example, that production of a particular good can be more efficiently undertaken in a different country, then producers of that good in already producing areas should cease production and find a new field of comparative advantage. In this way pure liberalism would dictate the disruption of domestic production, in already producing areas, for the greater benefit of the liberal community as a whole. This is what we mean by liberals adopting as their basic constituency not the nation state or even individuals within nation states but individuals within the larger liberal community.

The compensatory variant of liberalism has become decidedly more pronounced in the twentieth century such that it, rather than pure liberalism, tends to represent liberal orthodoxy.[60] However, compensatory liberalism is assuredly not purely a twentieth-century phenomenon. There are elements of compensatory liberalism in Mill but it first became more distinctive with the Montague and Green critiques of Mill. Thus, Green argued in 1879 for increased state intervention for the government to promote the moral development of that individual. Later, in 1911, Hobhouse added the argument that in order to promote liberty it was also necessary to promote greater social and economic equality. Particularly in Hobhouse the main parameters of compensatory liberalism are firmly set in place.[61]

Compensatory liberals most assuredly do not reject the pure liberal interpretation and conceptualization of the individual, and indeed if they did then the term liberal simply could not be applied to them. What does differentiate these two variants of liberalism is that the compensatory liberal argues that too much emphasis and too much faith is placed on the individual. Pure liberalism takes too extreme a view of individualism at the expense of having too stringent or restricted a view of community.[62] We can perhaps illustrate this divergence of emphasis by examining the position of the compensatory liberal on each of the six corollaries just identified.

Compensatory liberals make no claims whatsoever towards eradicating inequality. They do however hold a distinctly meritocratic view of equality. By this they mean that inequalities not only can be tolerated but indeed are desirable. The critical factor, however, is that such inequalities should only be based on individual merit. To amplify this point we need to turn to the second corollary.

Compensatory liberals do not share the same faith as pure liberals in the mutability of inequality. Indeed they argue that, in the absence of substantial intervention, inequalities are likely to be self-perpetuating. We may begin with one of several illustrations purely at the individual level. Thus, compensatory liberals argue for a tax on inherited wealth because without such taxes the offspring of the wealthy enjoy substantial advantages over others which they are likely to continue to enjoy on the grounds that, other things being equal, wealth begets wealth. This clearly contradicts meritocratic principles.

A second illustration points up a more important critique by the compensatory liberals, which is that pure liberals focus too exclusively on coercion of any one individual by another and fail to appreciate sufficiently structural coercion. By this they mean that structural features of society bestow much greater opportunities on some than others. For example the offspring of a manual worker have much less chance of, say, entry to university than the offspring of a professional worker. Once again this conflicts with meritocratic principles.

A third illustration might take up the regional one used above. In this context compensatory liberals would argue that a region may become sufficiently depressed that, even though wage rates and rental costs may be lower, it would not attract new investment which will tend to cluster around the dynamic centres of innovation. What can happen in this context then is that inequalities become frozen.

On the question of equality, then, compensatory liberals, while not being at all committed to absolute equality, argue that pure market forces, left to their own devices, can perpetuate inequalities and this is undesirable on meritocratic grounds. What in essence is happening here is that a critical belief of the pure liberals is being turned back against them. Talented individuals or groups may well be discriminated against and societies, in failing to utilize fully the talents of such individuals, are failing to maximize their creative potentials. In the illustrations we have used this argument would lead compensatory liberals to advocate wealth taxes, public schooling (combined with things like bussing or quotas or free university entry) and regional development grants or tax incentives. The common denominator through each of these particular policies is corrective intervention. This in turn explains the proclivity of compensatory liberals for more active and promotional government at the expense of the free market.

On the issue of efficiency, compensatory liberals do not really dispute the conceptualization of efficiency in terms of the optimum use of productive resources. What they do dispute is the centrality of efficiency and the market as the most efficient allocator. The argument is that the impersonal allocation by the market is not necessarily the most desirable allocation. Production accordingly to the compensatory liberals requires human decision-making, which, in turn, is based on human values. This then leads them to attach less importance to efficiency and give more attention to human needs.

This in turn leads to the next two corollaries, progress and welfare, which we can consider together. It is a mistake to think that the pure liberals' emphasis on the individual leads them to be oblivious to the community. However, while pure liberals approach the community through the individual, compensatory liberals follow either the opposite route or at least certainly give greater priority to community. This is manifested very explicitly in the conceptualization of welfare which is the satisfaction of at least basic needs of all members of the community. There is no precise stipulation of basic needs and indeed it is set very differently across different societies in terms of their levels of development. What is in fact interesting about this relativity is that it increases with development. In the West, welfare has come to be interpreted in terms of the Welfare State provisions of basic housing, education, health, social security and so on. The critical point here then is the conviction that the community has an obligation to provide at least basic provision for all its members. Trickle-down growth is not sufficient for compensatory liberals who wish to see explicit intervention so as to ensure the basic provision for all.

This in turn means a rather more substantive conceptualization of progress. Progress is not the spontaneous and unknown evolution profiled in pure liberalism. Rather, progress is a liberal community coming together through representative government to decide on which collective policies need to be pursued and then pursuing them. Progress to the compensatory liberal therefore entails much more planning and conscious direction than that of the pure liberal.

Finally, compensatory liberalism is just as much a universalizing doctrine as the pure variant. On account of compensatory liberalism's differential emphasis on the individual and community, it does tend to be more orientated towards the nation state. Thus there is a much stronger commitment to the government of any nation state being responsible first and foremost for the welfare of its own citizens. For example, compensatory liberals are decidedly more reticent about allowing, say, an industry to be displaced due to a new comparative advantage elsewhere. This more overtly 'nationalistic' tendency on the other hand is countervailed by an advocacy of an obligation of the more developed nation states to assist the less developed. What is happening here is that the domestic argument, that some individuals or groups may be structurally disadvantaged and hence require special assistance in the form of positive discrimination, is projected onto an international level. In other words, compensatory liberals profile a conceptualization of global welfare. Once again we see them turning round one of the pure liberal beliefs by arguing that intervention that succeeds in promoting the productive potential of less privileged nation states enhances global efficiency and in this way is of mutual gain to all concerned.

Notes

1. Following the convention in liberal discussion, freedom and liberty are taken as synonyms.
2. The significance of the 'human' interference is to emphasize that non-human obstacles are not seen as unfreedoms. For example, an inability to jump ten metres in the air is not regarded as an unfreedom.
3. I. Berlin, *Four Essays on Liberty*, Oxford, Oxford University Press, 1969, p. 122.
4. F.A. von Hayek, *Law, Legislation and Liberty*, vol. 3, London, Routledge & Kegan Paul, 1979, p. 129. Hayek's most popular work in this area is *The Road to Serfdom*, London, Routledge & Kegan Paul, 1976. The ideas contained in this book, originally published in 1944, are spelled out in more detail and sophistication in *The Constitution of Liberty*, London, Routledge & Kegan Paul, 1960; *Rules and Order*, *The Mirage of Social Justice*, *The Political Order of a Free People* (these last three books make up the three volumes of *Law, Legislation and Liberty*, published respectively in 1973, 1976 and 1979).
5. For an exposition of the difference between positive and negative freedom see Berlin, op cit. Further discussion of this contrast will be found in the next chapter dealing with the socialist paradigm.
6. M. Friedman, *Capitalism and Freedom*, Chicago, University of Chicago Press, 1962, p. 4.
7. Hayek, *Law, Legislation and Liberty*, vol. 3, p. 139.
8. F. Machlup, 'Liberalism and the Choice of Freedoms' in E. Streissler (ed.), *Roads to Freedom*, London, Routledge & Kegan Paul, 1969, p. 127.
9. Ibid. Hayek makes the same point when he comments: 'Probably nothing has done so much harm to the liberal cause as the wooden insistence of some liberals on

certain rules of thumb, above all the principle of laissez-faire.' (Hayek, *The Road to Serfdom*, p. 13).

10. For illustrations of the critique, see L. Crocker, *Positive Liberty*, London, Nijhoff, 1980; R. Dworkin, *Taking Rights Seriously*, London, Duckworth, 1977; A. Gutmann, *Liberal Equality*, Cambridge, Cambridge University Press, 1980; G. MacCallum, 'Negative and Positive Freedom', *Philosopical Review*, **76**, 1967; C.B. Macpherson, 'Berlin's Division of Liberty' in C.B. Macpherson (ed.), *Democratic Theory*, Oxford, Oxford University Press, 1973; D. Spitz, *The Real World of Liberalism*, Chicago, University of Chicago Press, 1982; C. Taylor, 'What's Wrong with Negative Liberty', in A. Ryan (ed.), *The Idea of Freedom*, Oxford, Oxford University Press, 1979.
11. Berlin, op. cit., p. 125.
12. Crocker, op. cit., p. 2.
13. S.I. Benn and W.L. Weinstein, 'Being Free to Act and Being a Free Man', *Mind*, **80**, 1971, p. 194.
14. Berlin, op. cit., p. xxxix.
15. Machlup, op. cit., p. 124.
16. For a variety of critiques, see for example: Friedman, op. cit.; L. von Mises, *Socialism*, New Haven, Yale University Press, 1951; K. Joseph and J. Sumption, *Equality*, London, Murray, 1979.
17. We do not imply that the compensatory position fuses liberalism and socialism to the point of consuming both. Rather it represents a partial acceptance of some socialist ideas and some liberal ones (generally in favour of the latter). There is still a distinctive socialist model.
18. Dworkin, op. cit., p. 273. Or again Dworkin comments: 'The sovereign question of political theory, within a state supposed to be governed by the liberal conception of equality, is the question of what inequalities in goods, opportunities and liberties are permitted in such a state, and why.' (loc. cit.). This would not be a 'sovereign question' for socialists.
19. There is no single term for the compensatory liberal goal (as there is with negative freedom for the pure liberal). Thus Crocker refers to positive freedom (which is rather confusing as it is not positive freedom as defined by Berlin); MacCallum argues for only one conception of freedom; Dworkin refers to liberal equality; Macpherson contrasts counter-extractive freedom (essentially negative freedom) with developmental freedom (one of the three uses of positive freedom confounded according to him in Berlin's positive freedom). The absence of a single term is only a handicap as far as a shorthand is concerned. The more critical point is that we can define the goal, which is essentially an amalgam of negative freedom and equality, where equality refers to opportunities or choices.
20. Hayek, *Law, Legislation and Liberty*, vol. 3, p. 74.
21. Ibid., p. 164.
22. Friedman, op. cit., p. 15.
23. One of the strongest statements on market transformations is found in Galbraith's work. While Galbraith undoubtedly has some arguments that the market has been superseded, he also argues that oligopolies do not preclude competition. See: J.K. Galbraith, *The New Industrial State*, Boston, Houghton Mifflin, 1967.
24. There are, furthermore, certain conditions under which oligopolies or monopolies are desirable. These include economies of scale, technological demands that require

25. Hayek, *The Road to Serfdom*, p. 26.
26. H.G. Johnson, *The World Economy at the Crossroads*, Oxford, Clarendon Press, 1965, p. 8.
27. Friedman, op. cit., p. 3.
28. R.A. Solo, 'The Economist and the Economic Roles of the Political Authority in Advanced Industrial Societies' in L.N. Lindberg *et al.* (eds.), *Stress and Contradiction in Modern Capitalism*, Lexington, D.C. Heath, 1975, p. 100.
29. This has been a dominant theme from Montesquieu and the reasoning of the Founding Fathers in drawing up the constitutional arrangements for the United States government.
30. Liberals are strongly committed to constitutional provisions but it is erroneous to equate a constitutional commitment with liberalism. Liberals are interested in particular types of constitutions, that is, those that limit governmental powers. It is perfectly conceivable to have a constitution that grants extensive power to government, which would be quite contrary to liberal convictions. Hayek emphasizes in this context the distinction between legislation, as the articulation of general rules of conduct, and government, as the allocation of particular means to particular purposes. The critical point is that government needs to be constrained by legislation. For a fuller discussion see especially Hayek, *Law, Legislation and Liberty*, vol. 3; and Hayek, *Constitution of Liberty*.
31. This particular component has tended to receive disproportionate attention. For recent discussions see R.A. Dahl, *Polyarchy*, New Haven, Yale University Press, 1971; and R.A. Dahl, *Dilemmas of Pluralist Democracy*, New Haven, Yale University Press, 1982.
32. See especially Hayek, *Law, Legislation and Liberty*, vol. 3.
33. Ibid., p. 123.
34. C.B. Macpherson, *The Life and Times of Liberal Democracy*, Oxford, Oxford University Press, 1977, p. 43.
35. The term 'democracy' is used in a multiplicity of very different fashions and consequently the question of whether a particular form of government is democratic is rather meaningless. Since the term has become a 'hurrah' word it is applied to virtually every conceivable form of government. The point to be emphasized here is that liberals are opposed to all populist or egalitarian conceptualizations of democracy. We might also add that what are commonly called the liberal democracies, i.e. the governments of the West, should not be taken by any stretch of the imagination to be prototypes of the desired form of pure liberal government. For general discussions of some of the varieties of democracy see R.A. Dahl, *A Preface to Democratic Theory*, Chicago, University of Chicago Press, 1967; C.B. Macpherson, *The Real World of Democracy*, Oxford, Oxford University Press, 1972.
36. It is primarily the fear of unrestrained government under popular sovereignty that leads Hayek to comment that 'an unlimited democracy may well be worse than limited governments of a different kind.' (Hayek, *Law, Legislation and Liberty*, vol. 3, p. 138) or Berlin: 'Some of my critics are made indignant by the thought that a man may, on this view, have more 'negative' liberty under the rule of an easy-going or inefficient despot than in a strenuous, but intolerant, egalitarian democracy' (Berlin, op. cit., p. lvii).

The liberal model   51

37. Hayek, *The Road to Serfdom*, p. 163.
38. F. Hirsch, 'Politicization in the World Economy' in F. Hirsch *et al.*, *Alternatives to Monetary Disorder*, New York, McGraw Hill, 1977.
39. A. Shonfield, *Modern Capitalism*, London, Oxford University Press, 1969.
40. Indeed so important is this new planning that Shonfield distinguishes various forms which he terms indicative planning, reinforced government powers and corporatism. The latter, which has subsequently received much attention, does not of necessity require explicit governmental intervention but rather the government plays a form of brokerage role in bringing together major groups, especially business and unions, into a single corporate whole.
41. Galbraith, op. cit.
42. Galbraith is one of several writers who have called attention not only to the impact of technology but also of the technostructure. See, for example: P.F. Drucker, *The Age of Discontinuity*, London, Heinemann, 1969; J. Elul, *The Technological Society*, New York, Knopf, 1964; J. Meynaud, *Technocracy*, London, Faber and Faber, 1968.
43. Galbraith, op. cit., p. 389.
44. Ibid., p. 390. For a response to this, see, for example, Z. Brzezinski, *Between Two Ages*, New York, Viking Press, 1970; or G.N. Halm, 'Will Market Economies and Planned Economies Converge?' in E. Streissler (ed.), *Roads to Freedom*.
45. J.N. Behrman, *Towards a New International Economic Order*, Paris, Atlantic Institute for International Affairs, 1974, p. 22.
46. Ibid., p. 10.
47. Ibid, p. 10.
48. J. Tinbergen *et al.*, *Reshaping the International Order*, New York, Dutton, 1976, p. 15.
49. Behrman, op. cit., p. 48.
50. Solo, op. cit., p. 101.
51. Ibid., p. 103.
52. Tinbergen, op. cit., p. 61.
53. Indeed in this context many writers taken to be central to the liberal tradition would not have identified themselves as liberal due to the term being employed only from the early nineteenth century. Furthermore there is some important variation in the use of the term 'liberal' in different countries which additionally complicates, if not entirely defeats, any simple lexicographical definition of liberalism. For a good succinct discussion of this and related points, see M. Cranston, *Freedom*, London, Longman, 1967.
54. By this we mean that different writers have had different substantive emphases, for example government (in Locke or Mill), economics (in Smith) or metaphysics (in Kant).
55. For example Locke was responding against the doctrine of the divine right of kings, or Montesquieu against tyrannical monarchs, or Madison against the demands of a whole new system of government, or de Tocqueville against the French Revolution or von Humboldt against the new Prussian bureaucracy, or in more recent times Schlesinger and Cohen in favour of New Deal type interventions or Hayek and Friedman against socialism.
56. For some general historical surveys, see for example: E.K. Bransted and K.J. Melhuish, *Western Liberalism*, London, Longman, 1978; Cranston, op. cit.; D.J.

Manning, *Liberalism*, London, Dent, 1976; G. de Ruggiero, *The History of Western Liberalism*, London, Oxford University Press, 1927.

57. If what we might call the 'positive' justification for some degree of inequality is dynamism, then the 'negative' argument against inequality is the point we have met above in the discussion of planning that attempts to eradicate inequality through intervention lead to coercion. Thus, a leading polemicist for pure liberalism argues: 'In an open and free society, political action which deliberately aimed to minimize, or even remove, economic differences [i.e. differences in income and wealth] would entail such extensive coercion that the society would cease to be open and free. The successful pursuit of the unholy grail of economic equality would exchange the promised reduction or removal of differences in income and wealth for much greater actual inequality of power between rulers and subjects. There is an underlying contradiction in egalitarianism in open societies.' (P.T. Bauer, *Equality, The Third World and Economic Delusion*, London, Weidenfeld and Nicolson, 1981, p. 8).

58. One of Hayek's major arguments in *The Road to Serfdom* is interesting in this context. Hayek argues that the very success of liberalism gave rise to the belief that man could control his own destiny. This issued in a propensity for intervention and planning, which in turn is undermining the very basis (that is, the spontaneity of the market) on which success had been achieved.

59. This point will be developed more in a later chapter. A common critique by the pure liberal of compensatory liberalism and especially of socialism is that they are guilty of almost an exclusive focus on distribution to the neglect of production. This point is commonly put in the form that pure liberals are much more interested in expanding the pie (and achieving greater welfare through this expanded pie) while compensatory liberals and especially socialists are preoccupied with dividing an existing pie. According to pure liberals, the interventions to redistribute the pie remove the potential for expansion and are thereby counter-productive.

60. It would be wrong to think of compensatory liberalism as the outgrowth of a now defunct pure liberalism. The latter is still very prevalent though unquestionably in domestic concerns compensatory liberalism has become the orthodoxy, rendering pure liberalism thereby more radical. On the other hand, as we shall see later, in international affairs it is difficult to decide which of the two variants represents the orthodoxy. We might also emphasize that it would be wrong to equate pure and compensatory liberalism with early and later liberalism. Even though compensatory liberalism has become more prevalent recently, pure liberalism has continued to evolve and should not as such be seen as being coterminous with early liberalism.

61. L.T. Hobhouse *Liberalism*, New York, Oxford University Press, 1964. Though the identification of 'firsts' is rather dangerous, a good argument could be made that Hobhouse presents certainly one of the first comprehensive statements of compensatory liberalism. In this context it is interesting to note that Hobhouse himself often uses the expressions of 'liberal socialism' and 'socialist liberalism'.

62. Thus Hobhouse, in arguing that the importance of an 'organic' or 'harmonic' view of society states 'while the life of society is nothing but the life of individuals as they act one upon another, the life of the individual in turn would be something utterly different if he could be separated from society. A great deal of him would not exist at all.' (ibid., p. 67). However, if 'the argument might seem to make the individual too

subservient to society', Hobhouse continues to emphasize the pure liberal commitment to individualism: 'Society consists wholly of persons. It has no distinct personality separate from and superior to those of its members.' (ibid., p. 68). Or again, having criticized socialists for being at times oblivious to 'elements of individual right and personal independence', and some Liberals for 'leaning its whole weight' on such considerations, Hobhouse continues: 'By keeping to the conception of harmony as our clue we constantly define the rights of the individual in terms of the common good, and think of the common good in terms of the welfare of all the individuals who constitute a society' (ibid., p. 108).

3 The socialist model

Goal

We take the major goal of the socialist model to be the promotion and protection of equality. Thus:

> Ask any socialist in a Western country today what his goals are, and his answer will at least include the following: greater equality in conditions of life, in particular the alleviation of the greatest conditions of need, a shift in priorities towards collective goals and needs, rendering the decision-making structures of society more responsive to citizens.[1]

Socialists are of course not alone in noting the widespread manifestation of inequalities in all areas of social life. There are, however, two characteristics which unequivocally distinguish the socialist view, of which the first is the conviction that inequality is not inevitable.

Neither the realists nor the liberals are directly concerned to promote and protect inequality, as is indicated quite clearly in their primary goal orientations.[2] The realists do, however, accept substantial inequality and are more concerned to manage inequality through mechanisms such as the balance of power rather than to eradicate it. While pure liberals regard some forms of inequality as undesirable, such as cartels or monopolies, other forms are seen as desirable. Thus, variations, that is to say inequalities, in individual initiative are one of the main driving forces of the pure liberal system. Compensatory liberals have a more ambivalent attitude toward inequality, being concerned in particular that an unregulated market can perpetuate inequalities that hamper the pursuit of negative freedom. None the less, the emphasis is on removing those inequities that hinder negative freedom rather than eradicating inequities *per se*.

To the socialist, however, inequality is assuredly not inevitable, except in the area of inequalities in individual physiology or talent which, short of genetic engineering, certainly not advocated, cannot be removed.[3] To the socialist inequality is only inevitable under non-socialist systems of social organization. Indeed most socialists would suggest that the kind of distinction made by realists and liberals, that is, no commitment to promote inequality but acceptance of some degree of inequality as inevitable, is too fine. Systems of social organization that are not explicitly committed to eradicating inequality must of necessity be guilty of systematizing it either directly or indirectly. For example, against the liberals it is argued that

> the combination of a market economy and political pluralism is one which makes the redistribution of advantages between social classes difficult to bring about ... A political system which guarantees constitutional rights for groups to organize in defence of their interests is almost bound to favour the privileged at the expense of the disprivileged ... Only if the main political contestants were to enjoy a roughly similar economic and social status could we say that pluralist democracy was a system of genuine political equality ... Thus, in the absence of socio-economic preconditions for political equality, pluralism is quite plausibly regarded as a philosophy which tends to reflect the perceptions and interests of a privileged class.[4]

Parkin goes on to argue that this explains why Social Democrats have not been successful in undermining privileges guaranteed by the market and private property. For the socialists, then, inequality is inevitable in any non-socialist form of social organization; only under a socialist system can genuine equality be achieved.

The second characteristic of the socialist approach to equality is its holistic and structural elements. Economic, political, social and cultural inequalities are all seen either as being reciprocally related or alternatively economic inequalities are seen as being the root of other inequalities. Consequently, any incremental or piecemeal approach to the eradication of inequality is totally inadequate: 'There is an economic, as well as social, stratification; a hierarchy of industry and labour, as well as of leisure and enjoyment. When the injustices of the second have been softened or abolished, it still remains to eliminate the tyranny of the first.'[5] The same author, commenting on the unequal powers and advantages of different classes, says:

> Till such powers and advantages have been equalized in fact, not merely in form, by the extension of communal provision and collective control, the equality established by the removal of restrictions on property and enterprise resembles that produced by turning an elephant loose on the crowd. It offers everyone, except the beast and his rider, equal opportunities of being trampled to death.[6]

The socialist approach is holistic in the sense that all inequalities are mutually reinforcing and need to be attacked simultaneously; it is structural in the sense that inequality is rooted in the basic institutions and organizations of society, which require wholesale and radical change.[7]

The pursuit of equality is therefore only possible under a socialist system of organization in which all the institutions and structural arrangements that harbour inequality have been removed. Equality entails the elimination of those features that perpetuate domination or control. Equality becomes that condition in which there are 'no barriers to reciprocal relations between relatively autonomous persons, who see each other and themselves as such, who are equally free from political control, social pressure and economic deprivation and insecurity to engage in valued pursuits, and who have equal access to the means of self-development.'[8] Or again, socialism is seen as entailing 'the creation of a social order in which there is the maximum feasible equality of access, for all human beings, to economic resources to knowledge, and to political power, and the minimum possible domination exercised by any individual or social group over any others.'[9] Equality for the socialist then becomes compatible with freedom, but this is not the negative freedom of the liberal but positive freedom. Thus when socialists talk of 'self-development' or 'self-realization', they are reflecting the conception of positive freedom as defined by Berlin: 'The "positive" sense of the word "liberty" derives from the wish on the part of the individual to be his own master. I wish my life and decisions to depend on myself, not on external forces of whatever kind.'[10] Such freedom can only be achieved with thoroughgoing equality. Thus:

> A society is free in so far, and only in so far, as, within the limits set by nature, knowledge and resources, its institutions and policies are such as to enable all its members to grow to their full stature, and to do their duty as they see it.[11]

In sum, the socialist conception of equality does not mean the type of equality, contemplated by realists or liberals, which is contingent essentially on balancing or countervailing inequalities. Nor does it mean the meritocratic pursuit of equality of opportunity. Nor does it mean a homogenization of society whereby individuals would be reduced to a collection of clones. Rather the pursuit of equality means the removal of relations of domination and exploitation in all areas of social life — or as Marx puts it: '[the] overthrow [of] all conditions in which man is a debased, enslaved, neglected and contemptible being' — such that collectively individuals are free to develop their own full potentials. It is the 'right to self-realization, an inalienable right of personal growth' in a context free of domination and exploitation that constitutes the core of the socialist goal of equality.

Structural arrangement

There are unquestionably difficulties in specifying the type of structural arrangement needed to sustain the goal of equality. Because inequality is so firmly rooted in the basic institutional organization of contemporary society, fundamental structural change is required; and major socialist writers, such as Marx, have been intentionally reticent when it comes to specifying in any detail the structure of the necessary future organization. None the less, socialists do have some explicit ideas on the structural arrangement of a socialist system (and indeed could not sustain a conceptualization of a goal if they did not). Furthermore, there is actually quite a marked consensus on the key structural features even though these are often expressed, of necessity, in rather general terms. There tends to be much greater controversy among socialists, which need not trouble us for the moment, on the strategies for achieving socialism.

Fundamental to the structural arrangement of the socialists is the reconstitution of the economic base of society. An important component of this reconstitution is the collective ownership of the means of production, often expressed as the socialization of the means of production. Such communal ownership would eradicate the juxtaposition between capital and labour and contribute toward the removal of the exploitation by the owners of capital of those who only have their labour to sell. Thus Bahro, for instance, calls for:

> The immediate socialization of the means and conditions of production, i.e. of past, objectified labour that was formerly concentrated in capital. The expropriation of the capitalists immediately divests all this wealth of its value form, reducing it to use value. It is therefore identical with the abolition of commodity production and money in which the alienation of the producers from the products of their activity finds concentrated expression.[12]

It is generally accepted by socialists that such socialization would need to be accompanied by a substantial degree of economic planning. The main reason for this is that the market, whether competitive or monopolistic, is seen as responsive only to the wealthier groups. It is these groups that establish patterns of demand and thereby patterns of investment and production (this is commonly referred to as the law of value). Under a socialist economy, investment and production decisions need to be set not by the unequal purchasing power of different classes but by the common needs of the whole of the populace (often expressed as use value). In this respect, then, the role of planning is to supplant what are seen as inequitable vagaries of a market, dominated and controlled by the wealthy, to produce a range of goods and services dictated by the communal needs of the populace as a whole. Thus:

> An economy governed by a plan implies ... that society's relatively scarce resources are not apportioned blindly ... by the law of value but that they are consciously allocated according to previously established priorities. In a transitional economy where socialist democracy prevails, the mass of the working people democratically determines this choice of priorities.[13]

Critical though collective ownership may be, it does not in isolation constitute a sufficient restructuring. While ownership represents an extremely important source of inequality, so too does the traditional division of labour. An excellent illustration of the thorough-going holistic conception of equality is therefore presented in the socialist contention that the division of labour needs to be eradicated and indeed without this eradication individual self-realization is impossible; thus:

> The abolition of the traditional division of labour, i.e. of the servile subjection of individuals to restricted and compartmentalized tasks. Two points have to be made here. First, the overcoming of the inherited social antitheses (inequalities) between man and woman, town and country, manual and mental labour, which are anchored in the entire structure of the former productive forces and relations. Secondly, the overcoming of the technical division of labour within the factory, within the sphere of necessary labour, by raising natural science to a higher level in production governed by scientific work.[14]

If communal ownership of an economy marked by an absence of the division of labour and geared to the satisfaction of collective need can be represented as one of the main keys to the socialist structural arrangement, the second must be the reconstitution of the polity in the form of mass popular democratization. The system of pluralistic liberal democracy whereby parties compete in regular elections is generally seen by socialists either as a sham or a deliberate mystification. As the quotation from Parkin above illustrates, socialists consider it absurd to pretend that equal popular participation and control can be exercized in a context of economic inequality.

Initially confusing here is what exactly is meant by democracy. Macpherson argues quite correctly that democracy has come to have a variety of different meanings and that, particularly in the West, there has often been a tendency erroneously to equate democracy with what is in effect only one particular variant, namely liberal democracy. MacPherson refers to liberal democracy as the 'narrow' usage but argues that there is also a 'broad' usage:

> Democracy has very generally been taken to mean something more than a system of government. Democracy in this broader sense has always contained an ideal of human equality, not just equality of opportunity to climb a class ladder, but such an equality as could only be fully realized in a society where no class was able to dominate or live at the expense of others.[15]

Socialists have some interest in the narrow usage, for example they certainly accept the utility of elections, but would argue that unless the techniques of democracy — the narrow usage — are contained within a context which guarantees the broad usage, then democracy is either meaningless or worse still a system of mystification by which privileged groups essentially fool dominated groups into granting their consent.

Mass popular democratization is not autonomously separated from the economy but rather pervades the economy in an organic manner:

> The appropriation of the means of production by the associated producers destroys the sharpest expression of the traditional division of labour and class rule, its political expression in the state machine, the state apparatus, and raises to a higher level the necessary social functions that the state has usurped on top of its rule over man, in a non-politicized administration of things which devolves not on specialized officials, but on elected delegates who are at all times responsible and can be effectively dismissed.[16]

Mass popular democratization requires:

> ... strict observance of the rule limiting incomes of the party and state functionaries to those of skilled workers, a strictly limited proportion of higher-paid elements in the representative bodies, strict respect of the

right of the rank and file to criticize and keep a check on those elements, access for the workers to all sources of information and means of education, socialist democracy in the political sphere, freedom of tendencies and for the establishment of parties basing themselves on socialism, freedom of discussion . . .[17]

Although the socialist conception of democracy unquestionably contains some elements, such as elections, that are to be found in liberal democracy, it also has some critically distinctive features. For socialists democratic participation is to be diffused throughout all areas of social life, especially in work settings, and democracy must avoid permanent officials who would be incompatible with the abolition of the traditional division of labour. Consequently, there are calls for part-time office holders, the circulation of office holders, and for shorter working hours so that people can acquire more information and education enabling them to participate more fully and actively in decision-making. In short, what socialist democracy attempts to achieve is full and equal participation and control.

This is not seen to be at odds with an ethic of planning. Indeed, it is mass democratization that controls planning. Thus

> the inevitable subordination of the individual producers to a conscious centralizing authority does not necessarily imply bureaucratism, authoritarianism, or despotism, once this authority is no longer designated from above and irremovable but is elected by the rank and file and can be recalled at the pleasure of the electors. Those critics who question the possibility of this . . . confuse the social sources of power with the technical forms of its implementation.[18]

A critical supporting structure for effective democratization is education. Once again socialists are extremely critical of education in capitalist society, arguing that it inculcates capitalist values, reifies the cult of the expert, institutionalizes class inequalities, and furthers capitalist production.[19] What is under attack is not education *per se* but a particular type of educational system. Indeed socialists place enormous emphasis on education, regarding it as a means to avoid the traditional division of labour, as a guarantor of democratization and as the avenue for self-realization. Thus Bahro praises 'the opening of unrestricted access for all to a general education embracing natural science and technique, society and art, at the highest [university] level, as the alternative to the differentiation of social strata according to levels of education and to socially incompetent bodies of specialists . . .'[20]

The development of democratized collective ownership and management would give rise to the withering away of the state. There is substantial controversy among socialists on the theory of the state in capitalist society, particularly over class and capital theoretic models and over instrumental versus relative autonomy interpretations.[21] In general, however, the capitalist state is seen as acting with varying degrees of autonomy through a variety of means ranging from repression to hegemony (the successful mobilization of the consent of dominated groups) to maintain the political and economic conditions for the reproduction of the capitalist mode of production. What is of greater concern for our immediate purposes is not so much the internal disputes but the generally held conviction that as the capitalist mode of production and/or system of domination that has been produced under capitalism is superseded by a socialist system based on the socialization and democratization of production, then the state would become redundant and politics as repression or the promotion of hegemony would be superfluous. Acceptance of socialist principles working through mass democratization would obviate the need for authority systems, creating in a sense a largely apolitical environment. The administration of people, and the domination inherent in that, would be replaced by what Bahro, for example, terms the 'non-politicized administration of things'.

We can amplify this analysis by considering the socialist critique of the Soviet Union. As we are defining socialism, the Soviet Union could not be considered a fully socialist system but at best proto-socialist. The socialist critique underscores the deviations of the Soviet Union from socialism. These deviations, then, are useful in gaining a complementary insight into what socialists see as a necessary and desirable form of social organization.

While it is generally conceded that the Soviet Union has achieved a relatively high level of collective ownership of the means of production, this has only been achieved at the expense of the intensification of the power of the state: 'Where the aim was the reabsorption of the state by society, we are faced with a desperate attempt to adapt the whole of living society into the crystalline structure of the state. Statification instead of socialization, in other words socialization in a totally alienated form.'[22] Or again, the Soviet Union is seen as having perpetrated a 'concentration of economic and political power in the hands of a bureaucracy on the one hand, and conversely in a lack of interest on the part of the mass of producers in the productive process. This deprives the work of building socialism of its potentially most powerful impetus.'[23] This statification has consequently prevented the Soviet Union from escaping many of the inequities inherent in capitalism:

> ... the cultivation of social inequalities that goes far beyond the spectrum of money incomes; with its perpetuation of wage labour, commodity production and money; with its rationalization of the traditional division of labour; with its almost clerical family and sexual policy; with its high official dignitaries, its standing army and police, who are all responsible only to those above them; with its official corporation for the organization and tutelage of the population; with its duplication of the unwieldy state machine into a state and party apparatus ...[24]

So far we have focused on the structural arrangement of a domestic community and this emphasis may appear rather odd in that we are committed to outlining a socialist conception of a global structural arrangement. The emphasis has, however, not been misplaced. Unlike the realist, the socialist does not see a major disjuncture between nation state and international levels of organization.[25] Rather the socialist anticipates a global organization based on a large number of socialist communities which would interact with each other to greater or lesser degrees on exactly the same principles that govern their internal organization. Thus the separate management of international relations is ultimately, unlike for the realist, of no concern to the socialist as international relations is simply not a distinctive area as socialist principles and practice of organization become diffused.[26] Thus the socialist anticipates

> a world where each part is a centre, spun together in a dense network of non-exploitative, participatory international organizations of various kinds. This would be the world of our dreams: many and smaller units ... woven together in a web of multilateral ties, substituting for the bilateral approach to global cohesion a much more multilateral approach.[27]

Or again:

> The answer lies in the discovery of the federative principle which is inscribed in the idea of free association ... association instead of subordination of individuals to their various subjective and objective purposes; association of their unions ... essentially into territorially grouped communes, as the decisive mediating links of the totality; association of nations in a contentedly co-operating world; mediation to each higher unity by delegates elected from the base.[28]

In sum, the structural arrangement of the socialists, deemed necessary for the effective promotion of equality, is a world of communities organized both internally and externally in terms of the democratized socialization of the means and conditions of production.

Belief system

Most historians of the socialist tradition, though accepting earlier precedents, generally see this tradition as a post-Enlightenment phenomenon.[29] While particular features of socialist thought are to be found in Voltaire and Rousseau, the early socialist writers, constituting the first phase of the socialist tradition, date from the later eighteenth century. Influenced by proposals for agrarian reform, the advent of the Industrial Revolution and the French Revolution it is in writers such as Babeuf, Blanc, Fourier, Robespierre and St Simon that we find the first relatively sustained critiques of the inequities of capitalism.

The second phase is coterminous with the works of Marx and Engels. The early works of Marx essentially continued and expanded the critique of capitalism in terms of socialist ethics and values.[30] It was, however, the later works of Marx that provided the major break with the early writers and in this respect Marx made a major addition to, and indeed could be represented as the single most important influence on, the socialist tradition. Not only did Marx provide a massively more comprehensive and empirically based analysis of capitalism but also through historical materialism afforded a scientific theory of the evolution of human society on a par with the scientific theory of biological evolution produced by Darwin.

The theories of Marx were evidently incomplete and, within a few decades of his death, the socialist tradition was clearly moving in a variety of directions. Thus, the revisionist movement was under way through writers such as Bernstein; some theorists, noting that capitalism was not collapsing in Western Europe, sought to extend Marx's theories by postulating a higher level of capitalism in the form of imperialism and monopoly capital — hence Hilferding or Luxemburg or Lenin; other socialists were trying to push a revolution through mass organization, hence Liebknecht and Luxemburg; still others were more militant and 'revolutionary' as opposed to 'evolutionary' — hence Lenin and the Bolshevik Revolution. This diversity has if anything continued and expanded. In general terms we can encapsulate the third, post-Marx, phase of the socialist tradition in terms of three related strands. On the one hand, there is the juxtaposition between non-Marxist and Marxist socialists, and within the latter camp, following a distinction made by Gouldner, between critical and scientific Marxists.[31]

Non-Marxist socialists are totally committed to socialist ethics and largely accept a good part of the early Marx. They would not accept the scientific theory of historical materialism or indeed much of the conceptual lexicon to be formed in Marx's analysis of capitalism. This often leads this strand to be dismissed by Marxists as utopian socialism, and its proponents as socialists who have failed to understand the laws and dynamics of historical materialism.[32] While the non-Marxist socialists for the most part readily accept a strong idealistic component and motivation, many would also emphasize that their writings are empirically founded also, albeit not in terms of Marxist science.[33]

Marxist socialists maintain a strong conviction in historical materialism though recognizing, in the light of the failure of 'competitive' capitalism to collapse, that the science of historical materialism requires substantial amendment and expansion. The scientific Marxists represent the more academic strain while the critical ones are willing to take more latitude and become more voluntaristic and activist in their attempts to promote socialism. They too, as a consequence, are sometimes attacked for being utopian by the scientific Marxists and in general stand closer to the non-Marxist socialists than do the scientific Marxists.[34]

The socialist tradition, as would be expected of any great intellectual movement, is multifaceted and has developed in diverse, sometimes cumulative and sometimes conflicting, ways over time. While recognizing some important diversity, there are none the less a number of core beliefs.

First, reflecting in some respects the legacy of the Enlightenment and the Renaissance, there is an optimistic evaluation of human nature or human potential. To the extent that humans interact in ways perceived to be detrimental to the general social good or well-being, this must be attributed not to any inherent perversity of human nature but to the institutional and structural arrangements created by human interaction.

Second, the history of human organization has, however, been a history of the creation of institutions that have engendered inequality and domination and thereby forestalled the full and equal development of human potential. While the explanation of inequality can vary, there is a common conviction that inequality and domination are structurally located and that this has been the continuing hallmark of human organization.

These two strands become joined in a third characteristic which is almost tantamount to a doctrine of salvation. Despite the pessimistic evaluation of human history, the optimistic evaluation of human nature means that socialism is a doctrine of progress and a doctrine which contains a condition and strategy for salvation. There are two aspects to the progress to salvation. Firstly, socialism profiles a system of social organization (what we label and have outlined above as the structural arrangement) under which inequality can be eradicated. Secondly, there is a conviction that this condition can be achieved. The stronger the commitment to historical materialism, the stronger is the belief that the historical unfolding of the laws of historical materialism will lead eventually and inevitably to socialism. While critical Marxists and non-Marxists may not share this conviction in the inevitability of socialism, this is usually compensated for by a willingness to contemplate and actively promote strategies for attaining socialism through human initiative. All socialists argue that, ultimately, through increasing consciousness, brought about either deterministically or voluntarily, human beings can rise above institutionalized inequality to engineer their own salvation through the establishment of socialism.[35]

A fourth belief is that socialism can only be achieved through large-scale structural change. There is substantial dispute among socialists as to the nature of the causal relationship between the economic base (the mode of production) and other aspects of political and social organization (the superstructure). While disputes on the nature of this 'topographical' relationship have importance in the calculation of strategies for the socialist revolution, none the less socialists agree that incremental or piecemeal change cannot succeed.[36]

This point can perhaps be clarified by contrasting socialism with compensatory liberalism. Socialism developed in part as a critique of liberalism and to some extent over time there has been a fusion of these two traditions. That fusion is represented by compensatory liberalism. The compensatory liberals readily agree that unfettered capitalism can either be counter-productive or can produce unacceptable inequalities. As such compensatory liberals can tolerate an extensive array of market interventions to correct for inequalities. However, these interventions are not designed in any way to supersede the market but simply to 'offset' some of its weaknesses.[37] For the socialists, it is not a question of offsetting but of totally replacing the market. Offsetting may help to promote equality of opportunity but the liberal meritocratic conceptualization of equality constitutes merely meritocratic inequality for the socialist.[38]

A fifth component of the belief system is the emphasis on cooperation. An important element of the socialist critique of capitalism is the attack on competition. Competition is seen as presupposing winners and losers. It bestows unequal rewards on winners and losers, and as long as there are unequal rewards then there can be every expectation that whatever means possible will be employed to win. Competition then becomes a means of institutionalizing and perpetuating inequality. Consequently competition is an important contributory factor to all manner of capitalist evils ranging from the creation of atomized individuals to its use as a rationalization for exploitation. Against competition, the socialists juxtapose cooperation as the only desirable basis for social organization. In place of an endless struggle to outdo one's fellows, the socialists prefer the virtues of community and solidarity. Only by eradicating the infinite regress of competition is it possible to overcome conflict and create a tension-free society. The emphasis on cooperation, and the conviction that this is the only viable means for conflict resolution, is found extensively in socialist writings not only on a prescriptive level — as in exhortations for solidarity and the end of alienation — but also on practical levels — as in collective ownership and control.[39]

The emphasis on cooperation and community should not be taken to imply that socialism is antagonistic towards the individual. Though socialists frequently engage in diatribes against bourgeois individualism, socialism advocates individual self-realization. What is attacked in bourgeois individualism is essentially a system whereby some individuals benefit at the expense of others. Liberal calls for the right to, say, universal education do not placate the socialist when not all benefit, or when different levels of educational attainment bestow different rewards. Universal rights are seen as pure mystification as long as each individual cannot enjoy these rights to an equal degree. The emphasis on community and cooperation does not, according to the socialist, preclude individuality and certainly does not entail homogenization. Socialists unequivocally recognize individual variation and indeed wish to sustain and enhance individual variety. They differ from liberals in their conviction that individual autonomy can only be achieved in a community of equals.[40]

Finally, socialism is a universal and universalizing doctrine. It is universal in that is is seen as the highest form of social development for any community. It is universalizing in the conviction that it needs to be established on a world-wide basis. A viable socialist community cannot be established as an isolated pocket in a world following other principles of social organization.[41] In this respect, nationalism is ultimately incompatible with and alien to socialism. Temporary preoccupations with nationalist revolutions should not be interpreted as inconsistent with this universalizing and cosmopolitan conviction of socialism. Socialists recognize the contemporary salience of the nation–state and, though committed to world revolution, accept that a world revolution is unlikely to happen simultaneously at all points in the world. Consequently, socialists will often attach substantial importance to the achievement of a national revolution (a socialist transformation in one state) or will oppose international developments or organizations which they see as inhibiting a socialist transformation. Thus on occasion socialists may appear to have territorially rather parochial concerns but this strategic necessity should not be taken to be at odds with their fundamentally universal preoccupation.

Notes

1. C. Taylor, 'Socialism and Weltanschauung' in L. Kolakowski and S. Hampshire (eds), *The Socialist Idea*, London, Quartet, 1977.
2. It is in fact relatively unusual to find in contemporary writings explicit attempts to justify actions in terms of defending inequality. However, as an illustration of an argument that some such attempts are made, see P. Green, *The Pursuit of Inequality*, Oxford, Martin Robertson, 1981.
3. A common misperception of socialism is the idea that socialists wish to pretend that all individuals are or can be made identical. This is clearly not the case. Thus Tawney writes: '. . . a mark of a civilized society to aim at eliminating such inequalities as have their source, not in individual differences, but in its own organization . . .' (R.H. Tawney, *Equality*, London, Allen & Unwin, 1964, p. 57).
4. F. Parkin, *Class Inequality and Political Order*, London, MacGibbon & Kee, 1971, p. 182.
5. Tawney, op. cit., p. 158.
6. Ibid., p. 111.
7. As an extension to this point, socialists are quite dismissive of equality of opportunity (which is certainly consonant with compensatory liberalism) on the grounds that it perpetuates a meritocracy of inequality or, as Tawney puts it, it offers 'equal opportunities of becoming unequal'.
8. S. Lukes, 'Socialism and Equality', in Kolakowski and Hampshire, op. cit., p. 82.
9. T. Bottomore, 'Socialism and the Working Class', in Kolakowski and Hampshire, op. cit., p. 133.
10. I. Berlin, *Four Essays on Liberty*, Oxford, Oxford University Press, p. 131.
11. Tawney, op. cit., p. 235. In effect freedom in the 'positive' sense and equality become synonyms. We use the term 'equality' rather than freedom mainly because this usage is more common with socialist writers.
12. R. Bahro, *The Alternative in Eastern Europe*, London, New Left Books, 1978, p. 29.
13. E. Mandel, 'Economics of the Transitional Period', in *Key Problems in the Transition from Capitalism to Socialism*, New York, Merit, 1979, p. 42.

68 Models of world order

14. Bahro, op. cit., p. 24.
15. C.B. Macpherson, *The Real World of Democracy*, Oxford, Oxford University Press, 1972, p. 22.
16. Bahro, op. cit., p. 29.
17. Mandel, op. cit., p. 50.
18. Ibid., p. 51.
19. For an illustrative amplification of this point, the work on the relation of science to capitalism is rather interesting. See, for example, H. Rose and S. Rose, *Science and Society*, London, Allen Lane, 1969; H. Rose and S. Rose (eds), *The Political Economy of Science*, London, Macmillan, 1976.
20. Bahro, op. cit., p. 274.
21. For a selection of books which cover most of the parameters of this debate, see J. Holloway and S. Picciotto (eds), *State and Capital*, London, Edward Arnold, 1978; B. Jessop, *The Capitalist State*, Oxford, Martin Robertson, 1982; R. Miliband, *The State in Capitalist Society*, London, Weidenfeld & Nicolson, 1969; N. Poulantzas, *State, Power and Socialism*, London, New Left Books, 1978; and J. Urry, *Anatomy of Capitalist Societies*, London, Macmillan, 1981.
22. Bahro, op. cit., p. 38.
23. Mandel, op. cit., p. 51.
24. Bahro, op. cit., p. 37. This is also why some analysts can find some substantial similarities between Soviet and Western patterns of stratification. See, for example: D. Lane, *The End of Inequality? Social Stratification Under State Socialism*, London, Allen & Unwin, 1982; or D. Lane, *The Socialist Industrial State*, London, Allen & Unwin, 1976.
25. In this respect there is some parallel between pure liberalism and socialism in that pure liberalism anticipates an extensive blurring of the national–international divide. This, we would argue, is far from coincidental. Unlike the realists, who are relatively unconcerned with domestic organization of nation states and who see the continued viability of nation states, both the socialists and pure liberals require respectively domestic socialist and liberal organization for a fully fledged socialist or liberal world system. Furthermore, both the socialists and liberals see the nation state as an ultimately, if not currently, anachronistic form of organization.
26. This does not mean that socialists are not currently preoccupied with international issues. Nor does it mean that international issues would not be of critical importance in the transition to the global establishment of socialism. What we are presenting here is neither a list of current issues nor strategies for transition but rather the final general form of socialist organization. That is why we make the argument that under a fully fledged socialist system international organization would be a non-issue.
27. J. Galtung, *The True Worlds*, New York, Free Press, 1980, p. 382.
28. Bahro, op. cit., p. 453.
29. The general overviews of the socialist tradition are legion. For relatively brief accounts see R.N. Berki, *Socialism*, New York, St Martin's Press, 1975; or A. Gray, *The Socialist Tradition*, London, Longman, 1946; or G. Lichtheim, *A Short History of Socialism*, London, Weidenfeld & Nicolson, 1970. For a much more extensive review, see the five volumes making up G.D.H. Cole, *A History of Socialist Thought*, 5 vols, London, Macmillan, 1954–60.
30. For an interpretation of the early works, see, for example, S. Avineri, *The Social and Political Thought of Karl Marx*, Cambridge, Cambridge University Press, 1968.

31. A.W. Gouldner, *The Two Marxisms*, London, Macmillan, 1980.
32. At the extreme, while scientific socialists attack the non-Marxists for being pathologically Utopian, the latter respond with charges of dogma. Thus, Hampshire, for example, likens the so-called science of historical materialism to 'this historical and social variant of theodicy' or to 'alchemy when chemistry had been invented'.
33. This strand has developed down through writers such as Bernstein and the Webbs. Currently good illustrations would be Galtung or Wallerstein.
34. Gouldner cites, as illustrations of the critical Marxists, writers such as Lukács, Korsch, Gramsci, Sartre, Goldmann, Bahro, Avineri, Claudin-Urondo, Perez-Dias, and much of the 'Frankfurt School'. Scientific Marxists include Volpe, Althusser, Poultantzas, Godelier, Glucksman, Bettelheim, Therborn and Blackburn. Gouldner emphasizes correctly that these are not discrete traditions and that Marx's writings contained both critical and scientific components. Indeed it is wrong to see writers as being either critical or scientific. None the less, there is substantial difference in emphasis.
35. The scientific Marxists emphasize much more strongly than the critical Marxists (and even more still than the non-Marxist socialists) that the socialist revolution presupposes the necessary objective conditions, which in turn require advanced capitalism. This leads the scientific Marxists in particular to be rather diffident towards if not completely dismissive of so-called socialist revolutions in the Third World. Socialism is seen as being achievable only under advanced levels of economic or material development and it is this that gives especially scientific Marxism a strong Eurocentric flavour. A further difference in this context is that non-Marxist socialists generally have less faith in the inevitability of socialism than the critical Marxists, who in turn have less faith than the scientific ones. Thus, Bottomore argues: 'We have to give up entirely that element in Marxism, and in some other socialist theories, which conceives the transition from capitalism to socialism as a historical necessity. Socialism is only a *possible* future.' (T. Bottomore, op. cit., p. 132).
36. Scientific Marxists are more prone to see the superstructure as derivative, that is, determined and caused by the substructure than critical Marxists. The 'topographical' debate is of much less interest to the non-Marxist socialists.
37. For a discussion of offsetting, see R.A. Solo, 'The Economist and the Economic Roles of the Political Authority in Advanced Industrial Societies' in L.N. Lindberg *et al.* (eds), *Stress and Contradiction in Modern Capitalism*, Lexington, D.C. Heath, 1975.
38. Thus, for example, while the ethos of the Welfare State, as manifested in Western Europe, may well have been inspired by socialist writings, it is a classic manifestation of the practice of compensatory liberalism and illustrates well the fusion idea. It should not, however, be seen as symptomatic of socialism. In this respect many of the major socialist parties of Western Europe, as distinct from a number of splinter parties, would be classed as compensatory liberal rather than socialist. Thus, the history of the first mass socialist party, the German Social Democratic Party, has been a history of the victory of the fusion of socialism and liberalism in compensatory liberalism over socialism.
39. The idea of a final salvation through community becomes particularly anathema to liberals. Thus, Berlin notes that positive and negative freedom may sound like

70 *Models of world order*

positive and negative ways of saying the same thing. It is however the implementation of positive liberty through some form of organic entity that causes problems for the liberal. Thus: 'But equally it seems to me that the belief that some single formula can in principle be found whereby all the diverse demands of men can be harmoniously realized is demonstrably false . . . Pluralism, with the measure of "negative" liberty that it entails, seems to me a truer and more humane ideal than the goals of those who seek in the great, disciplined, authoritarian structures the ideals of "positive" self-mastery by classes, or peoples, or the whole of mankind.' (Berlin, op. cit., pp. 169, 171).

40. We have emphasized above, in the discussion of goals, the importance of individual self-realization. It is at this point in particular that the libertarian element in socialism touches on the anarchist tradition. For a discussion of anarchism and its points of contact and departure from socialism, see G. Woodcock, *Anarchism*, Harmondsworth, Penguin, 1963.

41. Thus: 'Historically, the problems of building socialism will be solved only by world revolution. It is only in this context that the disproportions, the distortions, and the most extreme contradictions will be definitely overcome.' (Mandel, op. cit., p. 38).

4 The realist model

Goal

The goal of realism is to establish and maintain a society of sovereign states. There are two dimensions to this goal. In the first place, it entails that 'the principal concern of each state is to preserve its independence'.[1] In the second place, it presupposes that the independence of the state can only be secured within the framework of an international society. In contrast to many political theorists, realists insist that a state can only be comprehended in its international setting. As Northedge asserts, it is essential 'to define the state in terms of the context in which all states live'.[2] The state and the international society, therefore, are considered to be interdependent, so that it is impossible to consider one without the other.

The realist's goal is premised on the belief that the state can only maintain its independence and pursue its interests in an international society. As Watson has observed, the absence of diplomacy, which he sees as providing the bedrock for an international society 'would mean a world which would have to resign itself to a condition of anarchy and isolation, of chronic insecurity and war: something like what Hobbes called a state of nature. States would have to live by and for themselves.'[3] Realists see nothing to recommend the kind of monadic organization which would emerge in such an environment. To avoid this danger, therefore, realists argue that it is necessary to promote an international society. Bull argues that such a society emerges 'when a group of states, conscious of certain common interests and common values, form a society in the sense that they conceive themselves to be bound by a common set of rules in their relationship with one another, and share in the working of common institutions.'[4] Realists have paid a good deal of attention to both the state and the international society and, indeed, the realist goal can only be appreciated if the relationship between the two is understood. The relationship is based on sovereignty. Although often discussed in legal terms, realists prefer to identify sovereignty in terms of the internal and external power of the state.[5] Internal sovereignty exists when the state possesses a monopoly on the legitimate use of force within its boundaries.

As a consequence, the power of the state cannot be legitimately challenged. It is this power dimension of internal sovereignty which helps to distinguish the nation state from every other kind of social organization. As Laski has noted: 'All other forms of organization have a certain partial character about them.'[6] Realists accept that internal sovereignty is necessary to transform the state into a complete or total institution.

In practice, power resides with the government, which has control over the coercive machinery of the state. Realists deny, however, that a government, although subject to no higher authority, can exercise power in an arbitrary fashion and expect the state to survive. It is argued that the arbitrary use of power is counter-productive, undermining internal sovereignty. Instead, the realist requires the establishment of a contractual relationship between the state and the nation, with rights and duties on both sides. Meinecke, for example, when examining the emergence of a realist position, believes that even autocrats must establish

> a community of interest between the two [ruler and ruled] which above all contributes towards the bridling of the power-drive of the ruler. For he must also serve the interest of the subjects in some way, because the existence of the whole power system depends upon them; a satisfied people, willing and able to fulfil demands made upon it, is a source of power.[7]

Realists, however, accept that such a contract is not always established and indeed, from their perspective, a basic feature of the contemporary world is that many areas are

> under the sway of states that are not states in the strict sense, but only by courtesy. They are governments or regimes and exercise power over persons and control over territory: but they do not possess authority, as distinct from mere power; they do not possess enduring legal and administrative structures, capable of outlasting the individuals who wield power at any one time; still less do they reflect respect for constitutions or acceptance of the rule of law.[8]

The viability of many nation states is questioned by realists, therefore, not because power has failed to be monopolized by the central authorities, but because the exercise of power is not considered to be legitimate. They believe, moreover, that a sovereign state can only survive if a government can translate power into authority. This end is achieved when the nation accepts the legitimacy of the government. Legitimacy, therefore, represents a fundamental dimension of internal sovereignty.[9]

External sovereignty exists when the state is not subject to any higher authority. But in contrast to internal sovereignty, this freedom cannot be achieved on the basis of holding a monopoly on the instruments of coercion. In the international arena power is diffused; all states possess a power base. External sovereignty, therefore, only presupposes that the state possesses sufficient power to withstand any outside attempt to interfere in its domestic jurisdiction. This condition has important international consequences. It leads Fromkin to conclude that

> the first and essential condition that enables an entity to exist and participate in international politics — which is to say to be an independent state — is the possession of an adequate amount of power. That is the price of independence. What this means is that, in the first instance, all *international* politics necessarily are power politics, for only if a state achieves at least a minimum amount of success in power politics can it go on to engage in any other kind of politics. This condition of existence is what all states have in common with one another.[10]

This line of analysis has encouraged the popular belief that realists recommend a ruthless and unrestrained pursuit of power. But since all states would be required to follow a similar course, such a policy would give rise to a state of nature, and thereby undermine the realist goal of maintaining a society of states.

Realists, however, deny that state interest, or *raison d'état* as it was known in earlier centuries, must necessarily be defined in terms of pure power. The point is made explicitly by Northedge:

> *Raison d'état* was never in theory, though it may have been so bandied about in the practical arena of politics, equivalent to the crude and ruthless maximization of power in a particular state. It has generally and more accurately been regarded as a certain political and indeed moral obligation: the duty of government to study intensively and without pause what is required to preserve the security and satisfy the needs of the state in an anarchical system.[11]

Realists accept, therefore, that states must seek to defend themselves and protect their well-being but they do not believe that these endeavours must give rise to persistent conflict and perpetual trials of strength. These problems can be avoided in an international society, where there are rules and institutions to restrain the power capabilities of the member states, and state sovereignty is universally acknowledged.

The realist, therefore, is primarily concerned with preserving the sovereign independence of the nation state. This task, however, must be approached from two quite separate directions. In the first instance, it is essential that a nation acknowledges the legitimacy and accepts the authority of the state. These features relate to internal sovereignty. At the same time, it is also essential that the nation state operates within an international society where the members acknowledge each other's right to exist and pursue their own interests. These features relate to the external dimensin of soveriegnty. Realists insist that these two features of sovereignty cannot be considered independently. As Hinsley observes, the internal and external dimensions of sovereignty 'are complementary, they are inward and outward expressions, the obverse and reverse of the same idea'.[12]

Structural arrangement

The realist goal of sustaining a society of sovereign nation states gives rise to a well-defined structural arrangement. Within it, states are organized in terms of an anarchic hierarchy. So, although there is no overarching authority above the component nation states — thereby identifying an anarchic arena — there are power differentials between them — thereby establishing a power hierarchy. Relationships within this anarchic hierarchy are governed by two basic principles or guiding mechanisms. One is reciprocity on the basis of which states form rules and institutions to facilitate international cooperation. The other is the balance of power which discourages conflict and manages the disparities in power which exist among the nation states.

Before looking at these principles which maintain an international society, it is necessary to make some observations on the state itself. Realists argue that a state is defined by four attributes: a population, a territory, a government, and recognition by other members of the international arena.[13] To generate internal sovereignty, however, as already indicated, the government must establish not only a monopoly of power, but also authority and legitimacy. Realists, however, do not specify how this authority is to be achieved, acknowledging that there are different ways, all potentially legitimate, for managing power within the state. Kennan, for example, has asserted that the United States should not attempt to impede or embarrass internal arrangements in the Soviet Union. He argues:

It is her own laws of development, not ours, that Russia must follow. The sooner we learn that there are many mansions in the house of nations, and many paths to the enrichment of human experience, the easier we will make it for other people to solve their problems and for ourselves to understand our own.[14]

Realists, therefore, identify a norm of non-intervention which gives the state the freedom to pursue its own course of internal development unfettered by outside control. The norm of non-intervention is advocated primarily on the grounds of prudence. Morgenthau, for example, believes that 'we have come to over-rate enormously what a nation can do for another nation by intervening in its affairs — even with the latter's consent . . . in truth, both the need for intervention and the chances for successful intervention are much more limited than we have been led to believe'.[15] It follows, therefore, that even requests by one state to another for assistance in establishing or maintaining an internal political system need to be treated with extreme caution. Realists recognize that only in exceptional circumstances, to be touched upon later, can there be any justification for the members of the international society interfering in domestic politics.

The realist structural arrangement, therefore, is defined in the context of the international arena; it does not embrace any domestic political features. States are regarded as autonomous, independent entities. But the structural arrangement does include the power capabilities of states.[16] Although difficult to measure, it is accepted that these vary substantially from state to state and give rise to a power hierarchy in the international society. The basic elements which contribute to the power of a state are geography, which identifies the size and location of a state, natural resources, industrial capacity, military preparedness and the size of the population.[17] Although realists accept that it is impossible to place states on a specific rung on the international herarchy, they do insist that states can readily be located in the more general categories of great, medium and small powers.[18]

The existence of an international hierarchy complicates the task of establishing an international society because it tends to undermine the capacity of some states to maintain their sovereign equality. The two mechanisms identified by the realist, reciprocity and the balance of power, by working in conjunction, however, are intended simultaneously to maintain sovereign equality and to take account of the power inequalities. The two mechanisms need to be discussed separately before it can be shown how they reinforce each other.

Reciprocity, according to the realist, 'implies equality of treatment'.[19] It is seen, therefore, as the foundation for all cooperation in international society. Indeed, this mechanism can be seen as providing the genesis of international society. This is because the prerequisite condition for the establishment of an international society is the willingness of its members to acknowledge each other's independence. Watson has made this point explicitly:

> In a system of states where the policy of each affects the others, many states recognize that they have a joint interest in maintaining their independence; and they come to see in the independence of their fellow members the means to preserve their own ... From this practical and vital involvement in the independence of other states, the concept develops that states have a general right to be independent, and that those which want to exercise this right have an interest in supporting each other in asserting it. So states in systems come to recognize that the mutual acceptance of the principle of independence, even with exceptions, is a necessary condition of a society of states.[20]

The independence of states, therefore, can be seen to rest on the mechanism of reciprocity. Each state has a vested interest in ensuring that the principle of sovereign independence is observed, because violations serve to undermine the general principle. There is, therefore, a mutual interest in seeing the principle upheld. This mutual interest, however, is reinforced by the existence of self-help measures. If one state, for example, begins to criticize the internal political arrangements of another state in a public forum, thereby violating the norm of non-intervention, the criticized state is always in a position to retaliate. This ability reflects the essence of reciprocity. When a procedure operates to the benefit of two parties, it is not possible for one party to withdraw the benefit without running the risk of retaliation.

Realists argue, therefore, that this mechanism provides the basis for diplomacy, international law and international organizations. Schwarzenberger comments:

> In the rules of which those governing diplomatic immunity are typical, the influence of the principle of reciprocity becomes apparent. At a time when, in this sphere, international law was still in its formative stage, states were free to choose whether to interpret restrictively the rights of immunity granted to the representatives of foreign states or to give them a liberal construction. If, in the interest of their own

untrammelled sovereignty, states preferred the former course, nothing prevented them from taking this line. In this case, they could not, however, expect more generous treatment for their own envoys abroad than they themselves were prepared to grant to those of other states.[21]

On this basis, it becomes possible to see how a large and complex body of international law can be established. The nature of the law however, is different in character from domestic law which presupposes the existence of a central authority that holds a monopoly on the legitimate use of power. In the internaional arena where there are competing centres of power, this mechanism for maintaining law is absent. Nevertheless, realists insist that law can be established and maintained even in the absence of a central authority because, as Schwarzenberger observes, these rules derive 'their strength and their authority from the automatic working of the principle of reciprocity'.[22]

Realists have also observed that the growth of international institutions seems to have been influenced by the same principle. Many of these institutions have been established on the grounds that they bring mutual benefits to their members. It was on this basis that the Universal Postal Union, for example, was established in the nineteenth century. In the same way, Schwarzenberger notes how an international river commission can 'overcome on a footing of reciprocity the inconveniences of having a river community artificially segmented by the existence of several riparian states'.[23] Institutions persist, therefore, as long as the states are gaining mutual benefits. States operate within the rubric of an international institution because they know that if they do not, the institution will disintegrate as other states follow suit.

Realists, however, do not assume that interests invariably coincide. They acknowledge that interests often conflict, but they deny that a conflict of interest must necessarily lead to the exercise of force. In an international society, realists recognize that all states have legitimate interests and when a clash of interest occurs, some form of accommodation must be found wherever possible. As Thompson observes, 'there must be a reciprocal process of recognizing each other's vital interests and avoiding collisions and conflicts insofar as it is possible through the compromise of divergent interests'. Indeed, from Thompson's realist perspective 'the one thing which saves the idea of the national interest is its essential reciprocity'.[24]

Reciprocity, therefore, reinforces the independence of nation states and helps to build up the rules and institutions on which an international society depends. The existence of an international society, moreover, far from undermining the independence of states, is seen to consolidate it. The only occasion that the independence of the state conflicts with the existence of an international society is when the state fails to acknowledge the principle of reciprocity. This can happen when a regime comes to power and threatens to undermine the international society. The Bolshevik accession to power in 1917 was viewed in this way by the British. The British Foreign Office argued that it was not possible to establish any agreement with the Bolsheviks because they were 'fanatics who are not bound by any ordinary rules'.[25] Under these circumstances, realists accept therefore, that in order to safeguard the international society, it is appropriate to exclude the deviant state until its government accepts the established rules and institutions in the international society. It was on these grounds that the British Cabinet argued that there could be 'no question of entering into peace negotiations with the Bolsheviks until they had demonstrated their intention not to interfere, by propaganda or otherwise, in the affairs of their neighbours'.[26]

The second principle or mechanism identified by the realists to maintain an international society is the balance of power, which is seen to operate in conjunction with reciprocity. While reciprocity reflects and supports sovereign equality, the balance of power is seen to accommodate the disparities in power which exist among states. Realists acknowledge that the inequalities in power are an inevitable feature of an anarchic international arena and cannot be eliminated so long as states wish to preserve their independence. At the same time, it is also recognized that the existence of these power inequalities poses a constant challenge to state sovereignty, international society and reciprocity. In the event of a conflict between two states, widely separated in terms of their power capabilities, for example, the weaker state will have no alternative but to submit to the stronger state. If this course of action prevailed and was a characteristic feature of the international arena, then reciprocity would break down. As Bull observes: 'Where one state is preponderant, it may have the option of disregarding the rights of other states without fear that these states will reciprocate by disregarding their rights in turn.'[27] If this condition prevails, then it precipitates a world where states engage in a perpetual struggle for survival, without any regard for each other's interests. As a consequence, all forms of rules and institutions are disregarded. From this power-political perspective, the resulting balance of power operates in the absence of an international society. According to Bull:

> Doctrines which contend that there is, in any international system, an automatic tendency for a balance of power to arise . . . derive from a 'power-political' theory of this kind. The idea that if one state challenges the balance of power, other states are bound to seek to prevent it, assumes that all states seek to maximize their relative power position.[28]

Realists, therefore, distinguish between the balance of power in a state of nature and in an international society. They accept that a balance of power can emerge on the basis of states struggling to preserve their own existence. Schuman, for example, argues that 'the principle of the balance of power as an unformulated guide to state action is of great antiquity'.[29] But realists view this 'unformulated', 'automatic' balance of power as a rather primitive mechanism which exists in the absence of an international society. As a consequence, Schuman asserts that,

> in its elementary form, therefore, the balance of power principle is designed not to preserve peace or contribute towards international understanding, as later rationalizations would have it, but simply to maintain the independence of each unit of a state system by preventing any one unit from so increasing its power as to threaten the rest.[30]

As an elementary mechanism, therefore, the balance of power is simply concerned with the preservation of state independence. In such a balance of power, however, even small states may be able to maintain their independence by manoeuvring amongst the more powerful states. A threat to the independence of a state by a second, more powerful state, for example, can be offset by establishing an alliance with another powerful state. The existence of even an elementary balance of power, therefore, can help to preserve the independence of all the members of the international society.[31] Realists, however, often distinguish between the independence of small states and their capacity to pursue their own interests. As Tucker notes: 'If the balance of power often functioned to preserve the independence of small states, it also operated to sacrifice the interests of the weak.'[32]

Realists, therefore, observe a difference between a balance of power in a state of nature and in an international society. The latter only comes into existence when states recognize that they have a common interest in preventing the emergence of a hegemonial state and self-consciously pursue a policy which is designed to maintain an overall equilibrium. For the realist, then, the balance of power implies 'that each state should not only act to frustrate the threatened preponderance of others, but should recognize the responsibility not to upset the balance: it implies self-restraint as well as restraint of others'.[33] Realists recognize that this formulation of the balance of power is not inevitable or automatic. But they assert that in the context of a society, states will exercise restraint and not ruthlessly pursue power as a means of preserving their security. As a consequence in an international society, 'states are constantly in the position of having to choose between devoting their resources and energies to maintaining or extending their international power position, and devoting their resources and energies to other ends.'[34] In an international society, therefore, states will rely on other members of the society to assist in the task of maintaining a balance because it is recognized that a policy designed to maintain an international equilibrium constitutes a rule of 'prudence' or 'common sense'. As Aron notes, the rule involves 'manoeuvring in order to prevent a state from accumulating forces superior to those of its allied rivals. Every state, if it wishes to safeguard the equilibrium, will take a position against the state or the coalition that seems capable of achieving such a superiority.'[35]

At first sight, it may appear that there is no real difference between an 'automatic' balance of power whch emerges as the result of an international struggle for power and what Bull calls a 'contrived' balance of power which is based on the desire to prevent the emergence of a hegemonial state. But to the realist, the difference is substantial. A balance of power which emerges spontaneously is seen to be incompatible with an international society because it presupposes that states are guided purely by the desire to maximize their respective power capabilities. States guided by such a motive will not observe established rules or attempt to cooperate in international institutions. An unrestrained struggle for power will undermine the structural mechanism of reciprocity.

A contrived balance of power, on the other hand, is not only compatible with the establishment of an international society, it is seen to represent a necessary feature in such a society where power is located in a variety of centres and is unevenly distributed. If power was evenly distributed, then reciprocity could operate unassisted. But in a society where there is an uneven distribution of power, and no mechanism to manage power, then reciprocity will fail to operate. As Bull notes, rules and institutions which are the defining characteristics of an international society will not come into existence where there is no 'security for the observance of rules of international law other than the mere hope that a preponderant state will choose to be law abiding'. Bull then goes on to cite Oppenheim, who is only one of many international lawyers, of a realist disposition, who recognise that a contrived balance of power can provide a necessary precondition for the observation of international law. Oppenheim notes that 'the first and principal moral that can be deduced from the history of the development of the law of nations is that a law of nations can exist only if there be an equilibrium, a balance of power between the members of the family of nations'.[36] The relationship between the balance of power and international law exists because a state which disregards international law develops an obvious advantage over states which adhere to the law. If such a situation persisted, then the deviant state would, to all intents and purposes, be operating as a hegemonial power. In an international society, therefore, great powers will tend to police the actions of each other, defending the legal right of smaller states, and ensuring that the law operates amongst themselves.

There is, however, an obvious consequence of the balance of power which is not immediately apparent when international law is defined in terms of reciprocity. It is that the content of law must be aligned to the interests of the great powers, which will play the most important role in maintaining the law. For at least some realists, this situation is no different from domestic society. Niebuhr argues, for example, that 'the individual or the group which organized any society, however social its intentions or pretentions, arrogates an inordinate portion of social privilege to itself'.[37] But realists have always believed that the balance of power, while at one level undermining the equalizing capacity of reciprocity, at the same time introduces a restraining influence on the behaviour of the powerful states in the international society. It serves to 'moderate the mutual behaviour of the Great Powers'.[38] This benign view of the balance of power is unsurprising because this conception is directly associated with an internal counterpart. From the seventeenth century, it has been believed that a balance of power within government can avert the well-known dangers associated with the concentration of power. When an equilibrium is maintained by different centres of power pulling in opposite directions, then each centre must curb its own demands and endeavour to accommodate the interests of the other centres of power.[39] This internal mechanism is seen to preserve the freedom of the individual and, in the same way, it is argued that the international balance of power will provide the best possible protection of the interests of small states. The protection, however, is not absolutely assured. Realists recognize that under certain circumstances, the interests and even the independence of small states may have to be disregarded in order to prevent general conflagration within the international society. As Bull notes, 'from the point of view of a weak state sacrificed to it, the balance of power must appear as a brutal principle'. Nevertheless, he is quite certain that 'it is part of the logic of the balance of power that the needs of the dominant balance must take precedence'.[40]

To establish an international society, therefore, the realist recognizes that it is necessary to reconcile two conflicting conditions. One is the demand by states for equality, a condition which is inherent in the ideas of sovereignty and independence. The other is the recognition that states possess very unequal power capabilities, generating differential capacities to defend boundaries and pursue interests. The realist relies upon two main mechanisms to reconcile, though not eliminate, these conflicting conditions. The first is reciprocity, which encourages states to deal with each other on an equal footing, and to search for common interests. The second is the balance of power, which can, to some extent, accommodate power differentials in a way which does not lead to a state of nature. It provides the setting where reciprocity can flourish.

Beliefs

Contemporary realism is often misunderstood because of the failure to appreciate that it draws upon and pulls together two quite distinct historical traditions. One is the *Realpolitik* tradition which assumes that human beings are governed basically by a drive for power. Without some form of external constraint, therefore, individuals live in a state of nature, where there are no rules, no institutions, and no sense of morality. The state has been most frequently seen to provide the necessary constraint. The other tradition assumes that the defining characteristic of human beings is their sense of morality: an ability to distinguish between right and wrong. The consequence of this characteristic is that human beings have the capacity and the desire to live under social conditions where behaviour is restrained by the existence of rules and institutions and individuals exercise moral choice.

The first tradition can be traced back through Hobbes and Machiavelli to Thucydides; they all accepted, however, that the centralization of power within the state must inevitably give rise to a persistent struggle for power between states. Thucydides concluded, in the context of the Greek city states, that a state had no alternative but to strive to establish an empire because if it did not, there was an inevitable 'danger of coming ourselves under the empire of others'.[41] This conclusion was seen to be just as valid in Renaissance Europe. Machiavelli, it is argued, 'stated the case for imperialism as for "power politics" more clearly than any earlier or later thinker'.[42] According to this tradition, therefore, a ruler has a duty to promote the well-being of the state and must not be restrained from doing so because of either moral principles or weakness. In the interests of the state, moral principles must be cast aside and there must be an unending search for power. This amoral drive for power is often designated as Machiavellian power politics.

According to this tradition, then, society and civilization can develop and flourish within the state, but only at the expense of perpetuating uncivilized behaviour in the international arena. This tradition persists. Fromkin, for example, argues that barbarous and civilized behaviour 'spring from the same impulse'.[43] Civilized behaviour is a product of domestic politics, while barbarous behaviour represents the opposite side of the same coin and is a product of international politics. He criticizes contemporary realists on the grounds that when confronted by this truth about international politics, they search around for factors which can mitigate the effects of a pure struggle for power and prove 'unwilling to stare unblinkingly into the face of reality'.[44]

Contemprary realists find the *Realpolitik* line of argument unpalatable because they have been influenced by a second tradition, which insists that states can form an international society where common rules and institutions operate.[45] This tradition originated in the belief in natural law of the Stoics in ancient Greece. Natural law was premised on the assertion that there are principles, reflecting the rational and social nature of human beings, which are universally applicable.[46] This tradition was drawn upon by the Romans and it thereby found its way into medieval Christian thought. With the demise of the Christian Empire and the emergence of independent states, the belief in natural law provided the basis for the argument that the leaders of these new states were subject to social norms and institutions and that they could not behave in a completely unrestrained and amoral fashion. From the perspective of this tradition, therefore, it is incorrect to suggest that domestic and international politics are opposed and mutually incompatible forms of activity.

Contemporary realists, however, do not believe it is necessary to make a choice between these two traditions. By themselves, each of these traditions is inadequate. As Berki observes: 'Man's opposition to his fellow human-beings signifies a double-sided relationship; it means both friendliness and enmity. The one-sided emphasis on the latter produces no tenable realism, but only *Realpolitik*, a partial and incoherent conception.'[47] The same argument is made by Herz: 'The fundamental antagonism between co-operation and conflict, the need to depend on his fellow man, and at the same time the necessity for distrusting and possibly destroying him: this is the contradiction with which man is faced once he becomes conscious of his status in the world and society.'[48]

The confusion about contemporary realists has arisen because the second tradition was designated by realists as Utopian or idealist in character. It was assumed, therefore, that the school of self-styled realists, writing after the Second World War, must be reasserting the traditional *Realpolitik* line of thought. But, in fact, almost invariably, these realists were endeavouring to fuse the ideas of idealism with those of *Realpolitik*. They wished to acknowledge the importance of power, while at the same time indicating that there were some important factors which could serve to restrain the exercise of power. In particular, they wished to stress that the leaders of states recognized that they operate in a society and, as a consequence, share a number of common interests. The realists, therefore, were not opposed to the promotion of international law and institutions. Both were recognized to be essential features of any society. What the realists wished to stress, however, was that these rules and institutions would only function if they reflected the existing distribution of power in the international arena. This conviction reflected a number of basic beliefs shared by the realists.

In the first place, realists subscribe to the belief that the nation state is the best available type of political organization. In making this claim, realists are not, however, suggesting that the state must be coterminous with the nation. Since the time of the First World War, realists have acknowledged that national ties were far too complex and fragmented to support the contention that every nation has an a priori right to statehood.[49] The claims of nineteenth-century nationalists have come under increasing attack by realists during the course of the twentieth century.[50] It is accepted that support for the various nationalist movements which exist around the world would give rise to unlimited sources of controversy. Realists, therefore, now do no more than associate the nation with the population living within a state.[51] They retain the term nation, however, because it is recognized that the state is only a viable institution if the population accepts the legitimacy of the state institutions. The acceptance of common institutions is seen to bind the members of the population together.

But the realist belief in the nation state does not indicate an acceptance that the state is an ideal mode of political organization. Realists acknowledge that by supporting the state, they are simultaneously sanctioning the undesirable existence of an anarchic international arena. As far as realists are concerned, however, the only possible alternatives are either undesirable, as in the case of a world empire, where one state subjugates the others, or a world state, where the members of the international community agree to hand over their sovereign rights to a central world government. While some realists believe that this is the only possible mode of organization which could create a world without war, others believe that in practice, there is no difference between a world empire and a world state.[52] The reason is that no state is immune from the possibility of becoming a tyranny. From this perspective, therefore, the best opportunity for maintaining the freedom of the individual is to retain a plurality of states.

Following on from this central belief that the sovereign state represents the most effective form of political organization is the belief that all states must maintain a capacity to defend themselves. The necessity for these defensive arrangements arises, however, not because states possess an inevitable and insatiable drive for power, as adherents of *Realpolitik* assert, but because of the ambiguity and uncertainty which characterizes an anarchic international arena. These characteristics generate a 'tragic predicament' or 'security dilemma' for the component states.[53] There are two main features of the dilemma. The first is the product of the inability of the parties to a conflict to ascertain each other's motives. As a consequence, when two parties become locked into a conflict, each understands his own fear, but is unable to understand the counter-fear of the other party. There is, often, in other words, an unwillingness to recognize that the other party may have a legitimate cause for fear. The second facet of the dilemma, however, is that there will be occasions when the fear is justified and the one party in a conflict intends to destroy the interests of another. The predicament or dilemma arises, therefore, because there is no way of knowing for sure when a threat is real or apparent, because there is no certain way of identifying the motives of a putative enemy. The only rational course of action is to maintain a permanent capacity to defend the state and its interests, even when it is recognized that these actions will precipitate a reciprocal response by other states.

A third belief of the realists, therefore, relates to the need to assuage the effects of the security dilemma. It is argued that this can be done by ensuring that the interests of the state are restricted to the well-being of the nation. Realists then distinguish between core and peripheral interests and argue that it is rational and desirable for states to be willing to negotiate and compromise on the latter.[54] From the realist perspective, however, this conception of national interest is completely undermined when states define their interests in ideological terms, which extend across the state boundary.[55] The pursuit of these interests not only generates conflict, but also leads to counter-productive consequences, because as the scope of the interests extend, so also will the scale of the international opposition. Realists, therefore, argue that it is necessary to delimit the interests of the state and to be willing to compromise on any interest which does not involve survival or core values of the state. There are two caveats, however, often attached to this general belief. The first is that the idea of national security and national interest are highly elastic and can be used to stretch rather than restrict interests.[56] There is, therefore, a constant need to monitor policies pursued by the state, to ensure that they are not, intentionally or unintentionally, being extended beyond their requirements. The second caveat reflects the opposite tendency. Realists recognize that demands are often cast in ideological terms for purely rhetorical reasons. They are, as a consequence, deeply suspicious of demands for universal or sweeping changes, recognizing that often there is little substance behind the demands.[57]

A fourth belief of the realists, that power is a determining feature of relations in an anarchic arena, is then seen to provide a way of making a rational assessment of how extensively national interests can be defined. Realists believe that interests must be defined in the context of power. As the power of a state expands, so the interest of the state can become more extensive. But from the realist perspective, a state which extends its interests beyond its power capabilities is placing itself in a position of vulnerability. Realists recognize, therefore, that power is a relative commodity and that the power of a state must always be measured in terms of the power of other states. It is for this reason, of course, that a state must not only endeavour to identify its own interests, but also those interests of its potential enemies. Interests must then be trimmed in a way which is compatible with the interests and the power positions of these other parties.

A fifth belief of the realists is that, as a means of avoiding conflict, states must accept that their ability to shape the rules and institutions governing the international society must be dependent upon their position in the international power hierarchy.[58] In other words, states must acknowledge that their capacity to influence the structure of international society can only be commensurate with their power capabilities. In moving up the power hierarchy, therefore, a state can anticipate that its influence will increase, while a downward movement must result in a loss of influence. Failure to accommodate to this belief will, realists argue, engender conflict, because a state with power but no influence will be encouraged to violate the rules and disregard the resolutions of international institutions. On the other hand, when power and influence are commensurate, there will be a greater willingness to observe and enforce societal norms.

A sixth belief of the realists is that it is rational for states to promote an international society. Realists, therefore, draw a sharp distinction between an international system and an international society. A system exists when each state finds it necessary to take the presence of the other members into its calculations. Those who subscribe to a *Realpolitik* view of the world, therefore, recognize the need to acknowledge the existence of an international system. Relations in a system, however, are depicted in zero-sum terms. The increase in power by one state necessarily presupposes a loss of power by another state. It reflects a conflictual view of the world. Realists consider that this view is one-sided and fails to take account of the common interests which can exist and which need to be promoted between states. These interests, however, can only emerge and flourish in an atmosphere of trust. Such trust can only be built up, however, if Machiavellian statecraft is replaced by a form of diplomacy which is based upon permanent dialogue and an observation of established rules and institutions.

Realists believe that it is rational for states voluntarily to agree to accept societal restraints because under these circumstances, at least some of the uncertainty and ambiguity associated with an anarchical arena can be reduced. Moreover, under these circumstances, it is easier to extend mutual interests. Conflict and power remain important features of an international society, but their more destabilizing features can be controlled.

Finally, realists do not believe that there is anything immutable about either the state or the international society. They acknowledge that in the past there have been world empires and transnational societies. They see nothing in principle which would prevent the re-emergence of these structures. However, they do contend that, under existing circumstances, the state, operating within an international society, represents the optimum mode of global organization.

Notes

1. A. Watson, *Diplomacy: The Dialogue Between States*, London, Eyre Methuen, 1982, p. 36.
2. F. S. Northedge, *The International Political System*, London, Faber & Faber, 1976, p. 41.
3. Watson, op. cit., p. 22.
4. H. Bull, *The Anarchical Society: A Study of Order in World Politics*, London, Macmillan, 1977, p. 13.
5. International lawyers have never been happy with this development and believe that it has introduced an element of confusion into the discussion of sovereignty. See J.L. Brierly, *The Law of Nations*, 6th edn, Oxford, Clarendon Press, 1963, p. 13. Political

scientists, however, argue that sovereignty has no significance when it is divorced from power.
6. H.J. Laski, *The Foundation of Sovereignty and Other Essays*, London, George Allen & Unwin, 1921, p. 26.
7. F. Meinecke, *Machiavellism: The Doctrine of Raison d'Etat*, trans. D. Scott, London, Routledge & Kegan Paul, 1957, p. 10.
8. H. Bull and A. Watson (eds), 'Conclusion' in *The Expansion of International Society*, Oxford, Clarendon Press, 1984, p. 430.
9. See J.H. Herz, 'Legitimacy: Can We Retrieve It?', *Comparative Politics*, Winter 1978, 317-43.
10. D. Fromkin, *The Independence of Nations*, New York, Praeger, 1981, p. 23.
11. Northedge, op. cit., p. 56.
12. F.H. Hinsley, *Sovereignty*, London, C.A. Watts and Co., 1966, p. 158.
13. See R.H. Cox (ed.), *The State in International Relations*, San Francisco, Chandler Publishing Co., 1965, p. 11.
14. Cited in K.W. Thompson, *Political Realism and the Crisis of World Politics*, Princeton, Princeton University Press, 1960, p. 52.
15. H.J. Morgenthau, 'To Intervene or Not To Intervene?', *Foreign Affairs*, **45**, 1967, pp. 425-36.
16. For a justification of the need to include power capabilities in any conception of the international structure, see K.N. Waltz, *Theory of International Politics*, Reading, Mass., Addison-Wesley Pub. Co., 1979.
17. These elements are taken from H.J. Morgenthau, 5th edn, *Politics Among Nations*, New York, Alfred A. Knopf, 1973, Chapter 9. However, there are many similar accounts; for a rather more sophisticated assessment, see B. Buzan, *People, States and Fear*, Brighton, Wheatsheaf Books Limited, 1983, Chapter 2.
18. For an attempt to establish a more specific ranking, see W.H. Ferris, *The Power Capabilities of Nation States*, Lexington, D.C. Heath, 1973.
19. M. Palliser, 'Diplomacy Today' in Bull and Watson, op. cit., p. 379.
20. Watson, op. cit., p. 36.
21. G. Schwarzenberger, *Power Politics*, London, Stevens & Co. Limited, 1964, 3rd edn, p. 203.
22. Ibid., p. 203. The same point is made by Bull, op. cit., p. 108.
23. Schwarzenberger, op. cit., p. 229.
24. Thompson, op. cit., p. 169. See also Northedge, op. cit., p. 57.
25. Cited in R. Little, *Intervention*, London, Martin Robertson, 1975, p. 21.
26. Ibid., p. 22.
27. Bull, op. cit., p. 108.
28. Ibid., p. 111.
29. F.L. Schuman, *International Politics*, 4th edn, New York, McGraw Hill, 1948, p. 80.
30. Ibid.
31. See, for example, M. Handel, *Weak States in the International System*, London, Frank Cass, 1981.
32. R.W. Tucker, *The Inequality of Nations*, New York, Basic Books, 1977, p. 7.
33. Bull, op. cit., p. 106. For a discussion of this 'systemic' view of the balance of power, see H. Butterfield, 'Diplomacy' in R. Hatton and M.S. Anderson, *Studies in Diplomatic History*, London, Longman, 1970.

34. Bull, op. cit., p. 111.
35. R. Aron, *Peace and War*, New York, Praeger, 1967, p. 128.
36. Cited in Bull, op. cit., p. 109. See also A. and O.F. Vagts, 'The Balance of Power in International Law', *American Journal of International Law*, **73**, 1979, 555–80.
37. R. Niebuhr, *Moral Man and Immoral Society*, London, SCM Press, 1963, pp. 6–7.
38. Tucker, op. cit., p. 6.
39. For a discussion of the domestic balance of power, see W.B. Gwyn, *The Meaning of the Separation of Powers*, The Hague, Martinus Nijhoff, 1965. For a discussion of how the domestic and international dimensions of the balance of power have influenced each other, see J.H. Hutson, *John Adams and the Diplomacy of the American Revolution*, Lexington, University of Kentucky Press, 1980, pp. 142–3.
40. Bull, op. cit., p. 108.
41. Cited from 'The Peloponnesian Wars' in J. Herz, *Political Realism and Political Idealism*, Chicago, University of Chicago Press, 1951, p. 209. For a further discussion, see A.G. Woodhead, *Thucydides on the Nature of Power*, Cambridge, Mass., Harvard University Press, 1970.
42. Leo Strauss, *Thoughts on Machiavelli*, Seattle, University of Washington Press, 1958, p. 293.
43. Fromkin, op. cit., p. 154.
44. Ibid., p. 27.
45. See H. Bull, 'The Grotian Tradition', in H. Butterfield and M. Wight, *Diplomatic Investigations*, London, Allen & Unwin, 1966.
46. For a discussion of the origins of this tradition, see the interesting discussion of M. Donelan, 'Spain and the Indies', which looks at Vitoria's examination of the right of Spain to conquer Latin America, in Bull and Watson, op. cit., pp. 75–86.
47. R.N. Berki, *On Political Realism*, London, J.M. Dent & Son, 1981, p. 129.
48. Herz, op. cit., p. 16.
49. For a discussion of how realist views shifted on this issue, see the discussion of Meinecke's ideas on the subject in R.W. Sterling, *Ethics in a World of Power*, Princeton, Princeton University Press, 1958, p. 84ff and 192–5.
50. For a scathing attack, see E. Kedourie, 'A New International Disorder' in Bull and Watson, op. cit., p. 347–56. For a review of the relationship between state and nation, see L. Tivey (ed.), *The Nation-State*, Oxford, Martin Robertson, 1981.
51. See, for example, the definition of nation in J.G. Stoessinger's *The Might of Nations*, revised edn, New York, Random House, 1965, p. 10. Realists invariably use the terms 'state' and 'nation' interchangeably, as the titles of many texts by realists indicate. See, for example, H.J. Morgenthau, *Politics Among Nations*, op. cit.
52. Both Fromkin, op. cit. and Morgenthau, op. cit. pin their ultimate hopes on world government. However, Meinecke favours the persistence of a plurality of states. For Meinecke's views, see F. Meinecke, *Machiavellism*, trans. D. Scott, London, Routledge & Kegan Paul, 1957, pp. 93–6 and Sterling, op. cit., p. 99.
53. For a discussion of the tragic predicament, see H. Butterfield, *History and Human Relations*, London, Collins, 1951. For a discussion of the security dilemma, see J.H. Herz, op. cit. For more recent discussions, see R. Jervis, 'Co-operation under the Security Dilemma' in *World Politics*, **30**, 1978, pp. 167–214, and Barry Buzan, op. cit.
54. The distinction between core and peripheral interests is reflected in the writings of most realists. See, for example, H.J. Morgenthau, 'Another "Great Debate": The

National Interest of the US', in *American Political Science Review*, **46**, 1952, pp. 971–8. Northedge, op. cit., chapter 9.
55. The attack on ideological foreign policy emerges very clearly in Morgenthau, op. cit.
56. This point emerges very clearly in A. Wolfers, 'National Security as an Ambiguous Symbol' in *Discord and Collaboration*, Baltimore, John Hopkins University Press, 1962, Chapter 10.
57. This argument is implicit in Tucker's attack on the New International Economic Order, op. cit., and is also reflected in J. Piscatori, 'Islam in the International Order' in Bull and Watson, op. cit., p. 320, where he argues that 'Muslim Statesmen, like all statesmen, are guided more by the cold calculation of national interests than by the passionate commitment to ideological values'.
58. This argument is explored in the conclusion to R.W. Cox and H. Jacobson, *The Anatomy of Influence*, New Haven, Yale University Press, 1973; in R.O. Keohane and J.S. Nye, *Power and Interdependence: World Politics in Transition*, Boston, Little, Brown & Co., 1977; and in Tucker, op. cit.

PART III: GLOBAL ECONOMIC PROBLEMS AND SOLUTIONS

5 Liberal international economic problems and solutions

Problems

The first of two major manifestations of liberalism in the international economic system may be dated from the repeal of the Corn Laws in 1846, from which time Britain managed to translate many of the ideas of Smith and Ricardo into international practice.[1] The trade wars of the 1930s ended this first phase of liberalism but even during the collapse the first signs of the second phase began to appear.[2] This second phase crystallized in the aftermath of the First World War with the establishment of a liberal constitutional framework enshrined in three major new organizations.[3] The General Agreement on Trade and Tariffs (GATT) prescribed a liberal free trade system, which was underwritten by the Bretton Woods agreements, providing in turn the International Monetary Fund (IMF) that would alleviate balance of payments problems such that trade would not be restricted, and the International Bank for Reconstruction and Development (IBRD) that would provide investment finance.

Although the second half of the nineteenth century is often represented as the golden age of liberalism, the post-Second World War system has proved in many respects even more golden. For example, the free trade system of the nineteenth century was largely supported on a unilateral basis by Britain, as opposed to the multilateral reciprocity of the post-war period.[4] Britain engaged in substantial discrimination in its colonies, which has of course disappeared. The United States held very high tariffs until 1934, which again have all but disappeared. But perhaps most importantly, the post-war system was not based on any Cobdenite faith but on the conviction that restrictions on trade and payments (the latter being a further important novelty) could only be removed by explicit and formalized cooperation — hence the constitutional framework of the GATT, IMF and IBRD. Consequently in the post-war period we find such confident statements as: 'The framework of international economic cooperation and the commitment to basically liberal international economic policies developed by the major industrial countries over the post-war period have proved sufficiently strong to prevent wholesale reversion to the shortsighted economic nationalism of the 1930s.'[5] The post-war international economic system, which is broadly liberal, has endured. We begin our profile of liberal economic problems by considering the major challenges that this system has met.

The first of several successful challenges was the reconstruction of Western Europe. The Second World War had effectively caused the collapse of the Eurocentric system. The new system, initially a North Atlantic phenomenon organized pre-eminently by the United States could, however, not hope to survive unless the war damages of Western Europe were rectified. In this reconstruction the main roles were played not by the new international liberal institutions of the IMF and IMRD but by the Marshall Plan and the willingness of the United States to accept some degree of reverse discrimination. European recovery did proceed quickly, with currency convertibility being re-established in the late 1950s, such that at the start of the 1960s the new system was firmly rooted in the advanced economies, which for the most part were displaying impressive growth rates.

The second challenge concerned the Soviet Union. While the Bolshevik Revolution transformed the Soviet Union into a deviant regime (from the liberal perspective), the Soviet Union did not attract a great deal of attention in the inter-war period primarily because it was initially by Western standards rather backward and, under the doctrine of socialism in one country, rather inward looking. Stalin's forced industrialization programmes, however, transformed the Soviet Union into a major industrial power and, more significantly, the Soviet military performance during the Second World War demonstrated its massive military capability. In the vacuum of war-devastated Western Europe, the Soviet Union loomed as not only a detestable but also an extremely powerful regime.

The response to this threat was containment. Thus the Soviet Union found itself excluded from the new international economic organizations (GATT, IMF and IMRD), excluded from the Marshall Plan (for which one of the major rationales was to assist European recovery to contain the Soviet Union) and confronted by the military alliance of the North

Atlantic Treaty Organization (NATO). Irrespective of the accuracy of the perceived threat or the efficiency of the actual containment mechanisms, the Soviet Union has been excluded from Western Europe and containment, so defined, has been totally successful.

Although in the immediate aftermath of the Second World War the main preoccupation with the Soviet threat focused on Western Europe, it soon became apparent that this threat was also relevant outside the East–West confrontation in the Third World. The first of two forms this perceived threat could take was the demonstration of the Soviet model of economic and political organization. As many Third World countries moved to single party systems, adopted goals of rapid industrialization and engaged in formal centralized planning, the prospect appeared of many Third World countries developing a command-type economy and removing themselves from a liberal world economy. A second form of the threat was that the Soviet Union, through direct or indirect subversion, might induce regime changes in the Third World.

To some degree these threats have materialized, though for a variety of reasons the materialization has been very limited. Many Third World countries have not developed strong socialist parties and furthermore socialism, where it does appear, is more apparent in rhetoric than reality. Soviet aid and arms programmes, the main form of indirect subversion, though they have expanded rapidly have been relatively ineffective as instruments of social change. Finally Soviet direct subversion, the overseas deployment of its troops, has been limited.

A third challenge developed in the form of the so-called collapse of the Bretton Woods system. The main hallmarks of the IMF system (there has been no 'collapse' of the IBRD component) were an adjustable peg exchange rate regime, under which currencies were fixed to the dollar which in turn was fixed to gold, and the provision of additional reserves through drawing rights based on quotas. The IMF provided then an international monetary-management system affording market convertibility and a means for adjustment either through an exchange-rate change or IMF drawings that offered the possibility of accommodating payment problems without disrupting the free flow of trade or capital. Initially the system worked well, providing both the liquidity and convertibility to facilitate the promotion of an open market.[6]

The first major liberal critique of the working of the international monetary system argued that the demand for reserves was growing faster than the supply of gold, thereby creating a liquidity shortage which could only be alleviated by the United States running a payments deficit.[7] If the United States did this, however, the confidence in the dollar would be undermined as it could not be converted to gold. To break this vicious circle efforts were made to expand liquidity.[8]

These efforts were, however, overtaken by events as the United States financing of the Vietnam War, largely through monetary expansion, led to a surplus rather than a deficit of dollars. American inflation and the overvalued dollar meant a decline in the real value of the dollar to other countries. To this was added a further major difficulty in the form of speculation (which was not helped by being a riskless form of speculation). Any currency showing signs of weakness, that is, prone to devaluation, could expect a massive capital flight, while conversely a strong currency could expect a run. Such capital movements landed central banks with huge bills, disrupted domestic monetary arrangements and, to a large extent, undermined the effectiveness of any exchange-rate change.[9] In short, the Bretton Woods monetary arrangement contained a number of serious structural weaknesses: a gold–dollar convertibility that could not be maintained; a supposition that American inflation would always be low; undue pressure on deficit as opposed to surplus countries to adjust; and an inflexibility of adjustment that enhanced speculation.[10]

Over the period 1971–4, the Bretton Woods system was said to have collapsed. While there was undoubtedly an important change (from fixed to variable exchange rates with a dollar freed from gold convertibility), the extent of the collapse needs to be interpreted with care.[11] There is still a management system, the IMF continues (and is substantially more active), the dollar is still the major reserve currency, even gold survives as a component of reserves and there is still market convertibility.[12] Indeed, in a number of ways the current system is more functionally attuned to liberal goals than its earlier form. Not surprisingly therefore we can find such positive evaluations as:

> The international monetary system by adapting to a changing world environment during the last decade, showed its resilience and capacity for change without provoking a major crisis that might have seriously disrupted international trade and finance. Its movement has been evolutionary rather than revolutionary, and one can expect that the process of adapting the system to the requirements of a changing world economy will continue in the future. One of the hallmarks of the new international monetary system is that it provides for greater flexibility and scope for change than the Bretton Woods system it replaces.[13]

A fourth major challenge came in the form of the demands for a New International Economic Order (NIEO).[14] These demands were a function of the conjunction of increased Third World political organization, especially in the Non-Aligned Movement and UNCTAD, and an increasing preoccupation with an international dimension of development issues.[15] The demands may well have continued largely unheard had it not been for the crises precipitated by the IMF troubles and the OPEC oil-price rises. The OPEC cartel action seemed to be a harbinger of a new form of Third World power, namely commodity power, and the fear was not only that new commodity cartels would develop but also that OPEC would act as a vanguard of the Third World.[16]

The underlying sentiment of the NIEO demands was expressed very clearly in the Declaration on the Establishment of a New International Economic Order:

> ... our united determination to work urgently for the establishment of a new international economic order based on equity, sovereign equality, interdependence, common interest and cooperation among all states, irrespective of their economic and social systems, which shall correct inequalities and redress existing injustices, make it possible to eliminate the widening gap between the developed and developing countries and ensure steadily accelerating economic and social development and peace and justice for present and future generations.[17]

To achieve these ends, the NIEO package contained an extensive list of policy proposals.

The pure liberal response to these demands, which was one of acute opposition, centred on several factors. First, they disagreed totally with the UNCTAD type of explanation of Third World poverty. Second, they did not like the colossal oversimplification engendered in the juxtaposition of North and South. Third, they disapproved of cartels and the use of cartel economic power for political ends. Finally, they were adamantly opposed to the NIEO policy strategies most of which entailed large-scale discriminatory and interventionist techniques.[18] The pure liberal reaction to what was perceived to be 'a collection of self-serving less developed country theories of economic relations'[19] left no doubts on either the nature of the pure liberal evaluation or the severity of the threat:

> The NIEO demands are a signpost to disorder. They imply that everybody everywhere is entitled to a substantial income regardless of economic performance. Attempts to enforce the NIEO would lead to a Hobbesian war of all against all, to a spread of totalitarian government, and to a further erosion of the West.[20]

While the NIEO protagonists extracted a number of minor concessions, the NIEO demands as a whole made little progress. In the words of the UN Secretary-General:

> On most fronts... negotiations to attain those [NIEO] objectives have yielded results that fall considerably short of their initial targets or they have shifted focus from bold changes to attempts at partial adaptation. Indeed on a number of fundamental aspects of the new international economic order, progress has been negligible.[21]

A final challenge was the OPEC cartel action. Liberals strongly oppose cartels on the grounds of market disruption through price fixing and the use of monopolistic economic power for political purposes. Successful cartel action can only be executed under limited conditions, requiring essentially a small number of suppliers and a commodity for which there is a highly inelastic demand. These conditions were met in the 1973–4 oil-price rises, which stimulated substantial fears of world inflation and especially the market disruption that would be caused by the massive transfer of petro-dollars to OPEC countries.[22]

While the OPEC action undoubtedly caused some disruption, liberals can in general be extremely satisfied with the market adjustments which have largely diffused any major dislocation. For example, one of the dangers of price rises is that they can stimulate additional production from suppliers previously kept out of the market by too low a production price. This has indeed happened and OPEC domination of world oil supplies has declined so dramatically that from 1982 non-OPEC oil production exceeded that of OPEC.[23] In addition, price rises can stimulate the search for alternatives. In the case of oil there was some diversification, though more significantly there has been substantial conservation.[24] The market has also been quite successful in recycling the petro-dollars. Thus, OPEC imports expanded massively after 1974, with many of these coming from the West, or many of the petro-dollars were placed in commercial banks which have on-lent — albeit with some further problems that will be examined below.

The first part of our exposition of liberal problems suggests that the Western liberal economic system has responded rather successfully to a number of major challenges. It managed to launch and consolidate the system with the reconstruction of Western Europe, to forestall any serious erosion by the command economy of the Soviet Union, to adapt the original monetary arrangement, to withstand the discriminatory and dirigist NIEO demands, and to dissipate a serious threat from the OPEC cartel. The second part of the exposition considers a number of ways in which the international economic system has become more liberal.

The first, and arguably most important, way is the growth of multinational corporations.[25] The constitutional basis of the post-war liberal system did not anticipate a substantial role for capital flows and indeed until the 1960s the main dynamism came from trade. While trade growth rates have continued to be impressive (generally higher than those of total world production), the activities of multinational corporations now constitute the single most important engine of international economic intercourse.

While liberals undoubtedly see some problems inherent in multinational activity, the net benefits are strongly positive.[26] In the first place, multinationals show a marked propensity to reinvest and they increasingly raise capital in local markets (which is interpreted to mean either that idle investment funds are employed or that multinationals produce a higher marginal return on capital).

A second benefit of multinationals is their ability to blur the salience of national economies and thereby foster world market integration. Although the organizational design of many multinationals tends to be very national, liberals not only envisage a developmental progression from ethnocentric to polycentric to geocentric organization but also argue that lead multinationals are explicitly orientated in this direction:[27]

> For business purposes, the boundaries that separate one nation from another are no more real than the equator. They are merely convenient demarcations of ethnic, linguistic, and cultural entities. They do not define business requirements or consumer trends. Once management understands and accepts this world economy, its view of the market place — and its planning — necessarily expands. The world outside the home country is no longer viewed as a series of disconnected customers and prospects for its products, but as an extension of a single market.[28]

A third benefit of multinationals is that they are seen as embodiments of efficiency and comparative advantage. They move capital overseas when they perceive a higher marginal return. By operating in local markets, they can overcome tariff and exchange controls introduced by misguided national governments, they can break local monopolies and enhance competition, and they can adapt production to suit local needs. In addition to moving capital, they also transfer technology, expertise and management skills. In sum, global corporations make possible 'the use of world resources with a maximum of efficiency and a minimum of waste ... on a global scale'.[29] Or again: 'The MNC's integrated and rationalized operations in many lands make it incomparably efficient. It has proved to be the only really effective instrument for economic development.'[30]

A second encouraging development from the liberal perspective has been the growth of the Euromarket.[31] The term Eurodollar market is a misnomer in that the market is not merely European but world-wide and is based on currencies other than the dollar. The term reflects simply the origins of the market both by geography and currency.[32] The Euromarket is an international banking market in which loans and deposits are denominated in currencies other than that of the country in which the bank is located.[33] The market combines a credit market in which non-banks, mainly corporations, lend to and borrow from banks and a money market in which banks lend and borrow from each other. The attractions of this market, which grew rapidly through the 1970s, are that it is independent of official exchange controls, has no national boundaries and can move excess savings to points of investment:

> The market is extremely competitive and efficient. It facilitates movements of large volumes of funds from savers to investors across national borders at low cost. In doing so it helps to finance temporary current account imbalances and improves the efficiency of investment worldwide. It also exerts competitive pressure on domestic banking systems to be more responsive to their customers and to become more efficient.[34]

A third change concerns what might be called the formal constitutionalism of the post-war economic system, provided by the new inter-governmental regimes of the GATT, IMF and IBRD. Not only have these formal bases of the liberal system survived but they have become more flexible.

While the Articles of the GATT represented a clear commitment to free trade and provided a negotiating device in the form of reciprocity through the most-favoured nation clause, the negotiations still had to be executed. The first five rounds of negotiations were characterized by item-by-item negotiations, involving the difficulty that countries likely to gain from tariff reductions found themsleves opposed by those likely to lose. To instil a greater impetus Kennedy passed the 1962 Trade Expansion Act, which provided more extensive powers and resulted in good progress in the Kennedy Round of 1964–7. The Tokyo Round of 1973–9 produced a more elaborate formula for across-the-board reductions that could cope better with the variable tariff levels of different countries. On a number of issues, such as safeguard systems, agricultural protection, government procurement and other non-tariff barriers (NTBs), progress was unquestionably disappointing. Nonetheless, the source of the liberal optimism is that under GATT very real tariff reductions have been achieved, such that tariffs on industrial goods were reduced on average at the end of the Tokyo Round to 4.9 per cent — a historic low.

Perhaps the single most important achievement of the IMF system was the survival of the so-called collapse of 1971–3. There are, however, further sources of liberal comfort in the evolution of the IMF. First, it has not developed into an ossified dirigist organization and when it does intervene (when conditional drawings are required) the underlying criteria of its stabilization programmes are broadly liberal.[35] Second, it has proved adaptable, as for example in the First and Second Amendments to its Articles of Agreement or in the establishment of its special facilities.[36] Thus, after a rather quiescent start (in Triffin's words, 'condemned to impotence in the post-war decade'), the IMF has developed in a flexible manner, illustrated well in its contribution of substantially expanded lending after oil-price rise.

The generally optimistic evaluation of the World Bank is based on several arguments. First, the IBRD, together with its later adjuncts the International Development Association (IDA) and the International Finance Corporation (IFC), has grown, as from the early 1970s, into the single largest aid donor.[37] Second, the supply-side focus of the World Bank is seen as a useful complement to the demand-management focus of the IMF. Third, the World Bank has evolved a division of labour based on the graduation principle with the highly concessional loans of the IDA being concentrated in the poorest countries and the less concessionary IBRD loans in the better-off ones.[38] Fourth, while the IDA makes substantial financial calls on member governments, the IBRD's calls are relatively minor, which in turn explains in part the much larger loans of the IBRD (approximately four times those of the IDA).[39] Fifth, both the IDA and IBRD fund efficiently in the sense that substantial positive rates of return on their credits are consistently achieved. (The IBRD received an AAA credit rating in the mid 1950s and has held it ever since.) Sixth, the IBRD cannot be said to displace private investment. It is clearly attractive to private investors, raising around three-quarters of its funds on private markets. Furthermore, an increasing number, now almost half, of its projects are co-financed. Seventh, the World Bank does not simply pursue the public sector. By 1982, 43 per cent of total IDA and IBRD loans were to the private sector and the vast majority of the remaining loans to the public sector fell into a definition which would accord with the relatively small public sector of the United States.

Other things being equal, the pure liberal would prefer a reduction in the activities of the IDA and a matching increase in those of the IFC.[40] Overall, however, the performance of the World Bank has been impressive. Without displacing private investment and without promoting the public at the expense of the private sector, it has productively, using normal commercial accounting procedures, channelled substantial investment funds to the developing countries.

The fourth and final change relates to the underlying power structure of the international economic system. While both non-liberals and liberals would agree that the constitutional basis for a liberal international economic order was created in the aftermath of the Second World War, the liberal would not pretend for a moment that this was a perfectly liberal system. Rather it could be characterized as a quasi-liberal system in which the main deviation from a pluralistic diffusion of power rested in the hegemony of the United States. Indeed the formal constitutional liberal arrangement was launched against a decidedly illiberal underlying power distribution, though paradoxically the formal liberal system would not have been created at all without the monopolistic initiative and power of the United States. What is subsequently encouraging to the liberal is not that a pluralistic diffusion of power has been achieved but that there has been movement in that direction.

In this context some of the changes we have noted already in the growth of the Euromarket and increased multinational activity are highly pertinent. The main development has, however, been the decline in United States hegemony. With the economic recovery of Western Europe and the emergence of Japan, United States control in the major intergovernmental organizations has reduced, American backing of the international monetary system has relaxed, American trade, despite recent growth, is small relative to Western Europe's, and American domination of foreign direct investment has declined.

To recapitulate, the argument so far suggests, first, that in the wake of the Second World War a quasi-liberal international economic system was established; second, that this system has met a number of major challenges demonstrating a very real problem-solving capacity; third, that in a variety of important respects the quasi-system has become more liberal. To this argument two caveats must now be noted.

First, the presentation so far has been made primarily from the pure liberal perspective. In general, compensatory liberals would be decidedly less enthusiastic about a number of the changes or the way the challenges have been met. For example, they were much more sympathetic to the NIEO demands, are more inclined to see the current monetary arrangements as a non-system, are much less enthusiastic about multinationals or would emphasize the IDA over the IFC. Second, we have only presented the more positive side of the pure liberal case. Pure liberals have a number of problems and it is to these that we now turn. In so doing we shall try to amplify the pure and compensatory variations.

The first problem we consider is the new mercantilism or new protectionism. Mercantilism, according to Johnson, 'has remained a potent force in popular political thinking', which he holds to be 'scientifically and socially regrettable'.[41] The major contemporary manifestations are non-tariff barriers to trade which include labour subsidies, cartel agreements, subsidized loans, production subsidies, consumption subsidies, export subsidies, import quotas, government procurement, regional development grants, dumping and technical administrative obstacles.[42] The severity of neo-mercantilism to the pure liberal is beyond doubt: 'Today we are seeing a resurgence of mercantilism, whereby governments meet domestic economic demands with conscious policies of manipulation, passing the costs of these policies as much as possible onto other countries. This neo-mercantilism is a profoundly disruptive force in international relations.'[43]

A variety of factors underlie this concern. Non-tariff barriers do distort trade; the list is legion; many are difficult to detect and assess; the areas covered by them are extensive and varied (with the worst culprits being agriculture, steel, shipbuilding, textiles, cars and services). Furthermore, governments, which are primarily responsible for formally enacting the barriers, have shown great ingenuity (as in the multifarious technical obstacles) but also a marked propensity to violate the spirit if not the letter of the law (as with voluntary export quotas or orderly marketing arrangements). Perhaps the most acute source of concern is the relatively deep-rooted institutional basis of contemporary neo-mercantilism which is governmental involvement in the economy. In this context two factors in particular are held up for attack: the European Economic Community (EEC) and the growth of the welfare state.

The GATT rules provided for a number of exceptions, including free trade and customs unions, the main purpose of which was to assist smaller economies to integrate into larger markets. Since all trade and customs unions are trade-diverting mechanisms, they were never intended for large economies, though the EEC member countries have legitimately taken advantage of the exception provision. The EEC has, however, developed into an inter-governmental mechanism, which far surpasses trade diverting and which sees its most unfortunate development in the Common Agricultural Policy (CAP), which, among other crimes, absorbs most of the budget, is responsible for high food prices, discriminates against overseas producers, and creates massive surpluses which are dumped onto the international market. Allied with other developments such as the Lomé Conventions, the Davignon Steel Plan, or the regional development programmes, the CAP renders the EEC for Malmgren the 'ultimate in mercantilism' and for Johnson 'the epitome of modern mercantilism'.

The growth of governmental intervention is even more serious. In contrast to the old protectionism, which referred to trade-restricting (tariffs) and trade-expanding (export subsidies) devices, the new protectionism 'refers to how the totality of government intervention into the private economy affects international trade . . . what is new is the realization that virtually all government activity can affect international economic relations'.[44] This intervention, to the pure liberal, is based on the mistaken belief that the market cannot properly allocate resources and distribute income and on a false conception of welfare. Governments intervene to protect jobs and redistribute income, thereby making a redistribution from capital to labour, which in turn causes reduced savings, stagflation, and the maintenance of resources in low-productivity areas since it is these rather than high-productivity ones where jobs are threatened (hence protection in agriculture, shipbuilding, textiles and steel).[45]

The acute problems, to the pure liberal, created by the new mercantilism and protectionism, are decidedly less acute to the compensatory liberals, who have some substantial reservations about the market and are willing to tolerate those interventions that promote what they take to be economic justice and equality. While the difficulties caused by non-tariff barriers are generally appreciated, these barriers do not *ipso facto* constitute problems. Indeed the welfare state, far from being a problem, is in fact a solution to the types of problem that are likely to develop in an unregulated market.

A second general problem area centres on international monetary issues as these affect the smooth working of an open world economy. While the pure liberals are generally pleased, as we have documented above, with the evolution of the Bretton Woods system, some problems remain. There is concern that the Euromarket contains massive sums of money over which there is negligible control. There is also concern about the continued salience of the dollar and gold as the basis of foreign reserves. Perhaps the most important concern, and certainly the most widely discussed, is that of exchange-rate volatility. While the issue of exchange-rate volatility begs the question of how volatile is volatile, most observers would readily agree that there has been substantial volatility since 1973. While change is one of the desired results of the new system, there is certainly nothing to be gained by excessive change. More importantly, it is feared that volatility hinders trade by undermining expectations by which payments on trade are made.[46]

Pure and compensatory liberals do not diverge as much on international monetary issues as on the new mercantilism. In general, compensatory liberals are less pleased with new freedoms of exchange rates and Euromarkets and consequently are more vocal in their demands for control.

A third problem area concerns East–West economic relations, in which context pure and compensatory liberals have quite divergent perceptions. The compensatory liberal position has both an economic and security rationale for advocating increased economic intercourse. The economic rationale rests on the complementarity of the economies of the East and West and posits mutual gain for each region following its own comparative advantage.[47] The security rationale suggests that enforced economic isolation of the Soviet Union can only heighten tension while increased economic intercourse can create some degree of interdependence and thereby reduce tension. To the compensatory liberal, therefore, attempts to restrict East–West economic intercourse represent problems.

The divergent perception of the pure liberal is a function both of a greater pre-eminence given to security considerations and of a different conception of security. In some respects the Eastern bloc is not a major economic threat to the world market economy. The Soviet economy which dominates the Council for Mutual Economic Assistance (COMECON) is by Western standards rather backward and seemingly ever less adept at coping with the demands of a complex economy. Furthermore the COMECON market itself is far from impressive. It lacks a convertible currency, intra-COMECON trade is low (indeed it is not much higher than COMECON trade with the West), and, judging from COMECON hard currency debts to the West, the latter is rather more attractive than the Soviet Union. The main problem for the pure liberal does not pertain to the rival capacity of COMECON but to the issue of containment.

One response is to advocate the minimalization of economic intercourse on the grounds that economic exchange assists the Soviet Union.[48] A second is to advocate limited and selective exchange to be used either as leverage against the Soviet Union or as a means to entice the other COMECON members away from the Soviet Union.[49] These strategies, it might be noted, are by pure liberal standards highly illiberal in that economic exchange is used for political ends. They are justified of course by dint of being applied against an illiberal regime.

Thus, any expansion of East–West intercourse, other than the selective exchange, becomes a problem for the pure liberal and in this respect pure and compensatory liberalism hold diametrically opposed views. In actual practice one of the most notable features of East–West trade is its small size (around 3–4 per cent of OECD trade). Furthermore because of a number of major structural obstacles, such as managed COMECON trade or COMECON's lack of real reserves or convertible currency, this trade is likely to remain small and as such a source of comfort to the pure liberal and matching concern to the compensatory liberal.

A fourth issue area, that of West–South relations, offers arguably the most pronounced divergence between pure and compensatory liberals. The compensatory liberals begin from the North–South divide characterized in terms of a glaring inequality in standards of living. Appealing to 'human solidarity and a commitment to international social justice' the Brandt Report states: 'It cannot be accepted that in one part of the world most people live relatively comfortably, while in another they struggle for sheer survival.'[50]

The explanations of the gap are both varied and numerous. They include dualism, deteriorating terms of trade, vicious circles, backward linkages or the misapplication of Western planning techniques and development strategies.[51] The common denominator running through these varying explanations is the failure of the market both within and across nations. Thus Ul Haq declares that

> it is generally accepted by now that market mechanisms are neither efficient nor reliable instruments for allocating resources when the income distribution is very distorted ... there is an increasing realization that economic growth does not filter down automatically to the masses except in the modern urban sector and at very high rates of growth.[52]

Or, emphasizing the failure across nations, Brandt argues: 'In the world as in nations economic forces left entirely to themselves tend to produce growing inequality. Within nations, public policy has to protect the weaker partners. The time has come to apply this precept to relations between nations within the world community.'[53]

While the compensatory liberals see Third World development as a problem in that the condition of the South relative to the North affronts their conception of economic justice and equality, the pure liberal looks at Third World development as a problem for the extension of the market.[54]

The point of departure for the pure liberal is that the process of sustained economic development started in the West and has been gradually diffused to the rest of the globe.[55] What critically differentiates the West in aggregate from the Third World is that it has experienced a much longer period of sustained economic growth and consequently it is not surprising that there exist substantial variations (as opposed to inequalities) in standards of living.[56] In this respect there is an obvious explanation for the so-called divide. What disturbs the pure liberal is that a number of obstacles are either developing or have developed that are inhibiting the successful integration of the less developed countries into an expanding open world economy.

Some of these obstacles are domestically imposed by the Third World countries themselves. Thus many have failed to appreciate the principle of comparative advantage and have substituted excessive governmental intervention for private initiative and enterprise: 'The pursuit of private profit therefore guarantees that the right goods — in terms of the economy's overall factor endowment — will be chosen for production. . . . Free markets and comparative advantage are the bread and butter of intelligent development policy.'[57] This had led according to pure liberals to an emphasis on redistribution over growth and it is here that we see one of the most pronounced conflicts between pure and compensatory liberalism:

> One [approach] is to attempt to improve the standard of living of the poor alone. This requires zero-sum redistributionist methods, since with a stable economic pie one group can gain only at the expense of others. . . . Social Democratic strategists have misunderstood the process of economic development. They have placed too much emphasis on investments in social overhead and human capital and too little emphasis on private enterprise and private investment. In addition, they have imposed totally inappropriate goals of egalitarian income redistribution upon Third World countries that had virtually no surplus to redistribute . . . The Third World faces enough problems in achieving the imperatives of growth without being distracted by naive concepts of social justice.[58]

The obstacles are however not purely domestic but include a number of external factors introduced by the developed countries. These include several misguided interventionist programmes, such as the Generalized System of Preferences, the Lomé Conventions or several commodity agreements. A further externally induced obstacle is bilateral aid programmes. Far from being conducive to growth, these programmes hamper it by being directed at the public sector, promoting attitudes antithetical to self-help, encouraging corruption, and biasing development in favour of external prototypes. But perhaps the most serious obstacle is the inability of the developed countries to maintain their own dynamism through structural change. As growth has slowed in the high-income countries over the 1970s, this has removed a ready engine for Third World growth, that is, the demand for their exports. Or again, as interest rates have risen under excessive monetary growth and inflation, this has exacerbated debt-servicing problems. Or again, the new protectionism has often been geared to protecting precisely those industries in which the Third World enjoys a comparative advantage.

In sum, the pure liberal is attuned to the extension of the world market and sees Third World development problems in terms of obstacles to the free incorporation of Third World countries into an open world market. Lower standards of living are a function of a shorter history of development hampered by domestically or externally imposed barriers to free incorporation. The problem to the compensatory liberal is one of global inequity manifested in the gap in standards of living across the North–South divide, brought about by domestic and international market imperfections. We see here then a substantial divergence both in the conceptualization and explanation of the problem.

The final problem area, which to some extent underlies all those discussed above, concerns the overall management of the international economic system. The system created in the aftermath of the Second World War unquestionably contained a number of liberal components and indeed in some ways has become more liberal. It would be absurd, however, to pretend that the current system is the apotheosis of liberalism. The type of non-intrusive management system desired by pure liberals is thwarted in part by the relatively limited constitutional basis but much more importantly by deviations in the underlying power structure.

While pure liberals are given to declaring that 'the nation state is just about through as a unit of economic analysis', the nation state continues to thrive. Or again, liberalism has scarcely penetrated some nation states, such as COMECON, while its hold in others, much of the Third World, is rather tenuous. Furthermore, even within the core liberal club of the OECD, there are many illiberal tendencies and substantial variations in size or power which mitigate against a pluralistic base.[59]

Such deviations undermine the ideal of the non-intrusive management desired by pure liberals. Consequently the international economic systems become very vulnerable to the development of illiberal tendencies, such as the new protectionism. This in turn raises what for the pure liberal is a very awkward question of who is to be responsible for the protection of the development of a liberal international system.

The issue of management is also problematic for the compensatory liberals, albeit in a different form. Not sharing the pure liberal enthusiasm for market management, they wish to see stronger inter-governmental action. What is rather more critical, however, is the perceived need to diffuse controlling power within such organizations. Commenting on the previous history of informal cooperation among the OECD countries, Hirsch comments that 'the uneasy question remains as to how much this continued basis of informal cooperation is a depleting legacy of the earlier established order and must therefore be realistically expected to atrophy as the grounding of a clear set of international rules is progressively weakened'.[60] The compensatory liberal fear is that if management control is not 'democraticized' beyond the OECD club, then a liberal international economic system will not be able to extend and sustain itself.

Solutions

To the problem of the growth of the new mercantilism or protectionism, pure liberals offer a threefold solution, of which the first strand is an enhancement of GATT:

> The General Agreement must be revised and extended to provide detailed international codes or rules of acceptable behaviour governing non-tariff trade restrictions. In addition, an effective mechanism must be established to insure that new trade-distorting measures are not introduced as well as to facilitate multilateral negotiations designed to reduce existing distortions.[61]

A second strand is the use of adjustment assistance (which includes such factors as compensation for job loss, job retraining, tax credits and depreciation allowances for firms switching production) to ease the dislocations that can be caused by shifts in production dictated by comparative advantage:

> The case for adjustment assistance has been argued on the grounds of

efficiency, equity and practicality. On efficiency grounds, it would lead to greater flexibility in the allocation of resources. On equality grounds, the welfare gains to society as a whole resulting from the further trade would not be obtained at the expense of injury to the particular group of (inefficient) producers. On practical grounds, it is argued that adjustment assistance would weaken the protectionist trend which has begun to appear as increases in imports have threatened domestic producers.[62]

A third strand is for increased cooperation among the leading trade countries to forestall a progressive return to beggar-thy-neighbour policies. One successful illustration has been the initially informal attempt, subsequently insitutionalized, to ensure that export credit rates are linked to market interest rates.

While these mechanisms in principle are potentially powerful, there is no great optimism on the part of pure liberals for their extensive deployment. Thus, while NTBs have been discussed within GATT, the one 'achievement' of the Tokyo Round was the Code of Subsidies and Countervailing Duties, which merely legitimates counter-action rather than removing the root dislocation. Or again the prospects are slim of the CAP being replaced by a deficiency-payment system let alone being phased out under adjustment assistance. Or again, it is difficult to see major inroads being made against the welfare orientation of domestic government.

Though not wishing to countenance any return to restrictionism, compensatory liberals are substantially less perturbed about the facet of the new protectionism which is rooted in the development of the welfare state. On the contrary this development is likely to be seen as a solution to one of the problems associated with market imperfections. A further divergence, though one we shall discuss below, is the compensatory liberal commitment to increased preferential trade agreements with the South. Once the domestic or international welfare component is removed from the new protectionism, however, the compensatory liberal would concur with the proposals for the extension of GATT and the use of adjustment assistance.

The monetary problems have centred on exchange-rate volatility, excessive reliance on the dollar and control of Eurocurrency markets. Exchange-rate volatility is not in general a pressing concern for the pure liberal. This is partly because some degree of volatility is inherent in a floating system and partly because some control mechanisms already exist. In this latter context are speculation, forward markets and interventions by central authorities to dampen excessive movements.⁶³

Other things being equal, pure liberals favour diversification out of the dollar. The most prevalent suggestion is for the use of a Substitution Account in the IMF whereby dollar assets would be transferred to a credit balance denominated in SDRs. This account would transfer dollars to the United States Treasury in exchange for a new series of interest-bearing securities, thus effecting a foreign exchange diversification.⁶⁴

Pure liberals hold a generally favourable evaluation of the Eurocurrency market where their main concern is about the imposition of rather than the need for controls. One generally accepted control is that reserve requirements be imposed on Eurocurrency liabilities.⁶⁵

Compensatory liberals are, as we have noted, decidedly less sanguine about recent changes in the international monetary system and are prone to the 'non-system' view of Helmut Schmidt: 'The present "world monetary system" does not deserve the name. At best it is an unstable constellation or arrangement.'⁶⁶ On the other hand, there is no enthusiasm for a return to the old Bretton Woods system. In general, the compensatory liberals are in favour of establishing a greater degree of centralized control which at the extreme would entail a new International Central Bank functioning in terms of an international currency and having control over expansions and contractions of international liquidity (all of which is very reminiscent of the Keynes Plan). Less ambitiously, there are calls for stronger institutional cooperation. Thus, Schmidt argues that

> to overcome the crisis of the world's financial system needs even stronger, institutionalized cooperation between governments, central banks, bank supervisory authorities and private creditor banks. The International Monetary Fund and the World Bank must be considerably strengthened — not only in terms of funding but also in terms of their opportunities for surveillance of and influence on the national economic policies of debtor countries and creditors.⁶⁷

The third problem area dealt with East–West economic relations. In this context compensatory liberals argue for expanded intercourse and hence favour such measures as the extension of GATT, IMF and World Bank membership or inter-governmental deals such as the Siberian gas pipeline.

Pure liberals, who would prefer to see economic intercourse terminated, are committed, given that this is unlikely, to minimizing and coordinating Western economic exchange. The first of two strategies is to strengthen the coordinating Committee on Export Controls (COCOM) by providing it with a larger staff, a more extensive list of prohibited trade commodities and tighter controls.[68] A second strategy is to increase cooperation, outside the areas governed by COCOM, within the OECD countries. A good illustration of this is the informal agreement known as the 'consensus' operating within the OECD which sets floors on interest rates and maturity of loans. Thus, while compensatory liberals exhort governments to promote and extend economic ties, the pure liberals want governments to restrict the development of such ties.

The fourth problem area was defined for the pure liberal as obstacles to the extension of the world market to Third World countries, to which the solution is quite simply more extensive integration of the Third World into the open world economy.

The first of three major strategies for promoting development through integration is the pursuit domestically of a supply-side orientation.[69] Essentially this requires governments to remove numerous obstacles to private entrepreneurship, most of which have misguidedly been imposed by governments. These obstacles include price controls (especially over food production); state trading boards; the size and powers of central bureaucracies and planning agencies; redistribution policies; and savings taxes. The ideal is what Krauss terms 'the competitive growth state', where

> free enterprise rules for the most part; tax rates are low and business is by and large unregulated. But the competitive growth state is characterized by moderate and single-purposed government intervention in the private economy. The purpose of this intervention is to increase the economic growth of the private economy.[70]

The second strategy is the promotion of export-led growth whereby Third World countries explicitly promote their own comparative advantage and incorporate themselves into an international division of labour which they share with the West. Thus:

> Since most Third World countries have limited markets, 'exports' is the name of the game in the LDCs. If output is to grow, exports must grow. Exports free the personal income and consumption levels of domestic residents from the constraints imposed upon them by the limited size of domestic markets.[71]

Or again:

> The LDCs should be in the forefront of those who seek the

maintenance and strengthening of the 'rule of law' as embodied in the GATT Charter and Codes. Freer international trade in commodities, semi-processed goods and manufactures would bring them great benefits. This is the 'first best' solution to their problems.[72]

The third strategy is increased use of multinationals:

> The key institution in the world economy facilitating the transfer of prosperity from the industrialized countries to the developing ones is the MNC. The multinationals transfer technology to the LDCs that can be used to produce exports; they transfer capital to the LDCs that provides employment for LDC labour, and they also are a vehicle through which a considerable amount of North–South trade takes place. The multinationals, in other words, integrate the world economy. Otherwise fragmented labour markets, commodity markets and capital markets in the South are unified with their Northern counterparts by the MNCs to provide truly world markets for products and factors of production.[73]

In sum, the 'first best' solution to Third World development problems is for these countries to pursue a combination of the competitive state growth model harnessed to export-led growth and the maximization of the benefits of technology and investment transfer provided especially by multinationals. What the pure liberals want to see is not a massive income transfer along Welfare State lines but the transfer of the wherewithal for developing countries to expand their production: 'The essence of the economic development problem is the transfer of prosperity (i.e. the transfer of the ability to produce adequate amounts of real income) from the advanced countries to the less developed ones.'[74]

The first strand of the compensatory liberal solution to the problem of the North–South divide pertains to domestic changes, where there is an insistence on the responsibility of the developing countries to help themselves: 'The governments and people of the South have the primary responsibility for solving many of their own problems. . . . Only they can ensure that the fruits of development are fairly distributed inside their countries, and that greater justice and equity in the world are matched by appropriate reforms at home.'[75] These reforms are likely to require quite drastic changes not only in policy but in underlying political and economic power relations. They include the expansion of social services; agrarian reform; better tax administration; increased development expenditure; public ownership of major industries; maximum use of indigenous resources; and a new alliance of the worker, peasant and student against the army, bureaucracy, landlord and industrialist. What these reforms are intended to effect is a substantial reorientation of development. As opposed to an exclusive focus on production, development is to be defined initially in terms of consumption and more specifically in terms of consumption of those goods and services required to meet basic needs of minimum education, health, nutritional and housing standards. Production then is to be geared to meeting these consumption levels. Ul Haq spells out the objectives as follows:

- new development strategies must be based on the satisfaction of basic human needs rather than on market demand;
- development styles should be such as to build development around people rather than people around development;
- distribution and employment policies must be an integral part of any production plan: it is generally impossible to produce first and distribute later;
- a vital element in the distribution policies is to increase the productivity of the poor by a radical change in the direction of investment towards the poorest sections of society.[76]

The second strand is the fostering of collective self-reliance among the developing countries themselves.[77] This would entail such developments as increased South–South trade stimulated by preferential agreements; increased cooperation to control and monitor foreign investment (as in the Andean Pact); increased use of the Non-Aligned Movement as a truly non-aligned bloc or the use of exclusively Third World regional groups to solve local disputes (as for example in the Contradora Group). The underlying rationale is a twofold gain. First, increased South–South activity structured by basic needs stimulates self-help in its own right. Second, this would help to ease reliance and dependence on the North which itself has been one of the principal factors undermining South–South cooperation.

The third strand of the solution concerns the new cooperative relationship that needs to be developed between North and South. There is no hint of any secession by the South; the theme is, instead, the cultivation of mutual interests:

> We believe that the longer-term interests of the rich and the poor nations are mutually compatible in a fast shrinking planet. But this mutuality of interests must be established on new concepts of creative partnership, not on old patterns of dependency: on a dynamic view of future interdependence, not a revarnished image of past relationships.[78]

The basis of the new creative partnership is that the North makes a series of concessions which in effect constitute an international welfare system. Thus, Ward, commenting on the inequities that develop through an exclusive reliance on the market, argues: 'Within most developed societies, social mechanisms — public ownership, redistributive income tax, welfare schemes, social insurance — try to offset this trend. No such institutions are at work at the international level.'[79] While the suggestion that no mechanisms are at work is probably rather extreme, compensatory liberals would argue that existing mechanisms not only need to be revamped but also new ones need to be created to effect internationally the welfare correction that has come to be accepted domestically in Western welfare states.

What we might call the international welfare proposals, which are legion, include the following. First, the IMF should be strengthened, national currencies should be phased out in favour of SDRs, and, most importantly, SDRs should be allocated by need and not, as happens at the moment, by levels of development. (The most commonly cited practical scheme in this context is the SDR-link.) Furthermore, voting rights should not be tied to existing quotas, which give monopoly control to the West, but more evenly diffused. Or again, special windows (such as the Compensatory Finance Facility or the Extended Fund Facility) should be expanded and conditionality should be substantially relaxed. Second, something like the NIEO scheme for an integrated programme for commodities is required that would not only stabilize prices through buffer stocks but also provide assistance for structural change for export diversification or enhanced processing. Third, there needs to be a new body, say a World Food Organization, that would stabilize food prices, ensure adequate supplies and provide structural assistance. Fourth, there needs to be guaranteed long-term credit without strings to be provided through either an extended IMF or World Bank or a new International Development Fund. Or again in this context, a tax could be levied on rich countries (with popular tax bases being military expenditure or returns on commercial exploitation of the seabed). Fifth, there should be renegotiations of outstanding public and private debt and new codes of conduct for transnational corporations. Finally, the UN needs to be restructured to give greater control to the countries of the South.[80] In sum, these proposals call for greater equality within existing inter-governmental organizations and the creation of a plethora of new ones. Thus, Ul Haq calls for the establishment of a 'World Development Authority, supported by an International Central Bank, an International Development Fund, an International Trade Organization and a World Food Authority'.[81]

There is, then, a marked divergence between the pure and compensatory liberals on Third World issues. While problems for the former are market distortions which can only be solved by moving closer to a free market, the latter identifies problems in terms of basic inadequacies in the market and consequently wants to supersede the market to some degree through corrective devices of one form or another. Thus, compensatory liberal solutions become problems for the pure liberal, while conversely pure liberal solutions represent ways by which compensatory liberal problems are perpetuated or enhanced.

The final problem area outlined above concerned management of the international economic system. To the pure liberal, the ideal management system is the hidden hand of cobweb pluralism. However, in the absence of a pure liberal system, there is some need for active intervention to protect and promote liberalism. This intervention critically needs to come from the major OECD countries: 'Cooperation between North America, Japan and the EEC is essential for a healthy world economy ... If cooperation does not work in this triangle, then it will certainly not work in the very much more difficult polygon of the world economy.'[82] In the imperfectly liberal world a *primus inter pares* role is ascribed to the United States: 'Neither trilateral cooperation nor worldwide cooperation is imaginable at present without American leadership. That applies not only to the world's economic crisis but also to its political crisis.'[83] The emphasis on the major OECD countries as the main source of dynamism and initiative reflects of course the main concentration of liberalism in the world and the area from which the current quasi-liberal system developed. While this liberal core ideally should be extended, this should only happen so long as liberal principles are not corrupted. Although other countries should be encouraged to join the club, both for the interests of the club and its new members, the new members must abide by the rules. Corrupting these rules would be a self-destructive strategy.

For the compensatory liberal what might appear as a corruption to the pure liberal is nothing more than a desirable set of amendments. While the compensatory liberals do not anticipate anything like a centralized international welfare state, they do anticipate the diffusion of welfare state principles. To this end, the compensatory liberal envisages an enhanced degree of international dirigism or corporatism entailing a combination of massively extended inter-governmental organizational activity and a substantial diffusion of power. These changes need to be structured on the basis of positive discrimination so as to rectify some of the injustices and inequities inherent in the old liberal system.

In short, some desirable accommodations need to be made to expand the too restricted core. This new management system is well caught by Morse's idea of a tiered system. There is no pretence that the OECD countries should self-destruct. Indeed the governments of the developed countries need to cooperate 'to preserve their traditional liberal values, and to manage their mutual vulnerabilities'.[84] This part of the system however needs then to develop special arrangements to incorporate the Soviet bloc and the less developed countries into 'a tiered system into which other actors in the international economy would integrate themselves differentially without at the same time necessarily accepting fully either the goals or the rules of the essentially liberal Western system'.[85]

Notes

1. Britain succeeded in maintaining a free trade policy until the McKenna duties of 1916 and indeed remained relatively liberal until 1931. See P. Mathias, *The First Industrial Nation*, London, Methuen, 1969; or more generally N. McCord, *Free Trade Theory and Practice from Adam Smith to Keynes*, Newton Abbot, David & Charles, 1970.
2. For a discussion of the collapse, see for example C.P. Kindleberger, *The World Depression 1929–39*, Berkeley, University of California Press, 1973. As evidence of the re-emergence, the United States at the 1933 World Economic Conference was advising tariff reductions and the removal of exchange controls and in 1934 enacted the Reciprocal Trade Agreements Act.
3. For accounts of the emergence of the post-war trade and payments system, see G. Curson, *Multilateral Commercial Diplomacy*, London, Joseph, 1965; R.N. Gardner, *Sterling–Dollar Diplomacy*, Oxford, Clarendon Press, 1956.
4. There were some exceptions in the nineteenth century, for example the Cobden–Chevalier Treaty or some use of Most-Favoured-Nation treaties among the European states, though this does not detract from the general contrast of uni- versus multilateralism.
5. R.C. Amacher *et al.*, 'Introduction and Summary of the Conference', in R.C. Amacher *et al* (eds), *Challenges to a Liberal International Economic Order*, Washington, American Enterprise Institute, 1979, p. 1.
6. For a general history, see R. Solomon, *The International Monetary System, 1945–76*, New York, Harper & Row, 1977.
7. R. Triffin, *Gold and the Dollar Crisis*, New Haven, Yale University Press, 1960.
8. Among these strategies were the Gold Pool, the 'Roosa' bond, swap agreements and most notably the decision, and First Amendment to the Articles of Agreement, to create Special Drawing Rights.
9. For example, from March to August 1971 United States liquid liabilities to foreigners increased by $14.4 billion. Or from early 1971 to 10 May 1971 there was heavy buying of German marks resulting in an increase of official reserves of $5.2 billion (of which $2.6 billion arrived in the last three days). Or again, in the first week of February 1973 the German monetary authorities purchased $5.9 billion in an attempt to stop the mark appreciating against the dollar, and when the dollar

devalued a week later promptly lost over $2.0 billion on the country's exchange reserves.
10. Among the legion of accounts of the 'collapse' of Bretton Woods, see Solomon, op. cit.; and J. Williamson, *The Failure of World Monetary Reform, 1971–74*, New York, New York University Press, 1977.
11. As an illustration of discussions of how to resolve the 'mess' of the 'non-system' where it is far from clear what exactly is a 'mess', see R. Hinshaw (ed.), *Global Monetary Anarchy*, London, Sage, 1981. (In fairness, some commentators in this symposium are also struck with the same thought.)
12. See, for a full discussion, Williamson, op. cit.
13. H.R. Heller, 'The Changing International Monetary System' in Institute for Contemporary Studies, *Tariffs, Quotas and Trade*, San Francisco, Institute for Contemporary Studies, 1979, p. 84. Or for a further and similar evaluation, see O. Emminger, 'What Can We Learn From The Past', in J.S. Dreyer et al. (eds), *The International Monetary System*, Washington, American Enterprise Institute, 1980.
14. An early version of the NIEO demands was the Charter of Algiers, a series of recommendations prepared by the Group of 77 prior to UNCTAD II. Four years later, an expanded statement was issued at the preparatory meeting to UNCTAD III in the form of 'Declaration and Principles of the Action Programme of Lima'. The 1973 Conference of Non-Aligned Countries, meeting in Algiers, produced the 'Economic Declaration' and the 'Action Programme for Economic Cooperation'. These two statements formed the basis, at times verbatim, of the two main documents of the Sixth Special Session: 'Declaration on the Establishment of a New International Economic Order' (3201-SVI) and 'Programme of Action on the Establishment of a NIEO' (3202-SV1). These last two statements together with the UN Resolution (3281-XXIX) of December 1974, 'Charter of Economic Rights and Duties', constitute the main basis of the NIEO demands.
15. This international dimension of development issues was first popularized by Prebisch with the argument that the terms of trade were deteriorating constantly against Third World countries thereby condemning them permanently to an inferior position in the international economic system. Though this argument has been extensively criticized, the main general point, that of an international economic system institutionally loaded against the Third World, has continued.
16. For some more detailed accounts of the emergence and content of the NIEO demands, see H.O. Bergesen et al. (eds), *The Recalcitrant Rich: An Analysis of Northern Responses to the NIEO Demands*, London, Frances Pinter and New York, St. Martin's Press, 1982; E. Lazlo et al., *The Objectives of the New International Economic Order*, New York, Pergamon, 1978; K.P. Sauvant, 'Towards the NIEO' in K.P. Sauvant and H. Hasenpflug (eds), *The New International Economic Order*, Frankfurt, Campus Verlag, 1977; J.S. Singh, *A New International Economic Order*, New York, Praeger, 1977.
17. 'Declaration on the Establishment of a New International Economic Order' (3201-SV1).
18. For illustrations of pure liberal critiques of the NIEO demands, see, for example P.T. Bauer and B.S. Yamey, 'World Wealth Redistribution' in K. Brunner (ed.), *The First World and the Third World*, Rochester, University of Rochester Press, 1978; H. Friderichs, 'Basic Problems of the World Economy' in Sauvant and Hasenpflug, op. cit.; H.G. Johnson, 'The New International Economic Order' and 'The North–South Issue', in Brunner, op. cit.; C. Ries, 'The NIEO: A Skeptic's View' in Sauvant and

Hasenpflug, op. cit.; A.I. MacBean, *A Positive Approach to the International Economic Order*, London, British North American Committee, 1978.
19. P.T. Bauer and B.S. Yamey, 'Predatory Poverty on the Offensive', *Economic Development and Cultural Change*, 1976, p. 829.
20. P.T. Bauer and B.S. Yamey, 'World Wealth Redistribution', p. 193. This quotation is not uncoincidentally reminiscent of an often cited statement by Johnson: '. . . in some countries, there now appears to be a commitment not only for every man to be employed, but for him to be employed in the occupation of his choice, in the location of his choice and, it would sometimes seem, at the income of his choice (H.G. Johnson in G. Denton *et al.*, *Trade Effects of Public Subsidies to Private Enterprise*, London, Trade Policy Research Centre, 1975, p. xiii). Johnson is talking of the welfare state and the very explicit connection is that pure liberals conceptualized the NIEO demands as an attempt to establish an international welfare state.
21. Report of the Secretary-General to the UN General Assembly, 'Assessment of the Progress Made in the Establishment of the New International Economic Order', A/S–11/5, 7 August 1980, p. 123.
22. The 1979 price rises, despite the popular commotion, represented little more than a deflation correction to the 1973–4 rises.
23. Increased production has led to a saturated oil market which in turn has caused some real price declines in oil. Increased diversification combined with real price reductions has meant that OPEC's official foreign reserves, largely a function of oil earnings, have fallen as a percentage of total world reserves from 19.3 per cent in 1976 (up from 5.3 per cent in 1970) to 12.3 per cent in 1983.
24. Between 1970 and 1982, OECD GNP grew by 44 per cent while energy consumption increased only 14 per cent. Oil's share of total energy consumption over the same period dropped from 51 per cent to 44 per cent.
25. For some general discussion on the growth of multinationals, see J.H. Dunning (ed.), *The Multinational Enterprise*, London, Allen & Unwin, 1971; J.M. Stopford and J.H. Dunning, *Multinationals*, London, Macmillan, 1983; R. Vernon, *Sovereignty at Bay*, London, Longman, 1971.
26. See, for example, J. Diebold, 'Multinational Corporations: Why Be Scared of Them' in R.N. Cooper (ed.), *A Re-Ordered World*, Washington, Potomac, 1973; M. Gillis, 'MNCs and a Liberal International Economic Order' in R.C. Amacher *et al.* (eds), op. cit.; D. Robertson, 'Operations of MNEs in Perspective' in H. Corbet and R. Jackson (eds), *In Search of a New World Economic Order*, London, Croom Helm, 1974; R.D. Tollinson and T.D. Willett, 'Foreign Investment and the MNC', in Institute for Contemporary Studies, op. cit.
27. For the characterization of this development progression, see A. Perlmutter, 'The Tortuous Evolution of the Multinational Corporation', *Canadian Journal of World Business*, 4, 1969.
28. This is a statement by the president of the IBM World Trade Corporation, quoted from R.J. Barnet and R.E. Muller, *Global Reach*, New York, Simon & Schuster, 1974, p. 14 (which in the first two chapters contains numerous fascinating world views as expounded by major corporate heads).
29. Quoted from Barnet and Muller, op. cit., p. 14.
30. Diebold, op. cit., p. 141.
31. On the development of Euromarkets, see E.W. Glendenning, *The Euro-dollar Market*, Oxford, Clarendon Press, 1970; F. Machlup, 'The Eurodollar System and its

Control' in F. Machlup et al., *International Monetary Problems*, Washington, American Enterprise Institute, 1972.
32. One irony in the development of the Euromarket is that it was stimulated in part by the Soviet Union which did not wish to hold its dollars in the United States for fear of their being frozen.
33. Eurobanks now cover all the major idustrial countries as well as the offshore banking centres. This market, though still dominated by Europe, which held a 60 per cent market share in 1983, is continuously diversifying.
34. H.C. Wallich, 'The Need for Control over the Eurocurrency Market' in J.S. Dreyer et al. (eds), *The International Monetary System*, Washington, American Enterprise Institute, 1980, p. 298.
35. The main ingredients of the stabilization programmes are an abolition or liberalization of foreign exchange and import controls, devaluation and domestic anti-inflation programmes (including control of bank credit, higher interest rates, abolition of subsidies, reductions in government deficits, control of wage rises and tightening of taxation procedures).
36. The First Amendment of 1968 created SDRs, while the Second amendment of 1978 legalized the variety of exchange-rate systems. The specialized facilities include the Compensatory Financing Facility, established in 1963 mainly to meet shortfalls in the export earnings of primary producers; the Oil Facility of 1974-6; the Extended Fund Facility; the Supplementary Financing Facility; and the Trust Fund.
37. The IFC was established in 1956 and the IDA in 1960. The IDA and IBRD have the same staff and President, as distinct from the IFC. Following the usual convention, the World Bank will apply to both the IDA and IBRD. For a general history, see E.S. Mason and R.E. Asher, *The World Bank since Bretton Woods*, Washington, Brookings Institute, 1973.
38. In 1980 prices, the per capita income ceilings for IDA loans are set at $730 and for IBRD loans at $2,650. In fact IDA loans are very heavily concentrated in the poorest countries, with around 80 per cent of its loans going to countries with per capita incomes below $411.
39. IDA capital, given its almost pure grant form, has to be contributed by member governments (achieved through replenishments). The IBRD, apart from a small amount of paid-in capital, raises its finances on the commercial markets through bonds.
40. The IFC, which works purely in the private sector, has indeed been expanding rapidly in recent years.
41. H.G. Johnson, 'Mercantilism: Past, Future and Present', in H.G. Johnson (ed.), *The New Mercantilism*, Oxford, Blackwell, 1974, p. 2.
42. See R.E. Baldwin, *Nontariff Distortions of International Trade*, Washington, Brookings, 1970. This contains a detailed discussion of the different ways in which non-tariff barriers distort trade.
43. H.B. Malmgren, 'Coming Trade Wars? Neo-Mercantilism and Foreign Policy', *Foreign Policy*, 1, Winter 1970-71, p. 120. For further statements, see: R.E. Baldwin, 'Protectionist Pressure in the US' in Amacher et al. (eds), op. cit.; J. Tumlir, 'The New Protectionism, Cartels and the International Order', in ibid.; B. Belassa, 'The New Protectionism', in ibid.
44. M.B. Krauss, *The New Protectionism*, New York, New York University Press, 1978, p. 36. For an interesting attempt that tries to assess the scale of managed trade, see S.

Page, 'The Management of Internatioal Trade', Discussion Paper 29, National Institute of Economic and Social Research, London, 1982. This paper illustrates well the measurement problems in detecting contemporary trade distortions but points to a general increase.
45. Krauss, op. cit., goes on to argue that the welfare state, while resting on productivity increases, actually undermines them. He thus sees a fundamental contradiction, the obverse of the traditional Marxist one, of consumption outstripping production.
46. Rates of growth of trade have been lower under the floating system but many other indicators have performed less well over the same period. The control problems of trying to isolate the impact of floating rates are substantial, though an accumulating body of evidence indicates that there is no deleterious effect. See, for example: T.D. Willett, 'The Causes and Effects of Exchange Rate Volatility', in J.S. Dreyer *et al.* (eds), op. cit.
47. Despite its size, the Soviet economy is relatively backward and is ideally suited to exporting primary products (especially oil and gas) in exchange for Western European manufactures or loans.
48. This position is classically stated by Secretary of Defense Weinberger: '... without access to advanced technology from the West, the Soviet leadership would be forced to choose between its military-industrial priorities and the preservation of a tightly controlled political system. By allowing access to a wide range of advanced technologies, we enable the Soviet leadership to evade that dilemma.' Quoted in the *Economist*, 22 May 1982, p. 69, from Weinberger's annual budget report to Congress of February 1982.
49. The leverage case was illustrated in the grain embargo. Given that the Soviet Union is a small trader, well aware of leverage problems, and that embargoes are notoriously difficult to manage, this strategy is not very promising. The leverage logic explains, however, the antagonism of some to the oil and gas pipelines (that is, it would give leverage to the Soviet Union). The enticing strategy can be seen for example in the extension of IMF membership to Romania in 1972 and Hungary in 1982. Both of these strategies are explicitly antagonistic and in this respect quite dangerous. The Soviet Union has demonstrated several times that not only is it quite uninterested in liberalization but will use force to resist liberalization.
50. Independent Commission on International Development Issues, *North–South*, London, Pan, 1980, p. 64. Hereafter this is referred to as Brandt Report 1, to be distinguished from the second report, *Common Crisis*, London, Pan, 1983.
51. For some general reviews, see, for example, H. Brookfield, *Interdependent Development*, London, Methuen, 1975; P. Donaldson, *Worlds Apart*, Harmondsworth, Penguin, 1971; M. ul Haq, *The Poverty Curtain*, New York, Columbia University Press, 1976; H. Singer and J. Ansari, *Rich and Poor Countries*, London, Allen & Unwin, 1977; B. Ward *et al.* (eds), *The Widening Gap*, New York, Columbia University Press, 1971; B. Ward and R. Dubos, *Only One Earth*, Harmondsworth, Penguin, 1972.
52. Ul Haq, op. cit., p. 60.
53. Brandt Report 1, p. 32.
54. There is an important terminological and conceptual issue at stake here. The term Third World is a legacy from the Cold War when the residue countries that did not fall in the East–West bipolar system became the Third World. Compensatory liberals tend to use now the North–South (rather than World) terminology to

emphasize the distinction between economic haves and have-nots. This is generally opposed by pure liberals who think more in terms of a graduation of per capita incomes and levels of development not only across but within countries. As such the North–South juxtaposition is seen as a 'political' oversimplification causing people to think in terms of redressing a gap that is artificially created by the terminology of North–South itself.
55. For a general discussion, see S. Kuznets, *Economic Growth of Nations*, Cambridge, Harvard University Press, 1971; A. Maddison, *Economic Growth in the West*, London, Allen & Unwin, 1964. It might be emphasized here that pure liberals do not accept the argument that the West has harmed development prospects. Thus: 'Far from the West having caused the poverty of the Third World contact with the West has been the principal agent of material progress there.' (P.T. Bauer, *Equality, the Third World and Economic Delusion*, London, Weidenfeld & Nicolson, 1981, p. 70.)
56. Thus: 'The problem of speeding development in backward, relatively isolated countries is not amenable to swift or dramatic solution. Their progress will take time.' (MacBean, op. cit., p. 49).
57. M.B. Krauss, *Develoment Without Aid*, New York, McGraw Hill, 1983, p. 50.
58. Ibid., p. 45.
59. For example, interest rates are very much nation state phenomena and it would be absurd to pretend that say the Danish interest rate is as important as the American one.
60. F. Hirsch and M.W. Doyle, 'Politicization in the World Economy', in F. Hirsch *et al.*, *Alternatives to Monetary Disorder*, New York, McGraw Hill, 1977, p. 20.
61. Baldwin, op. cit., p. 185.
62. S. O'Cleireacain, 'Adjustment Assistance to Import Competition', in H. McFadzean *et al.*, *Towards an Open World Economy*, London, Macmillan, 1972.
63. It is commonly suggested that IMF approval should be sought for substantial interventions. See, for example, Willett, op. cit.
64. See, for example, E.M. Berstein, 'The Future of the Dollar and Other Reserve Assets' in J.S. Dreyer *et al.* (eds), op. cit.
65. See, for example, D.W. Henderson and D.G. Waldo, 'Reserve Requirements on Eurocurrency Deposits' in J.S. Dreyer *et al.* (eds), op. cit.; F. Machlup, 'The Eurodollar system and Its Control', in F. Machlup *et al.*, op. cit.; H.C. Wallich, 'The Need for Control over the Eurocurrency Market' in J.S. Dreyer *et al.* (eds), op. cit.
66. H. Schmidt, 'The Inevitable Need for American Leadership', *Economist*, 26 Feburary 1983, p. 24.
67. Ibid., p. 22.
68. COCOM, established shortly after the Second World War, has a list of so-called 'strategic' exports and any export to Soviet Russia that is on this list must be cleared unanimously by all fourteen member countries. COCOM, however, has no permanent headquarters and a small staff, which consists mainly of trade officials who regularly grant permission.
69. For general statements on a supply-side focus, see, for example, G. Gilder, *Wealth and Poverty*, London, Buchan and Enright, 1982; M. and R. Friedman, *Free to Choose*, London, Martin and Secker, 1980. For general statements more explicitly attuned to Third World issues, see P.T. Bauer, *Dissent on Development*, London, Weidenfeld & Nicolson, 1971; Bauer, *Equality, The Third World and Economic Delusion*; Krauss,

Development Without Aid; MacBean, op. cit.
70. Krauss, *Development Without Aid*, p. 4. The competitive growth state is an amalgam of Johnson's two models of Competition and Government Control. See H.G. Johnson, 'A Word to the Third World', *Encounter*, October 1971. The architypal competitive growth-state model is Japan. The current models for the Third World are the newly industrializing countries.
71. M.B. Krauss, *Development Without Aid*, p. 60. See also B. Belassa, *The Process of Industrial Development and Alternative Development Strategies*, Princeton, International Financial Section, 1980; A. Kreuger, 'Alternative Trade Strategies and Employment in LDCs', *American Economic Review Papers and Proceedings*, **68**, 2, 1978: R.I. McKinnon, *Money and Capital in Economic Development*, Washington, Brookings Institute, 1973.
72. MacBean, op. cit., p. 49.
73. Krauss, *Development Without Aid*, p. 127. See also in this context: H.G. Johnson, *Technology and Economic Interdependence*, London, Macmillan, 1975.
74. Krauss, *Development Without Aid*, p. 109.
75. Brandt Report 1, p. 41.
76. Ul Haq, op. cit., p. 28. For a general review of basic needs orientation, see P. Streeten, *First Things First*, Oxford, Oxford University Press, 1981.
77. This idea is far from novel, having been articulated in the 1950s by people such as Peron, Nehru, Nkrumah and Sukarno.
78. The Third World Forum, Special Task Force, *Proposals for a New International Economic Order*, Mexico and New York, 1975.
79. B. Ward, Report on the UNEP–UNCTAD Symposium, *Patterns of Resource Use, Environment and Development Strategies*, Cocoyoc, Mexico, 1975.
80. See classically Brandt Reports 1 and 2.
81. Ul Haq, op. cit., p. 202. We should perhaps emphasize that this threefold strategy goes not represent the single agreed compensatory liberal programme. There is variation in emphasis across the three stands. Very typically, however, compensatory liberal proposals work at all three levels.
82. Schmidt, op. cit., p. 30.
83. Ibid.
84. E.L. Morse, 'Political Choice and Alternative Monetary Regimes', in F. Hirsch *et al.*, op. cit., p. 96.
85. Ibid., p. 123.

6 Socialist international economic problems and solutions

Problems

The major goal for socialists is the pursuit and promotion of equality and as such problems are defined in terms of manifestations of inequalities. A major characteristic of socialist thought is the contention that these inequalities are deeply rooted in the basic structural organization of society. In the contemporary world, capitalism is the structural organization which is seen to foster and perpetuate inequality and consequently it is only with the overthrow of capitalism and the superseding establishment of socialism that inequities can be eradicated.

The demise of capitalism, as originally envisaged by Marx, has clearly not happened. While many underlying contradictions of capitalism are seen to be continuing, it is clear that capitalism in the short term has succeeded in postponing its collapse. Rather than identifying problems in terms of an almost endless list of the inequities inherent in capitalism, it seems more profitable to present the problems as perceived by the socialists in terms of those adaptations that have permitted the postponing of the collapse of capitalism. Thus, capitalism as the embodiment of inequalities constitutes the core problem for socialists and whatever changes have happened in capitalism have done nothing to shake this conviction. In the shorter term, it is the adaptation or extension of capitalism that becomes the critical problem for socialists since it is this adaptation that has facilitated the perpetuation of a system of inequality. The two most critical adaptations are the growth of the bourgeois state and imperialism. We begin our presentation of the twin problems of the state and imperialism by focusing on the traditional capitalist core.[1]

For a variety of reasons, socialists have recently become preoccupied by the idea of the state. These include the relative 'absence of systematic political theorization on the part of Marx'. Or again, as Miliband and others point out, Marx's writings, despite a high level of nomothetic content, were still 'for the most part the product of particular historical episodes and specific circumstances'.[2] Marx, at his death in 1883, had not seen the growth of the state to the point at which it consumes upwards of

30 per cent of GNP or employs up to half of the work-force. But of even more importance for our purposes is the reason for the attention to the state which is a function of the perception that the growth and development of the state in advanced capitalist societies has been one of the major means whereby capitalism has postponed its demise and thereby perpetuated a social system founded on and fostering equality.

The recent preoccupation with the state has triggered a number of controversies of which one critical one has been between instrumentalists and relative autonomists.[3] In general, the weight of opinion lies with the latter. Thus Urry argues for the need to incorporate a consideration of civil society 'as that set of practices outside both the state and the relations and forces of production'. Deploying the idea of civil society, Urry produces an explicit statement of relative autonomy:

> Thus the relative autonomy of the state stems from the existence of civil society and the fact that there are patterns of interrelations between the two. Although certain practices in civil society are determined by the economy, and the form of the state is given by its need to attempt to preserve the overall conditions for profitable accumulation, these interrelationships are partially autonomous of the capitalist economy. It is these interrelationships between the state and civil society which guarantee the relative autonomy of the former and partial independence of certain practices within the latter.[4]

Following a line closer to the relative autonomy rather than the cruder instrumentalist position, we can now survey what is more critical for our immediate concerns, namely a consideration of the roles of the state.

A key role of the state continues to be repression, to which end the state holds a monopoly of a highly developed set of means of coercion. It is, however, the non-overtly repressive roles which are more important. The major contribution and extension introduced by Gramsci was in his reappraisal of state power and the shift from seeing the state purely as a coercive instrument to one based on a mixture of coercion and hegemony. Indeed, it is recognized very explicitly that it is the very development of hegemony in advanced capitalist societies that has made it very difficult to overthrow the state as opposed to those states, such as Tsarist Russia, where state power was based purely on force and consequently was very vulnerable to popular counter-force.[5]

A further extension to the non-overtly repressive role of the state is, following Poulantzas in particular, that set of activities whereby the state organizes bourgeois fractions. Thus, the state not only promotes hegemony but also unifies bourgeois class fractions into a coherent power bloc. As such the state may often act against certain bourgeois fractional interests to preserve a larger bourgeois interest. In this context there is explicit recognition of some conflict of interest and the unitary interest view, characteristic of state monopoly capitalist theories, is seen as erroneous.[6] Repression, but more saliently, hegemony and fraction organization constitute the functions of the state in providing the political conditions for the reproduction of the capitalist mode of production.

Parallel to and reciprocally related with the maintenance of the political conditions, the state also provides the economic conditions for the reproduction of capitalism. In this context, Mandel lists the general technical preconditions of production (postage, transportation), the general social preconditions (law, currency), and the reproduction of intellectual labour (education).[7] In similar manner, Jessop lists formal facilitation (money, legal or administrative systems), substantive facilitation (production of the infrastructure), formal support and substantive support.[8]

Despite some undoubted controversy on the precise roles of the state or on how these roles can be founded in Marxist theory, there is, none the less, some consensus on several important points. First, the state in late capitalism is geared essentially towards 'providing and sustaining those conditions appropriate for capital accumulation'. Second, the state has displayed an impressive capacity for adaptation. Third, though unquestionably manifesting several important contradictions, the particular form that state development has taken in advanced capitalist societies means that the state represents a very formidable obstacle to socialism.[9] Thus, by dint of facilitating the extension and development of capitalism, the state has served to extend the lifespan of the domination and inequality inherent in capitalism. It is this capacity of the state to forestall socialism that constitutes it as such a major problem in the socialist model.

An important corollary to the development of the state in advanced capitalist societies is the change in ideology. Under emergent capitalism, the dominant ideology was a belief in the omnipotence of competition. This has been superseded by an ideology of 'technical rationalism', proclaiming organization and regulation and the belief that through continuing growth benefits can be diffused to all:

> Belief in the omnipotence of technology is the specific form of bourgeois ideology in late capitalism. This ideology proclaims the ability of the existing social order to eliminate all chance of crises, to find a 'technical' solution to all its contradictions, to integrate rebellious social classes and to avoid all political explosions.[10]

The end of ideology proclaimed by bourgeois writers, such as Bell, is seen as an ideology in its own right or as false consciousness whose 'objective function is simply to convince the victims of alienated labour that it is senseless to rebel against it'.[11] Thus, once again, we are confronting, in this changing ideology, a problem in that 'technical rationalism' serves to perpetuate capitalism and thereby a system of domination and inequality.

The second core problem has been the development of imperialism. As in the case of the state there is no single theory and indeed the analysis of imperialism is the subject of some considerable controversy. In general, the controversy is most acute on the sources or theoretical underpinnings of imperialism, which does not directly concern us, rather than on the form and impact of imperialism, which is of more concern. Rather paradoxically, a good part of the controversy is based on a common consensus among the socialist writers. Thus, there is an unequivocal agreement that imperialism is not to be equated with colonialism and consequently decolonization did not spell the end of imperialism. While there is no single, generally accepted definition of imperialism, the manifestation of it pertains to the external relations of inequality and domination of capitalism. Thus, imperialism constitutes 'a complex of economic, political and military relations by which the less economically developed lands are subjected to the more economically developed. . . . Imperialism remains the best word for the general system of unequal world economic relations.'[12] The complication, as far as the controversy is concerned, is that imperialism is seen as an integral part of capitalism and that a comprehensive understanding of imperialism is predicated upon a full understanding of capitalism. Furthermore, as capitalism has changed and developed, so too has imperialism. Thus, in analysing imperialism, socialists are coterminously analysing capitalism and it is this high level of analysis that accounts for much of the controversy.

Modern imperialism has developed alongside monopoly capitalism. As such, it was an outgrowth of the free trade imperialism characteristic of competitive capitalism, which in turn was an extension of mercantilist imperialism and the feudal mode of production.[13] Although Marx did not develop a full theory of imperialism in his exposition of surplus value, the tendency of the rate of profit to fall and the concentration of capital, he did provide the main building blocks on which Lenin formulated an explicit theory.[14] Though Lenin borrowed extensively for this work, it has none the less come to assume a position of central importance in the exposition of modern imperialism.

The motivation to accumulate surplus value from labour was seen to promote the increasing concentration and centralization of capital. Central to this development was the concentration of banking and the merger of bank and industrial capital in finance capital. The main features of modern imperialism were the concentration of production and capital; the merger of bank and industrial capital in finance capital; an increasing emphasis on the export of capital as opposed purely to commodities; the formation of international monopoly capitalist associations; and the territorial division of the world.

Two points in particular are worth emphasizing from the early expositions on imperialism. First, the state is seen as playing an increasingly important role in contrast to the minimal role of the state under the free trade imperialism of competitive capitalism:

> Finance capital needs a strong state which recognizes finance capital's interests abroad and uses political power to extort favourable treaties from smaller states, a state which can exert influence all over the world in order to be able to turn the entire world into a sphere of investment. Finance capital finally needs a state which is strong enough to carry out a policy of expansion and to gather in new colonies.[15]

There is, in other words, a symbiotic relation between the development of the state and the development of imperialism both of which are a function of but also reflect the changing underlying structure of capitalism and particularly the continuing concentration and centralization of capital.

A second point of emphasis is that Lenin sees imperialism as 'the highest stage of capitalism' or the 'eve of socialism'. In this Lenin departs from Hilferding, who sees imperialism as a policy choice, in stressing that imperialism is an integral feature of capitalism. Furthermore, it is seen as an inevitable development of capitalism and in particular a way in which capitalism could temporarily forestall the contradiction inherent in the falling rate of profit:

> As long as capitalism remains what it is, surplus capital will never be utilized for the purpose of raising the standard of living of the masses in a given country, for this would mean a decline in profits for the capitalists; it will be used for the purpose of increasing those profits by exporting capital to the backward countries. . . . The necessity for exporting capital arises from the fact that in a few countries capitalism has become 'over-ripe' and . . . capital cannot find 'profitable' investment.[16]

The inevitability component and the underconsumption explanation have become sources of controversy.[17] However, the continuing validity of the law of falling profits is of more concern to the scientific integrity of Marxism than our exposition. What is critical is that Lenin introduced the idea, from which there is no really significant deviation even among his socialist critics, that the development of imperialism facilitates the continuing expansion and perpetuation of capitalism.

The outline of imperialism by Lenin is essentially one of national capitals becoming increasingly concentrated and in their enforced outward movement coming into conflict. The themes of concentration and rivalry are continued in later writings. Thus, Mandel sees monopoly capital as characterized by national concentration and centralization resulting in overcapitalization and the need to export capital. This created international concentration but not international centralization: 'The international concentration of capital did not mainly take the form of an international centralization of capital, but pitted national imperialist monopolies against each other as antagonists on the international market for commodities, raw material and capital. Only very rarely was there any actual international fusion of capital.'[18] This antagonism found its most acute expression in the chaos of the 1930s and in the two world wars which are seen as inter-imperial wars.

> Each national monopolistic bourgeoisie had its own demarcated national market plus a territorially demarcated colonial enclave from which it excluded the others by force of arms. With tariff and other barriers protecting the market, the sources of raw and auxiliary materials, and the outlets for capital exports, the colonial system was perfected. Efforts to gain entry into these colonial preserves necessitated a repatriation or redivision by force of arms. The result of this was the two imperialist World Wars.[19]

Capitalism and imperialism clearly did not collapse with the Second World War and indeed both are seen by the socialists as continuing in an enhanced form in the post-war period. This enhancement was intially promoted by the post-war reconstruction directed under American hegemony and took the form of the movement towards multilateral monopoly imperialism.[20]

The move towards multilateralism had its roots, however, in very national concerns. Though imperialism was never equated with colonialism, colonialism was a product of the territorial initiatives or imperatives of antagonistic national capitals. Thus, the initial capitalist leader states had succeeded through their colonial drives in closing off a good part of the world to United States capital. The Second World War placed the United States in an excellent position to develop some leverage over the Europeans. Thus a *quid pro quo* of the first Lend-Lease Agreement was to gain access to British colonial markets. Or again, the American commitment to promoting independence for colonial territories was not to assist national liberation movements but rather to remove the formal colonial power to permit American capital penetration.

The wartime devastation was, however, also a source of major concern to the United States. Thus, the United States saw itself to be confronted by what it perceived to be an aggressive socialist power in the form of the Soviet Union. The Soviet Union might either have been tempted by the devastation to annex Western Europe or alternatively it might have taken advantage of the economic instability to foster domestic socialist revolutions. The loss of Western Europe would have been a devastating blow to the United States as not only would a critical region be excluded from the capitalist sphere but also the United States itself was strongly tempted by Western Europe, seeing in it enormous trade and investment potential in which it could unleash its booming economy.

The devastation of the war created a situation in which the United States could effect a substantial readjustment of the advanced capitalist economies. The critical point, however, is that it could only promote its own capitalist interests by ensuring the continued viability of Western European capitalism — in short, by providing some form of multilateral framework.

The solution was provided in the form of the 'Open Door' and containment policies, which took practical form in the guise of the Bretton Woods system, the Marshall Plan and NATO. In this single stroke the Soviet Union was to be contained and isolated, a constitutional framework for the free flow of goods and capital was established, and European recovery was to be assisted to provide a market for United States capital and trade.

On the one hand, there was a substantial projection of United States capitalist interests:

> This tendency was already observable in the First World War, and in the course of the Second World War and its aftermath it found spectacular expression in the world-wide political and military hegemony of US imperialism, It basically corresponds to . . . decisive control over an increasing share of the international apparatus of production by the owners of a single national class of capitalists, with foreign capitalists participating at most as junior partners.[21]

The directing hand of the United States was very clear in its control of the IMF, IBRD, and NATO or in its conditions for Marshall Aid or in the enormous imbalance of capital flows. On the other hand, the reconstruction under American hegemony was multilateral in the sense that American interests could only be fostered by promoting and protecting Western European capitalism:

> By working out the multilateral strategy, United States imperialism undertook to underwrite the other capitalist states and provide them with a 'security' cover, both for themselves and for their neo-colonial puppets in exchange for which the United States was henceforth entitled to an 'Open Door' red carpet under the new umbrella of redivision.[22]

In much the same way the theorists of the state, looking primarily at domestic developments, have emphasized its role in facilitating the reproduction of capitalism, so too have those looking at post-war imperialism emphasized the same facilitating role played by the United States government in post-war reconstruction except that the focus is now on an international scale.[23]

The American concern to support capitalism in Western Europe also explains its general enthusiasm for the European integration movement.[24] Conversely, the European Economic Community (EEC) is strongly opposed by the socialists.[25] At a particularistic level, they object to the lack of attention to social and economic justice. Thus, the Regional Fund receives little attention, or the Common Agricultural Policy assists larger farmers. Or again, they object to the development of a stultifying bureaucracy or the feeble popular assembly or the dominant position of technocrats for whom there is no public accountability. However, these objections are merely detailed manifestations of the generalized antagonism which is founded on the charge that the EEC is nothing more than a technical device designed to promote and protect monopoly capital interests:

> There is no doubt that the Common Market of Europe was a reactionary set-up aimed against socialism in Europe, national liberation in the colonies and general United States superiority. There can also be no doubt that it was a temporary agreement of European capitalists against workers of Europe and the workers and peasants of the colonial and neo-colonial Third World.[26]

Once again, the salience of the state as a facilitator of international capitalism is well illustrated in the EEC context.

Within multilateralism, a further important development could take place in the form of the growth of multinational corporations. Given the opportunity of larger markets, international concentration could be enhanced and, furthermore, develop into international centralization: '. . . the international concetration of capital henceforward started to develop into international centralization. In late capitalism, the multinational company becomes the determinant organization of big capital.'[27] Multinational corporations were of course not new but they did experience a massive growth in the post-war period, reflecting the continuing expansion and development of capital:

> The new giant corporations that arose represented a more developed stage in the concentration of production and circulation of both goods and capital. Whereas a simple cartel divided the market between independent monopolists, a syndicate organised the centralized sale of their output, a trust gathered under a single management the sale of goods; a concern managed simultaneous enterprises of various sectors by way of production integration, and a cartel of trusts divided markets at an immeasurably higher level, the transnational corporation combined all these forms of monopolization and thus raised it to a qualitatively higher level.[28]

The expansion of multinationals, underwritten in a variety of ways by the state, has further enhanced imperialism:

> The United States would not seek hegemony so avidly were it not for the American multinational companies which have installed themselves all over the planet. It is to defend the actions and the development of these companies that American power is brought to bear. . . . Conversely, these companies are imperialism's pawns. Subtly and almost irresistably, like gigantic squids, they spread their tentacles.[29]

American hegemony, characteristic of the period up to the late 1950s, has unquestionably declined. Thus, whether one looks at world output or world investment flows the relative contribution of the United States has declined. This decline has on occasion triggered serious crises in international capitalism whenever a direct structural component of American hegemony has been unable to meet demands placed upon it, as for example in the overextension of the dollar underlying the Bretton

Woods collapse. However, the most significant characteristic of the decline of American hegemony has been that it had been brought about by the re-emergence of European and Japanese capitalism. Thus while American hegemonic interests dictated a multilateral foundation which in turn has destroyed American hegemony, the 'triumph' of multilateralism has been that American hegemony could reduce without weakening international capitalism.

In concluding this discussion of the capitalist core we can consider three short-term scenarios for capitalist development outlined by Mandel. These are useful in that they underscore the close affinity of the developments of the state and imperialism. Supra-imperialism essentially profiles the dominance of a single imperial power and is held to be unlikely (though this condition was approximated during American hegemony). Ultra-imperialism entails a fusion of capital across states, which would entail a victory of capital over the state and which is again held to be unlikely as it would require a substantial expansion of international centralization. The third, and deemed by Mandel most likely, is inter-imperialist competition:

> Although the international fusion of capital has proceeded far enough to replace a larger number of independent big imperialist powers with a smaller number of imperialist super-powers, the counteracting force of the uneven development of capital prevents the formation of an actual global community of interest for capital. Capital fusion is achieved on a continental level, but thereby intercontinental imperialist competition is all the more intensified.[30]

The emphasis thus far on the capitalist core is not misplaced in that this core has provided the engine or driving force of capitalism. In turning our attention now to the Third World, we find a conceptualization of Third World 'development' issues couched in terms of contingency on the developments of capitalism in the Western core.[31] The key to the conceptualization of Third World development issues is that capitalism has not been confined to this core but, particularly through imperialism, has created a world capitalist system:

> My thesis is that underdevelopment as we know it today, and economic development as well, are the simultaneous and related products of the development on a world-wide scale and over a history of more than four centuries at least of a single integrated economic system: capitalism. I suggest that the experience with mercantilism and

capitalism should be understood to be part not only of a single historical process, the development of capitalism, but of the development of a single, integrated system, the capitalist system, which came to attain world-wide scope.[32]

Or again:

> The rise of capitalism, and the industrialization of the advanced countries to which it led, brought into being a world market and an international division of labour. It was through their relation with the world market that the national capitalist states acquired their specific physiognomy and that the less developed areas, as they were brought into contact with the world market, assumed a position of dependence.[33]

The idea of a world capitalist system presupposes a substantial degree of integration. The critical feature of the integration brought about by the diffusion of capitalism is that it has produced an integration of substantial inequality between the capitalist core and the Third World periphery: 'International integration has led to national disintegration and dependence in the Third World. This is reflected in growing national and international inequality, the absolute impoverishment of a minority in poor countries, and greater social differentation among the ex-colonial people.'[34] The hallmark of unequal integration is Third World dependence:

> By dependence we mean a situation in which the economy of certain countries is conditioned by the development and expansion of another economy to which the former is subjected. The relation of interdependence between two or more economies, and between these and world trade, assumes the form of dependence when some countries (the dominant ones) can expand and can be self-starting, while other countries (the dependent ones) can do this only as a reflection of that expansion . . .[35]

This condition of dependence or underdevelopment in the Third World is the 'other face' of capitalist development in the core: 'Underdevelopment is not just the lack of development. Before there was development there was no underdevelopment . . . underdevelopment developed in intimate relation with the development of the now-developed countries as simultaneous results of the historical process of capitalist development . . .'[36]

In sum, the diffusion of capitalism from the core has created a world market and world division of labour which has entailed an enforced integration of Third World territories into the world capitalist system. This enforced integration has been one of unequals with the consequence that capitalist penetration has arrested the development of the Third World, structuring it so as to accommodate the interests and demands of the capitalist core. Third World development, the epitome of domination and exploitation, can only be understood in terms of dependent development:

> This system is reproduced as a dependent one when it reproduces a productive system whose development is limited by those world relations which necessarily lead to the development of only certain economic sectors, to trade under unequal conditions, to competition with international capital under unequal conditions, to imposition of relations of super-exploitation of domestic labour force.[37]

The dependent development of the Third World is a process that has been underway since the emergence of mercantilist imperialism. Not surprisingly, therefore, the transmission mechanisms have changed over time. Furthermore, the point in time at which particular territories became incorporated into the world capitalist system has also varied. These two factors mean that there is some variation across Third World territories in their manifestations of imperialism. What, however, has been constant is the domination and exploitation inherent in the unequal relationship of dependency.

The transmission mechanisms of imperialism in the post-war period are both varied and extensive, covering official and non-official bodies, national and international agencies, deliberate and conscious interventions as well as more enduring structural influences. Thus, included in this long list are to be found aid and arms transfers, multinational corporations, technology transfers, trade, international bodies such as the IMF and World Bank, or more general structural features such as the international division of labour.[38] It would be erroneous, however, to see all the transmission mechanisms as being purely 'external'. Capitalist penetration is not limited to international exchange but has transformed the whole social, economic and political fabric of underdeveloped societies. In the process it has developed a 'bridge-head' or 'comprador national bourgeoisie' which acts to promote and protect core capitalist interests in the periphery.[39]

> At the same time the post-colonial international system has helped to create a harmony of interests between the elites of the Third World and

those of the industrialized world, and in the process a conflict of interest between rich countries and poor has been partially transformed into a conflict between the masses and the elite within the poor countries.[40]

This is what underlies the commonly used model of the centre and periphery each containing their own centre and periphery.[41] In this respect, there is a strong 'domestic' content to Third World development problems, albeit a domestic content that finds its source in the world capitalist system. This explains why socialists, though having some sympathy for Prebisch-type arguments on the terms of trade, would not accept Prebisch correction strategies. Such a strategy (essentially import substitution) is far too limited in its explanatory base. Or again, this general point explains why socialists were uninterested in the New International Economic Order movement which again was almost exclusively premised on external change and did not contain any important prescriptions for domestic transformation.

Like the liberal, the socialist is likely to see so-called development problems, such as food or unemployment or domestic conflict, as symptomatic rather than causal characterizations of the main problem.[42] Where they do differ radically from the liberals is firstly in the conception of development. While the liberals emphasize diffused growth, the socialists want equality under redistribution and the satisfaction of collective needs. The second difference pertains to structural arrangement. Thus, while the liberals want integration into an open world market, the socialists want to abolish this market in favour of the socialist structural arrangement.[43]

The final context in which we examine the development of the state and imperialism is that of the Soviet Union. While socialist writers, as we have profiled socialism, are willing to grant a number of major achievements to the Soviet Union, they also see it as an example if not of a 'revolution betrayed' then certainly of an embryonic or distorted form of socialism. What is interesting for our purposes is that it is a combination of arguments on the state and imperialism that explain not only how 'actually existing socialism' deviates from socialism but also why this deviation has developed.[44]

The main point in the elaboration of the deviation from socialism manifested by 'actually existing socialism' concerns the 'statification' of the Soviet Union. It is the massive concentration of power in the state apparatus that is seen as responsible for the ossification of Soviet society and for the perpetuation of inequality.[45] As a statified corruption of socialism the Soviet Union has been led into 'bureaucratic imperialism' particularly in its structuring effects on the development of Eastern Europe but also in the Third World. Thus, Bahro, for example, who initially described the invasion of Prague in 1968 as 'the greatest crime of the USSR since World War II', later substituted Afghanistan as the greatest crime, describing it as a manifestation of the 'naked face of great power chauvinism, or bureaucratic imperialism'.[46]

The explanation of the deviation is seen firstly in the inappropriate conditions for socialism. Thus Mandel, in accounting for the development and the deviation in these societies that have tried to make a socialist revolution, argues: 'Instead of concentrating on a process of creating new productive relations and new norms of distribution, the leaders of transitional societies have had to concentrate their efforts on expanding the productive forces themselves.'[47] This has resulted, according to Mandel, in the 'bureaucratic deformation and degeneration of the transitional society'.[48] A second critical factor has been that the Soviet Union was obliged not only to respond to existing Western capitalist penetration but more importantly subsequently found itself encircled by imperialist capitalist powers. In failing to promote a permanent revolution and in opting for socialism in one country in what initially was a relatively backward area, the Soviet Union found itself developing a 'fortress neurosis'. This in turn has enforced a form of reactive imperialism on the Soviet Union which finds itself obliged to respond to capitalist encirclement on capitalism's own terms. Thus in trying to escape from containment, the Soviet Union has been seduced not only in domestic terms, such as its permanent arms economy, but also externally in creating the type of spheres of influence or satellites so beloved by the major capitalist powers.

A very curious and somewhat paradoxical achievement of world capitalism, then, has been to contribute in part towards the corruption of the development of socialism in or from the Soviet Union. While there is no pretence that the Soviet Union is identical in economic or political structure to major Western states and while its imperialism takes different forms, by virtue of becoming engaged in a major superpower rivalry with the United States, the Soviet Union reinforces a global system of imperialism and in this respect constitutes an obstacle to socialism.[49]

In summary, capitalism, for the socialist, is the embodiment of inequality and as such is the root cause of the myriad manifestations of domination and exploitation found in the world today. From its initial consolidation as competitive capitalism, capitalism has succeeded in extending itself both in terms of its stages of development and in terms of its geographical extent. By dint of evading its demise, originally anticipated under anticipated under competitive capitalism, capitalism has extended and enhanced global inequalities. The two critical pillars of the extension of capitalism are the developments of the state and imperialism and it is in this respect that they constitute the core problems for the socialist.

Solutions

All three models have no difficulty in identifying what, from their perspectives, are a series of important problems, and in this respect the socialists are no different from the liberals or realists. A major difference between the socialists, on the one hand, and the realists and liberals, on the other, does appear in the context of solutions. While neither the liberal nor the realist would see contemporary global structure as conforming to their own desired models of structural arrangement, it is none the less the case that they can identify many structural features that do correspond to their models. Consequently, their solutions have a pronounced incremental content for the very simple reason that they have already existing building blocks on which changes can be effected. This is not the case for the socialists and consequently their solutions entail radical, qualitative change with the result that socialist solutions simply cannot be specified with the same type of detail that characterizes much of, say, liberal solutions.[50]

This is not to imply that the socialists do not have any solutions. Indeed, on the contrary, the solution is staggeringly clear. Since the root cause of all problems resides in capitalism and since the socialists have a structural arrangement that can overcome these problems, then the solution quite logically is to overthrow capitalism:

> All these searing problems will remain insoluble so long as control over the forces of production is not wrested from the hands of the capital. The appropriation of the means of production by the associated producers, their planned application of priorities determined democratically by the mass of the workers, the radical reduction of working time as a precondition of active self-administration in economy and society, and the demise of commodity production and money relations are the indispensable steps to their solution. The final abolition of capitalist relations of production will be the central objective of the mass revolutionary movement of the international working class that is now approaching.[51]

Two factors in particular make the overthrow of capitalism a solution of substantial magnitude. In the first place, the replacement of capitalism has to be world-wide, partly because, as we have seen, capitalism has become a world system and partly because socialism would be vulnerable unless enacted on a world scale: 'Historically, the problems of building socialism will be solved only by world revolution. It is only in this context that the disproportions, the distortions, and the most extreme contradictions will be definitely overcome.'[52]

The second factor is the socialist conviction that inequality cannot be overcome within capitalism and consequently 'technical solutions' cannot be effected within capitalism:

> These structures are strong. They have a great absorption capacity and can distort, even pervert, many well-intended measures. So the basic thesis as to strategies of development would be that technical solutions are likely to be either irrelevant — or in the worst case — counterproductive, partly by mystifying and masking the problem, partly by strengthening the structures of dominance. Fundamental structural change is indispensable, in order to create a world in which some of the more technical solutions would be meaningful, meaning both destroying and building new structures.[53]

Two illustrations serve to enhance this general point. We have seen that the liberals have some misgivings about the World Bank and consequently have a series of proposals for amending its structure and workings. Payer, in her analysis of the World Bank, totally eschews any technical solutions:

> In summary, the World Bank is perhaps the most important instrument of the developed capitalist countries for prying state control of its Third World member countries out of the hands of nationalists and socialists who would regulate international capital's inroads, and turning that power to the service of international capital.[54]

The conclusion that it should be terminated follows quite logically. On a larger scale we can consider a second illustration that focuses on the Brandt Report, which figures very prominently in compensatory liberal solutions. Commenting on the Brandt Report, Hayter argues:

> Thus its proposals for reform are designed first and most crucially to ensure that the existing world economic system functions smoothly. Second, if possible, the reforms are to be designed in such a way that they achieve some alleviation of extreme poverty in underdeveloped

countries. But the Report, like most of the orthodox literature on development, notably omits to explain why the poverty exists in the first place. If it attempted such an explanation, it might come to the embarrassing conclusion that the poverty is caused precisely by the economic system which its proposals are supposed to protect.[55]

Once again, technical fixes are quite inadequate. What is required rather is global socialism:

> We need societies in which what is produced is determined by need rather than by the profit calculations of individual business people ... socialism is a form of society in which decisions are made consciously by the people as a whole, who control democratically what is produced, how it is produced and how it is distributed.[56]

The socialists, then, have a clear conception of problems. They also have an equally clear conception of the solution. What does become rather problematic are the strategies for implementing the solution of the replacement of capitalism by global socialism. These difficulties in strategies turn essentially on the rejection by the socialists of technical solutions within capitalism in favour of a holistic revamping of global structural organization. It is the magnitude of required change or the absence of any already existing building blocks that makes the socialist solution of a qualitatively different form from those of the realist or liberal.

There is within the socialist model a generally high level of consensus on the solution of the need to establish global socialism. Where this consensus begins to break down somewhat is on the strategies for delivering this solution. The controversy centres on two issues in particular: the location of the impetus for the restructuring and the means for achieving the restructuring.

The location controversy turns on whether the impetus would come from the developed capitalist states or from the underdeveloped periphery. For these writers who see imperialism in terms of a simple confrontation between a metropolitan core and an impoverished periphery, the location for change can be placed in the latter. Thus Baran and Sweezy, seeing an internationalization of the proletariat, argue: 'The revolutionary initiative against capitalism, which in Marx's day belonged to the proletariat in the advanced countries, has passed into the hands of the impoverished masses in the underdeveloped countries who are struggling to free themselves from imperialist domination and exploitation'[57] Many of the dependency writers also take up a periphery focus. Thus

Amin, while accepting that 'socialism can only come into existence on a world scale' argues that the periphery has a choice between dependent development and autocentric develoment. There can be no progress for the Third World if it remains within the capitalist system and consequently it must contract out: 'the periphery cannot just overtake the capitalist model; it is obliged to surpass it'.[58]

For most Marxists, however, the location for the overthrow of capitalism resides unequivocally in the advanced capitalist countries. For the scientific Marxists this is because the objective conditions can only be met under advanced capitalism. A further reason is that socialism, as envisaged by most European Marxists, presupposes a high level of industrial and technological development which has only been achieved by the advanced capitalist countries. Indeed a major task of the more developed countries would be to transfer resources to the less developed. Another reason is that socialist revolutions in the less developed countries would leave them encircled by more powerful and hostile capitalist countries, which would thwart the socialist development of the poorer countries (even assuming that socialist revolutions were allowed to happen in the first place). This is the type of reasoning we have seen already from Bahro and Mandel, among many others, used to explain in part the failure of the development of socialism in the Soviet Union.

As for the means whereby the structural change is to be effected, these resolve into two main categories. One of these relates to a sudden collapse in capitalism brought about by the failure of capitalism to resolve its inherent contradictions. A critical feature, particularly of scientific socialism, is the proposition that capitalism contains the seeds of its own destruction.[59] The evolution of capitalism under the developments of the state and imperialism has afforded capitalism with a way of avoiding major contradictions. This avoidance is seen not as a final and successful resolution, however, but rather in terms of the postponement of the collapse. Thus while the bourgeois state has prolonged its existence by moving from pure repression to the development of hegemony, it none the less remains a state that acts in the interests of capitalism. Consequently, Mandel, for example, sees many illustrations of crisis in, for instance, the high level of decomposition of the repressive apparatus, in the broad development of popular power by workers or in the crisis of legitimacy.[60] Or again in the context of imperialism, numerous contradictions are manifested in, for example, inter-state rivalry or the clash between governments and corporations or the failure to control business cycles. Thus, the collapse of Bretton Woods or international stagflation are seen as symptomatic manifestations of contradictions.[61]

A second route, which is more gradual than the collapse brought through contradictions, is consciousness raising. This effectively entails conversion to the socialist belief that capitalism needs to be overthrown and replaced with socialism. Its importance is accepted by all socialists and is never presented as an alternative to contradictions, though there can be variability on the relative importance of consciousness raising and contradictions.

Within the area of consciousness raising there is controversy over where such consciousness raising is to take place. The traditional Marxist view is that it should be founded in the proletariat essentially for the simple reason that the bourgeoisie will not transform itself to self-destruct. Within this tradition, however, there has always been a strong emphasis, found in very explicit form in Lenin's vanguard ideas, that intellectuals would play a strong role in fostering proletarian consciousness.

Critical Marxists and non-Marxist socialists have generally placed much less faith, and at the extreme virtually no faith at all, in the traditional alliance of intellectuals and the working class. Thus Bottomore does not want 'to cast the intellectual in a Lukacsian role, as party theorists who are able to express the "correct class consciousness of the proletariat" by virtue of some privileged insight into the ultimate meaning of history'.[62] Or again Bahro comments: 'It is no longer probable that the crisis of bourgeois society will find its solution in the sense of the proletarian revolution traditionally expected.'[63] This view, though not for an instant rejecting the need to establish socialism, tends to reject a good part of the basis of scientific Marxism and in particular the determinate interpretation of the sub- and superstructures:

> Since history itself had thoroughly discredited all hopes of an economically grounded 'mechanism' of emancipation, it is not only necessary for a theoretical analysis to take into account entirely new constellations of 'bases' and 'superstructures'; in fact, the criticism and alteration of the 'superstructure' have a new and decisive importance for the movements of liberation.[64]

The failure of proletarian radicalism is not a source of pessimism for these socialists primarily because radicalism, in their view, should never have been expected from the working class. Real hope for emancipation and liberation does exist and indeed is a function of the continuing develoment of capitalism. That hope lies in a 'new working class' made up of the technical, professional and most qualified sectors of production. Thus, commenting on May 1968, Touraine argues that this indicated that sensibility to the new themes of social conflict was not most pronounced in the most highly organized sectors of the working class. The railroad workers, dockers and miners were not the ones who most clearly grasped its most radical objectives. The most radical and creative movements appeared in the eonomically advanced groups, the research agencies, the technicians with skills but no authority, and, of course, in the university community.[65]

In short, as capitalism develops, it produces ever more educated groups who wish to exert control over all areas of their political, social and economic lives and it is these groups, 'incubated within the womb of the capitalist order', that will gradually effect the socialist transformation.

In summary, the core problems for the socialist are the developments of the state and imperialism in that these are the main agencies that have facilitated the extension and perpetuation of capitalism and thereby sustained the relations of inequality and domination inherent in capitalism. The socialists do have an eminently clear and consistent solution, namely the overthrow of capitalism and its replacement with socialism. The extremely comprehensive and holistic conceptualizations of both capitalism and socialism, the perceived irreconcilability between capitalism and socialism, and the world-wide dominance of capitalism make this solution one of enormous magnitude. This explains why socialists generally do not profile detailed or issue specific solutions and also why the strategies for achieving the solution are cast in rather general terms. As such there is understandable controversy on where the socialist transformation is to be effected and what agents or forces will be responsible. None the less, whether founded on a scientific basis or not, or on varying degrees of optimism or pessimism, or on greater or lesser inevitability, there is a conviction that national socialist revolutions triggered by some combination of contradictions and increasing consciousness will diffuse to issue in the creation of global socialism and a world order that will be problem free.

Notes

1. Reciting inequities would at the descriptive level constitute problem identification. However, since capitalism embodies every conceivable form of inequity, such a descriptive elucidation would almost be endless. More importantly, given the socialist location of inequities in the structural organization of society, it would largely miss the point. Following the discussion of problem identification in terms of description with explanatory content, it therefore seems more profitable for us to pursue the avenue of indicating those developments within capitalism that have

enabled it to extend itself and, by dint of thereby postponing its demise, to perpetuate inequality.
2. For a fuller discussion, see R. Miliband, *Marxism and Politics*, Oxford, Oxford University Press, 1977 (from which the brief quotations are taken).
3. For a fuller discussion of this and other controversies, see J. Holloway and S. Picciotto (eds), *State and Capital*, London, Arnold, 1978; B. Jessop, *The Capitalist State*, Oxford, Martin Robertson, 1982; R. Miliband, *The State in Capitalist Society*, London, Weidenfeld & Nicolson, 1969; N. Poulantzas, *State, Power, Socialism*, London, New Left Books, 1978; J. Urry, *Anatomy of Capitalist Societies*, London, Macmillan, 1981.
4. Urry, op. cit., p. 122.
5. In this context some socialist writers point to universal suffrage, competitive elections, tolerance of pressure groups as illustrations of the functional fit between liberal democracy and capitalism. Some writers, such as Urry, attack as absurd the idea that the franchise was extended as a deliberate ploy to mystify the proletariat. While Urry sees nothing inevitable in the growth of liberal democracy, the general point of interest to us still holds that, whether deliberately or inevitably or not, liberal democracy has served to promote hegemony.
6. State monopoly capitalist theories have come largely from official Communist parties. Such theories envisage the imposition of economic interests of a dominant fraction on other fractions and classes. Poulantzas in contrast argues that the economic fractioning of the bourgeoisie can only be overcome by the state. For a fuller review, see, for example, Jessop, op. cit.
7. E. Mandel, *Late Capitalism*, London, New Left Books, 1975.
8. Jessop, op. cit.
9. The contradictions are multiple. For an interesting discussion of a major contradiction, see J. O'Connor, *The Fiscal Crisis of the State*, New York, St Martin's Press, 1973.
10. Mandel, op. cit., p. 501.
11. D. Bell, *The Coming of Post-Industrial Society*, New York, Heinemann, 1973. The quotation is from Mandel, op. cit., p. 503. For a discussion of alienation contingent on capitalist consumption, as opposed to production, see H. Marcuse, *One Dimensional Man*, London, Routledge, 1964.
12. M. Barratt Brown, *After Imperialism*, New York, Humanities Press, 1970, p. viii.
13. Mercantilist imperialism is essentially primitive accumulation based on plunder. Some non-Marxist writers, usually employing a less elaborate conceptualization of capitalism, attach more significance to mercantilist imperialism as the initial diffusion of capitalism. See, for example: A.G. Frank, *World Accumulation*, London, Macmillan, 1978; I. Wallerstein, *The Capitalist Economy*, London, Cambridge University Press, 1979. Marxists tend to begin their expositions more with the free trade imperialism of the nineteenth century at which point competitive capitalism was becoming firmly established.
14. V.I. Lenin, *Imperialism: The Highest Stage of Capitalism*, New York, International Publishers, 1977.
15. R. Hilferding, quoted in M. Barratt Brown, 'A Critique of Marxist Theories of Imperialism' in R. Owen and B. Sutcliffe (eds), *Studies in the Theories of Imperialism*, London, Longman, 1972, p. 49.
16. Lenin, op. cit., p. 63.

17. See, for example, P. Baran and P.M. Sweezy, *Monopoly Capital*, London, Monthly Review Press, 1966. Baran and Sweezy wish to substitute 'the law of rising surplus for the law of falling profit'. Or, see M. Barratt Brown, 'A Critique of Marxist Theories of Imperialism'. Brown is critical both of the overly deterministic element in Lenin and of underconsumption. Rather, following Myrdal among others, he points to 'capital accumulation at one pole [which] creates impoverishment at the other' but emphasizes that 'this is a theory that fits well enough in Marx's model of capitalist economic relations'. This emphasis on continuity with Marx does not, however, prevent Baran and Sweezy or Brown from being severely attacked by others who see themselves as more orthodox Marxist-Leninists. See, for example, the critique contained in D.W. Nabudere, *The Political Economy of Imperialism*, London, Zed Press, 1977.
18. Mandel, op. cit., p. 314.
19. Nabudere, op. cit., p. 185.
20. As illustration of several studies that cover the following exposition see Baran and Sweezy, op. cit.; F.L. Block, *The Origins of International Economic Disorder*, Berkeley, University of California Press, 1977; Y. Fitt et al., *The Word Economic Crisis*, London, Zed Press, 1980; J. Kolko, *America and the Crisis of World Capitalism*, Boston, Beacon Press, 1970; G. Liska, *Imperial America*, Baltimore, John Hopkins, 1968.
21. Mandel, op. cit., p. 326.
22. Nabudere, op. cit., p. 154.
23. This explains why some see the United States government in the pocket of private capital while others cede more autonomy to the government. The former position is a restatement of instrumentalism and the latter of relative autonomy.
24. This enthusiasm has not been unqualified. Initially European integration was seen as a further bulwark for capitalism against the Soviet Union. Over time, however, the potential has developed for European autonomy and antagonism towards the United States which would have been trivial on a bilateral basis but is more significant on a regional one.
25. See, for example, S. Holland, *Uncommon Market*, New York, St Martin's Press, 1980; or, for more general and theoretical considerations, J. Galtung, *The European Community*, London, Allen & Unwin, 1973; or E. Mandel, *Europe vs. America*, London, New Left Books, 1970.
26. Nabudere, op. cit., p. 155.
27. Mandel, *Late Capitalism*, p. 316. See also, in this context, S. Hymer, 'The Efficiency (Contradictions) of Multinational Corporations', *American Economic Review*, **60**, 1970.
28. Nabudere, op. cit., p. 186.
29. Fitt, op. cit., p. 1. For an extensive discussion, see also R.J. Barnet and R.E. Miller, *Global Reach*, London, Cape, 1975.
30. Mandel, *Late Capitalism*, p. 332.
31. In general, European socialists (albeit with some exceptions) have concentrated more on the forces within the advanced capitalist countries that gave rise to imperialism and in this respect the Third World often seems to be somewhat overlooked. Much of the writing on the Third World comes from Third World dependency writers who in turn tend to concentrate more on the impact rather than causes. While there are some real conflicts on occasion between 'North' and 'South' writers, in general the distortion caused by imperialism is taken for granted by the

writers of the 'North' while equally the source of distortion is taken for granted by writers of the 'South'. In this respect we are simply seeing different and equally ethnocentric points of emphasis. For an interesting discussion, see, for example, T. Hodgkin, 'Some African and Third World Theories of Imperialism' in Owen and Sutcliffe, op. cit. The dependency literature itself is legion. For some major representative statements, see, for example, S. Amin, *Unequal Development*, London, Monthly Review Press, 1976; S. Amin, *Imperialism and Unequal Development*, London, Monthly Review Press, 1977; F.H. Cardoso, *Dependency and Development in Latin America*, Berkeley, University of California Press, 1979; A. Emmanuel, *Unequal Exchange*, London, Monthly Review Press, 1972; A.G. Frank, *On Capitalist Underdevelopment*, Bombay, Oxford University Press, 1975; C. Furtado, 'Elements of a Theory of Underdevelopment', in H. Bernstein (ed.), *Underdevelopment and Development*, Harmondsworth, Penguin, 1977; T. dos Santos, 'The Structure of Dependence' in K.T. Fann and D.C. Hodges (eds), *Readings in US Imperialism*, Boston, Porter Sargent, 1971.

32. Frank, *On Capitalist Underdevelopment*, p. 43.
33. T. Kemp, 'The Marxist Theory of Imperialism', in Owen and Sutcliffe, op. cit., p. 20.
34. K. Griffin, *International Inequality and National Poverty*, London, Macmillam, 1978, p. 2.
35. Dos Santos, op. cit., p. 226. More commonly the term dependency is used rather than dependence but here they are synonyms.
36. Frank, *On Capitalist Underdevelopment*, p. 1.
37. Dos Santos, op. cit., p. 226.
38. This list of factors is assuredly not a disparate one. Indeed, a common hallmark of dependency writings is that each of the elements on such a list is integrally related to others. None the less, the emphasis can vary. For more specific writings on this sample list, see, for example, S. Weissman, *et al.*, *The Trojan Horse*, San Francisco, Ramparts Press, 1974; J. Oberg, 'Arms Trade with the Third World as an Aspect of Imperialism', *Journal of Peace Research*, **12**, 3, 1975; Hymer, op. cit.; F. Stewart, *Technology and Underdevelopment*, London, Macmillan, 1977; C. Payer, *The Debt Trap*, Harmondsworth, Penguin, 1974; C. Payer, *The World Bank*, London, Monthly Review Press, 1982; F. Frobel *et al.*, *The New International Division of Labour*, Cambridge, Cambridge University Press, 1980.
39. For a discussion of 'collaboration', see R. Robinson, 'Non-European Foundations of European Imperialism' in Owen and Sutcliffe, op. cit. While seeing the object of imperialism as lying in the drive by a metropolitan country to 'reshape [the dominated country] in its own interest and more or less in its own image', Robinson also argues that 'no society, however dominant, can man-handle arcane, densely-peopled civilizations or white colonies in other continents simply by projecting its own main force upon them. Domination is only practicable in so far as alien power is translated into terms of indigenous political economy.' This critique is levelled in part against an over-centralist interpretation of some earlier theories of imperialism. This point has become generally accepted in later writintgs. For a somewhat idiosyncratic but very powerful exposition on the domestic support of imperialism, see F. Fanon, *Black Skins White Masks*, London, Paladin, 1970.
40. Griffin, op. cit., p. 2.
41. The centre–periphery model in each of the centre and the periphery (expressed very

clearly in J. Galtung, *The True World*, New York, Free Press, 1980) is now commonly employed. It is more popular than a simple centre–periphery juxtaposition (found for example in Baran and Sweezy, op. cit., or P. Jalee, *The Pillage of the Third World*, London, Monthly Review Press, 1968). However, it must be emphasized that centre–periphery terminology is used more extensively in non-Marxist socialist literature and some Marxists attack this terminology quite strongly (see, for example, Nabudere, op. cit.). However, it would seem that centre–periphery translates itself quite easily to class models.

42. For example on food issues, see, as illustrations, S. George, *How the Other Half Dies*, Harmondsworth, Penguin, 1977; or F.M. Lappe and J. Collins, *Food First*, Boston, Houghton Mifflin, 1977.
43. In the conceptualization of development and the structural arrangement necessary to pursue development, the pure liberals have no points of contact with the socialists. As would be expected, compensatory liberals come closer to the socialists but there is still a substantial gulf. This is well illustrated by the socialist critiques of the Brandt Report. See, for example, T. Hayter, *The Creation of World Poverty*, London, Pluto, 1981.
44. The phrase 'actually existing socialism' is the one used by Bahro to characterize Soviet socialism. See R. Bahro, *The Alternative in Eastern Europe*, London, New Left Books, 1978.
45. To save repetition the reader is referred back to Chapter 2 for a fuller discussion of this point.
46. The invasion of Prague in 1968 was a 'crime' in that the Soviet Union was seen to be killing off a genuine revolt against statification. Afghanistan is a greater crime in that, while the Soviet Union was wrong to invade Czechoslovakia, it did, because of Western pressure, have some 'rightful' concern for developments in Eastern Europe. There is no such partially mitigating justification for Soviet involvement outside Eastern Europe. See R. Bahro, *Socialism and Survival*, London, Heretic Books, 1982.
47. E. Mandel, *Key Problems in the Transition from Capitalism to Socialism*, New York, Merit, 1979, p. 35.
48. Or again, Bahro, *The Alternative*, points to factors such as the semi-Asiatic past of Russia, the tradition of Tsarist autocracy, and the psychology of the masses trapped in primary patriarchy.
49. For non-Marxist profiles of Soviet imperialism, see, for example Galtung, *The True World*. As an illustration of the reciprocal nature of superpower rivalry, see N. Chomsky *et al.*, *Superpowers in Collision*, Harmondsworth, Penguin, 1982.
50. This is not to imply that incrementalism is an inherent feature of liberalism. If global structure were currently socialist, then liberalism would appear radical and would be engaged with precisely the same qualitative change that currently typifies socialism. Realists on the other hand are much more inclined to make a virtue of incrementalism.
51. Mandel, *Late Capitalism*, p. 589.
52. Mandel, *Key Problems*, p. 38.
53. Galtung, *The True World*, p. 150.
54. Payer, *The World Bank*, p. 20.
55. Hayter, op. cit., p. 15.
56. Ibid., p. 121.

57. Baran and Sweezy, op. cit., p. 9.
58. S. Amin, *Unequal Development*, p. 383. The viability of revolution in the periphery, held to by many dependency theorists, then leads to admittedly more detailed propositions for self-reliance, South–South cooperation, and basic needs.
59. The notion of contradictions is not peculiar to Marxists, let alone the scientific ones. Thus, Wallerstein explicitly uses the idea of contradictions; see 'The Rise and Demise of the World Capitalist System', in Wallerstein, op. cit.
60. E. Mandel, *Revolutionary Marxism Today*, London, New Left Books, 1979.
61. See, for example, Block, op. cit.
62. T. Bottomore, 'Socialism and the Working Class', in L. Kolakowski and S. Hampshire (eds), *The Socialist Idea*, London, Quartet, 1977, p. 132.
63. Bahro, *Socialism and Survival*, p. 45.
64. A. Wellmer, *Critical Theory of Society*, New York, Herder & Herder, 1971, p. 121.
65. A. Touraine, *The Post-Industrial Society*, New York, Random House, 1971, p. 18.

7 Realist international economic problems and solutions

Problems

Realism is commonly charged with an almost total neglect of economics. It has to be conceded that there is no counterpart in realist writings to Smith or Marx; the development of realist theorizing has come primarily through politics and history rather than economics; the very label of realism, though well known to students of international politics, is largely unknown or unused by students of economics.[1] Indeed, that strategic and foreign policy studies rather than economics constitute the core subject matter of realist investigation is a view that is held not only by critics of realism but by many realists also.

This does not mean, however, that realists are uninterested in economics. If there is any lack of interest then it is in a pure or autonomous study of economics. There is, however, a very distinctive realist approach to political economy. Since this is not only not well known but also relatively poorly articulated by realists themselves, it is worthwhile outlining the basic parameters of the realist approach to political economy before presenting the realist profile of international economic problems.

The charge that realism ignores economics stems essentially from a *Realpolitik* or Machiavellian characterization of realism. While Machiavelli did indeed largely separate economics from politics, to focus almost exclusively on the latter, he was soon followed by the mercantilists. This school equally explicitly reunited economics and politics, arguing that wealth and power were inextricably linked.[2] Though it would be absurd to make a simple equation of realism with mercantilism — in particular the 'bullion' approach to trade is totally defunct — realist political economy finds its intellectual roots very much more in mercantilist than Machiavellian conceptions.

Consequently, it is no surprise to find that Gilpin, citing Viner's study of mercantilism, indicates with approval a postulated reciprocal relation between power and wealth. Power and wealth are not only mutual prerequisites but they are also harmonious:

> We label 'economic' those sources of wealth upon which national

power and domestic welfare are dependent ... Understood in these broader terms, the economic motive and economic activities are fundamental to the struggle for power among nation states. The objects of contention in the struggles of the balance of power include the centres of economic power.[3]

Economic capabilities, such as gross national product or gross domestic fixed capital formation or international liquidity holdings, are a major component of national power. Such capabilities not only critically underwrite military capabilities, but in their own right constitute important sources of status and influence. From this perspective it is not surprise that Schelling, taking trade as a synonym for many economic interactions, can argue:

> Aside from war and preparations for war, and occasionally aside from migration, trade is the most important relation that most countries have with each other. Broadly defined to include investment, shipping, tourism and the management of enterprises, trade is what most of international relations are about. For that reason trade policy is national security policy.[4]

Economic policy can become national security policy in a variety of ways. Trade, investment or monetary interactions lend themselves to a host of means of influence or coercion.[5] Even when such interactions are not deliberately transformed into means of influence, states can find themselves subject to a variety of vulnerabilities, or what Cooper terms disturbance, hindrance or competitive effects, all of which can be seen as threats to sovereignty.[6] But perhaps most importantly, economic considerations play a critical role in influencing and structuring the development of the whole international power distribution. Indeed in the longer term, as Gilpin argues, economic factors can take priority over political ones:

> In the short run, the distribution of power and the nature of the political system are major determinants of the framework within which wealth is produced and distributed. In the long run, however, shifts in economic efficiency and in the location of economic activity tend to undermine and transform the existing political system. This political transformation in turn gives rise to changes in economic relations that reflect the interests of the politically ascendant state in the system.[7]

Or again, writing against a background of assumed stability in nuclear deterrence, Hunter comments:

> We are rapidly leaving the era in which military strength has been the prime measure of national power and a principal arbiter of war and peace. We are moving to an era dominated by economic power ... threats to economic peace become much more salient. In other words, tomorrow's threats to peace (as a state of international order) will be contained largely in challenges to the relative distribution of economic, not military power.[8]

There can be no doubt that political economy is of vital significance to realists. This significance, furthermore, derives directly from their goal of promoting sovereignty within a society of states. Economic considerations are not tangential to sovereignty but an integral component of it. Equally the management of international economic interaction is a critical component of the maintenance of a society of states.

What is rather peculiar to the realist political economy is that it does not contain any enduring or invariant economic principles. There is no counterpart, for example, to the law of falling profit or to free trade and comparative advantage. Furthermore, there are no economic prescriptions to any absolute level or intensity of international economic intercourse. Depending on circumstance, very different profiles of foreign economic behaviour, ranging for instance from a relatively open economy to autarchy, can be tolerated. This absence of invariant economic principles should not be interpreted to indicate indifference. Not only are economic considerations of critical importance but also international economic relations need to be modelled in a particular way otherwise international order can be seriously jeopardized. Furthermore, the requirements for the arrangement of international economic relations are firmly written into the goal, strctural arrangement and belief system that make up the realist model. More specifically the nature and conduct of international economic behaviour must satisfy two principles.

In the first place, governments have a duty to monitor and manage their international economic interactions. States have an obligation to ensure in whatever network of international economic intercourse they find themselves lodged or which they choose to pursue that the national interests of their citizens are promoted. Even though force may be the ultimate arbiter of sovereignty, sovereignty in a *de facto*, as opposed to a *de jure*, sense can be eroded by economic vulnerability and permeability. Governments, then, must monitor and manage their foreign economic policies so as to ensure that economic sovereignty is maintained and that the interests of their basic constituents, their national populace, are not damaged.

The second principle contains two major clauses. While it is incumbent on governments to pursue and protect the national interest of their citizens, this is not intended by realists to provide a *carte blanche* for the unbridled pursuit of national interest. Indeed such a situation would be viewed as catastrophic. In pursuing their national interest, states must, and this is the first clause, take into account the interests of others.[9] Accommodation of the interests of other states is not, however, equally distributed throughout the international system. The international system is characterized by a high degree of inequality and this inequality means that accommodation or reciprocity is also unequally distributed. States at similar levels in the international power hierarchy must take greater account of each other's interests than of the interests of a state at the bottom of the hierarchy. While realists see the unequal or hierarchical organization of states to be relatively enduring, they do emphasize that the location of states within this hierarchy can change. As states move within this hierarchy then adjustments must be made, in reciprocity, to match such movements. The second clause, then, requires that, as a state moves down the hierarchy, it should expect to exercise less influence and conversely a greater accommodation of interest would be ceded to a state moving up the hierarchy. The second principle requires that not only must states take account of the interests of others but such accommodation must both reflect location within the international hierarchy and be sensitive to changes in it.[10]

In sum, we would unquestionably be disappointed if we searched within realism for any invariant economic principles or any single desirable economic configuration. Indeed, one of the hallmarks of realist thought is that it specifically eschews such things. This does not for a moment, however, mean that realism is unconcerned with economic matters. In fact, given the core connection of power and wealth, economic considerations could scarcely be more important. Though very deliberately avoiding any prescription of invariant economic principles or forms of economic organization, realism does none the less have relatively enduring prerequisites of how international economic behaviour needs to be structured. These prerequisites take the form of the two principles we have just outlined and it is these principles that provide the bench-marks against which problems can be assessed. Using these principles as organizing devices we can now profile realist international economic problems in the post-war period.

Viewing the post-war period as a whole, the international economic system was perceived to be relatively problem free through to the mid-1960s. Rather curiously, however, this relatively problem free period had rather inauspicious origins in the cold war.

Prior to the onset of the cold war, generally set by realists at 1945, there had been real hopes that some accommodation might be achieved between the two new superstates of the Soviet Union and the United States.[11] Within the American administration itself there was clearly some preference in the Treasury for the Soviet Union to be accommodated both within any inter-governmental organizations and in an American economic assistance programme geared to reconstruction.[12] With the death of Roosevelt and the victory of the State Department over the Treasury, such hopes were not to be fulfilled and with substantial realist misgivings an offensive liberal impetus from the Truman administration put the seal on the development of the cold war.

While, from a liberal perspective and particularly a pure liberal one, the cold war was in effect inevitable, this was not the case for realists. The inevitability for the liberal was primarily a function of the clash between diametrically opposed ideologies of liberal democracy and communism. Since the realist is concerned to demote the salience of ideological factors, the inevitability simply did not exist. As Steel emphasizes: 'As far as the national interest is concerned it makes little difference what kind of ideology a government professes, so long as it does not follow policies which are hostile or dangerous.'[13] On the other hand, it would have to be conceded (quite apart from the fact that ideologies matter if those in power hold ideology to be critical) that for the Soviet Union and United States to have achieved an immediate *modus vivendi* would have been a tall order. Even putting aside the different ideologies profiled by these two states, the Soviet Union and the United States manifested a major power rivalry in the context of a vacuum created by the collapse of the Eurocentric system. As Gilpin explains, while the cold war was certainly not inevitable, it was equally the not unlikely consequence of great power rivalry:

> The efforts of each to forestall the other merely increased the insecurity of the other, causing it to redouble its own efforts. Each, in response to the other, organized its own bloc, freezing the lines of division established by the victorious armies and wartime conferences. As in the case of every great power, both the United States and the Soviet Union desired an international environment congenial to their own economic and security interests. . . . The origins of the Cold War, therefore, may

indeed be said to be economic, but in the mercantilist sense of interstate competition for control of industrial power and of the economic resources that determine the international distribution of power.[14]

The American response to the cold war in the economic field was to establish the Bretton Woods system. Though established against an unfortunate, albeit understandable backdrop, the Bretton Woods system met with general approval from the realist.

This may in the first instance seem rather strange as the Bretton Woods system unequestionably established a bipolar world economy. As far as one of the key powers, the Soviet Union, was concerned, this was not, however, seen as particularly troublesome. Since 1917 the Soviet Union, largely of its own volition, had pursued an essentially autarchic foreign economic policy. Realism contains no absolute prescriptions as to whether autarchy is good or bad. If a major state chooses an autarchic policy and in so doing does not damage the interests of other key states, then the autarchic option is eminently justifiable. Both of these conditions were met. At the same time the United States chose a commitment to an open international economy. Since this reflected an enduring American position and was not injurious to the interests of others, then equally this option was satisfactory.

Within the Bretton Woods world economy the United States clearly adopted a dominant leadership position. Once again this was not problematic from the realist perspective. Since the turn of the century the United States had emerged as the single most important economic power and the First World War had transformed it very critically from a debtor to a creditor state. In fact, far from the dominant leadership position proving problematic, there would have been much greater dangers had the United States adopted an isolationist position. A good part of the traumas of the inter-war period could be explained in terms of an unsynchronized international economic system. During this period the European powers, and Britain in particular, had clung on to a leadership role which they were clearly unable to sustain. The dislocations caused by the recourse to economic nationalism were in large part a function of inadequate leadership and management whereby non-leader states attempted to play a leadership role. Thus, though Steel is critical of the later way in which the Pax Americana developed, he also argues that the Pax was based on good motives of 'welfare imperialism' rather than 'base motives of profit and influence'.[15]

A third source of realist approval was that not only did the United States assume the responsibilities of leadership but also the design itself of the

Bretton Woods system was consonant with realist principles. In particular, while rightly playing a hegemonic role, the United States also displayed an appropriate degree of reciprocity. For example, the United States neatly accommodated Europe and through the Marshall Plan not only assisted European economic recovery, providing coterminously a suitable market for a booming American economy, but also helped to assure that Europe could meet any Soviet political threat.[16] Or again, the United States permitted a degree of discrimination against itself to facilitate further European recovery. Or again, although the Bretton Woods system had a high liberal content, it also manifested a suitable number of safeguards. Thus, the dollar was established as the key currency, the United States held a dominant position in both the International Monetary Fund (IMF) and the International Bank for Reconstruction and Development (IBRD), the General Agreement on Trade and Tariffs (GATT) principles contained many caveats and in any event could only be pursued through government initiative and negotiation, or the United States could, and indeed did, easily bypass these institutions if it so chose.

Had a pure liberal system appeared then this would have proved problematic for the realist. In the event the quasi-liberal system underwritten by a hegemonic United States was almost perfect. There was an explicit management system with the United States rightfully playing a strong leadership role. At the same time the United States proved suitably sensitive to Europe. Finally, the Soviet Union could continue to follow its autarchic preference.

The economic dimension of the Pax Americana performed rather well until around the mid-1960s and during this period the realists were confronted with a largely problem-free environment. By the mid-1960s, however, a series of developments were under way which were to produce a number of more pressing problems. Two developments in particular were critical for the realists. In the first place, the relatively open world economy ushered in by Bretton Woods led to a substantial increase in the volume and speed of economic intercourse. Couched in such intensity terms the international economic system experienced a major stimulant to interdependence. Second, although bipolarity was maintained in the military field, there was a major change in the economic arena. The Soviet Union broadly remained within its own 'world economy' but the Bretton Woods 'world' economy moved to a position of asymmetrical multipolarity as American hegemony declined in the context of the resurgence of Europe, Japan and the appearance of a number of critical Third World states.

We turn now to consider the major problems that have developed since the mid-1960s. These problems are defined in terms of transgressions of the two critical principles, outlined above, and consequently these principles can now serve as organizing devices. In the context of the first principle, that governments should manage and monitor their external economic interactions, four main problems have developed.

One of these centres on the growth and development of multinational corporations. Multinational corporations *per se* are held to be neither inherently good, for example as vehicles of economic efficiency, nor inherently bad, for instance as instruments of capitalist expansion. From the realist perspective any such conditions are largely irrelevant. A variety of factors have coalesced to stimulate the development of multinational corporations and against this background the critical question is not whether multinational corporations should exist but rather how should they be managed.

Multinational corporations become problematic when they threaten the capacity of a government to implement that range of policies it deems necessary to pursue the national interest. The sheer magnitude of the resources commanded by multinationals can affect a host of government policy areas, such as balance of payments, or taxation, or money supply. In the longer term multinationals can influence critical areas of a state's production structure as a whole and in this context transfer to alien hands a vital control over strategies and paths of economic development. Furthermore, as was demonstrated in Chile, multinationals can influence government tenure.

In this context many of the concerns expressed by dependency writers would receive a sympathetic hearing from realists. Where the latter do differ very distinctively is in emphasizing that multinationals can have many of the same deleterious consequences for their states of origin. In particular, there is a concern firstly that capital benefits at the expense of labour: 'In sum, labor wants to keep a careful and detailed record on what multinationals are doing, wants them to pay their proper share of taxes, wants their freewheeling with money and technology regulated, wants the flow of foreign goods placed under controls.'[17] A second and more expansive concern is that the whole domestic production structure can be damaged by the transfer of resources overseas:

> In a world of competing nation-states, wherein power rests ultimately on an industrial base, foreign investment contributes to an international redistribution of power to the disadvantage of the core.... This dependence of the declining core on the rising periphery becomes a source of political vulnerability.... there is an inherent danger in an

overemphasis on foreign investment to the neglect of the rejuvenation of the domestic economy and of foreign trade.[18]

A second problem, defined again from the perspective of the failure of government management, concerns the development of the Eurocurrency markets. As in the case of multinationals, it is the sheer magnitude together with largely private controls that concerns the realist. Ruggie criticizes both banking and monetary authorities for thinking of Eurocurrencies as a 'neutral transmission belt'.[19] The availability of very substantial sums of money outside any clear national control can seriously disrupt control of domestic money supplies.

More generally, international banking as a whole, of which the Eurocurrency system is a major part, has grown substantially and for the most part outside government supervision. A classic illustration of the specific type of problem that can develop under such circumstances is provided by recent loans to the Third World. Following their massive liability increases in the wake of the oil-price rises, private commercial banks have rushed in a largely uncontrolled manner to make loans to Third World governments, which all too frequently had woefully inadequte investment plans. As Calleo explains:

> Even the international growth of American banks may, in due course, prove a greater liability than benefit. Much of the expansion is the 'recycling' of borrowed oil funds to underdeveloped countries. Some of the flow has undoubtedly financed real growth in Third World countries. But much of it has financed unrealistic levels of consumption, including a prolonged failure to adjust to new energy prices. The increasing shakiness of the world's financial structure is the obvious consequence.[20]

The possibility of default could seriously damage the Western banking system as well as precipitate conflict between the governments of countries of the North and South. At a less dramatic level than default, the size of the debt incurred by several Third World countries has seriously compromised their own policy-making latitudes.

A third problem centres around a cluster of topics dealing with international liquidity, reserves and exchange rates. Under the initial Bretton Woods system, exchange rates, which could only be changed by governments, were fixed to the dollar, which in turn was backed by gold. This system worked well as long as the United States was a hegemonic economic power, which both could keep its inflation in check and also had sufficient gold reserves to underwrite the international reserve role of the dollar. During the 1960s both of these preconditions began to fail. American gold reserves were insufficient to cover foreign dollar liabilities while domestically American inflation increased as the demands of overseas commitments, especially Vietnam, and an enlarged domestic welfare programme were met, not through higher taxation, but through the printing of money. American inflation was exported, the dollar was overvalued and other countries found themselves in effect funding American overseas commitments including their own Americanization.[21]

Over the years 1971–3 the Bretton Woods system collapsed. What concerns the realist is not so much that this system collapsed, indeed the collapse was somewhat overdue, but that it has not been replaced by any new system. Terms such as chaos, anarchy or non-system are common epithets used by realists to describe the post-1973 monetary arrangements. What had become one of the most inappropriate features of the old Bretton Woods system survives as the dollar remains the most dominant reserve currency. Furthermore, as the principal currencies float, exchange-rate volatility has become pronounced. This in turn means that countries can find their reserves fluctuating markedly in value as their currency changes against the dollar, they become extremely susceptible to American domestic monetary policy, and trade becomes vulnerable as stable currency expectations, at which trade exchange can take place, are destroyed.

A fourth problem pertains to a very different type of trade vulnerability. As we have noted, realists do not adopt any absolute position on levels of trade, positing that states should choose that level which, other things being equal, suits their national interest. Any state has a responsibility, assuming some commitment to trade, to ensure that it does not find itself in a situation of dependence, whereby another state can use the threat of or an actual cut in trade as a means of coercion. The most critical illustration of states failing to live up to their responsibilities of protecting against dependence has been seen in the context of oil.

Oil production, outside the communist bloc, developed almost entirely under the auspices of a small number of oil companies. Under the management of these companies oil prices remained low with the result that oil came to enjoy an ever increasing share of energy consumption. From the early 1950s oil-producing countries began increasingly to assume a greater control of their oil resource, culminating in 1960 in the establishment of OPEC. Strategies such as cartel formation and nationalization with compensation are perfectly legitimate as far as realism is concerned and indeed reflect an entirely praiseworthy commitment for the establishment of sovereignty over national resources. In this context the 1973 UN Economic and Social Council Resolution is entirely compatible with realism, recognizing

> that one of the most effective ways in which the developing countries can protect their national resources is to promote or strengthen machinery for cooperation among them having as its main purpose to concert pricing policies, to improve conditions of access to markets, to coordinate production policies, and, thus, to guarantee the full exercise of sovereignty by developing countries over their national resources.[22]

The blame for the variety of crises that came in the wake of the 1973–4 oil embargo and price rises did not rest so much with the OPEC countries but rather with the oil-importing countries, which had not developed any safeguard systems against a good for which they had a highly inelastic demand.[23]

We now turn to consider the second set of problems, which are those defined from the second principle. What is of critical issue in this context is that there has been a number of important changes in the economic dimension of the international power hierarchy. The changes, essentially the move to asymmetrical multipolarity, are not in themselves problematic. What is of critical concern is that reciprocity calculations be adjusted to accommodate these changes.

The single most important change has been the relative decline of the United States set against what Calleo calls 'the revival of the world':

> As Europe and Japan have revived and the Third World developed, the international system has grown more plural. With strategic parity, the superpowers have themselves grown more equal. These changes have inevitably affected America's world position. They represent not so much the decline of America as the revival of the world.[24]

It is this decline in the United States' power that leads Tucker to call for an American foreign policy of 'maturity'[25] and Steel to argue: 'There is no more urgent task for the United States diplomacy than to find a path away from the benevolent imperialism of Pax Americana and towards a reconciliation with a world shattered into a plurality of nation states.'[26] Or again, Whitman, in calling for 'leadership without hegemony', argues that the United States, in adjusting to a new role, needs to find a 'trade-off between policies that would promote the achievement of specific national economic or political goals, on the one hand, and those likely to promote the viability of a coherent international economic system in the long run on the other'.[27]

The critical, though not sole, readjustment needs to be made by the United States. This is not of course a coincidence but a reflection of the hegemonic role played in the design and management of the international economic system by the United States after 1945. Furthermore, the widespread calls for readjustment are not intended as a major critique of American policy throughout the whole of the post-war period. The role played by the United States until the mid-1960s was by and large well suited to the demands of that time. This arrangement only began to falter as the United States ceased to be the hegemonic power. As Hunter warned at the start of the 1970s

> there will be major problems in adjusting to changes in relative power among countries in the world today and tomorrow — relative power represented increasingly in economic terms. These problems could prove as demanding as those problems of power that led to other major international upsets in this century, including world wars.[28]

These changes in relative power can be surveyed by examining briefly the major new poles of the current economically asymmetrical system. Due in no small measure to American largess the OECD countries have made an amazing recovery. What is critical for the realist in this context is not only that Western Europe and Japan need to be ceded greater weight but also that they have shown markedly less enthusiasm for an American-dominated open system.

The establishment and development of the European Economic Community generally receives a favourable evaluation from the realist. It is a development which rightly has been dominated by intergovernmentalism. Furthermore, critical policy areas, such as the Common Agricultural Policy or the European Monetary System, are eminently understandable drives to protect key interests. Japan too is seen as following a very sensible line of development. Just as pure liberals condemn the European Economic Community as the 'epitome of neo-mercantilism' and accuse Japan of taking a 'free-rider' advantage of an open system without extending the benefits to others, realists argue that these developments represent salutary governmental interventions orientated towards the protection of national interests.

A second area of critical change that demands readjustment is the Third World. What Steel terms the 'spectacular appearance of Africa, Asia and Latin America' is 'by any standard, one of the great revolutions of modern times, even more important that the Russian revolution of 1917. By their assertion of equality with the older nations of the West, the underdeveloped states of the Third World have transformed the world power structure.'[29] Many Third World countries face horrendous problems. As Ajami rather bluntly expresses it: 'Much as they rant and rave about new worlds and new orders, many Third World rulers preside over crippled societies. Side by side with the talk of autonomy and power that fills the air has come an accumulation of some basic and deadly troubles.'[30] Put rather more mildly there is no doubt that many Third World countries are experiencing major difficulties in establishing domestic legitimacy. Furthermore, such legitimacy is an essential prerequisite for state existence. None the less, Third World development is unequivocally in the direction of establishing domestic legitimacy and pursuing externally their national interests. As Tucker argues, 'the challenge of the Third World is one made by states and on behalf of states'. The emergence of the Third World is not a major challenge to the desired structural arrangement but a substantial supplement to it:

> What we find in the demands of the developing countries is not a challenge to the essential structure of the international system but a challenge to the distribution of wealth and power within this system. It is not the state system *per se* that is condemned, but the manner in which the system operated in the past and presumably continues to operate even today. It is primarily through the state that the historically oppressed and disadvantaged nations seek to mount a successful challenge to what governing elites of developing countries view as persisting unjust inequalities.[31]

Consequently, the political mobilization and organization of Third World states in the Non-Aligned Movement or in UNCTAD are entirely legitimate from the realist perspective. Furthermore, the pressing of demands through commodity cartels or through such movements as the New International Economic Order debate or through actions to protect their own resources are eminently understandable and praiseworthy. This does not mean that the realists favour any major hand-outs to the Third World and indeed have nothing but scorn for the 'new egalitarians'.[32] None the less it is incumbent on the more developed states to recognize the Third World concern, as Steel expresses it, 'with economic development, political influence, and racial equality'. Attempts by the superpowers to interfere in the domestic affairs of Third World countries are seen as highly problematic, while, more generally, greater recognition needs to be ceded to the Third World[33]

The final area in which some accommodation is required concerns the Soviet Union. The change in this context is rather different from those we have just reviewed for the OECD countries and the Third World. Both of these latter groups represent dimensions of the 'revival of the world', which as a consequence need appropriate accommodation. The concern with the Soviet Union is rather different and can only be understood in the context of security policy.

In the military sphere, realists are under no illusion but that bipolarity continues: 'Yet in an important sense bipolarity persists, and the failure to understand that, or to keep it sharply in mind, constitutes one of the great dangers of the coming decade.'[34] While the United States and the Soviet Union will continue to be 'the primary military powers', the United States does need to recognize that 'American superiority is a thing of the past', that the superpowers are locked into 'an inevitable partnership', and that it is foolish to think that the Soviet Union will change its political system. None the less, even though the United States needs to accept parity, it must still not relax its military vigilance.

It is in this context that an economic dimension becomes critical. Realists are fond of a 'two-track system'.[35] The one track pertains to the military dimension where firmness is the key word; the second task pertains to the economic dimension where cooperation is the key word. This leads the realists to have two critical concerns. First, they are adamantly opposed to the use of trade or investment as a means of leverage against the Soviet Union. In this context the grain embargoes or the attempts at specific linkage have been illegitimate.[36] Second, they see the failure to promote trade and investment as a major opportunity lost. Economic interactions are an ideal means to pursue *détente* and denial of this therefore undermines one of the two tracks.[37]

In sum, the post-war international economic system has undergone a marked change. The essentially liberal Bretton Woods system was well suited to the needs of international reconstruction in the aftermath of the collapse of the Eurocentric system. The subsequent developments of the need to pursue *détente* in a relation of parity with the Soviet Union, of the 'revival' of Europe and Japan, and of the 'spectacular' emergence of the Third World have undermined the liberal arrangement managed under American hegemony. As Bresand argues: 'The capacity of the hidden hand to bring about not only efficiency at the world level but also harmony and shared interests among nations will continue its decline.'[38] The basic principles that guided international economic intercourse are no longer suited to the new world of multipolarity. While the major onus for readjustment falls on the former hegemon, other critical states need to join the United States in 'the creation of a new international bargain, a cumulative approach to a negotiated settlement among several strong, although very unequal partners, without a single hegemon to impose it'.[39]

Solutions

With the possible exception of the management of the international monetary system, the problems we have just outlined are not seen as being particularly acute. The first of the two main reasons for this is that states are playing an ever increasing role in economic management: 'More and more governments are organizing the adjustments of their domestic economies. They reject profoundly the notion that social and economic structure should be left to the international market to determine.'[40] Second, states are manifesting a marked propensity through 'negotiated settlement' to achieve 'a new international bargain'.

The capacity of governments to respond to new challenges is illustrated perhaps no more clearly than in the area of multinational corporations. As Zysman and Cohen argue:

> The Japanese first showed that a government could act as doorman to the national economy, breaking up the package of management, finance, technology, and control represented by the MNC and forcing the pieces to be recombined under national authority. Other countries quickly learned these lessons. Government and politics had mattered all along; their influence had simply been obscured.[41]

Although multinational corporations can indeed cause difficulties, sovereignty is decidedly not at bay. Working individually or in regional associations (such as the Andean Common Market or the European Economic Community) or through UN bodies, states have a whole host of measures whereby multinationals can be harnessed to their own interests.[42] Some commentators, particularly those emphasizing the costs to the domestic economy of the export of jobs, capital and technology would like to impose greater restrictions on foreign private investment in favour of increased trade:

> A dollar earned from trade is worth more than one earned from foreign investment. The dollar earned from trade contributes more to government revenues; it generates greater domestic economic development; and it is more evenly distributed between labor and

capital. Therefore, even if a decrease in direct foreign investment meant a decreased American economic presence in the world economy, the cost/benefit ratio of trade rather than investment would on the whole favor the American national interest.[43]

Even this more extreme position lies within the capacity of government to effect.

In general, there is less tranquillity about the Eurocurrency markets. There is certainly substantial scope for governments to impose greater reserve requirements and closer monitoring of commercial banks. On the other hand, the debt scares since 1980 have unquestionably caused banks to be more cautious and to cooperate more actively. Furthermore, forums, such as the Paris club, have been quite successful. None the less, governments still need to be more interventionist in this area. Particularly in the context of Third World loans, there is scope either for more direct lending by the IMF and IBRD to pre-empt commercial banks or for more joint action of these bodies with commercial banks.[44] Though not pretending that these problems have been solved, realists are generally encouraged by the way states are responding. Thus, commenting on both multinational corporations and the Eurocurrency market, Zysman and Cohen argue: 'It is not that multinational corporations and private international financial markets have diminished in size or importance, but rather that state strategies to shape markets have become more prevalent, more powerful, and more central to the future shape of the international economic order.'[45]

Perhaps the greatest challenge concerns the management of the international monetary system. While in the longer term realists can look forward to the possible establishment of a true world bank with a true international reserve currency,[46] the shorter-term aspiration is towards parallel currencies in a decentralized and regionalized system.[47]

A return to an arrangement such as the Bretton Woods system is out of the question as 'even if the purchasing power of the dollar were now to be stabilized, only a politically more balanced international monetary arrangement would prove acceptable today'. The emphasis on the 'politically more balanced' aspect is highly symptomatic of realism and reflects the perception of the changed international power distribution. Equally symptomatic is the commitment to eschew the ideal arrangement because it is politically unfeasible in the short run. Thus:

> Between an ideal but impossible supranational monetary order and the anarchy of the present system, a new path to monetary stability can

perhaps be found. An arrangement of this kind may grow out of the present effort of European countries to stabilize their currencies against each other, and to harmonize their monetary policies, under the new European Monetary System or EMS.[48]

The EMS receives very strong support and indeed there are calls for its immediate strengthening. The EMS is, however, merely part of what Giscard d'Estaing terms the 'phased march' toward a new monetary system. Regional monetary systems, based on the European currency unit (ECU), the dollar and the yen, would integrate through 'target zones' in a looser interregional version of the EMS. This decentralized system would provide the basis from which in the longer run a new world monetary system, based on fixed but adjustable exchange rates and backed by a new international reserve currency, would develop. The regionalized interim system with its parallel currencies would not be ideal, but it would be a marked improvement on the current system:

> A regionalized monetary system of this kind would not be as open or as politically harmonious as was the dollar system in its heyday. The conflicts of interest between blocs over exchange rates might be serious. Tendencies toward regional trade preferences already evident would be confirmed and strengthened. Yet this regional ordering of international monetary relations would probably be preferable to the realistic alternative — a continuation of present anarchic tendencies.[49]

On the problem of trade vulnerabilities, realists have a host of solutions including diversification, stockpiles, commodity agreements, counter cartels and the development of substitutes. In general realists take the view that while the problem of trade vulnerability may be ever present, the problem can normally be relatively easily circumvented as long as governments are not negligent in deploying the appropriate defence measures.

The one issue of trade vulnerability that has attracted the bulk of attention has been oil.[50] While no commentator would pretend that the oil issue has been finally solved, three factors have allayed at least some of the worst fears. First, there has been a distinct political response from the West, including, among other measures, stockpiling and collaboration in the form of the International Energy Agency.[51] Second, the new-found wealth of the OPEC countries has made them vulnerable to some degree to counter-measures. Third, there have been signs of reciprocity from the OPEC countries in attempts to index oil prices to general price changes in the West. Some writers are rather more pessimistic and, pointing particularly to the instability of the Middle East and Soviet activity there, argue for the need to retain a military option in a guise such as the Rapid Deployment Force.[52]

Extending our discussion somewhat, it is noticeable that, in general, trade issues have not attracted a great deal of attention from realists. This is in part because, unlike the liberals, they have no automatic interest in high or increasing levels of trade. But, perhaps more importantly, realists see trade as having been generally well managed. The GATT system is run by governments, it contains numerous loopholes, and it involves intergovernmental negotiation. While facilitating trade, and more critically pre-empting trade-based conflicts, the GATT system has not ushered in a period of uncontrolled and uncontrollable free trade. Like the liberals, realists see some changes taking place: 'On the whole, our trade environment will be less transparent and more conflictual. Trade interests will be complex and will not lend themselves to the traditional forms of regulation developed in the golden age of trade liberalization.'[53] In contrast to the pure liberals in particular, for whom some of the recent changes are highly problematic, the realists do not see any major difficulties. Indeed many of the problems reviewed for the liberals under the heading of neo-mercantilism are in fact realist policies. An unwavering commitment to free trade, for example, is a nonsense to the realist who can see that domestic production and jobs can be lost. On the other hand, the realist does not countenance blind protectionism for fear of trade wars. Thus, ideal strategies for the realist are such devices as voluntary quotas or orderly marketing agreements, which permit trade albeit in a context negotiated and agreed among governments. The recent growth of state involvement in trade, subject always to the proviso of reciprocity, meets with realists' approval and explains their relative lack of concern with trade issues as a whole.

Finally, we can turn to consider the readjustments required to suit the new asymmetrical multipolar system. In the OECD arena while there are unquestionably conflicts, and will continue to be conflicts, there is no major strain. There is a broad complementarity of interests and an established tradition of inter-governmental negotiation. Indeed in this latter vital context there has been the encouraging development of annual summit meetings of the seven largest OECD countries: 'Annual economic summitry has made clear both the widespread perception that coordination of macro economic policies is essential in an interdependent world, and the difficulties that confront efforts to implement the concept.'[54] The only further ingredient is for the United States to accept what Tucker terms 'maturity' or Hoffmann calls 'modesty'.[55] The United States must retain its leadership role while at the same time accommodating other OECD country interests.

This balancing of leadership and accommodation can be illustrated in what is perhaps the most crucial area, that of monetary arrangements. There can be no doubt that the dollar will continue to be very important:

> Although the inflation of the past decade has destroyed much of the dollar's central function in the international economy, the size of the United States economy and the depth of its capital markets ensure that the decisions of the Federal Reserve concerning monetary policy still have a major influence on economic conditions throughout the world.[56]

Despite this unquestioned 'major influence', Triffin makes very explicit that the United States must not attempt to return to hegemony: 'We should be averse as foreign countries — or more so — to incurring again the awesome political responsibilities and inflationary temptations inseparable from the exorbitant, but poisoned privilege of having our *national* currency used as the main international currency of the world.'[57] Or more specifically, in the context of the EMS:

> Thus, the most urgent task of the United States is to help the new European Monetary System to succeed, and to insert itself into a worldwide monetary order, rather than become at best a mere inward-looking oasis, or at worst a total failure, condemned by our lack of cooperation to live in a world of continuing monetary chaos.[58]

More generally Schmidt, in his call for the 'inevitable need for American leadership', echoes realist sentiment perfectly. Cooperation among the United States, Japan and the EEC is absolutely vital. Within this trilateral arena the United States must take and be granted leadership; but it must be a leadership sensitive to the interests and aspirations of the other partners: 'Neither trilateral co-operation nor worldwide co-operation is imaginable at present without American leadership ... Leadership among the free and sovereign states of the West cannot consist of instructions and orders ... It must be based on the principle of "give and take".'[59]

While the single most important readjustment, due to power requirements of the international hierarchy, needs to take place in the

OECD arena, attention must also be paid to the Third World. Although many Third World states may be suffering quite severe dislocations in establishing their domestic legitimacy, these countries are seen as being committed to nation state development. Consequently not only must they be given the opportunity to create their own legitimacy but they must also be incorporated into the international society of states. At a general level, this entails, as Steel explains, 'standing back to allow the new nations to work out their own destiny as they see fit within their own frontiers'.[60] Or, as Jay comments: 'It will have to offer a world political and economic order that makes small countries feel secure, poor countries confident of development, aggressive countries fearful of retribution, and all countries properly independent within their necessary interdependence.'[61]

More specifically, this requires, in the first place, that attempts to influence the internal development of Third World states should cease. In this context realists are adamant that the ideological conflict between communism and capitalism is of little relevance to the Third World. While it is of little relevance, attempts, particularly by the superpowers, to pursue such a conflict, through such instruments as aid and arms-sales programmes, are potentially very dangerous. The path for the Third World is non-alignment: 'The search for that "third way" that was launched at Bandung and that still survives in pockets of the Third World — battered, compromised, but nonetheless still there — ought to be encouraged.'[62] In the second place, there is a need for an accommodation of what Bergsten terms 'the legitimate aspirations of the developing countries', which at the most general level requires

> effective participation by the Third World in the decision-making process on international economic issues. These countries quite rightly reject the imposition on them of rules and institutional arrangements created solely by the industrialized nations ... Inclusion of more countries in the decision-making process may make it more difficult, but there is no prospect of a viable system without it.'[63]

While often being quite contemptuous of the 'new egalitarianism', realists also emphasize that failure to respond to some demands is foolhardy. In practical terms, this leads them to be sympathetic to developments such as an enhanced role for the World Bank and IMF, the Generalized System of Preferences, the Lomé Conventions, or the creation of commodity agreements.[64]

Finally, some readjustment is required *vis-à-vis* the Soviet Union. The basic realist convictions in this context are that the United States and

Soviet Union are locked into an 'inevitable partnership', that this partnership does and will continue to entail conflict, that the United States and the West in general need to display a simultaneous mix of firmness and cooperation, and that the primary means of the cooperative track must come from increased economic interaction. This does not mean, it must be emphasized, that any blind commitment to trade should be made. Indeed, recognizing that state control of economic interaction is much more highly developed in the Soviet Union, there is an emphasis on the 'supervision needed to protect against the hazards of unregulated trade'.[65] As well as rejecting an unregulated trade option, there is also rejection of a trade strategy geared to leverage or the extraction of concessions — a strategy characterized by Caldwell as the 'Trojan Horse'. The appropriate trade option is rather, to use again Caldwell's terminology, the 'Yankee Trader':

> It holds that trade does have political effects, but its time horizon is longer than that of the Trojan Horse strategy. Trade by itself opens the Soviet system. Moreover, it encourages the modest, incremental, political adaptation promised by the modernist persuasion in Soviet political life. The Yankee Trader strategy, then, offers higher levels of trade turnover, a more stable climate of economic relations, and the prospect that by bringing the Soviet Union into a long-term economic relation with the other industrialized nations Soviet interest in a cooperative international system is increased.[66]

In summary, problems for the realist develop to the extent that governments fail to manage international economic intercourse so as to protect the national interests of their citizens and to the extent that international management as a whole fails to accommodate in a differential manner the interests of states as dictated by their location in the international power hierarchy. While the post-war international economic system emerged from a set of circumstances, in the form of the cold war, about which the realists had serious reservations, it none the less performed remarkably well until the turn of the 1960s. By this time threats to state sovereignty, contingent particularly on increased investment and monetary interdependence, combined with a fairly pronounced change in the movement to a symmetrical multipolarity, brought to the fore a number of more pressing problems. Of these perhaps the least adequately resolved is that of international monetary management, though even here a viable solution is readily within grasp. For the most part, however, without being at all complacent, realists are generally well satisfied with

168 *Global economic problems and solutions*

the responses to these problems. States do seem to be learning to accept an increased management role; furthermore, either through more formal channels, such as inter-governmental organizations, or less formal ones, such as summitry, critical states are displaying sensitivity to each other's interests and a serious commitment to negotiation. As long as states, individually and collectively, continue to manifest the kind of strategies and solutions that they have developed as the world has evolved out of the era of the Pax Americana, then realists can envisage in at least the near future that conflict and tension, though inevitably enduring, will be confined within manageable bounds.

Notes

1. The charge that realists attach a pre-eminence to politics with a concomitant neglect of economics finds a curious counter-echo on the part of realists who are inclined to accuse liberals and Marxists of focusing too exclusively on economics to the neglect of politics. See, for example, D.P. Calleo and B.M. Rowland, *America and the World Political Economy*, Bloomington, Indiana University Press, 1973; R. Gilpin, *US Power and the Multinational Corporation*, London, Macmillan, 1976.
2. For an interesting discussion of this general area, see A.O. Hirschman, *National Power and the Structure of Foreign Trade*, Berkeley, University of California Press, 1980.
3. Gilpin, op. cit., p. 38.
4. T.C. Schelling, cited in R.N. Cooper, 'Trade Policy is Foreign Policy', *Foreign Policy*, **9**, 1972–3, p. 32.
5. For a general discussion, see, for example, K. Knorr, *Power and Wealth*, London, Macmillan, 1973.
6. R.N. Cooper, *The Economics of Interdependence*, New York, McGraw Hill, 1968.
7. Gilpin, op. cit., p. 43.
8. R.E. Hunter, 'Power and Peace', *Foreign Policy*, **9**, 1972–3, pp. 38 and 44.
9. Thus Hoffman argues: 'If the purpose of the exercise of power is to influence the behaviour of others, the first requirement is to understand the concerns, interests, and fears of those one tries to affect and the costs and limits of control.' (S. Hoffman, 'Requiem', *Foreign Policy*, **42**, 1981, p. 5).
10. For a fuller discussion of the general content of these two principles, see for example: Calleo and Rowland, op. cit.; Gilpin, op. cit.; S.D. Krasner, *Defending the National Interest*, Princeton, Princeton University Press, 1978; R.W. Tucker, *The Inequality of Nations*, London, Martin Robertson, 1977; K.N. Waltz, *Theory of International Politics*, Reading, Addison-Wesley, 1979.
11. W. Lippman, *The Cold War: A Study in US Foreign Policy*, New York, Harper & Row, 1972; R. Steel, *Pax Americana*, New York, Viking Press, 1967.
12. For a fuller discussion, from a non-realist writer, see F.L. Block, *The Origins of International Economic Disorder*, Berkeley, University of California Press, 1977.
13. Steel, op. cit., p. 322.
14. Gilpin, op. cit., p. 103.
15. Steel, op. cit., p. 16. Similarly Gilpin emphasizes the almost obligatory leadership

role that the United States assumed: '... the United States had to use foreign economic and military aid to maintain its influence, acquire strategic positions, and protect American overseas economic interests. In short, for military and political reasons, economic relations provided a vital element in the organization of Pax Americana.' (Gilpin, op. cit., p. 105).

16. Although realist commentators on the cold war argue that the United States exaggerated the *military* threat from the Soviet Union, they did not dispute a *political* threat. In particular, the war-ravaged economics of Western Europe was seen as being vulnerable to domestic discontent, which could provide an opening for domestic communist insurrection. In this context the Marshall Plan was a perfect antidote.
17. G. Tyler, 'Labor's Multinational Pains', *Foreign Policy*, **12**, 1973, p. 132; or for a further similar account, see D.H. Blake, 'Labor's Multinational Opportunities', *Foreign Policy*, **12**, 1973.
18. Gilpin, op. cit., p. 78.
19. J.G. Ruggie, 'The Politics of Money', *Foreign Policy*, **43**, 1981, p. 148.
20. D.P. Calleo, 'Inflation and American Power', *Foreign Affairs*, **59**, 4, 1981, p. 790.
21. See, for example, H. van Buren Cleveland, 'How the Dollar Standard Died', *Foreign Policy*, **5**, 1971–2; Calleo, op. cit.; R. Triffin, 'The International Role and Fate of the Dollar', *Foreign Affairs*, **57**, 2, 1978.
22. Quoted in Z. Mikdashi, 'Collusion Could Work', *Foreign Policy*, **14**, 1974, 58.
23. Realists could argue, as we will indicate later, that the OPEC oil action of 1973–4 came dangerously close to a neglect of reciprocity. For a general discussion of the several crises precipitated by the OPEC action, see C.F. Bergsten, 'The Threat from the Third World', *Foreign Policy*, **11**, 1973.
24. Calleo, op. cit., p. 804.
25. R.W. Tucker, 'America in Decline: The Foreign Policy of "Maturity" ', *Foreign Affairs*, **58**, 3, 1979.
26. Steel, op. cit., p. 336.
27. M.v.N. Whitman, 'A Year of Travail: the United States and the International Economy', *Foreign Affairs*, **57**, 3, 1979, p. 528.
28. Hunter, op. cit., p. 45.
29. Steel, op. cit., p. 38.
30. F. Ajami, 'The Fate of Nonalignment', *Foreign Affairs*, **59**, 2, 1980, p. 371.
31. Tucker, 'America in Decline', p. 471.
32. Tucker, *The Inequality of Nations*.
33. See for example, C.F. Bergsten, 'The Response to the Third World', *Foreign Policy*, **17**, 1974–5; J.P. Cot, 'Winning East–West in North–South', *Foreign Policy*, **46**, 1982; R.D. McKinlay and A. Mughan, *Aid and Arms to the Third World*, London, Frances Pinter, 1984.
34. L.T. Caldwell and W. Diebold, *Soviet–American Relations in the 1980s*, New York, McGraw Hill, 1981, p. 25.
35. See, for example, ibid.; and R. Legvold, 'Containment Without Confrontation', *Foreign Policy*, **40**, 1980.
36. See, for example, J.B. Bingham and V.C. Johnson, 'A Rational Approach to Export Controls', *Foreign Affairs*, **57**, 4, 1979.
37. See, for example, G. Agnelli, 'East–West Trade: A European View', *Foreign Affairs*, **57**, 4, 1979; H.D. Genscher, 'Toward an Overall Western Strategy for Peace,

Freedom and Progress', *Foreign Affairs*, **61**, 1, 1982; Legvold, op. cit.
38. A. Bressand, 'Mastering the "Worldeconomy"', *Foreign Affairs*, **61**, 4, 1983, p. 758.
39. J. Zysman and S.S. Cohen, 'Double or Nothing: Open Trade and Competitive Industry', *Foreign Affairs*, **61**, 5, 1983, p. 1135.
40. Ibid., p. 1124.
41. Ibid., p. 1117.
42. For a general review, see P.A. Tharp, 'Transnational Enterprises and International Regulation', *International Organization*, **30**, 1, 1976.
43. Gilpin, op. cit., p. 169.
44. See, for example, W.H. Bolin and J. Del Canto, 'LDC Debt: Beyond Crisis Management', *Foreign Affairs*, **61**, 5, 1983; P.P. Kuczynski, 'Latin American Debt', *Foreign Affairs*, **61**, 2, 1982; K. Lissakers, 'Money and Manipulation', *Foreign Policy*, **44**, 1981; C.F. Meissner, 'Debt: Reform Without Governments', *Foreign Policy*, **50**, 1983; H.J. Shaw, 'Debts and Dependency', *Foreign Policy*, **50**, 1983.
45. Zysman and Cohen, op. cit., p. 1117.
46. Realists, in the long term, would approve Triffin's suggestion for a new reserve asset, to replace the dollar and gold, to be issued by the IMF, or some equivalent, to 'adjust growth of world monetary reserves to noninflationary requirements of feasible growth in world trade and production'. (Triffin, op. cit., p. 285).
47. For general discussions, see, for example, H. van Buren Cleveland and T.F. Huertas, 'Stagflation: How We Got Into It — How To Get Out', *Foreign Affairs*, **58**, 1, 1979; Cleveland, op. cit.; B.J. Cohen, 'Europe's Money, America's problem', *Foreign Policy*, **35**, 1979, V. Giscard d'Estaing, 'New Opportunities and New Challenges', *Foreign Affairs*, **62**, 1, 1983; Triffin, op. cit.
48. Cleveland and Huertas, op. cit., p. 115.
49. Cleveland, op. cit., p. 51.
50. For general discussions, see, for example, S.D. Krasner, 'Oil is the Exception', *Foreign Policy*, **14**, 1974; W.J. Levy, 'Oil and the Decline of the West', *Foreign Affairs*, **58**, 5, 1980; J.S. Nye, 'Energy Nightmares', *Foreign Policy*, **40**, 1980; R.S. Pindyck, 'OPEC's Threat to the West', *Foreign Policy*, **30**, 1978; S.F Singer, 'Limits to Arab Oil Power', *Foreign Policy*, **30**, 1978; J.D. Theberge, 'A Mineral Raw Materials Action Program', *Foreign Policy*, **17**, 1974–5.
51. Liberals argue that the oil threat has been diffused through market-related mechanisms rather than through a political framework. For an interesting contrast of view in this context, see H.B. Chenery, 'Restructuring the World Economy: Round II', *Foreign Affairs*, **59**, 5, 1981.
52. See, for example, W.J. Levy, 'Oil: Agenda for the 1980s', *Foreign Affairs*, **59**, 5, 1981. For an illustration of an argument for caution on the military option, see, for example, C. van Hollen, 'Don't Engulf the Gulf', *Foreign Affairs*, **59**, 5, 1981.
53. Bressand, op. cit., p. 758.
54. Whitman, op. cit., p. 538.
55. See Tucker, 'America in Decline'; 'modesty' as opposed to 'primacy' is a persistent theme of Hoffmann's writing, see, for instance, S. Hoffmann, *Gulliver's Troubles*, New York, McGraw Hill, 1968; 'Choices', *Foreign Policy*, **12**, 1973; 'Hoffmann, 'Muscle and Brains', *Foreign Policy*, **37**, 1979–80; Hoffmann, 'Requiem'.
56. Cleveland and Huertas, op. cit., p. 119.
57. Triffin, op. cit., p. 284.

58. Ibid., p. 286.
59. H. Schmidt, 'The Inevitable Need for American Leadership', *The Economist*, 26 February 1983, p. 30.
60. Steel, op. cit., p. 332.
61. P. Jay, 'Regionalism as Geopolitics', *Foreign Affairs*, **58**, 3, 1979, p. 514.
62. Ajami, op. cit., p. 386.
63. Bergsten, op. cit., p. 28.
64. See ibid.; or C.F. Bergsten, 'The Threat from the Third World', *Foreign Policy*, **11**, 1973; or Tucker, *The Inequality of Nations*.
65. Legvold, op. cit., p. 95.
66. Caldwell, op. cit., p. 114.

PART IV: GLOBAL SECURITY PROBLEMS AND SOLUTIONS

8 Liberal International Security Problems and Solutions

Problems

Most analysis in the field of security has traditionally been designated as realist in orientation. Liberalism has been deemed to have relatively little to say about what are often depicted as the intractable problems of international security. This is not because liberals have been seen to lack a theory of international relations or have failed to develop a conception of security but because their approach indicates that, following the successful implementation of a liberal world order, problems associated with security would be effectively eliminated. The liberal solution to problems of security has been considered to require a transformation of the international arena; it has been identified by sweeping, Utopian reform rather than by the pragmatic solutions normally associated with international security. It is realists who have generally been seen to be concerned with preserving the security of the state.

In the eighteenth and nineteenth centuries, there was, without doubt, a good deal of truth to this assessment. At that time, realist ideas were extremely influential; liberal thinkers simply stood on the sidelines, insisting that realist solutions were, in practice, exacerbating the problems of international security. But in the contemporary era, this traditional assessment of liberalism requires wholesale revision.

First, it fails to take account of a major division which has developed since the end of the nineteenth century between those defined in Chapter 3 as pure liberals, who wish to see the role of government curtailed, and compensatory liberals, who argue that individual freedom requires the role of government to be expanded. This dispute has extended into their analysis of international security, where it is found to have important implications.

The traditional assessment of liberalism also fails to take account of the growing influence of liberalism on government policy during the course of the twentieth century. In the first half of this century, the views of the compensatory liberals began to have a major impact on international affairs. Their interest in international organizations, for example, proved to be particularly significant. In the second half of the century, however, with growing scepticism about the capacity of international organizations to resolve security problems, the views of pure liberals have come to play a crucial role in the formulation of security policy in the Western world. Contrary to conventional wisdom, then, in recent years realists have very often been left the unhappy observers of international events with liberal solutions being seen to precipitate a deteriorating world order.

Realist views prevailed when Europe dominated the international arena. The liberal approach to security has become influential in the twentieth century mainly because of the growing power of the United States. Earlier liberal assessments of international relations were regarded in Europe as radical and subversive. Such ideas, however, flourished in the United States, in part, because North America was physically isolated from Europe. The United States has always been regarded, particularly by Europeans, as the bastion of liberalism. As Tom Paine noted in *The Rights of Man* at the end of the eighteenth century: 'What Athens was in miniature, America will be in magnitude. The one was the wonder of the Ancient World. The other is becoming the admiration of the present.'[1] During the twentieth century, however, the United States has ceased to be simply a model of liberalism for other societies to follow but the active defender of liberalism. After the Second World War, as Huntington has put it, 'the future of liberalism' became 'intimately linked to the future of American power'.[2]

The Second World War marked a watershed for both pure and compensatory liberal approaches to security. In the past, the future of liberalism had always seemed to be assured. There were two major reasons for this conviction. Liberals believed, first, that the inherent superiority of their ideas of all alternatives was so obvious that it was only a matter of time before these ideas came to prevail. Second, the adoption of liberalism in the United States seemed to establish an unchallengeable bulwark behind which liberalism would always prosper. The security of the United States provided the ultimate sanctuary for liberalism in the rest of the world.

This liberal optimism was severely shaken by the rise of Communism and Fascism.[3] The emergence of state-sponsored ideologies, inimical to liberalism, was extremely threatening. In the nineteenth century the progress of liberalism appeared to be inexorable; but in the twentieth century, liberal societies fell victim to governments pursuing rival and hostile ideologies. The problem became acute after the Second World War as liberals contemplated the spectacular military successes of the Soviet Union and took note of the dramatic advances in military technology. It was unequivocally clear that the security of liberalism even in the United States was not now assured. Once the United States lost its nuclear monopoly, the threat to liberalism loomed very large. As Strausz-Hupé put it at the beginning of the 1960s: 'For the first time in history there exist weapons permitting a technologically armed superpower to conquer the entire world . . . The potentiality is inherent in nuclear explosives and global-range delivery systems and constitutes a fundamentally new development in world affairs.'[4]

These changes were particularly disturbing to the compensatory liberals who had been confident that security problems could be adequately managed by the establishment of a liberal world economy and an international security agency. The hostile attitude of the Soviet leaders to both these institutions left the compensatory liberals bereft of ideas about how to deal with the emerging post-war security problems. It was left to the pure liberals to define the nature of these security problems and to devise an appropriate solution. The problem was associated primarily with the rise of Communism, and the response took the form of a containment strategy which has in a variety of guises remained the basis for Western security policy ever since the late 1940s.[5] In the initial instance, compensatory liberals accepted this assessment and the consensus was sustained throughout the 1950s. It was only in the 1940s that it began to break down and compensatory liberals began to acknowledge that containment, very far from providing a solution to the problems of international security, was constituting the major source of these problems. Ironically, pure liberals were also becoming increasingly disturbed by the growing number of security problems associated with the inadequate management of containment.

Before examining these problems, however, it is necessary to discuss the emergence of containment because, in practice, this strategy represents a radical departure from the way pure liberals have traditionally approached the question of security. For them, containment does not represent an ultimate solution to the problems of security but rather a mechanism for managing the problems until liberalism has become universal.

Pure liberals, in contrast to realists, have always started from the premise that there is no need to develop a distinctive theory of international relations. As Parekh has observed, to the extent that the pure liberal has a theory of international relations, it is, in fact, 'only his theory of interpersonal relations projected on the international scene'.[6] All the main threads of the pure liberal approach to international relations had been gathered together by the end of the eighteenth century. Thomas Paine, for example, in *The Rights of Man*, provided 'a gospel which was to be preached virtually without alteration by Western liberals until our day'.[7] At the heart of this gospel lay the belief that peace was 'fundamentally a question of the establishment of democratic institutions throughout the world'.[8]

But the pure liberal was as much concerned with the universal delimitation of government as with the spread of democracy; governments were seen to be the major cause of international conflict and insecurity. As a consequence, a sharp distinction was drawn between inter-governmental and international relations — a distinction which has become blurred with the passage of time.[9] But in the nineteenth century, from the perspective of the pure liberal,

> whereas there was a natural disharmony between governments and states, there was a natural harmony between nations and societies. These factors produced the belief that progress was destined to replace inter-governmental relations by the free play of enlightened public opinion between societies. And when the day dawned — when international relations became relations between nations of peoples — war which was materially profitless and absurd and morally wrong, would be replaced by free and peaceful economic competition and such sources of dispute as still remained would easily be settled by judicial procedure.[10]

Pure liberals, therefore, consistently echoed Richard Cobden's call for 'as little intercourse as possible between *Governments*, as much connection as possible between *nations* of the world'.[11] To implement this solution, however, it was evident that the prevailing autocratic governments would have to give way to liberalism.

These early pure liberals were aware, of course, that the autocratic regimes in Europe were not going to disappear voluntarily. They possessed arms and the support of powerful vested interests within the state. But the major obstacle to the removal of these regimes was the balance of power. Cobden, for example, asked himself how the Austrian government had persisted during the nineteenth century, given its aversion to progress. He answered:

> Why, the state system of Europe which goes under the name of the Balance of Power. This it is which alone preserves the integrity of the Austrian Empire, and deprives the nationalities of a chance of overthrowing the incubus. It is because the other Governments of Europe consider it necessary at whatever cost of internal mismanagement to keep intact a great member of the states system, rather than allow it to suffer disruption and take a new form, that these tyrannies propped up from without seem to threaten to be eternal.[12]

Although pure liberals did not believe that these 'tyrannical' governments would remain a permament feature of the international arena, they accepted that there was no method for bringing about their immediate demise. It would take time for a truly liberal world order to emerge. In the meantime, illiberal regimes would continue to rely on the balance of power, this 'foul idol' as John Bright called it, to sustain themselves and they would thereby precipitate conflict which would engulf the entire system. Bright insisted that 'it is not possible for the eye of humanity to scan the scroll upon which are recorded the sufferings which the balance of power has entailed upon this country'.[13] Despite these appalling costs, no method was devised for speeding up the process of bringing about a liberal world order. It was acknowledged that liberalism could not be implemented in infertile political conditions. Liberals were resolutely opposed to military intervention as a means of promoting their beliefs. Intervention, argued J.S. Mill, could only be sanctioned as a means of counteracting autocratic intervention designed to uphold illiberal regimes.[14] But pure liberals were confident that, as the virtues of liberalism became more widely appreciated, autocratic regimes must come under sustained internal pressure to implement liberal reforms. But these demands for change could not be artificially or externally generated. The use of force, then, had no role to play in bringing about a liberal world order.

The emergence of state-sponsored ideologies transformed this assessment. With the rise of Fascism, but more particularly Communism, pure liberals recognized that the very existence of liberalism was coming under threat. There were two dimensions to the Communist threat. First, it was argued that the freedom displayed in the West represented a threat to the survival of the Communist system. As John Foster Dulles put it, 'to Soviet Communists, freedom is frightening. To them it is inconsistent with order. That is why they feel they will not be safe until they have liquidated freedom as a major force in world politics.'[15] Second, it was argued that the Soviets had a messianic desire to spread communism.

By 1950, this liberal assessment of communism was firmly entrenched in the American defence establishment where it was concluded that only the United States could provide an adequate counter to this Soviet threat to liberalism. The reasoning behind this position was revealed in a classified document NSC68, written in 1950, although not made public for the next twenty-five years. The Soviet Union and the United States were intractable enemies because the idea of freedom is peculiarly and intolerably subversive of the idea of slavery' and, as a consquence, 'the implacable purpose of the slave states to eliminate the challenge of freedom has placed the two great powers at opposite poles'. It followed that 'the United States, as the principal center of power in the non-Soviet world and the bulwark of opposition to Soviet expansion, is the principal enemy whose integrity and vitality must be subverted or destroyed by one means or another if the Kremlin is to achieve its fundamental design'.[16] Nothing in the intervening years has suggested at least to pure liberals that the basic aim of the Soviet Union has changed. Pure liberals continue to argue that

> Soviet foreign policy has two major aims: maintaining control over the areas in which power has already been established and extending Soviet influence over the rest of the world. It would be dangerous to argue that the Soviet leaders have reached the limit of their ambitions and are now basically on the defensive . . . Soviet spokesmen repeatedly emphasize that there can only be one outcome in the present 'ideological struggle' between the two social systems: the 'complete and final victory of socialism and communism on a world-wide scale'.[17]

It was obvious to pure liberals in the late 1940s that it was not possible to rely on the power of persuasion to defend liberalism against such a desperate and determined enemy. They began, as a consequence, to reassess the balance of power which, while unquestionably responsible for precipitating wars, had at least ensured the survival of states, including those with pretentions to defend liberalism. This argument was made plain in NSC68 where it was asserted that

> for several centuries it had proved impossible for any one nation to gain such preponderant strength that a coalition of other nations could not in time face it with a greater strength. The international scene was marked by recurring periods of violence and war, but a system of foreign and independent states was maintained over which no state was able to achieve hegemony.[18]

Whatever its failings, then, it was acknowledged that the balance of power helped to preserve the existence of liberal states and had, in consequence, played a part in the survival and promotion of liberalism. The balance of power began to look even more attractive when contrasted with the Manichaean system which had emerged after the Second World War, when liberalism was confronted by the aggressive and expansionist forces of Communism — without the support of the balance of power.

The future of liberalism was seen to depend upon the ability of the non-Communist world to combine forces, maintain a position of military superiority and, ultimately, to defeat Communism. Only after Communism had been eliminated as a state-sponsored ideology could the security of liberalism be assured. The strategy designed to achieve this objective has come to be known as containment. The conception originated with George Kennan, a State Department official and the first head of the United States Policy Planning Staff. He argued in 1947 that

> it will be clear that the Soviet pressure against the free institutions of the Western world is something that can be contained by the adroit and vigilant application of counter-force at a series of constantly shifting geographical and political points, corresponding to the shifts and manoeuvres of Soviet policy . . .[19]

Although Kennan's statement was unquestionably influential, the main foundation stones for containment were laid down in NSC68. The document has been described as the 'definitive statement of American national security policy'[20] and because of the hegemonial position of the United States in the non-Communist world, it also provided the basis for Western defence policy.

The desire of pure liberals to uproot Communism is very apparent in this document. The case for an early 'preventative' war against the Soviet Union is examined, for example, and only rejected on the grounds that a quick defeat of the Soviet Union could not be guaranteed; instead it was indicated that there would probably be 'a long and difficult struggle during which free institutions of Western Europe and many freedom-loving people would be destroyed'.[21]

Preference was therefore given to a rapid build-up of political, economic and military strength in the non-Commnist world:

> The frustration of the Kremlin design requires the free world to develop a successfully functioning political and economic system and a

vigorous political offensive against the Soviet Union. These, in turn, require an adequate military shield under which they can develop. It is necessary to have the military power to deter, if possible, Soviet expansionism, and to defeat, if necessary, aggressive Soviet or Soviet-directed actions of a limited or total character.[22]

At the centre of the containment doctrine, therefore, lay the idea of an integrated alliance system embracing the non-Communist world. It was also recognized that the strategy could not be purely defensive in character. It was argued that

> there is now and will be in the future no absolute defence. The history of war also indicates that a favourable decision can only be achieved through offensive action. Even a defensive strategy if it is to be successful, calls not only for defensive forces to hold vital positions while mobilizing and preparing for the offensive, but also for offensive forces to attack the enemy and keep him off balance.[23]

However, the document made clear that the defensive strategy was only a temporary phase and would, when adequate preparations had been made, give way to more strenuous efforts to eliminate Communism: 'it is clear that a substantial and rapid building up of strength in the free world is necessary to support a firm policy intended to check and roll back the Kremlin drive for world domination'.[24] It was argued, however, that such a strategy could not be contemplated until the necessary military strength had been achieved and confidence in the non-Communist world had been restored. Talk of roll back, therefore, had to be avoided because

> any announcement of the recommended course of action could be exploited by the Soviet Union in its peace campaign and would have adverse psychological effects in certain parts of the free world until the necessary increase in strength had been achieved. Therefore, in any announcement of policy and in the character of the measures adopted, emphasis should be given to the essentially defensive character, and care should be taken to minimize, so far as possible, unfavourable domestic and foreign relations.[25]

Nevertheless, even in the short term, it was recommended that

> we should take dynamic steps to reduce the power and influence of the Kremlin inside the Soviet Union and other areas under its control. The

objective would be the establishment of friendly regimes not under Kremlin domination. Such action is essential to engage the Kremlin's attention, keep it off balance and force an increased expenditure of Soviet resources in counter-action.[26]

Containment, therefore, as originally conceived, was designed not only to counter the threat of Communism, but in the long term, to eliminate Communism, if necessary, by military means. It was designed, however, to appear purely defensive in orientation.

Ever since the formulation of the containment strategy, pure liberals have been dissatisfied with the way it has been implemented. They have always felt that the nature of the threat has been underestimated and insufficient attention has been paid to counteracting the threat. As Strausz-Hupé and his colleagues noted in the early 1960s, for example: 'There is no assurance that we shall confound the all-too-obvious purpose of the Communists unless we and the peoples of our side join in an effort in the cause of freedom much greater than we have thought thus far worth our while.'[27] The failure to implement containment effectively has been manifested in three major areas.

The first is associated with the failure to counter the fact that ever since 1945, the Soviet Union has been, as NSC68 put it 'a great and growing center of military power'.[28] More important, however, the Soviets have succeeded at every stage in eroding areas of strength possessed by the United States and its allies. In 1945, the Americans were reasonably confident that it would take the Soviets at least a decade to develop a nuclear bomb. But within five years, the Soviets had bridged this technological gap. Then, during the 1950s, the Soviets developed the capacity to deliver nuclear weapons into American territory. The Soviets went on to match the American nuclear capacity and, by the late 1960s, a position of rough parity had been achieved. The pure liberals, however, were quite certain that having equalled Western capabilities, the Soviets would continue to build up their military position. During the 1970s, the Soviets were observed to make advances in a number of key areas. They established their superiority in theatre nuclear weapons targeted on Europe; they enlarged and modernized their ground forces deployed in Eastern Europe and Western Russia; they transformed their tactical air forces from a defensive force, dependent primarily on short-range interceptors, to an offensive force based upon long-term multipurpose aircraft capable of extending the air war deep into NATO territory; they transformed their surface navy from what was largely a coastal defence force into a powerful 'blue water' force capable of challenging American control of the seas; and finally they eliminated NATO's qualitative advantage in many technologies, especially those associated with land warfare.[29]

These developments have not been a reaction to earlier American programmes. As Gray argues, 'such an interpretation is not consistent with the available evidence concerning Soviet style in defense preparation . . . the strategy framework for Soviet defense programmes was determined well prior to the American action that some people claim triggered the Soviet military buildup'.[30] But pure liberals acknowledge that the Soviet task has been assisted by the unwillingness of the West to respond. Podhoretz notes that, 'despite all the easy talk . . . about an arms race, the United States responded to this relentless marathon not by running but by standing still and even slipping back'.[31]

A second problem area relates to the persistent attempts to accommodate rather than to contain the Soviets. Pure liberals have observed a dangerous tendency to promote strategies designed to reach a settlement or accord with the Soviet Union and its allies. This tendency was exemplified by the establishment of the Conference on Security and Cooperation in Europe (CSCE) in 1975 which legitimized the status quo established at the end of the Second World War in Eastern Europe. The conference has been viewed as part of a general policy of East–West *détente*, intended to reduce the level of tension between the two political systems. Pure liberals, however, have persistently attacked any attempt to reach a political accommodation with the Soviet Union: 'Under this policy the leadership of the Western world would pass to Moscow and the United States would surrender its political birth-right.'[32] The same point is made more graphically by George Meany in an attack on the attempts by Nixon and Kissinger to establish *détente* with the Soviet Union. He argues that

> we are not building lasting structures of peace. We are building castles of sand on the watery foundations of petty greed, wishful thinking, irresponsibility and plain old ignorance. The inability to face the world as it is, and to understand clearly the nature of freedom's enemies everywhere, is really the greatest threat to peace today. That threat is nowhere more clearly posed than in the delusion we call *détente*.[33]

Pure liberals argue that very often, particularly in Western Europe, there has been a failure to see that the Soviet Union has been deliberately encouraging the West to lower its guard. As Handlin puts it: 'The common Marxist rhetoric that many well-intentioned writers in Western Europe shared with the Reds persuaded them to accept verbal assurances that the Soviet Union laboured toward the same objective as they, and blinded them to the realities of Russian aggressiveness.'[34] From the pure liberal's perspective, *détente* can only serve the interests of the Soviet Union. Indeed, they coincide exactly with the Soviet policy of peaceful coexistence. Payne notes that 'peaceful coexistence is the theoretical basis of the CPSU policy to create conditions favourable for the expansion of communism while simultaneously avoiding nuclear war. The new opportunities for anti-Western activity entailed by the Soviet view of peaceful coexistence imply the encouragement of an intensified assault on Western interests.'[35] *Détente*, therefore, overlooks a very basic feature of the Communist threat:

> Different political systems can exist side by side, but not when one system is aggressive, geared to conflict and bent on conquest. The nature of the Soviet system exacerbates the problem of arriving at a settlement, because the communists can appear to renounce aggression for a few years in order to lull the West to sleep.[36]

Attempts to reach agreements with the Soviets, therefore, must never ignore both the long-term aggressive intentions of the Soviets and their willingness to engage in 'protracted' conflict.

Pure liberals have found the attempts to maintain mutual deterrence and to promote arms-control agreements particularly disturbing because they are so compatible with the Soviet desire for peaceful coexistence. Both are premised on a willingness to collaborate with the enemy. Although the pure liberals were prepared to tolerate deterrence while the Soviet Union was in a position of strategic inferiority, the idea became suspect from the moment that the Soviets achieved parity. The unease existed even when the Americans retained a position of strategic superiority. It was noted that 'deterrence for all its merits, is too speculative and too negative a concept' and considerable concern was expressed that 'we appear to be adopting, without a real national debate on its implications, a single strategy, that of "finite deterrence" — an essentially "no defense" posture based on the assumption that any nuclear war will result in mutual suicide.'[37] The dangers of deterrence were spelled out more frequently once the Soviets achieved nuclear parity. Mutual deterrence only works as a strategy if the two 'partners' are willing to leave themselves equally vulnerable to an attack from the other side. Pure liberals argued that the Soviets were not willing to 'cooperate' and were aiming instead at a war-winning strategy.

Rather than the Western focus upon mutual deterrence, political bargaining, and punitive strikes, the Soviets appear to take a classic approach to strategic doctrine. In the event of a strategic war, Soviet doctrine (according to declaratory policy) envisages a traditional strategy: destroy the opponent's war-making capability, survive enemy attacks, and consumate a politically meaningful victory.[38]

The attack on deterrence was inevitably extended to the field of arms control. From the start, arms-control negotiations were seen to demonstrate that the West was frightened of nuclear war and could therefore be seen to reflect a lack of resolve. As Spanier and Nogee put it,

> the very fear of war that the West has betrayed in its arms-control proposals has only served to reassure the Russians that the West is unlikely to launch a first blow, and that they can therefore safely proceed to employ the threat of war to frighten the West. In the final analysis, arms control is exactly the kind of device one would expect from a status quo power seeking only peace and stability — a power that, by the very nature of its society and position, has surrendered the initiative to the opponent. For the same reason, the revolutionary power must be expected to reject it — and, indeed, to exploit the other side's yearning for 'normalcy'.[39]

Subsequent critics have gone on to assert that the advocates of arms control have also failed to recognize that the Soviets do not even share a common conception of strategic stability. In an attack on some of the early advocates of arms control, it has been argued that

> arms control was held to be capable of contributing to the stability of the military environment by means of conscious cooperation (explicit or tacit) or even collaboration, between potential adversaries . . . The possibility that Western notions of stability might not be shared in Moscow, or that stability might not be chosen as a goal of armament policy (even by those who were familiar with Western arms control theory) were thoughts that appear but briefly in the classical works [on arms control].[40]

From this perspective, therefore, it is extremely difficult to achieve meaningful arms-control agreements because the strategic interests of the Soviets and the Americans are not symmetrical. But the task becomes not only difficult but positively dangerous if the Soviets are aiming to establish a position of strategic superiority. The problem has been further complicated, however, by the enthusiasm for arms control inspired by its advocates. Gray notes that:

> Absurd though it really is, evidence of 'belief' in and commitment to arms control has come to be required for a reputation as a responsible leader. It is difficult for a government to approach the prospect of, let alone believe in, arms control negotiations in a prudent manner when its domestic (and allied) constituency demands evidence of commitment and perhaps evidence of 'progress', while the adversary partner holds to an instrumental view of the arms control process as a tool of political warfare.[41]

This leads to the conclusion that the outcome of arms-control talks in the past has almost inevitably favoured the Soviet Union because of the American need to satisfy the demands made by domestic and international opinion to reach some kind of agreement. SALT I and SALT II have both been attacked, for example, on the grounds that they jeopardized the security interests of the United States and its allies.[42]

The third problem area arising from the unsuccessful implementation of containment relates to the competition between liberalism and Communism in the Third World. From the moment that decolonization got under way after the Second World War, it was apparent that there was no guarantee that the historical alliance between Western Europe and the former colonies would be maintained. It was equally apparent that the Soviet Union intended to make a detemined effort to win control in these areas. The difficulty for the liberals was how to encourage the growth of liberal values in the Third World without becoming susceptible to the charge that they were attempting to maintain the former colonial relationship.

Communism had an irresistible appeal for many politicians in Third World countries because of its established link with anti-imperialism. The collapse of the Kuomintang regime in China in 1949 demonstrated the strength of the Communist opposition. It became evident that the West was confronting a world-wide challenge and that, without an adequate response, events would favour the Communists. Pure liberals were drawn to the metaphor of falling dominoes. It was believed that once one country fell to the Communists, this would have an immediate knock-on effect and neighbouring countries would also succumb.

Pure liberals have insisted that, as Soviet strength has increased and as the West has searched to reach a political accommodation with the Soviet

Union, so the capacity to influence events in the Third World has diminished. As Handlin has note, 'the clatter heard out of Angola, Ethiopia, Afghanistan and Iran was the sound of falling dominoes, as awareness of Western paralysis eased restraints form within and without.'[43] By the 1980s, pure liberals observed that, as the strategic positions of the United States deteriorated, so the threat of Communism could come closer to home. Sanchez, for example, has argued that 'Americans are now finding it hard to accept the fact that the Soviet Union is abetting an assault on the security of this hemisphere more dangerous than the post-war threat to Western Europe'.[44] The generally deteriorating position of liberalism in the world is, therefore, seen by the pure liberals to be the result of an interaction between Soviet expansionism and Western passivity.

Although compensatory liberals have always had a different conception of the security problem to the pure liberals, since the 1960s the gulf has become wide and acrimonious. As already indicated, in the early years of the cold war, they accepted the pure liberal assertion that accommodation with the Soviet Union in either the economic or security spheres was simply not feasible and they acknowledged the need for a policy of containment.

Compensatory liberals had always believed that the pure liberal approach to security was flawed and, as the deleterious effects of the cold war persisted and worsened, so the compensatory liberals returned to their criticism of the pure liberal position. The early compensatory liberals had been critical on two major counts. First, they questioned the pure liberal proposition that the promotion of the untrammelled activities of individuals across state boundaries was sufficient to bring about a peaceful world. Hobhouse, for example, noted how 'one nation may act as selfishly, callously and cruelly in relation to another as one class in relation to another'.[45] More important, on the second count, was the recognition by compensatory liberals that governments had a crucial part to play in the promotion of individual freedom and that it was necessary for the role of governments to expand rather than contract, so compensatory liberals were also unwilling to accept that peace could only be encouraged by the contraction of governments. This departure from two of the basic tenets of pure liberalism meant that the compensatory liberals had to devise their own solutions to the problems of security.

Their approach developed in two phases. During the first, compensatory liberals recognized that 'the improvement of international relations and the avoidance of war required an international organization with some at least of the attributes of government'.[46] This idea achieved fruition during the course of the First World War. Compensatory liberals from a variety of countries advanced similar peace plans which all included the demand for an international agency sufficiently strong to protect its members against aggression.[47] These schemes received a tremendous fillip when the idea was adopted by President Woodrow Wilson who incorporated their ideas into his Fourteen Points which laid out his plans for the post-war world. But Wilson's support for a collective security organization simply accorded with established American liberal proclivities which had always opposed the European desire to maintain the balance of power.[48]

Wilson insisted that 'There must be, not a balance of power but a community of power; not organized rivalries but an organized common peace.'[49] Wilson saw the new League of Nations, therefore, as a completely new and independent force capable of overriding the animosities and conflicts which had traditionally beset Europe. This assessment, however, overlooked the importance of economics — always a central feature in any liberal plan for peace. Only three of Wilson's fourteen points touched on economic issues and according to Hofstadter, as a consequence, it had to be accepted that the League was inadequate as a mechanism for preserving peace because it left existing commercial and industrial relations intact. It was a 'political peace in which the fundamental economic arrangements of nineteenth century Europe were taken for granted'.[50] He goes on: 'No matter how historians may dramatize Wilson's struggle with Clemenceau and Lloyd George, it was not a struggle between an Old Order and a New Order, but merely a quarrel as to how the Old Order should settle its affairs.'[51]

The inadequacy of the League of Nations as a solution to the problems of security soon became painfully apparent. It gave rise to the second phase in the development of the compensatory liberals' approach to security. Events in the 1920s and 1930s served to reconfirm their appreciation of the economic dimension of peace. Liberals argued that the growing international turmoil was largely a product of the economic dislocation precipitated by the creation of economic blocs. As Cordell Hill, Secretary of State to President Roosevelt, saw it,

> unhampered trade dove-tailed with peace; high tariffs, trade barriers and unfair economic competition, with war. Though realizing that many other factors were involved, I reasoned that if we could get a freer flow of trade — freer in the sense of fewer discriminations and obstructions — so that one country would not be deadly jealous of another and the living standards of all countries might rise, thereby eliminating the economic dissatisfaction that breeds war, we might have a reasonable chance for lasting peace.[52]

But in contrast to the nineteenth-century free traders, Hull and his compatriots believed that free trade could only be achieved if it was supported by a framework of international organizations. When the United States entered the Second World War, therefore, these compensatory liberals were determined not to repeat the error perpetrated by Wilson. As Kolko notes:

> the United States did not simply wish to repair the pre-war world economy, but to reconstruct it anew. There was remarkable unanimity in Washington on this objective and it was by far the most extensively discussed peace aim, surpassing any other in the level of planning and thought given to it.[53]

The role of the compensatory liberals in creating a liberal world economy has already been discussed in Chapter 6. As an economic venture, it was remarkably successful. But from a security perspective, it proved a complete failure once the Soviet bloc was excluded from the reconstructed world economy. The pursuit of a liberal world economy negated the solution to the security problem devised by the compensatory liberals. All that was left was the United Nations. But as their attitude to the League of Nations made clear, such an institution could not hope, on its own, to resolve the knotty security issues associated with a world of separate competing economic blocs. At the onset of the cold war, therefore, compensatory liberals found that their proposed solution for security problems had proved as inadequate as that of their First World War forebears and they had to reassess their approach.

It took some time for a complete reassessment to take place. Initially therefore, the compensatory liberals latched on to the approach advanced by the pure liberals. Containment was accepted as the most acceptable method to defend liberalism. But, from its inception, compensatory liberals were opposed to containment being defined in anything other than defensive terms. Events, however, have encouraged compensatory liberals to take an increasingly critical view of containment. Three major problem areas have been identified.

The first relates to the danger of nuclear war. The event which began to unhinge the alliance between the pure and compensatory liberals on this issue was the 1962 Cuban missile crisis. Compensatory liberals have endorsed the view of Robert Kennedy, who described the crisis as a 'confrontation between the two giant atomic nations, the United States and the USSR, which brought the world to the abyss of nuclear destruction and the end of mankind'.[54] Thereafter, the danger of nuclear war has been seen to be the most important problem in the area of security. For compensatory liberals technological developments have made it impossible to envisage any form of society surviving a major exchange of nuclear weapons. They have no doubt, therefore, that neither liberalism nor Communism would emerge from a war between the superpowers. They believe that

> no past war can help us understand the impact of a nuclear war. In the Second World War, despite the astronomical death-toll and appalling barbarism, there was no massive breakdown of society or morale ... An all-out nuclear war would create a degree of chaos and confusion for which humanity is totally unprepared, and for which it can never prepare. It could mean the end of life itself.[55]

From the perspective of the compensatory liberal, moreover, the prospects of a nuclear war are steadily increasing because of the persistence of the arms race and the steady deterioration in the international climate. It is believed that the world, having recovered from the Second World War, is 'marching towards the brink of a new abyss, towards conflicts whose consequences would exceed experience and defy imagination'.[56] Compensatory liberals, therefore, conceive of a tightly integrated set of policies associated with nuclear weapons which are collectively moving the global community into increasingly dangerous postures. The Palme Report notes that 'every year has uncovered new evidence that humanity may eventually confront the greatest danger of all — world wide nuclear war'.[57] Two key interrelated factors are considered to enhance the threat of nuclear war. The first is the pure liberal conception of the Soviet threat, and the other is the strategic consequences which flow from the way the threat is perceived. Compensatory liberals have become disconcerted by the credence given to the pure liberal assertion that the Soviet Union is more concerned with winning a nuclear confrontation than with maintaining mutual deterrence. It is argued that this assessment is based on a distorted evaluation of views which, under any circumstances, have only been expressed in the theoretical writings of a group of Soviet military officers. After a survey of this literature, Kaplan has concluded that

> Soviet military literature does emphasize what happens after nuclear war begins more than American literature does; but this concern seems to grow out of a genuine fear of an attack on the Soviet Union by the United States or its allies; this fear has historical basis. In any event, the

Soviets have not apparently worked out a decent operational definition of 'winning' a nuclear war or how to get there from here. Finally, the Soviets seem just as horrified about the prospects and consequences of nuclear war as anybody.[58]

The draconian image of the Soviet Union has had very important strategic consequences. It has helped to justify a strategy which incorporates a role for counterforce weapons. The existence of these weapons had made it possible for the United States to contemplate a war-winning strategy. In practice, both the Soviet Union and the United States have now developed weapons systems which can make it appear to the other side that there are plans 'to fight a limited nuclear war as a matter of policy'.[59] Such a development can only add to the existing danger.

A second problem area identified by the compensatory liberals relates to the tendency by the United States to use its military power in an effort to promote or protect liberalism. The major event which caused compensatory liberals to reassess this dimension of containment was the American involvement in Vietnam. Even after the Cuban missile crisis, compensatory liberals continued to accept that it was important to curb the spread of Communism. The war in Vietnam caused the compensatory liberals to reflect not so much on the aim as on the methods which were being employed to pursue the aim. Compensatory liberals began to talk about the 'abuse' and the 'arrogance' of power. It was observed that military intervention was becoming the habitual response of the United States to political problems. Such a response was also observed to be counter-productive. Very far from undermining the Communists, it seemed to be strengthening their position.

For many liberals, the American involvement in the Vietnam War proved traumatic. Events there made it impossible to sustain the image of the United States as the untarnished leader of liberalism. The American role in the international arena, since the Second World War, and in earlier periods, was re-evaluated. Compensatory liberals began to argue that the pure liberal account of the cold war was too simplistic and that the United States was equally, if not more, culpable for the course of events after the Second World War.[60] The nature of the problems as seen by Draper was that 'we cannot continue to live wholly in the moment, holding on to every status quo, however rotten and unstable, to maintain the line against Communism at whatever cost. In the new worship of power, we are squandering our power by using too much too· frequently and too maladroitly.'[61] Since the war in Vietnam, compensatory liberals have adhered to the traditional liberal view that military intervention can never help to foster liberalism. They have argued further that the American justifications of intervention have also been employed by the Soviets precipitating what Frank and Weisband call the 'echo-effect'. It occurred when the arguments used by the United States to account for their intervention into the Dominican Republic in 1965 were reiterated by the Soviet Union when they invaded Czechoslovakia. The Brezhnev Doctrine, which indicated that the Soviet Union had the right to prevent any attempt to 'roll back the socialist commonwealth',[62] is depicted as the mirror image of the Johnson Doctrine which indicated that the United States would 'not permit the establishment of another communist government in the Western hemisphere'.[63] Frank and Weisband note, however, how

> few Western observers noted that the Russians were echoing the very words used by the hardheaded realists in Washington to defend America's Latin American policy. By failing to listen to themselves as if they were the enemy speaking, American policy makers had made it easy and cheap for Russia to reassert the dark side of its nature.[64]

This problem has been exacerbated as growing military strength has given the Soviets the potential to pursue the kind of wide-ranging strategy of intervention which previously only the Americans had been able to pursue. The Soviets were, as a consequence, encouraged to leap-frog over the boundary of containment in their endeavours to emulate the United States.

The ideological struggle between East and West has also helped to promote a steady stream of weapons into Third World countries, thereby exacerbating the widespread number of conflicts between Third World societies which are, all too often, a legacy of post-colonial settlements. As the Palme Report notes: 'The Third World now includes some sixty-two states with populations of less than one million, thirty-six of which have populations below 200,000. Their very smallness and weaknesses tempts others to pursue territorial and political ambitions through military intervention.'[65] Containment, therefore, has not only encouraged a pattern of reciprocal intervention in the Third World, it has also simultaneously fuelled indigenous conflict in these areas.

A third major security problem area for the compensatory liberal relates to the economic and social consequences of military spending. They argue that these consequences have grown spectacularly in the last hundred years with the dramatic increase in military spending. Compensatory liberals focused on this problem area as they became more aware of the global economic crisis in the 1970s.[66] They have observed a perverse mismatch between the willingness to increase military spending and the unwillingness to take firm actions to improve the global economy. Part of the problem arises because 'economic cost itself is seen as the prime index of military effort. Spending more money on defense becomes an end in itself ... Military security is counted in inputs (money) rather than outputs of "security" or even of military goods or services.'[67] The vast increases in military expenditure have not enhanced security. The constant improvements and renewal of military equipment have simply become a self-perpetuating exercise.

Compensatory liberals, however, are not only concerned with what they see as the wasteful aspects of military expenditure but also the opportunity costs. By diverting resources into the military, negative economic and social consequences arise which are not immediately apparent:

> Military spending is a charge on the economic future of all countries, the richest and the poorest, those who import and those whose export arms, the East and the West. Its economic consequences are in certain respects similar in the most diverse countries. Everywhere, it demands resources which are scarce and which are becoming yet more scarce.[68]

The economic benefits of military expenditure are considered to be trivial in comparison to the economic costs. These costs can include increased unemployment, as well as reductions in economic growth, investment, and scientific research. It is accepted that the importance of these costs will vary from country to country, but because societies are now interdependent, it follows that 'all countries are hurt if military spending reduces the economic well-being of major participants in the world economy. All are hurt if military demands on government finances limit aid or commercial lending to developing countries.'[69] While the economic and social costs have always been high, these costs are obviously magnified as military expenditure rises and interdependence ensures that the effects are increasingly diffused. So for compensatory liberals, containment, which seeks to establish a political division in the international arena, runs directly counter to economic and technological trends which are drawing nations into a more closely-knit interdependent world. In such a world, containment simply serves to decrease the general level of security.

Solutions

Pure liberals have never discarded their traditional belief that, ultimately, the only real solution to the problems of security is the establishment of a liberal world order. As Dean Acheson observed: 'We are children of freedom. We cannot be safe except in an environment of freedom.'[70] Huntington has argued, in the same vein, that a liberal-democratic system 'can only be secure in a world system of similarly constituted states'. He goes on, moreover, to say that, whereas in the past, not a great deal of weight was attached to this argument, it has become progressively more important:

> Given the increasing interactions among societies and the emergence of transnational institutions operating in many societies, the pressures towards convergence among political systems are likely to become more intense. Interdependence may be incompatible with coexistence. In this case, the world, like the United States in the nineteenth century or Western Europe in the twentieth century, will not be able to exist half-slave and half-free. Hence, the survival of democratic institutions and values at home will depend upon their adoption abroad.[71]

In a world where liberalism is not universal and peaceful coexistence is precluded, pure liberals have identified containment as the best strategy for preserving liberalism. It is acknowledged, however, that containment inevitably generates a paradox. In the context of the United States, for example, there exists, according to Huntington, a 'contradiction between enhancing liberty at home by curbing the power of the American government and enhancing liberty abroad by expanding that power'.[72] Communism, therefore, can only be curbed abroad at the expense of bridling liberalism at home. Pure liberals, therefore, see containment as a conservative strategy because 'the greatest need is not so much the creation of liberal institutions as the successful defense of those which already exist. This defense requires American liberals to lay aside their liberal ideology and to accept the values of conservatism for the duration of the threat.'[73] While acutely conscious that their solutions to contemporary security problems involve the negation of pure liberalism, pure liberals accept containment because of the rise of state-sponsored Communism. More disturbing than the rise of conservatism is the failure to establish a viable defence.

To restore containment it is necessary, first, to reassert the strategic superiority of the non-Communist world. While pure liberals do not underestimate the difficulty of achieving this end they do insist that it is possible. Two factors are involved. It is essential, first, to convince all the non-Communist countries that their security interests are identical. As Sonnenfeldt has argued, from the perspective of the non-Communist world: 'Security *vis-à-vis* the USSR is indivisible.'[74] The essence of containment is collective security. Once it is accepted that there is a shared responsibility for the security of liberalism, then it is also essential, secondly, to convince all non-Communist countries that it is necessary to spend more on defence. If the economic resources of the non-Communist world are harnessed to the task of serving strategic superiority, then there is no possibility that the Communists can compete. As Strausz-Hupé argues: 'The economic resources of the Free World are so much greater than those of the communist bloc that, combined with a masterful exploitation of technology, a strategy based on overwhelming military means is well within our reach.'[75] These two factors have both been stressed in a report on the security relationship between Japan and NATO. It argues that

> Japan and Europe can no longer put off, nor relegate to the United States, the commitment of greater resources to their collective security. There can in fact no longer be individual national security for any of the advanced industrialized nations — only collective security in which all participate according to their capabilities . . . The allies can only lose control of their own future destiny and progress if they lose sight of what is required to earn those benefits by investing more heavily in their own future security.[76]

When the resources of the non-Communist world are aggregated, therefore, the task of maintaining a position of strategic superiority is obviously possible. Containment is a strategy which encourages this conception of collective responsibility.

The second problem identified by the pure liberals relates to the attempts to reach an accommmodation with the Communists. To counter this danger it is necessary to heighten the differences which exist between Communist and non-Communist societies. It is essential for the free world to recognize

> its own identity [and the] absolute moral differences that separate it from regimes with which it shares the globe. And the time left will be wasted upon those who fail to understand that they inhabit one world with others and must summon up the will to defend values from the past that are still valid for the future.[77]

An appropriate strategy to contend with the present threat involves drawing upon the strengths of the free world and playing upon the weaknesses of the Communists. The two major assets of the West are its economic power and its technological skills. Strategy must, therefore, utilize both of these features. Pure liberals, therefore, favour strategic developments which will move the West into a position of strategic superiority. Attempts must be made, therefore, to preserve the strategy of flexible response. The logic behind flexible response was laid out at the end of the 1950s by General Maxwell Taylor.

> This name suggests the need for a capability to react across the entire spectrum of possible challenge, for coping with everything from general atomic war to infiltrations and aggressions such as Laos and Berlin in 1959. The new strategy would recognize that it is just as necessary to deter or win quickly a limited war as to deter a general war.[78]

The underlying aim of flexible response is escalation dominance. If the West has superiority across the 'entire spectrum of possible challenge' then the Communists are precluded from attaining any military advantage from escalating a conflict. This involves maintaining Western superiority at conventional, tactical, theatre and strategic levels. Currently there are plans to extend the logic of flexible response so the United States can display strategic superiority in space. Since it is not possible that the Soviets would willingly accept a position of inferiority, flexible response successfully undermines *détente.*

In addition to vertical escalation dominance, pure liberals also favour a policy of horizontal escalation dominance, achieved when the West can extend war from areas where the enemy possesses strength to areas where weaknesses are displayed.[79] Simes has argued that such a capacity would 'increase Soviet caution and temper its inclination to conduct a diplomacy of force'. He goes on:

> If, for example, Moscow meddles in the Horn of Africa, the United States should resist the understandable temptation to demonstrate its power and will by automatically and immediately countering the Soviets ... Rather it should communicate to Moscow that if the Soviet Union seeks to undermine the US global positions, the United States will not preclude responding in areas that matter to the Soviets and where their positions are particularly shaky, including in their own East European backyard.[80]

Pure liberals also favour the pursuit of policies designed to maximize the chances of surviving and winning a nuclear war. They are concerned with offensive and defensive capabilities rather than deterrence. To achieve an adequate defence, pure liberals have favoured building more fall-out shelters and creating an effective ballistic missile defence system (BMD).[81] In conjunction with BMD, they also favour an improved counterforce strategy. Such a policy is seen to be infinitely safer than relying upon a system of mutual deterrence which depends on the goodwill of the Soviet Union and which, if it failed, would bring about the mutual destruction of both the United States and the Soviet Union. Such a policy appears to the pure liberal to be self-defeating, dangerous and immoral.

The popular demand for arms-control agreements and the propaganda advantage which the Communists can reap if the West refuses to engage in arms-control talks has meant that pure liberals have had to consider a strategy for managing such talks. Pure liberals favour the strategy identified by Spanier and Nogee as gamesmanship. The strategy was developed during the disarmament talks which took place in the 1950s. It arose

> because one side's security could be gained only at the expense of the opponent's security, [which meant that] neither side could accept a *compromise* agreement. Every disarmament plan offered has therefore inevitably contained at least one element — the 'joker' —that the other could not possibly accept. This joker has served a dual function: to compel a rejection of the whole plan and thus place the onus for the deadlock on the other side, and to protect the vital interests of the proposing side.[82]

Given the climate of domestic and international opinion, pure liberals believe that there is no alternative but to extend this tactic into the arms-control arena. Such tactics are essential to sustain flexible response.

The final problem area identified by the pure liberals is associated with the growing number of states which the free world has 'lost'. Pure liberals have argued that these losses took place because the West lacked the courage of their convictions and have operated a double standard. All too often, it is argued, the United States has withdrawn support from regimes under attack from Communists on the grounds that the existing regime is insufficiently democratic, while maintaining relations with Communist states which are often substantially more undemocratic. As Kirkpatrick observes, for example: 'The Carter administration's conception of national interest bordered on doublethink: it found friendly powers to be guilty representatives of the status quo and viewed the triumph of unfriendly groups as beneficial to America's true interests.'[83] She goes on to argue that such a policy

> failed not for lack of good intentions but for lack of realism about the nature of traditional versus revolutionary autocracies. Only intellectual fashion and the tyranny of Right/Left thinking prevent intelligent men of good will from perceiving the *facts* that traditional authoritarian regimes are less repressive than revolutionary autocracies, that they are more susceptible of liberalization, and that they are more compatible with US interests.[84]

Huntington has argued further that liberalism has flourished most when the United States has been powerful and prepared to intervene on the side of freedom. He notes, for example, how American intervention in Nicaragua, Haiti, and the Dominican Republic in the 1920s and 1930s 'produced the freest elections and the most open political competitions in the history of those countries'.[85] It follows, therefore, that pure liberals believe that it is better to support conservative autocracies than to undermine them when they are threatened by a potential revolutionary autocracy. It is also argued that the liberal prohibition on intervention should be ignored when liberalism is confronted by state-sponsored Communism. Pure liberals, therefore, advocate an increased capacity for intervention. Betts notes that in regional conflicts, the Middle East, for example, pre-emption is the only sound strategy for the superpowers:

> preemption not in terms of strikes against each other's forces but in terms of reaching the scene first. Once one of the superpowers' troops are on the disputed ground, counterintervention becomes a much more reckless venture for the other, because he has the 'last clear chance' to avoid the dangers inherent in undertaking the unprecedented action of combat between two nuclear-armed states.[86]

Pure liberals also argue that the legitimacy of the action can be enhanced by operating under the banner of collective security. It has, therefore, been argued that

> less well disciplined nations cannot be permitted to disrupt the continuing progress and evolution of the world through barbaric and terrorist acts designed to intimidate civilized government or corrode the fabric of accepted international institutions. If and when military

actions are required to preserve allied security, the legitimacy of such actions will be substantially enhanced in the eyes of all observers if they carry the weight of international cooperation and shared responsibility.[87]

Pure liberals believe, therefore, that force still has a vital role to play in the task of preserving freedom and that, in order to contain the threat of Communism and defend freedom, countries in the 'free world' must be ready and willing at all times to exercise force. Containment can, moreover, only succeed if the free world ensures that it is in a position of all-round strategic superiority. Under such conditions, the potential to push the Communist world in a more liberal direction may also become feasible. Once all societies have become liberal, then the whole charcter of the security problem is transformed and the need to maintain armaments will be largely eliminated.

For the compensatory liberal, the threat of Communism has become secondary to the threat of nuclear destruction. This represents their first major problem area. The solution to this problem, therefore, lies in the recognition that throughout the globe there are overriding common security interests which transcend more parochial political interests. It is necessary for all states to rethink their security policies:

> States can no longer seek security at each other's expense; it can be attained only through cooperative undertakings. Security in the nuclear age means common security. Even ideological opponents and political rivals have a shared interest in survival . . . *A doctrine of common security must replace the present expedient of deterrence through armaments.*[88]

Disarmament can be achieved if the reality of common security is acknowledged and states adopt a building block approach to the task. The 'task of diplomacy is to limit, split and subdivide conflicts, not to generalize and aggregate them'.[89] The central building block has to be the agreements between the United States and the Soviet Union on their strategic arms. An intensification of the SALT-START approach is favoured. Counterforce weapons and anti-satellite weapons must be outlawed. At the same time, the ABM agreement reached in 1972 must be reconfirmed and reinforced. These agreements must then be extended to embrace a ban on biological and chemical weapons.

Compensatory liberals have also argued that the reduction in armaments between the Soviet Union and the United States and the movement towards general disarmament could be substantially enhanced by demilitarizing central Europe, where the military forces of Communism and liberalism currently confront each other. Such a development would obviously have to take place in stages and an initial step could be the reduction of conventional troops in the area. This must be followed by the elimination of tactical weapons. The area could then be established as a nuclear, chemical and biological weapon-free zone.[90]

The need for these moves toward disarmament can be seen to be logical and necessary once the importance of common security is recognized. However, compensatory liberals also acknowledge that the distrust and hostility which has built up between liberal and Communist societies is not going to evaporate quickly or easily. Progress will be slow and frustrating. They are, therefore, very attracted to the idea of confidence-building measures which are designed to increase trust and reduce tension between enemies. An approach towards implementing confidence-building measures began in 1975 at the Conference on Security and Cooperation in Europe. They are intended to reduce fears of a surprise attack taking place in Europe. The measures require each side to provide information about troop manoeuvres and military exercises and to open military installations to observation.[91] The objective of both arms-control negotiations and the establishment of confidence-building measures, therefore, is to break down the barriers which have been built up over the years as the result of implementing a containment strategy.

The second major problem area relates to the persistent tendency of liberals and Communists to encourage military conflict in Third World societies. Compensatory liberals accept that if these countries are going to be persuaded to participate in a comprehensive disarmament plan, then it will be necessary to satisfy their security concerns. The Palme Report argues:

> We believe that to a significant degree these special needs of Third World countries can be met. Moreover, we feel that this can be accomplished largely within the framework of existing international and regional institutions and mechanisms, principally by strengthening the role of the United Nations on the basis of partnership between the great powers and the other members.[92]

The solution involves moving the United Nations beyond its restricted peace-keeping role towards the much more comprehensive and active collective security role which was originally described in the UN Charter. The Palme Report suggests that border disputes could provide a practical starting points. The aim would be to deter states from endeavouring to resolve border disputes by force. To develop an effective deterrent, however, Article 43 of the Charter, which envisages agreements between the UN and member governments on the provision of standby forces, would have to be resurrected. Compensatory liberals also favour strengthening regional collective security arrangements.[93] By increasing the strength of the UN and regional organizations like the Organization for African Unity, the siege mentality encouraged by a containment strategy can be reduced.

The third problem area of the compensatory liberals relates to the economic and social costs associated with the arms race. Compensatory liberals believe that, in order to increase awareness of these costs, it becomes important to encourage a redefinition of security. It is argued that security in the past has been much too narrowly defined in terms of military threats. As a consequence, too little attention has been paid to the fact that malnutrition, unemployment, pollution and a whole host of other factors can also pose a threat to the individual and the nation. As the Brandt Report observes:

> An important task of constructive international policy will have to consist in providing a new, more comprehensive understanding of 'security' which would be less restricted to the purely military aspects. In the global context true security cannot be achieved by a mounting up of weapons — defence in the narrow sense — but only by providing basic conditions for peaceful relations between nations, and solving not only the military but also the non-military problems which threaten them.[94]

The money spent on the arms race which only serves to generate insecurity must, therefore, be redirected into improving living standards which serves to reduce insecurity. The Brandt Report suggests that military expenditure and arms exports could be liable for international taxation which could be used for development purposes. The compensatory liberal considers that the solutions to economic problems in general, therefore, represent a fundamental contribution to the solution of security problems. Indeed, the distinction drawn between economic and security problems to a very large extent conflicts with the compensatory liberal's demand for a redefinition of security.

As far as the compensatory liberal is concerned, therefore, the emphasis on containment has encouraged a narrow and overly militaristic conception of security. It has diverted attention away from the need to develop a broader conception of security which takes account of the well-being of the individual. A direct link is drawn between security and prosperity so that the promotion of economic development becomes indistinguishable from the promotion of common security.

Notes

1. M. Howard, *War and the Liberal Conscience*, London, Temple Smith, 1978, p. 29.
2. S.P. Huntington, 'American Ideals versus American Institutions', *Political Science Quarterly*, **97**, 1982, 1–37, p. 35.
3. See Z. Brzezinski, *Between Two Ages: America's Role in the Technetronic Age*, New York, Viking Press, 1970, pp. 115-6, for a review of the rise of pessimism in the twentieth century.
4. R. Strausz-Hupé et al., *A Forward Strategy for America*, New York, Harper Bros., 1961, p. 14.
5. For a review of the changing character of containment, see J.L. Gaddis, *Strategies of Containment: A Critical Appraisal of Postwar American National Security Policy*, Oxford, Oxford University Press, 1982.
6. B. Parekh, 'Liberalism and Morality' in B. Parekh and R.N. Berki *The Morality of Politics*, London, George Allen & Unwin, 1972, p. 82.
7. See Howard, op. cit., p. 31.
8. Ibid.
9. The term international was in fact first coined by Jeremy Bentham in the nineteenth century: see H. Suganami, 'A Note on the Origin of the Word ' 'International' ', *British Journal of International Studies* **4**, 1978, 226–32.
10. F.H. Hinsley, *Power and the Pursuit of Peace*, Cambridge, Cambridge University Press, 1967, p. 111.
11. Cited in Howard, op. cit., p. 43. It is worth noting that with the development of literature on interdependence in the 1970s, this view came very much into vogue again: see, for example, R.O. Keohane and J.S. Nye, *Power and Interdependence: World Politics in Transition* Boston, Little Brown & Co., 1977.
12. Cited in C. Holbraad, *The Concert of Europe: A Study in German and British International Theory 1815–1914* London, Longman, 1970, p. 154.
13. Cited in Howard, op. cit., p. 43.
14. For a discussion of Mill, see R.J. Vincent, *Non-Intervention and the International Order*, Princeton, Princeton University Press, 1974.
15. Cited in Gaddis, op. cit., p. 138.
16. Cited in T.H. Etzold and J.L. Gaddis, *Containment: Documents on American Policy and Strategy, 1945–1950*, New York, Columbia University Press, 1978, p. 387.
17. P. Towle et al., *Protest and Perish: A Critique of Unilateralism*, London, Alliance Publishers Ltd., 1982, p. 36.
18. Cited in Etzold and Gaddis, op. cit., p. 385.
19. Ibid., p. 87. Paradoxically, George Kennan has also been seen as a major opponent of containment. He maintained, at the time, and later, that he disliked the way that containment was being implemented. He was, in fact, a realist rather than a liberal. There has always been an element of mystery about his initial position on containment. See C. Gati, 'What Containment Meant', *Foreign Policy*, 7, 1972, 24–36.
20. Ibid., p. 431.
21. Ibid.
22. Ibid., p. 432.
23. Ibid., p. 434.

24. Ibid., p. 434.
25. Ibid.
26. Ibid., p. 435.
27. Strausz-Hupé, op. cit., p. ix.
28. Cited in Etzold and Gaddis, op. cit.
29. This assessment is taken from J. Record, *Revising U.S. Military Strategy: Tailoring Ends to Means*, Washington, Pergamon-Brassey's, 1984, p. 33–4.
30. C.S. Gray, *Strategic Studies: A Critical Assessment*, London, Aldwych Press, 1982, pp. 123–4.
31. N. Podhoretz, *The Present Danger*, New York, Simon & Schuster, 1980, p. 40.
32. Strausz-Hupé, op. cit., p. 28.
33. Cited in K.B. Payne, *Nuclear Deterrence in U.S. Soviet Relations*, Boulder, Westview Press, 1982, p. 110.
34. O. Handlin, *The Distortion of America*, Boston, Little, Brown & Co., 1981, p. 66.
35. Payne, op. cit., p. 97.
36. Strausz-Hupé, op. cit., p. 8.
37. Ibid., p. 122.
38. Payne, op. cit., p. 126.
39. J.W. Spanier and J.L. Nogee, *The Politics of Disarmament: A Study in Soviet American Gamesmanship*, New York, F.A. Praeger, 1962, p. 179–80.
40. C.S. Gray, *Strategic Studies and Public Policy*, Lexington, University of Kentucky Press, 1982, pp. 76–7. Gray is referring to writers such as T.C. Schelling and M.H. Halperin, *Strategy and Arms Control*, New York, The Twentieth Century Fund, 1961.
41. C.S. Gray, *Nuclear Strategy and Strategic Planning*, Philadelphia Policy Papers, Philadelphia, Foreign Policy Research Institute, 1984, p. 117.
42. See R. Burt, 'The Relevance of Arms Control in the 1980s', *Daedalus*, 1981, pp. 159–77.
43. Handlin, op. cit., p. 125.
44. N.O. Sanchez, 'The Communist Threat', *Foreign Policy*, 51, 43–50, p. 44.
45. Cited in Howard, op. cit., p. 68.
46. Hinsley, op. cit., p. 117.
47. For a discussion of the liberal peace plans, see A.S. Link, *Wilson the Diplomatist*, New York, New Viewpoint, 1974, Chapter 4.
48. Wilson's view of the balance of power was, however, rather more complex than is sometimes suggested. See E.H. Buehrig, *Woodrow Wilson and the Balance of Power*, Bloomington, Indiana University Press, 1955.
49. Cited in E.C. Rozwenc and T. Lyons (eds.), *Realism and Idealism in Wilson's Peace Program*, Boston, B.C. Heath & Co., 1965, p. 9.
50. R. Hofstadter, 'Wilson's Peace Program' in ibid., p. 62.
51. Ibid., p. 64.
52. Cited in G. Kolko, *The Politics of War: Allied Diplomacy and the World Crisis of 1943–45*, London, Weidenfeld and Nicolson, 1968, p. 244.
53. Ibid., p. 245.
54. R.F. Kennedy, *13 Days: the Cuban Missile Crisis*, London, Macmillan, 1968, p. 27.
55. Olaf Palme, Chairman of the Independent Commission on Disarmament and

Security Issues, *Common Security: A Programme for Disarmament*, London, Pan Books, 1982, p. 58–9.
56. Ibid., p. 1.
57. Ibid.
58. F.M. Kaplan, *Dubious Specter: A Skeptical Look At The Soviet Nuclear Threat*, Washington, Institute for Policy Studies, 1980, p. 24.
59. Palme, op. cit., p. 44.
60. See, for example, T.G. Peterson 'Introduction' in T.G. Peterson (ed.), *Cold War Critics*, Chicago, Quadrangle Books, 1971.
61. T. Draper, *Abuse of Power: U.S. Foreign Policy from Cuba to Vietnam*, Harmondsworth, Penguin Books, 1967, p. 215.
62. T.M. Frank and E. Weisband, *Word Politics: Verbal Strategy Among the Superpowers*, New York, Oxford University Press, 1971, p. 345.
63. Ibid., p. 75.
64. Ibid., p. vii.
65. Palme, op. cit., p. 126.
66. Attention was drawn to this issue by Willy Brandt, Chairman, Independent Commission on International Development Issues, *North–South: A Programme for Survival*, London, Pan Books, 1980, Chapter 7.
67. Palme, op. cit., p. 74.
68. Ibid., p. 95.
69. Ibid., p. 96.
70. Cited in Gaddis, op. cit., p. 108.
71. Huntington, op. cit., p. 21.
72. Ibid., p. 35.
73. S.P. Huntington, 'Conservatism as an Ideology', *The American Political Science Review*, **51**, 1957, 454–73, p. 473.
74. H. Sonnenfeldt, 'Security vis-à-vis the USSR is not Divisible', *Atlantic Community Quarterly*, **19**, 1981, 393–406.
75. Strausz-Hupé, op. cit., p. 102.
76. U.A. Johnson and G.R. Packard, 'The Common Security Interest of Japan, the United States and NATO' *Atlantic Community Quarterly*, **18**, 1980, 485–501, p. 490.
77. Handlin, op. cit., p. 152.
78. M.D. Taylor, *The Uncertain Trumpet*, New York, Harper Bros., 1959, pp. 5–7.
79. See Record, op. cit., Chapter 4; and K.A. Dunn and W.D. Standenmaier 'Strategy for Survival', *Foreign Policy*, **51**, 1983, 22–41.
80. D.K. Simes, 'Disciplinary Soviet Power' *Foreign Policy*, **43**, 1981, 33–52, pp. 50–1. See also S.P. Huntington, 'Conventional Deterrence and Conventional Retaliation in Europe', *International Security*, **8**, 1983–4, 32–56, who argues in favour of developing an offensive conventional capability in Europe.
81. See K.B. Payne and C.S. Gray, 'Nuclear Policy and the Defensive Transition', *Foreign Affairs*, **62**, 1984, 819–42; and Gray, *Nuclear Strategy and Strategic Planning*, for a discussion of strategy based on defence rather than deterrence.
82. Spanier and Nogee, op. cit., p. 5.
83. J.J. Kirkpatrick, *Dictatorships and Double Standards*, New York, Simon & Schuster Inc., 1982, p. 44.
84. Ibid., p. 49.

85. Huntington, 'American Ideals', op. cit., p. 29.
86. R.K. Betts, *Surprise Attack: Lessons for Defense Planning*, Washington, The Brookings Institute, 1982, p. 262.
87. Johnson and Packard, op. cit., pp. 496–7.
88. Palme, op. cit., p. 139. Emphasis in original.
89. Ibid., p. 140.
90. This line of argument has been developed, for example by Robert S. McNamara in 'The Role of Nuclear Weapons: Perceptions and Misperceptions', *Foreign Affairs*, **62**, 1983, 59–80. See also the demand for a posture on nuclear weapons of 'no first use' in Europe, by McGeorge Bundy *et al.*, 'Nuclear Weapons and the Atlantic Alliance', *Foreign Affairs*, **60**, 1982.
91. See International Peace Research Association, 'Building Confidence in Europe: An Analytical and Action Oriented Study', *Bulletin of Peace Proposals*, **11**, 1980, 150–66; and W. Multon *et al.*, 'Some Reflections on the Confidence Building Process', *Bulletin of Peace Proposals*, **11**, 1980, 306–11.
92. Palme, op. cit., p. 127.
93. For an extensive discussion of regional collective security, see M.W. Zacher, *International Conflict and Collective Security*, New York, Praeger, 1979.
94. Brandt, op. cit., p. 214.

9 Socialist international security problems and solutions

Problems

Although the foundations were laid in the nineteenth century, the contemporary socialist conception of security was mainly developed after the onset of the First World War. Since that time, the socialists have formulated a very distinctive approach to security, although they have made little contribution to the established literature on strategic studies.[1] Indeed, this literature is viewed as ideological, helping to desensitize the population to the real issues at stake.[2] Before examining how socialists assess contemporary security problems, we shall briefly examine how their current conception of the global security environment emerged.

From its inception, war, violence and repression have been viewed as major problems in socialism. As Friedrich observes: 'In all socialist thought, the problem of war has played a major role.'[3] Socialists have persistently maintained that violent conflict is an unnecessary evil, perpetrated and perpetuated by exploitative modes of social organization; and that it will only disappear once the existing world order has been replaced by socialism which will provide both a 'means to and a guarantee of universal peace'.[4] While Marx may have said little about 'perpetual peace', Hinsley has insisted that this is because 'he believed that it would follow automatically upon the withering away of the state'.[5] In terms of its origins and development, therefore, socialism has continuously been associated with the creation of a peaceful world. The association persists. Markovic, a contemporary Yugoslavian Marxist, asserts that 'Socialism by definition means the transition period in which men evolve towards a non-violent classless society'.[6]

There is, therefore, a direct parallel between socialism and liberalism. Both believe that war can be eradicated, but only if their own conception of order is universalized. However, while for the liberal, it is only in the twentieth century that communism and, by association, socialism, have come to replace the balance of power as the major impediment to a liberal world order, by contrast, socialists have always viewed liberalism as the major obstacle to their preferred world order. As Lichtheim observes, 'the socialist movement from the start defined itself as a critique of liberalism'.⁷ The opposition arose because liberalism was seen to provide the ideological underpinning for capitalism. The conjunction of capitalism and liberalism was regarded as constituting the chief obstacle to the elimination of inequality.

The early socialists largely bypassed the international arena in their analysis. Marx, for example, as Cox has observed, developed his conception of capitalism primarily in the context of a 'closed society'.⁸ This did not mean that issues associated with conflict and violence were overlooked, but they were generally explored within the boundaries of the state. The focus of attention was not on the clash of arms between states, but on the conflict between classes inside the state. The whole history of human intercourse is depicted by socialists in terms of confrontation and, as Schurmann has observed, the 'nature of the enemy' is, in consequence, central to this mode of analysis. It reflects a 'combative philosophy, for it views class struggle as the central fact of all human existence. Peace is simply an illusion which masks real struggles.'⁹

From the onset, therefore, socialists attacked the idea that the state had come into existence to preserve the security of its citizens. Such an assessment was viewed as a historical distortion. Marx and Engels, for example, asserted that, in primitive communities, where there was no surplus production, there did exist pre-political institutions which were formed to safeguard common interests and to provide protection against external enemies. But the nature of these institutions changed when surpluses were generated by the economy and inequalities began to develop in their distribution. Then, it was argued, with the divergence in distribution, *class differences* emerge. Society divides into classes, the privileged and the dispossessed, the exploiters and the exploited, the rulers and the ruled.'¹⁰ The emergence of classes necessitated the creation of officials to mediate and resolve the conflicts of interest between the competing groups. As Marx put it, 'out of this very contradiction between the interest of the individual and that of the community, the latter takes an independent form as the *state*.'¹¹ The major *raison d'être* for the state, therefore, was to defend the interests of the owners of property against the dispossessed. Schurmann argues that 'it is class war, not class, that produces the state'.¹² From an early socialist perspective, therefore, the state had to be viewed as a divisive institution, for it promoted the security of one section of the community at the expense of another. This view persists. Cockburn argues that, from a Marxist perspective, the state is an 'instrument of class domination' and its 'characteristic function is repression'. As a consequence, the state is associated, above all, with the armed forces, the police, the judges and the courts of law.¹³

It seemed to Marx and Engels that there was no possibility that class divisions could be eradicated peacefully. In the *Communist Manifesto* there were no qualms about how change should be implemented. It proclaimed: 'The Communists refuse to hide their views and purposes. They declare openly that their ends can only be achieved through the violent overthrow of the entire existing social order.'[14] Friedrich observes that both Marx and Engels 'preached war, the class war or class struggle, as the only road to peace'.[15] The advocacy of open, violent revolution continues. Muste notes, for instance, that 'in a world built on violence one must be a revolutionary before one can be a pacifist'.[16]

To the extent that the early socialists did develop an international view point, they gave their class analysis a global perspective which cut across the established state barriers. It was in this context that Ernest Jones, an English socialist, writing in the mid-1850s, asserted that

> my country is the world, and the nation I belong to is the most numerous of all: the nation of the oppressed. I acknowledge but two nationalities in existence, the tyrant and the slave. To me the world forms but two great camps: the rich and the poor — and in the latter I am a soldier.[17]

International relations, therefore, were depicted in terms of a transnational class struggle which was seen to take precedence over states and nations. Marx argued, for example, that international war was a product of 'governmental humbug' and was designed 'to defer the struggle of classes, and to be thrown aside as soon as the class struggle bursts out into civil war. Class struggle is no longer able to disguise itself in a national uniform, the national governments are as one against the proletariat.'[18] The international system was seen by the early socialists to be divided into two classes. Conflicts between states were considered to arise from superficial disputes within the international bourgeoisie which could, when necessary, always be resolved in the face of a revolt by the proletariat. Marx observed, as a consequence, when the Prussians helped the French to crush the Paris Commune that it was 'only the old story. The upper classes always united to keep down the working classes.'[19]

As socialists saw it, then, the international arena generated a condition of double jeopardy for the working classes. On the one hand, in the event of international conflict, the major costs were invariably borne by the working classes, while, on the other, the transnational ties which existed between the international bourgeoisie were sufficiently strong to ensure that there would be transnational collaboration to crush any revolution by the working class within the state. Nevertheless socialists were, from the start, divided over their attitude to violence. Although some of the early socialists such Fourier were pacifists,[20] others, such as Proudhon saw war as a 'necessary albeit barbarous means of promoting justice'.[21] But as the international links between working-class movements developed, with the establishment of the Second International, socialists began to recognize that these links could be used simultaneously to prevent war and promote socialism.[22]

Moderate socialists such as Jean Jaurès and Kier Hardie began to argue at the beginning of the twentieth century that socialists 'can force even capitalists to live at peace. This they can do in a number of ways culminating in the threat of general strike and insurrection against any government that undertakes war.'[23] It was believed that a policy of systematic non-cooperation could not but fail to tame the ruling classes in all states. Only if this strategy failed did the moderates believe that a resort to force would be necessary. As Jaurès argued: 'We will not go to war against our brothers! We will not open fire on them. If the conflagration breaks out despite everything, there will be war on another front, there will be revolution.'[24] Working-class solidarity at the international level, then, was seen to provide the way forward, preventing war and promoting reform.

Although socialists continue to see the international arena in terms of transnational class divisions, events in the twentieth century have caused them to modify considerably this image. Four major developments have influenced the socialist assessment of the international arena. First, there was the traumatic collapse of transnational working-class solidarity at the outbreak of the First World War. Mandel observes how 'under the pretext of "national defence", Social Democracy in each country plunged into virtually unqualified support of the enterprise of plunder by its own imperialist bourgeoisie'.[25] This catastrophic development has subsequently been attributed, in part, to the 'class collaboration' which went on during the previous decades when the reformist influence of Social Democracy had prevailed. During this period, 'the multiplication of benefits the officials of the Social Democratic party enjoyed within the bourgeois-democratic state eventually created a community of interest between those officials and the bourgeoisie',[26] and this interest had the effect of undermining any revolutionary perspective and rendering socialist leaders incapable of modifying their established gradualist tactics.

The failure of working-class solidarity served to increase the divisions about how to promote socialism. After 1919, two of the major socialist theorists, Trotsky and Kautsky, were divided on this issue. While Trotsky believed that progress could only be made when a socialist revolution had taken place throughout the world, Kautsky argued that revolution was not necessary in the Western world and that socialism could be achieved using the tool of parliamentary democracy.[27] In both cases, however, the conviction that socialism was a realistic possibility remained firm.

The second development affecting the socialist view of the international arena was the Bolshevik Revolution in 1917. With the establishment of the Soviet Union, there was now a state in a position to protect socialism. The ability of the Soviet Union to survive in a capitalist world, however, was initially doubted by socialists. It was believed that the country would either revert back to capitalism under pressure from the capitalist states, or alternatively provide the springboard for a world-wide socialist revolution. Neither of these alternatives materialized. Instead, with the emergence of Stalin, the progress of socialism in the Soviet Union was seen to be virtually halted. Moreover, as a result of the Second World War, the Soviet Union was able to consolidate its power and extend its influence into Eastern Europe. However, although most socialists were appalled by developments under Stalin, they acknowledged that the Soviet Union provided the only real bulwark against the progress of capitalism.[28]

The third development which modified the socialist image of the international arena was the promotion of the United States to a position of hegemony at the end of the Second World War, with the result that capitalism strengthened its grip throughout the Western world. Non-socialist writers are prone to assert that the 'supreme event in socialist history was the Russian Revolution',[29] but many socialists have seen the consolidation of capitalism after the Second World War as being just as significant. As Anderson has observed, after that point, there could be no doubt that 'an oppressively stable, monolithically industrial, capitalist civilization was now in place'.[30] He goes on to assert that with this development, the horizon of future change has become closed so that the West has become locked into an 'interminably recurrent present'.[31] After the Second World War, he argues, 'the image or hope of revolution faded in the West. The onset of the Cold War, and the Sovietization of Eastern Europe, cancelled any realistic prospect of a socialist overthrow of advanced capitalism, for a whole historical period.'[32]

The fourth development affecting the socialist view of the international arena has been the rapid process of decolonization which has taken place since the Second World War. This has had the effect of radicalizing many sectors in the former colonies and revolutions in some areas has even brought into existence a new set of 'proto-socialist' states.[33]

As a result of these developments, socialist theorists have found it necessary to make radical amendments to the transnational class model. It has been recognized, first, that there must be much greater provision made in socialist analysis for the state as an autonomous entity and, second, that it is necessary to view the international arena in terms of interactions amongst a set of independent states.

Ever since the failure of the Second International either to prevent the First World War or to promote revolution, socialists have become increasingly aware of the independent power of the state to generate support and loyalty from the population. The consolidation of capitalism in the West after the Second World War reinforced the need to understand the ability of the capitalist bourgeois state to maintain its legitimacy despite its capacity to undermine the interests of the working classes. It is argued that the capitalist state has successfully ensured that the population views the world through ideological blinkers which justify and therefore perpetuate established social structures. For example, as Bunyan argues,

> the liberal-democratic belief that the state acts as a neutral arbiter has an important legitimating function since it implies that the state acts for the benefit of society as a whole. Working-class political action is therefore not seen for what it is, a confrontation of capital and labour, but as action against the interests of all. In this way the class nature of democratic institutions and of the state are continually denied as a reality.[34]

Merleau-Ponty asserts, as a consequence, that 'to understand and judge a society, one has to penetrate its basic structure to the human bond upon which it is built'.[35] When this is done, it is found that capitalism 'not only tolerates but even requires violence'.[36] Using a variety of ideological techniques, the capitalist state has successfully diverted attention from this fact. First, the implications of structural violence have been systematically obscured.[37] Structural violence occurs when a social system promotes needless suffering. So, pain and death associated with malnutrition and illness constitutes structural violence in any system where a redistribution of resources could have alleviated these afflictions. Markovic notes that while the ruling class in capitalist states

> demand that the people use only peaceful means, they seem to overlook the fact that the whole system is based on enormous amounts of built-in, institutionalized 'structural' violence. In contrast to direct, physical violence that hits individuals in a dramatic immediately observable

way, structural violence affects large masses of people indirectly, slowly, invisibly through the system and its legal institutions.[38]

He goes on to assert that the number of people who die from starvation and pollution 'is certainly no less than the number of those who are killed by bullets'.

Socialists have also argued, however, that the capitalist state has been remarkably successful at ensuring that acts of physical violence designed to protect capitalism are defined as legitimate, while similar acts designed to undermine capitalism are deemed to be illegitimate. Chomsky and Herman argue, for example, that

> the words 'terror' and 'terrorism' have become semantic tools in the Western world. In their dictionary meaning, those words refer to 'intimidation' by the 'systematic use of violence' as a means of both governing and opposing existing governments. But current Western useage has restricted the sense, on purely ideological grounds, to the retail violence of those who oppose the established order.[39]

Elsewhere, Chomsky has argued that Western scholars have also become deeply implicated in this process and that scholarship has as a consequence been subordinated to the needs and interests of a counter-revolutionary position.[40]

Socialists argue, therefore, that the development of capitalism has been accompanied by a systematic process of mystification which helps to maintain the status quo. The ruling classes have benefited from an ideology which associates insecurity with the danger of internal and external threats of violence. The state is then depicted as the primary instrument for minimizing this danger and thereby generating security. However, once the ideological gloss has been peeled away, it can be seen, argues the socialist, that for the vast majority of people, a major source of insecurity derives from the threat of structural and physical violence created or endorsed by the state. At best, then, the state establishes what Galtung calls 'negative peace' which is characterized by an absence of physical violence. Socialists, however, are interested in 'positive peace' where both physical and structural violence has been eradicated.[41]

In addition to paying closer attention to the autonomy of the state, socialists have also begun to pay more attention to the international setting in which states now reside. As Baran and Swezy acknowledge 'from its earliest beginnings in the Middle Ages, capitalism has always been an international system'. They go on to argue, moreover, that many features of capitalism cannot be understood if it is not examined in its international context. 'In particular, it would be quite impossible to understand the role of armed force in capitalist society without placing the international character of the system at the very centre of the analytical focus.'[42] Lenin, of course, played an important role in moving socialism beyond the transnational class model when he developed his theory of imperialism. In the first place, he acknowledged that conflicts between capitalist states could be structural rather than superficial in character, and in the second place, he identified that there could be objective sources of conflict between the proletariat at the centre and the periphery of the capitalist world economy.[43]

Since the Second World War, however, socialism has found it necessary to extend beyond Lenin's position. It is apparent now that the international arena is made up of both capitalist and proto-socialist states. The progress of socialism is proving to be incremental, as a world-wide revolution has failed to materialize. Nascent revolutions, therefore, are occurring in an international arena made up of states adhering to competing ideologies. As a consequence, socialists have had to define security issues in the context of a world made up of capitalist and proto-socialist states. They acknowledge, therefore, that superimposed on the transnational class divisions is a state system which can be divided into three separate categories. There is a First World, led by the United States, made up of liberal bourgeois states; a Second World, led by the Soviet Union, made up of industrialized proto-socialist states; and a Third World, made up of ex-colonial states. Socialists accept that these three worlds are interdependent and that, as a consequence, the security problems in all three worlds are interrelated, although there is considerable disagreement about the structure of this interdependent world.[44]

Having examined the emergence of the analytical framework currently used by socialists, we can go on to explore their assessment of contemporary security problems. The assessment takes place under two major headings. The first relates to the security of the working classes. Socialists believe that the security of individuals in the working classes in all societies is increasingly being jeopardized by the universal strengthening of state institutions. The second area of problems relates to the steady encroachment of capitalist imperialism which is posing a constant and growing threat to the established forces of socialism around the world. We shall look first at the problems associated with the growing power of the state in the First World.

In the years immediately after the Second World War, it quickly became apparent that the West, far from succumbing to the forces of revolution, was embracing capitalism with renewed enthusiasm. Socialists, as a consequence, began to focus on the hegemony of bourgeois ideology, paying particular attention to Gramsci, as a means of explaining the acquiescence of the proletariat in this development. By the late 1960s, however, as the capitalist world economy began to falter, and there was growing evidence of urban decay and disaffection in the Western world, socialists once again turned their attention to the role of the state as a repressive agent for capitalism. It was argued that Gramsci had overestimated the capacity of the bourgeois state to maintain the consent of the masses and overlooked both the sophistication of the technology of repression in the West and the widespread acceptance of the coercive powers of the liberal state.[45]

Socialists are now recognizing that the instruments of repression in the West represent a fundamental and growing problem to the promotion of an egalitarian society. Liberal-democratic theory has, of course, never denied that the state possesses instruments of coercion, but they are always depicted as 'operating over and above the different sectional interests within society'.[46] Socialists are now drawing attention to the fact that the military, the police, the prisons and the courts can not be seen as 'subservient to government, as the liberal democratic notion suggests, but rather as interdependent centres of state power'.[47] As a consequence, these instruments of repression serve the interests of capitalism. Bunyan argues that a survey of these institutions 'demonstrate class interests explicitly present in their creation and imbued in their later practices'.[48] He goes on to assert, moreover, that, since the early 1960s, these agencies have all begun to use new and more sophisticated methods and have adopted an increasingly aggressive role. The underlying causes of this development 'are located in the general crisis faced by British capitalism which, although centred on economic instability, produces equally serious political and social dislocation'.[49]

The liberal democratic state, however, confronts an obvious dilemma in situations where the repression required to maintain the existing social and economic order has to be applied against protesting citizens. The dilemma has encouraged the growth of what Ackroyd *et al.* call a 'technology of political control' which is designed for 'situations in which the state's repression needs to be at least partially masked. The development of these technologies is therefore especially stimulated by major social conflicts which for political reasons cannot be "solved" by open repression by the state — which needs a velvet glove to sheath the iron fist.'[50] They argue that these technologies have been promoted in liberal democratic states and were developed very rapidly in the 1970s in context of Northern

Ireland where they 'provided the state with a subtler range of options than was previously available for damping down mass dissent'.[51] The technologies have subsequently been extended to mainland Britain and involve, for example, changes in the law, such as the 1974 Prevention of Terrorism Act in Britain, to restrict democratic rights; infiltration and electronic surveillance as a means of gathering information; the development of new riot-control weapons; and the establishment of new methods of interrogation. Ackroyd and her colleagues suggest that very little is heard about these developments because 'capitalist states just like Eastern European ones are intensely secretive about their means of repression'.[52]

Although socialists attach considerable importance to the development of these covert methods of repression, they also acknowledge that the population is nevertheless aware of the overt power of the state. As a consequence, oppressed minority groups fail to revolt against their conditions because of a strategic calculation of the costs of doing so. Castells uses this argument to account for why there is no reaction against the authorities in the black ghettos in America where unemployment has risen to 70 per cent.

> Police repression is brutal and effective. Massive expenditures on weapons, manpower and training during the Nixon administration produced a real change. Blacks know that any attempt to revolt could lead to a massacre, and they have learned to appreciate this power relationship since the political impasse in the aftermath of the 1967–1968 riots. The indoctrination and training of 'special police' forces in addition to the regular police trained in riot control are a major threat to any community that might wish to express massive discontent in the future.[53]

It is argued by socialists that the increase in repression represents a general trend. As Bunyan argues:

> Britain is not alone in experiencing the increased attention of the repressive agencies — informed by many years of colonial and imperialist counter-insurgency being turned inwards against the people themselves. All the countries of the advanced capitalist world, most of whom have liberal-democratic political systems, are each in their own way reacting to the global challenge confronting capitalism.[54]

It is clear to socialists that, in the First World, sophisticated and elaborate exercises have already been designed to deal with any possible future political upheaval. In the Second World, on the other hand, it is generally acknowledged that, in the Soviet Union at least, the potential for future upheaval has been minimized as the result of past repression. It is argued that the proletariat in the Second World has been subjected to massive repression in the years after the Bolshevik Revolution. Socialists are, however, unable to agree on their explanation of this phenomenon. They accept that the state in Eastern Europe and the Soviet Union has been bureaucratized and that the members of the bureaucracy have used their power monopoly in order to acquire material and social privileges which they are determined to defend. They accept also that the bureaucracy is 'a parasitic formation on the body of the wage-earning class',[55] and has consistently relied on repression to maintain control. On the other hand, socialists are unable to agree about whether the bureaucracy constitutes a distinctive class and whether or not the economy is still capitalist in formation.[56] In any event, as in the First World, the state is seen to justify its use of repression in terms of 'defending the Soviet people from the attack from without and within'.[57]

But it is also admitted that there have been vast changes in the Eastern bloc since the death of Stalin with 'the elimination of mass terror' and a 'considerable reduction in the power wielded by the apparatus of repression'.[58] Socialists also argue that, despite the phenomenon of Stalinism, progress has been made towards a socialist society in the Eastern bloc. Throughout all the repression by the state, efforts have been made to increase the sense of security experienced by the proletariat by way of housing, health facilities, and employment. Anderson argues that Stalinism has not eliminated the 'slow work of socialist construction'.[59] But the cost of Stalinism in terms of the development of socialism has, nevertheless, been enormous. As Mandel observes:

> The most disastrous result of Stalinism, worse even than all the institutions of political repression and terror — although in part a function of these — is the huge process of depoliticization of the Soviet working class. This class, which represents, together with the American working class, the numerically largest sector of the world proletariat, has today an extremely low level of political interest and consciousness, although it tenaciously clings to whatever tangible remains of the conquests of the October revolution survive in its eyes, not the least of which is the much higher level of job security and much lower work rhythm than that which exists in capitalist societies.[60]

In the Second World, socialists argue that the instruments of repression, resulting in the depolitization of the proletariat, have been wielded by the state bureaucracy. We turn now to the Third World where socialists have also identified a growing militarization of the emerging political and social structures in these new countries. To some extent, however, socialists accept that this militarization is a legacy of colonialism because in most Third World countries

> both army and state were in a real sense created or restructured by the expansion of the central capitalist powers. Their military hierarchies are based on imposed organizational blueprints. The state machinery as a whole is weak, narrowly based and as much the artefact of international as of national domination. And to shore up its fragile structure the military function is inverted: the armed forces being more often used to repress internal dissent than to maintain international security.[61]

From the socialists' perspective, it is also necessary to note that militarization is not directly associated with the emergence of military regimes which often represents only a superficial political change. They argue that 'the military's formal participation in politics is less important than the question of how far the state superstructure is or is not held together by organized coercion'.[62] This form of militarization is seen to be increasing as Third World countries rely on repressive rather than ideological mechanisms for retaining control. This trend is reflected, for example, in the growing arms trade with the First World.[63]

Socialists have, moreover, never suggested that the military in Third World societies is simply the tool of the domestic ruling class, or of international capital. They acknowledge cases where the military has intervened to assist minority or peripheral groups. But it is asserted that the military establishment, none the less, has, in general, a

> vested interest in what military ideologists call 'national security' and what its opponents call state and class domination. The natural response of professional soldiers is to suppress class struggle when it appears because it divides the nation, undermines the international economic standing of the economy — causing flights of foreign capital — and imposes certain real costs — casualties, disruption of routine, threats to its structure and its monopoly of organized force — upon the military establishment itself.[64]

As Third World societies become progressively more integrated into the capitalist world economy, the perceived need for domestic stability increases. But ironically, as the integration takes place, so existing local conflicts are exacerbated. Although socialists are not agreed on how the Third World is integrated into the world economy, they acknowledge that the process has precipitated internal dislocation in Third World countries. Sunkel and Fuenzalida note how the link with the capitalist world sets off a 'process of internal polarization, involving the expropriation of local entrepreneurial groups, the disruption of indigenous economic activities and the concentration of property and income'.[65] It follows, therefore, that the level of repression must increase in proportion to economic development. As Senghaas argues:

> Under prevailing conditions, militarism within the Third World is more and more an inherent and constitutive dimension of growth-oriented accumulation processes. The more Third World economies are mobilized, the more social conflict potential will there be, and the more social warfare will there be waged to preserve the general pattern.[66]

The consequences for the urban and agricultural proletariat in such societies are seen to involve inevitable and substantial repression and a high probability that the authorities will successfully promote the 'political *demobilization* and the *depolitization* of the poor peasants the proletariat and the critical intelligentsia'.[67]

In addition to these militarized states on the periphery of the capitalist economy, it is also the case that in the period since 1945, a large percentage of the Third World's population has come to live in countries which have 'rejected more or less comprehensively capitalist modes of development and adopted various forms of socialist development strategy'.[68] As with the Soviet Union, progress towards socialism in these countries is proving to be tortuously slow. Progress is hindered, moreover, by the structures established to precipitate the revolution. As White indicates, they contribute to a 'pervasive militarisation of society, ideologically and institutionally, a heavy security consciousness which tends to retain its strength' after the actual level of threat has receded.[69] As a result, nationalism turns into chauvinism, which can contribute to isolationism, and the state is strengthened. Far from solidarity emerging amongst the proto-socialiast states, against all socialist expectations, there has been a spate of wars between them.[70]

In all three sectors of the world, then, the growing power of the state has been associated with an increased capacity to exercise repression. This development has diminished the sense of personal security experienced by members of the proletariat around the world; it has also had the effect of decreasing the willingness of the proletariat to engage in actions designed to reduce global inequality. The power of the state has, therefore, been expanded at the expense of socialism. But socialists also argue that this development needs to be seen in conjunction with the expansion of imperialism which has not only exacerbated the threat to the security of the proletariat, but has also endangered the progress already made towards a socialist world order.

Socialists have developed a very extended conception of imperialism. It is no longer concerned simply with the acquisition of overseas territory; it now involves the survival and expansion of world capitalism. Since the Second World War, the United States has been seen as the architect of imperialism, when it took on the role of managing the internationalization of capital. Smith and Smith observe that, because there is no world state to regulate the different requirements and competing interests of individual capitalist states, 'the functions of international regulation tend to be performed by a single nation state which has economic, political and military predominance. Coercion and influence enable this state to hold a position of hegemony.'[71] They note how the United States assumed this role after the Second World War and thereby created the conditions for the long period of expansion in the capitalist world economy which lasted until the early 1970s. In order to police and control the world economy, therefore, the United States, like Britain in the nineteenth century, had to maintain a position of military pre-eminence. But, as Baran and Sweezy argue, there is a major contrast between the United States and Britain because the latter did not display a 'mounting need for military strength'. They assert that, during the nineteenth century 'British experience would seem to support the view that the very existence of an undisputed leader would have the effect of stabilizing the needs of all the units in the capitalist hierarchy including those of the leader itself'.[72] By contrast, with the rise of the United States to hegemonic status, the arms industry has come to play a crucial role in its economy. Moreover, as Mandel has observed, there are no indications that the 'tendency towards a permanent war economy will diminish'.[73] Socialists are, however, divided as to the effect of this development on the capitalist world economy. Socialists have argued about whether weapons production has come to provide the major mechanism for regulating the capitalist world economy. But although there is no agreement as to the economic consequences of the arms economy, it is widely accepted that the impetus behind the creation of an arms economy has been the need to defend capitalism and to counteract socialism. As Baran and Sweezy assert, it is the 'rise of a world socialist system as a rival and alternative to the world capitalist system which accounts for the American arms economy'.[74] The arms economy is, in other words, seen to be a product of contemporary imperialism and has had a fundamental impact on the West's relationship with both the Second and Third Worlds.

Until recently, socialists have failed to develop an integrated view of imperialism, so as to include the Second as well as the Third World. Traditionally, socialists have focused on the relationship between the First and Third worlds, defining imperialism in terms of the links between the centre and the periphery of the capitalist world economy. There have, as a consequence, been few attempts to provide a theoretical link between the permanent arms economy and the strategic relationship between the United States and the Soviet Union. Socialists have had relatively little to say about the cold war or nuclear strategy. Davis, for example, acknowledges the pertinence of the 'critique of socialist theory for not generating an original analysis of the specificity of the strategic arms race or the transformation which it has wrought in world politics'.[75] However, for reasons which will become more apparent when we look at the socialist solutions, this hiatus began to be filled in the 1980s, with the deterioration in relations between the Soviet Union and the United States — a deterioration often designated by socialists as the onset of a second cold war.[76]

Socialists now generally accept that there is a very high degree of interdependence between internal repression within the First World, the difficulties generated by East–West conflict and the problems created by the imperialist link between the centre and periphery of the capitalist world economy. In the first place, socialists acknowledge that internal repression is often justified in terms of the East–West conflict. As Williams argues:

> What is now most dangerous in capitalist societies is the powerful attempt already too widely successful, to achieve a symmetry between the external (military) threat — directly identified as the Soviet Union — and the internal threat to the capitalist social order which is primarily constituted by an indigenous working class and its organizations and claims.[77]

At the other extreme, socialists have come to identify in recent years a close link between the cold war conflict and the relationship between the centre and periphery of the world economy. Bourgeois mystification has helped to dissociate these two tightly connected phenomena. But because of the close interrelationship, socialists deny that the bipolar conflict between the United States and the Soviet Union can be seen as the 'dominant level' of world politics. Instead, it is considered more accurate to place the conflict in the context of a world-wide, violent and protracted transition from capitalism to socialism — which is how revolutionary Marxists have always conceptualized the modern age. Davis asserts, therefore, that the cold war should be characterized as a 'process of *permanent revolution* arising out of the uneven and combined development of global capitalism'.[78]

The cold war, argue the socialists, should always have been characterized in these terms, but the link between the East–West conflict and Third World imperialism has only become clearly defined since the 1970s when the United States openly sought a 'trade-off between nuclear parity and the containment of Third World revolution. "Linkage" in the jargon of Kissinger meant the US codification of the strategic arms status quo in exchange for Soviet ratification of the socio-political status quo in the Third World.'[79] Such a bargain, however, could never be implemented, according to the socialists, because neither side were in a position to deliver their part of the bargain. The Soviets, for their part, had no direct control over revolutionary movements in the Third World. Far from revolutions being stemmed, as Halliday demonstrates, the 1980s came to be characterized in terms of a 'revolutionary upsurge' and 'Third World defiance'.[80] By the same token, as socialists have often observed, the arms economy in the United States has given rise to a military industrial complex and a host of vested interests which are opposed to any attempt to disband the arms race. By the early 1970s, despite talk of 'parity' the plans for a new round of weapons systems, which was to materialize in the 1980s, were already in place.

In earlier decades, the West had used two major mechanisms to stem Third World revolution. The first was military assistance. Since the Second World War, there has been a massive transfer of arms by the West to the Third World. The arms trade is seen by socialists to be a defining characteristic of imperialism. Albrecht and Kaldor argue that it is the cement which holds the world economy together. They believe that the 'acquisition of modern military technology is one mechanism whereby third-world countries are drawn into the global confrontation between the super-powers and a world division of labour that limits the full potential of development'.[81] The second mechanism used to constrain revolution has been direct military intervention. Events in Vietnam in the late 1960s, however, served temporarily to render this mechanism domestically unacceptable. At the same time, as the Soviets moved towards parity, intervention also began to appear strategically dangerous.

From the socialist's perspective, therefore, the second cold war was an orchestrated event designed, first, to allow the United States to justify its decision to move once again into a position of strategic superiority and, second to undermine the domestic and allied resistance to imperialist intervention. Once these restraints had been dealt with, it became possible once more for the United States to intervene in the Third World.[82] Socialists recognize, moreover, that the link between the cold war and imperialism is not new. As Wolfe argues,

> the architects of the postwar economic order devoted a tremendous amount of time to ensuring that political attitudes would keep pace with material transformations. In essence, they were forced to flame the Cold War in order to bring about the required transformations in both the structure of the U.S. state and popular attitudes compatible with U.S. domination over the world economy.[83]

The problems associated with the threat of nuclear destruction cannot, at the analytical level, be separated from those relating to the general exploitation of the proletariat. As Davis argues, 'the strategic arms race must be conceived as a complex, regulative instance of the global class struggle'.[84]

Solutions

As indicated earlier, socialists have always been divided about how to bring about a socialist world order. Before the Second World War, the division was between advocates of revolution and reform. Since 1945, however, with the consolidation of the capitalist world economy, the split has been exacerbated and complicated by a debate between socialists who believe that social forces throughout the world are dictated by a world capitalist system and those who believe that the course of human history can be influenced by human intervention. The former group believe that capitalism will only be destroyed as the result of the historical working out of its internal contradictions. For these socialists there can, therefore, be no immediate transition to socialism and only with the 'demise of the dominance of the world-capitalist system, envisaged over a time-span of centuries rather than decades, can such a transition be on the historical agenda'.[85] The latter group of socialists insist that it is naively deterministic to believe that historical forces must necessarily work in favour of socialism. It ignores the fact that the human world is an open or unfinished system and the same radical contingency which threatens it with discord also rescues it from the inevitability of disorder and prevents us from despairing of it, providing only that one remembers its various machineries are actually men and tries to maintain and expand man's relation to man.[86]

These activists divide into two categories. First, there are those who advocate a strategy of world revolution. From this perspective, 'the solution lies not in opting out of the world economy, but in smashing it'.[87] In the same vein, Callinicos attacks Althusser, a major French Marxist, for his failure to examine the unity of theory and practice and to show how to 'detonate an explosion that would bring down the capitalists'.[88] Second, there are those socialist reformers who believe that socialism can be achieved incrementally. These reformers consider that in the First World, the revolutionary position is 'essentially utopian' because it offers 'little if any help in a real-world situation'.[89] Given the modern techniques available to counter-insurgency forces, the attempt to promote violent revolution in any urban centre of an advanced capitalist society is considered to be 'doomed'.[90] These socialists argue in favour of a democratic reform strategy. Oppenheimer, for instance, asserts:

> In general I agree with Christopher Lasch that the political left must create a party of its own, not primarily for electoral activity as such, nor even to register protest votes or try to act as a lever on the other parties. Rather such a party must try to 'introduce socialists perspectives into political debate, to create a broad consciousness of alternatives not embraced by the present system, to show both by teaching and example that life under socialism would be preferable . . . [91]

Such a posture contains echoes of Kautsky and it is unsurprising that there is a new interest in his writings, after years of neglect.[92]

Despite their strategic differences, socialist reformers and revolutionaries agree that it is vital to identify, monitor and take advantage of the systemic or structural contradictions which can be observed in capitalist societies. Socialists have, in consequence, paid considerable attention to the 'deep conflict between the legitimation and accumulation functions of the capitalist state'.[93] The modern state, it is argued, is required to perform two functions which are quite contradictory. On the one hand, it is required to promote the accumulation of capital, while on the other, it must obtain and maintain mass loyalty to the system. Repression, for example, which is designed to protect the process of capital accumulation inevitably has the effect of undermining the legitimation function of the state. At the same time, attempts to promote legitimacy take place at the expense of the accumulation function.[94] The pursuit of both functions, moreover, involve heavy expense and can generate a vicious circle which thereby precipitates a fiscal crisis for the state.[95]

Liberals have been very impressed by the socialist line of argument.[96] They have recognized and acknowledged, moreover, that when the legitimacy of the state is questioned, members of the proletariat may become more politically active. Certainly Huntington, a prominent liberal, has frankly admitted, 'some of the problems of governance in the United States today stem from an excess of democracy . . . Needed, instead, is a greater degree of moderation in democracy'.[97] Socialists have come to recognize that they must resist this desire for moderation and instead exploit the contradiction between accumulation and legitimation so as to create sufficient space to manoeuvre their own policies into position.

Internal repression, the arms trade and nuclear weapons have all been recognized by socialists as critical issues around which it should be possible to mobilize mass support and thereby exacerbate the conflict between accumulation and legitimacy. Yet there are no illusions that the task of mobilizing support will be easy. As Taylor and Pritchard note: 'The ethos of our contemporary state capitalist, bureaucratic society encourages the view that complex matters should be "left to the experts" and that ordinary people should concern themselves only with their own immediate problems and development.'[98] Socialists, therefore, have formed a particular interest in the reasons why initially successful mass movements such as the Campaign for Nuclear Disarmament collapsed after a promising start. Taylor and Pritchard came to the conclusion that

> because the movement in the U.K. was one of middle class radicalism *par excellence* and was therefore largely unconcerned with the basic issues of jobs, investment alternatives and so on, it failed to make the crucial breakthrough to the working class. It thus failed to build up sufficiently powerful forces to confront the massive vested interests of the military/industrial State complex.[99]

The failure could, from the perspective of the advocates of revolution, have been anticipated. As far as they are concerned, such movements always run the danger of cooptation.[100] They could, for example, cite the way that corporate interests in the United States have attempted, by means of judicious funding, to structure the development of the peace movement in a way which deflects attention and criticism away from the existing socio-economic structures of capitalist society.[101] Because of the danger of cooptation, Mandel argues that '[i]t is better to combat all the seeds of reformism, gradualism and class collaboration from their inception, for their ultimate fruits will indeed be bitter ones. The threat is not indigestion but generalized cancer.'[102] As far as Mandel is concerned, the 'masses of the world have to take the matter of the nuclear arms race out of the hands of governments, into their own hands. The problems of nuclear disarmament will not be solved at diplomatic conference tables but in the streets and the factories.'[103] It follows, therefore, that only a revolution by the working class can resolve problems associated with repression and armaments.

This traditional viewpoint, which defines all issues in terms of a class struggle, has been subjected to substantial criticism, not only on the grounds that the objective is Utopian, but also on the grounds that it reflects an inadequate theoretical analysis of contemporary capitalism. Socialists of a more reformist predisposition have been impressed by the growth of grass-roots social movements which cut across class divisions. The peace movement is viewed as a prime example of such a movement. Socialist activists have begun to set about identifying ways of fostering this opposition to government defence policies. A central suggestion has been that socialists must accept the plurality of interests aroused by this issue and avoid 'counterposing and isolating themselves from broader currents of opinion by an exclusive and one-sided insistence on their own objectives and forms of struggle'.[104] To avoid the dangers of cooptation, however, socialists also acknowledge that there must be full recognition given to socialist modes of analysis and mobilization.[105] It is argued, against Mandel, that success can be helped by a broad-based assault, since the state is more likely to accede to demands when it can be shown that a failure to do so would precipitate a widespread erosion of its legitimacy. The peace movement is seen to be a particularly instructive example of socialist activism which has combined the use of democratic channels in conjunction with non-violent resistance. Hinton has argued that

> the 'politics of resistance' are, indeed fundamental to the prospects of the peace movement. Direct action has done much to force the nuclear issue onto the political agenda and keep it there. Non-violent resistance plays an important part in exposing the unacceptable face of Thatcherism ... Moreover, the peace movements' politics of resistance have provided a forcing house for ideas of radical change ... it would

be unwise to underestimate the contribution that the less orthodox parts of the peace movement may have to make to the future of radical politics.[106]

In conjunction with the activists, socialist theorists have also been exploring the theoretical implication of these new demands to extend the principles of democratic control to the field of national defence. The implications are seen to be serious. As Laclau and Mouffe argue: 'Discourse concerning defense policy — traditionally the enclosed preserve of restricted military and political elites — is thus subverted as the democratic principle of control lodges itself at its heart.'[107] To understand this process, however, the new theorists argue that it is necessary for contemporary analysis to be extended substantially beyond the original reformist ideas expressed by Kautsky and Gramsci. In contrast to the revolutionaries, Laclau and Mouffe argue that their theoretical analysis leads them to conclude that

> [t]he achievement of socialism, therefore, does not arise from an absolute moment, represented by a radical break consisting of the seizure of power. It must instead be the result of a series of partial ruptures through which the ensemble of relations of forces existing in a society will be transformed.[108]

This line of argument, therefore, leads them to reject the dichotomy usually drawn between reform and revolution. They assert:

> The defense of a democratic socialism, then, has nothing to do with a necessary 'peaceful road' or a slow accumulation of reforms. What it refers to is a novel conception of the radicalization and the politicization of social struggles, one which enlarges the field of confrontation and struggle to the whole of civil society.[109]

Socialists in the First World, therefore, need to radicalize and politicize issues associated with the arms race and repression in a way which transcends class divisions. In doing so, according to this view, they are helping to rupture the existing capitalist system and promote a socialist democracy.

In the West, therefore, there are disagreements amongst socialists about whether the problems associated with peace and security should be solved by reform, rupture or revolution. At first sight, none of these options appear to be available in the Second World. In the Soviet Union, because the population has been largely depoliticized, the state does not confront the difficulties associated with maintaining legitimacy found in the West. There is, therefore, considerable pessimism about resolving existing problems in this proto-socialist state. Socialists are agreed, however, that change cannot be imposed from outside. Attempts by governments in the West to precipitate internal changes in the Soviet Union can only prove to be counter-productive or ineffective. Socialists in the Soviet Union, such as Roy Medvedev, moreover, are extremely sceptical of efforts made by such governments which he argues are primarily interested in defending the interests of the ruling classes in their own states. He goes on:

> Right-wing circles in the West, on the contrary, exploit any shortcomings in the USSR and any acts of oppression by the Soviet State for their own demagogic ends; their aim is not to assist the victory of a 'socialism with a human face' but to discredit both socialism and communism, and thereby strike a blow above all against the forces of the Left in their own countries.[110]

Although he acknowledges that world public opinion can help to curb repression in the Soviet Union, he insists that 'the prime impulse towards democratization in the USSR must necessarily come from within Soviet society itself'.[111] The population, however, he argues, has 'learnt to become silent' so that there is no possibility of any 'mass movement capable of bringing about any real political change'. The movement towards social democracy will only come as the result of 'certain initiatives "from above" supported "from below" '.[112] Although he is not optimistic about immediate or rapid developments in this direction, he believes that the 'mass discontent' which can be found within the Soviet population will have an effect on the Soviet leadership in 'very complicated and round-about ways'.[113].

At the other extreme to this reformist solution lie the revolutionaries, such as Mandel, who insist that the idea of reforms initiated 'from above' is an illusion and could never represent more than 'concessions made by the ruling caste in order to defend and perpetuate its privileges and its power'.[114] Only a politically active and conscious working class can, from Mandel's perspective, precipitate change. Dissenters in the Soviet Union must, therefore, look for ways to politicize the Soviet workers. The task of socialists in the West, meanwhile, is to struggle for a socialist revolution to provide a new 'model' which can help to reactivate working-class consciousness in the Soviet Union.

Many socialists in the West are sceptical of such 'Utopian' solutions.

They recognize that it would, as Deutscher notes, be extremely difficult to activate the depolicized worker who is under the 'watchful eye of the ubiquitous and hostile state apparatus'.[115] They are, therefore, much more impressed by the evidence provided by Medvedev of 'polemical disputes and factional struggles within the higher echelons of the Central Committee of the CPSU'.[116] They note, moreover, that the experience of Czechoslovakia in 1968 also confirms the view that, in practice, change can come 'from above'. Nevertheless, such examples are also seen as no more than straws in the wind and, overall, socialists remain pessimistic about any immediate prospects for significant change in the Eastern bloc.

While socialists find little room for hope in the Second World, events in the Third World have provided the grounds for considerable optimism. Some of the most resounding defeats of capitalism since the Second World War have taken place on the periphery of the capitalist world economy. The reason for this development is seen to be self-evident. As Davis argues:

> It is not necessary to share an eschatalogical vision of the World Revolution to recognize that the development of capitalism on a planetary scale has likewise internationalized the forces of revolt against it. True, the emergence of these forces displays no simple, evolutionary tendency, but rather the most baffling pattern of contradiction, retrogression and sudden rupture. Yet it seems to me indisputable that the major trend in modern history has been the tectonic action of these elemental class struggles within and upon the international state system.[117]

The major instrument for waging this class struggle in the Third World has been guerrilla warfare which has been seen to be 'destroying the last vestiges of feudalism and of the old colonialism'. Taber goes on to argue that guerrilla warfare,

> in its total effect, is creating new alignments and a new confrontation of powers that vitally relates and yet transcends the Cold War. It is a confrontation in its essence, of the world's *haves* and the world's *have-nots* of the rich nations and the poor nations. It is reshaping the world that we have known, and its outcome may well decide the form and substance of the foreseeable future, not only in the present theatres of war, which are vast and shadowy, but everywhere.[118]

Although Taber has been criticized for endeavouring to view guerrilla warfare as an undifferentiated phenomenon,[119] the fact remains that since he was writing, in the late 1960s, guerrilla warfare has continued to provide a remarkably successful instrument for the advocates of socialist resolution. The success, moreover, has not been attributed primarily to a successful application of military strategy, but to the capacity of the guerrilla to mobilize the population. For politicization to be successful, however, the preconditions must be right:

> The guerrilla is subversive of the existing order in that he is the disseminator of revolutionary ideas; his actions lend force to his doctrine and show the way to radical change. Yet it would be an error to consider him as being apart from the seedbed of revolution. He himself is created by the political climate in which revolution becomes possible.[120]

From this perspective, then, the primary goal of the guerrilla fighter is to 'raise the level of revolutionary anticipation and then of popular participation, to the crisis point'.[121] Politicization can, moreover, take place directly. Kaldor notes, for example, how the development of counter-insurgency tactics in Brazil in the early 1960s required a decentralization of command and, as a result, the technical role of the sergeants was raised without any corresponding social and economic upgrading. As a result, they began to make common cause with the trade unions.[122] But despite this emphasis on the importance of politicization in the theory of guerrilla warfare, socialists of a gradualist predisposition remain extremely sceptical of the relevance of guerrilla warfare for many Third World countries. In Latin America, for example, it is argued that in the appeals for guerrilla warfare 'the analysis of social problems is allotted only a little space. The tendency is rather to limit or even suppress altogether studies to deal with class structure and relations.'[123] In the absence of any theoretical analysis of how the structure of society affects politics, the guerrilla fighter is destined to fail. Following the death of Che Guevara, the gradualists in Latin America were more than ever convinced that the road to socialism must be of a reformist character.[124]

No matter how the structure of a society is analysed, however, socialists of all persuasion recognize that imperialism or the international forces of capitalism represent a major threat to socialism in the Third World. Guerrilla warfare has provided a major obstacle to capitalist imperialism, but socialists acknowledge that very often these revolutionary movements would not have been successful without the presence and sometimes the assistance of the Soviet Union. Mandel, for example, has noted how 'Soviet nuclear strength affords a measure of protection to anti-imperialist revolutions'.[125] And as Muslow sees it, the international divide between East and West has been vital for those countries attempting a socialist transition on the periphery. The Eastern bloc has been able to provide the military hardware necessary for Third World revolutionaries to take power and keep it. Muslow accepts that this assistance has its pitfalls but he sees it as providing a genuine alternative to the forces of capitalism.[126] Trotsky argued that the Soviet bureaucracy would prove to be an unequivocally counter-revolutionary force in the international arena. But Anderson insists that, in practice, although the role of the Soviet Union has proved contradictory, it has assisted revolutionary parties in the Third World. As a result, 'paradoxically, the exploited classes *outside* the Soviet Union may have benefited more directly from its existence than the working class inside the Soviet Union'.[127]

Finally, it is necessary to turn to the emergence since 1945 of conflicts between socialist states. Socialists accept that it is essential to examine the specific circumstances which account for these conflicts, but that it is not necessary to find grounds for justifying them. Caldwell argues, for example, that 'we now have revolutionary regimes in power, which can in a certain sense look after themselves — they don't need apologists, they don't need voluntary ambassadors, they've got their own apparatus of propaganda and their own wireless; they're installed in power and, one assumes, irreversibly so'.[128] These states are not yet socialist. They are in a state of transition and, therefore, it is to be expected that there will be distortions in their attempt to pursue socialist policies. By the same token, they are operating in an international arena of states, and inevitably, this also affects policy formation. As Kleinen observes, 'the current turmoil in Southeast Asia is best understood in terms of the kind of rivalries inherent in an international order organized around states'.[129] From the socialist perspective, it is unreasonable to demand all the benefits of socialism from a world where many of the necessary preconditions have yet to materialize.

Notes

1. Marx and particularly Engels, however, were fascinated by the mechanics of war. See B. Semmel (ed.), *Marxism and the Science of War*, Oxford, Oxford University Press, 1981.
2. See the discussion by E.P. Thompson in E.P. Thompson and D. Smith, *Protest and Survive*, Harmondsworth, Penguin Books, 1980.

3. C.J. Friedrich, *Inevitable Peace*, Cambridge, Mass., Harvard University Press, 1948, p. 210.
4. K.E. Miller, *Socialism and Foreign Policy: Theory and Practice in Britain to 1931*, The Hague, Martinus Nijhoff, 1967, p. 2.
5. F.H. Hinsley, *Power and the Pursuit of Peace*, Cambridge, Cambridge University Press, 1967, p. 112.
6. M. Markovic, *The Contemporary Marx*, Nottingham, Spokesman Books, 1974, p. 154.
7. G. Lichtheim, *The Origins of Socialism*, London, Weidenfeld & Nicolson, 1968, p. 5.
8. O.C. Cox, *Capitalism as a System*, New York, Monthly Review Press, 1964, p. 214.
9. F. Schurmann, *The Logic of World Power*, New York, Pantheon Books, 1974, p. 325.
10. H. Draper, *Karl Marx's Theory of Revolution: State and Bureaucracy*, Vol. 1, New York, Monthly Review Press, 1971, pp. 244–5.
11. Ibid., p. 190.
12. Schurmann, op. cit., p. 131.
13. C. Cockburn, *The Local State: Management of Cities and People*, London, Pluto Press, 1977, p. 42.
14. Quoted in Friedrich, op. cit., p. 211.
15. Ibid.
16. Cited in Markovic, op. cit., p. 166.
17. Cited in Miller, op. cit., p. 17.
18. Cited in V. Kubálková and A. Cruickshank, *Marxism-Leninism and the Theory of International Relations*, London, Routledge & Kegan Paul, 1980, p. 49.
19. Draper, op. cit., p. 259.
20. Lichtheim, op. cit., p. 73.
21. Ibid., p. 86.
22. The Second International was established in Paris in 1889. See J. Joll, *The Second International 1889–1914*, London, Routledge & Kegan Paul, 1974.
23. K.N. Waltz, *Man, the State and War*, New York, Columbia University Press, 1959, p. 128.
24. Cited in E. Mandel, *From Stalinism to Eurocommunism*, trans. J. Rothschild, London, New Left Books, 1978, p. 9. But see, also, the view on Jaurès of Friedrich, op. cit., pp. 214–5.
25. Mandel, op. cit., p. 9.
26. Ibid., p. 10.
27. For a very critical account of parliamentary socialism, see P. Foot, 'Parliamentary Socialism' in N. Harris and J. Palmer, *World Crisis: Essays in Revolutionary Socialism*, London, Hutchinson, 1971.
28. For a brief discussion of the dilemma confronting many socialists following the Second World War, see J. O'Neill's introduction to M. Merleau-Ponty, *Humanism and Terror*, trans. J. O'Neill, Boston, Beacon Press, 1969 (originally published in 1949).
29. J. Vaizey, *Capitalism and Socialism: A History of Industrial Growth*, London, Weidenfeld & Nicolson, 1980, p. 210.
30. P. Anderson, 'Modernity and Revolution', *New Left Review*, **144**, 1984, 96–113, p. 106.

230   *Global security problems and solutions*

31. Ibid., p. 109.
32. Ibid., p. 107. The same argument is also made by E.H. Carr, 'The Russian Revolution and the West' *New Left Review*, **111**, 1978, 25–36.
33. The designation of states in the 'socialist' camp is very troubling for socialists, since none have yet achieved socialism. Proto-socialist is the term used by G. White *et al.* in *Revolutionary Socialist Development in the Third World*, Brighton, Wheatsheaf Books Ltd., 1983, p. 2.
34. T. Bunyan, *The History and Practice of the Political Police in Britain*, London, Julian Friedmann, 1976, p. 2.
35. Merleau-Ponty, op. cit., p. xiv.
36. Ibid., p. xiii.
37. The concept of structural violence was developed by J. Galtung 'Violence and Peace Research', *Journal of Peace Research*, 1969, 167–91.
38. Markovic, op. cit., p. 168.
39. N. Chomsky and E.S. Herman, *The Washington Connection and Third World Facism*, Vol. 1, Nottingham, Spokesman, 1979, p. 85.
40. N. Chomsky, *American Power and the New Mandarins*, London, Chatto & Windus, 1967, p. 26.
41. See Galtung, op. cit.
42. P.A. Baran and P.M. Sweezy, *Monopoly Capitalism*, Harmondsworth, Pelican Books, 1968, p. 178.
43. For a detailed account of Lenin's view of international relations, see Kubálková & Cruickshank, op. cit., pp. 84–109.
44. The debate centres on the degree of autonomy experienced by the proto-socialist states. Most socialists believe that these states could, in principle, develop self-reliant policies. But this position has been challenged by the world systems theorists led by I. Wallerstein, *The Capitalist World-Economy*, Cambridge, Cambridge University Press, 1979. For a review of this debate see C.K. Chase-Dunn (ed.), *Socialist States in the World System*, Beverly Hills, Sage Publications, 1982.
45. See P. Anderson 'The Antimonies of Antonio Gramsci', *New Left Review*, **100**, 1976–7, 5–80.
46. Bunyan, op. cit., p. 2.
47. Ibid., pp. 2–3.
48. Ibid., p. 289.
49. Ibid., p. 290.
50. C. Ackroyd *et al.*, *The Technology of Political Control*, 2nd edn, London, Pluto Press, 1980, p. xvii.
51. Ibid.
52. Ibid., p. xv.
53. M. Castells, *The Economic Crisis and American Society*, Oxford, Basil Blackwell, 1980, p. 248. This idea of strategic decision making in conflict situations is explored in D.F.B. Tucker, *Marxism and Individualism*, Oxford, Blackwell, 1980.
54. Bunyan, op. cit., p. 290.
55. E. Mandel, 'The Social Forces Behind Détente' in K. Coates (ed.), *Détente and Social Democracy*, Nottingham, Spokesman Books, 1975, p. 44.
56. For a review of the disputes see P. Corrigan, *et al.*, 'Bolshevism and the USSR', *New Left Review*, **125**, 1981, 45–60.
57. E.P. Thompson, 'Détente and Dissent' in Coates, op. cit., p. 124.

58. R. Miliband, 'Social Democracy' in Coates, op. cit., p. 62.
59. P. Anderson, 'Trotsky's Interpretation of Stalinism', *New Left Review*, **139**, 1983, 49–59, p. 57.
60. Mandel, 'The Social Forces Behind Détente', p. 46.
61. R. Luckham, 'Militarism: Force, Class and International Conflict' in M. Kaldor and A. Eide, *The World Military Order: The Impact of Military Technology on the Third World*, London, Macmillan, 1979, p. 243.
62. Ibid., p. 244.
63. See Kaldor and Eide, op. cit.
64. Luckham, op. cit., p. 251.
65. Cited in M.D. Wolpin, 'Arms Transfer and Dependency in the Third World' in A. Eide and M. Thee, *Problems of Contemporary Militarism*, London, Croom Helm, 1980, p. 251.
66. D. Senghaas, 'Military Dynamics in the Contemporary Context of Periphery Capitalism' in Eide & Thee, op. cit., p. 203.
67. Ibid., p. 199.
68. G. White, *et al.*, op. cit., p. vii.
69. Ibid., p. 6.
70. For a discussion of some of these conflicts, see W. Burchett, *The China, Cambodia, Vietnam Triangle*, London, Zed Press and Vanguard Books, 1981; A. Barnett and J. Pilger, *Aftermath: The Struggle of Cambodia and Vietnam*, K. Gough 'Roots of the Sino-Vietnamese Conflict: A Comment', *Monthly Review*, **35**, 1983–4, 40–52; J. Kleinen, 'Roots of the Sino-Vietnamese Conflict', *Monthly Review*, **34**, 1982–3, 16–36; M. Caldwell 'Background to the Conflict in Indo-China', *Monthly Review*, **31**, 1979, 1–20.
71. D. Smith and R. Smith, *The Economics of Militarism*, London, Pluto Press, 1983, p.47.
72. Baran and Sweezy, op. cit., p. 183.
73. E. Mandel, *Late Capitalism*, trans. J. De Bres, London, Verso, 1980, p. 274.
74. Baran and Sweezy, op. cit., p. 184. The argument in favour of the arms economy as a tool of economic management is developed by M. Kidron, *Western Capitalism Since the War*, London, Weidenfeld & Nicolson, 1968; the argument against is developed in Mandel, *Late Capitalism*.
75. M. Davis, 'Nuclear Imperialism and Extended Deterrence' in New Left Review (eds.), *Exterminism and Cold War*, London, Verso, 1982, p. 35.
76. See F. Halliday, *The Making of the Second Cold War,*, London, Verso, 1983.
77. R. Williams, 'The Politics of Nuclear Disarmament', *New Left Review*, **124**, 1980, 25–42, p. 30. See also P. Laurie, *Beneath the City Streets*, 2nd edn, St Albans, Granada, 1979.
78. Davis, op. cit., p. 44. For a discussion of 'combined and uneven development' see M. Lowy, *The Politics of Combined and Uneven Development*, London, Verso, 1981.
79. Davis, op. cit., p. 51.
80. Halliday, op. cit., Chapter 4. See also M. Ougaard, 'The Origins of the Second Cold War', *New Left Review*, **147**, 1984, 61–75.
81. U Albrecht and M. Kaldor, 'Introduction' in Kaldor and Eide, op. cit., p. 15.
82. See J. Petras, 'U.S. Foreign Policy: The Revival of Interventionism', *Monthly Review*, **31**, 9, 1980. 15–27.
83. A. Wolfe, 'Trilateralism and the Carter Administration: Changed World Realities

vs Vested Interests' in H. Sklar, (ed.), *Trilateralism*, Montreal, Black Rose Books, 1980, p. 537–8.
84. Davis, op. cit., p. 53. This argument runs directly counter to the argument put forward by E.P. Thompson in terms of exterminism. Thompson depicts the cold war in completely symmetrical terms. See E.P. Thompson, 'Notes on Exterminism, the Last Stage of Civilization', New Left Review, *Exterminism*. Most socialists argue that the United States precipitated the cold war and the arms race.
85. I. Wallerstein, cited in B. Muslow 'Is Socialism Possible on the Periphery', *Monthly Review*, **35**, 1983, 25–39, p. 25.
86. Merleau-Ponty, op. cit., p. 188.
87. A. Callinicos and J. Rogers, *Southern Africa After Soweto*, London, Pluto Press, 1977, p. 208, cited in Muslow, op. cit., p. 26.
88. A. Callinicos, *Althusser's Marxism*, London, Pluto Press, 1976, p. 103.
89. Muslow, op. cit., p. 26.
90. M. Oppenheimer, *The Urban Guerrilla*, Chicago, Quadrangle Books, 1969, p. 169.
91. Ibid., p. 171. The quotation from C. Lasch comes from 'The New Politics: 1968 and After', *New York Review of Books*, 11 July 1968.
92. See M. Salvadori, *Karl Kautsky and the Socialist Revolution 1880–1928*, New Left Books, 1979; and G.P. Steenson, *Karl Kautsky 1854–1938: Marxism in the Classical Years*, Pittsburgh, University of Pittsburgh Press, 1978.
93. A. Wolfe, 'Capitalism Shows Its Face: Giving up on Democracy' in Sklar, op. cit., p. 301.
94. The idea of a legitimation crisis has been developed by J. Habermas and C. Offe. For a review of their ideas see D. Held and J. Krieger, 'Accumulation, Legitimation and the States: The Ideas of Claus Offe and Jürgen Habermas' in D. Held *et al.*, *States and Societies*, Oxford, Martin Robertson, 1983.
95. J. O'Connor, *The Fiscal Crisis of the State*, New York, St Martin's Press, 1973.
96. See, for example, K. Middlemas, *Politics in Industrial Society*, London, André Deutsch, 1979, who draws on the work of Habermas and Offe.
97. Cited in Sklar, op. cit., p. 37.
98. R. Taylor and C. Pritchard, *The Protest Makers*, Oxford, Pergamon Press, 1980, p. 141.
99. Ibid., p. 140.
100. Cooptation occurs when the demand for reform is absorbed by the system without, in fact, implementing any change: see T. Mathiesen, *Law, Society and Political Action*, New York, Academic Press, 1980; and E. Dammann, *Revolution in the Affluent Society*, trans. Louise Makay, London, Heretic Books, 1984. Chapter 8.
101. T. Wright, *et al.*, 'Corporate Interests, Philanthropies and the Peace Movement' *Monthly Review*, **36**, 1985, 19–34.
102. E. Mandel, 'The Threat of War and the Struggle for Socialism', *New Left Review*, **141**, 1983, 23–50, p. 45.
103. Ibid., p. 44.
104. L. Magri, 'The Peace Movement and European Socialism', *New Left Review*, **131**, 1982, 5–19, p. 6.
105. R. Williams, 'The Politics of Nuclear Disarmament', *New Left Review*, **124**, 1980, 25–42, p. 37.
106. J. Hinton, 'The Case for the Defence', *Marxism Today*, April 1985, 15–18, p. 18.

107. E. Laclau and C. Mouffe, *Hegemony and Socialist Strategy*, trans. W. Moore and P. Cammack, London, Verso, 1985, p. 165.
108. E. Laclau and C. Mouffe, 'Socialist Strategy: Where Next?' *Marxism Today*, January 1981, 17–22, p. 20.
109. Ibid., p. 20.
110. R. Medvedev, 'Problems of Democratization and Détente' in Coates, op. cit., p. 22.
111. Ibid., pp. 26–7.
112. Ibid., p. 18.
113. Ibid., p. 20.
114. Mandel, 'The Social Forces Behind Détente', p. 45.
115. T. Deutscher, 'Reflections on Roy Medvedev's "Democratization and Détente" ', in Coates, op. cit., p. 37.
116. Medveder, op. cit., p. 16.
117. Davis, op. cit., p. 44.
118. R. Taber, *The War of the Flea: Guerrilla Warfare Theory and Practice*, St Albans, Paladin, 1970, p. 16–17. See also W.J. Pomeray (ed.), *Guerrilla Warfare and Marxism*, London, Lawrence and Wishart, 1969.
119. See T.H. Heinricken 'People's War in Angola, Mozambique and Guinea Bissau', *Journal of Modern African Studies*, **14**, 3, 1976.
120. Taber, op. cit., p. 19.
121. Ibid., p. 23.
122. M.H. Kaldor, 'The Significance of Military Technology' in Eide & Thee, op. cit., p. 229.
123. L.M. Vega, *Guerrillas in Latin America: The Technique of the Counter State*, London, Pall Mall Press, 1969, p. 3.
124. This attitude changed, however, after the success of the Sandinistas in Nicaragua in 1979. See W. Bollinger, 'Revolutionary Strategy in Latin America', *Monthly Review*, **34**, 1983, 27–33.
125. Mandel, 'The Threat of War', p. 29.
126. Muslow, op. cit., p. 35.
127. Anderson, 'Trotsky's Interpretation of Stalinism', p. 58.
128. Caldwell, op. cit., p. 2.
129. Kleinen, op. cit., p. 34.

10 Realist international security problems and solutions

Problems

Because realists believe that we have much to learn from the past, their views on contemporary security essentially distil the experience of statesmen who were responsible for maintaining the balance of power in Europe in previous centuries. For realists, in contrast to the liberals and socialists, the international arena has never been characterized by absolute insecurity and nor could it ever be compared to an anarchic state of nature. On the contrary, while statesmen have never managed to abolish war, realists argue that they have ensured that in the past states survived and experienced prolonged periods of peace. De Porte, for example, observes that the conspicuous characteristic of the European state system 'was that most of the member states survived all fluctuations of power, rank, and frontiers for 500 years or more. As all things changed, the states themselves persisted, along with the fundamental structure of the relations among them that made their survival possible.' He goes on to note that we take this 'truly extraordinary phenomenon' for granted simply because it is so familiar.[1]

In previous centuries realism, therefore, has played an important role in the way that security problems and solutions were formulated. It is still often assumed that realism continues to hold sway in the twentieth century.[2] But, as was indicated in Chapter 8, since 1945, realists have more often than not found themselves in the role of critic rather than spokesman. So, for example, they were from the outset opposed to the security policies initially implemented by the Soviet Union and the United States after the Second World War. But paradoxically, the conjunction of these policies had the unintended effect by the early 1960s of forcing both parties to accept a position of mutual deterrence which was compatible with the basic tenets of realism. The optimism which emerged, as a consequence, amongst realists proved to be short-lived. Realists are now pessimistic about the contemporary global security arena. But before surveying their current assessment it is necessary, first, to examine their general conception of security; second, to explain why they believed in 1945 that this conception was being abandoned; and third, to show how their view of global security was reassessed in subsequent years.

Realists believe that security can only be achieved if it is defined in relative terms. Osgood notes, for example, that 'national security, like danger, is an uncertain quality; it is relative not absolute'.[3] The reasoning behind this proposition has been examined by Kissinger, who argues that 'since absolute security for one power means absolute insecurity for all others, it is never obtainable as part of a "legitimate" settlement and can be achieved only through conquest'.[4] Security, therefore, requires all states to modify their own ambitions and find some means of reconciling their competing interests. For realists, therefore, international relations involves 'a delicate adjustment of power to power, a mutual exploration of intentions and capabilities, so as to find and preserve an order which, though fully satisfying to nobody, is just tolerable to all.[5] Kissinger draws out the implications of this position for the realist understanding of security. He argues that

> paradoxically, the generality of their dissatisfaction is a condition of stability, because were any one power *totally* satisfied, all others would have to be *totally* dissatisfied and a revolutionary situation would ensue. The foundation of a stable order is the *relative* security — and therefore the *relative* insecurity of its members.[6]

The condition of relative security is seen by realists to provide a solution to what they refer to as the security dilemma. The dilemma exists for so long as any party in the international arena persists in trying to achieve absolute security. Relative security can be achieved but only if all parties cooperate in the endeavour. The structure of the dilemma is clearly revealed when expressed in matrix form as in Figure 1.

	Antagonistic search for absolute security	Cooperative search for relative security
Antagonistic search for absolute security	Absolute insecurity for States A and B	Absolute insecurity for State B; absolute security for State A
Cooperative search for relative security	Absolute insecurity for State A; absolute security for State B	Relative security for States A and B

STATE A (right axis)

STATE B (bottom axis)

Figure 1: *A Matrix of the Security Dilemma*

Butterfield argues that the dilemma remains 'the basis of all tensions of the present day, representing even now the residual problem that the world has not solved, the hard nut that we still have to crack'.[7] Because of their fear and distrust of each other,. states always and yet self-defeatingly rely upon armaments to preserve their security. Butterfield believes that 'in international affairs it is this situation of Hobbesian fear which, so far as I can see, has hitherto defeated all the endeavour of the human intellect'.[8]

In so far as Butterfield is referring to the failure to achieve disarmament, all realists would unquestionably accept this pessimistic assessment. But relative security can be achieved provided that states are willing, as they often have been in the past, to rely on reciprocity and the balance of power. Herz has noted that

> the security dilemma, while always existing, could be attenuated. There were always a number and variety of competing powers from which one could select allies and with which one would try to balance would-be hegemony power: there was the possibility of shifting alignments; there were 'balancers' and mediators . . . it all amounted to a system with such strongly 'conservative' features that its members could feel relatively secure once certain minimum requirements of security — generally modest ones — had been satisfied.[9]

But the sense of balance and reciprocity which generates relative security and has traditionally ensured the survival of the international state system must, according to the realist, be based upon a political settlement which is mutually acceptable to the members of the international arena. This approach to the security dilemma first emerged clearly at the Treaty of Westphalia, which ended the Thirty Years War in 1648 and provided the basis for the contemporary international system. From that time onwards European states saw the balance of power

> as the most practical norm for the maintenance of European peace; they hoped that — given an order in which every state, large and small, had its reasonable claims satisfied — the united action of the community of satisfied states would then be strong enough to prevent such an equilibrium from being overthrown. They would defend it if only for reasons of self-interest.[10]

From an early stage in the development of the European state system, therefore, the balance of power, underpinned by reciprocal or mutual interest in the maintenance of the balance, was seen to provide the necessary foundation for the preservation of a society of states. But by the beginning of the twentieth century there were obvious signs that Europe would be unable, in the future, to maintain a stable global security system. The intervention of the United States into the First World War provided an early warning signal of the impending demise of the European balance, although the reluctance of the United States and the Soviet Union to move on to the centre of the world stage delayed the final collapse. By 1945, however, it was impossible to disguise that the European states had become pawns in a global security debate. The terminal stage in the decline of the European balance of power had been reached. Prescient observers had forecast this event in the nineteenth century, as they noted the growing power of Russia and the United States.[11] But no one had foreseen the sudden catastrophic and absolute decline of the European powers brought about by the Second World War.[12] With the collapse of the European balance of power, realists were very conscious that the problems of re-establishing a stable global security environment were formidable, if not insuperable. There were two major obstacles: first, the two emergent great powers had no interest in drawing upon realist principles; second, material changes militated against the possibility of restoring a balance of power.

The American distaste for the balance of power was well known. It had been publicized by President Wilson during the Versailles Peace Conference in 1919. This attitude persisted. It is reflected, for example, in a statement made in 1943 by Francis Sayre, an influential State Department official, concerning the prospects for a post-war peace settlement. He argued that 'if we are to build for lasting peace, we must abandon the nineteenth century conception that the road to peace lies through a nicely poised balance of power. Again and again world experience has told us that no peace dependent upon a balance of power lasts.'[13] The Americans were particularly suspicious of the way balance of power policies subordinated the interests of smaller states to the purpose of achieving a stable security environment. As a consequence, the American government failed to come to terms with Soviet demands for the creation of 'friendly' governments in Eastern Europe. Churchill, on the other hand, wanted to reach an accommodation with the Soviet Union on this issue before the war was over. He feared that in the absence of an agreement, naked power would decide matters. Churchill met Stalin, therefore, and established a spheres-of-influence solution which delimited the extent of Soviet control in Eastern Europe.[14] The Americans refused to sanction the agreement but failed to develop any contingency plans for post-war political and territorial arrangements.[15] After the war, they had no clear views about how to contend with the Soviet presence in Eastern Europe. Their desire to see the Soviets withdraw failed to come to grips with the realist contention that Soviet security interests would have to be accommodated if a stable security environment was going to be re-established.

There were also grounds for believing that the Soviet Union was unconcerned about the need to establish and maintain a new global balance of power. Soviet leaders were seen to dislike the mechanistic assumptions associated with a balance of power and considered that it stood in the way of the forces of history. The balance represented an impediment to change and was antithetical to Marxist teachings.[16] The two new dominant members of the international arena were, therefore, ideologically opposed to each other and unwilling to exercise the necessary restraint required to generate and preserve a society of states. It followed that international relations would be moving into a dangerous and unstable era. Neither of the two superpowers were interested in maintaining a balance of power; instead, their policies were dictated by what Morgenthau called nationalistic universalism, identified by the desire to spread a particular ideology across the globe. As Morgenthau saw it:

> This struggle for the minds of men, advancing rival claims to universal dominion on the part of different nations, has dealt the final, fatal blow to that social system of international intercourse within which for almost three centuries nations lived together in constant rivalry, yet under the common roof of shared values and universal standards of action. The collapse of that roof has destroyed the common habitat of the nations of the world, and the most powerful of them each assert the right to build it anew after their own pattern. Beneath the ruins of that roof lies buried the mechanism that kept the walls of that house of nations standing: the balance of power.[17]

Ironically, European realists were more concerned with the possibility that the United States might withdraw and return to an isolationist policy. It was clear that Britain could no longer provide the necessary ballast to act as a counter weight to the Soviet Union. To restore the balance of power in Europe, therefore, an alliance with the United States was essential. European realists began to urge the United States to retain its link with Europe. A very direct appeal was made by Churchill in his 'Iron Curtain' speech given in Fulton, Missouri in the spring of 1946. He identified a new type of security system. When confronted by a potentially dangerous enemy, he argued, 'the old doctrine of the balance of power is unsound'; Churchill wanted preponderance, not equilibrium. If the British and Americans collaborated, he asserted, 'there will be no quivering, precarious balance of power to offer temptations to ambition or adventure. On the contrary there will be an overwhelming assurance of security.'[18] Since Churchill knew perfectly well that in a balance of power the members always collaborate and establish a preponderance of power to deter a revolutionary state from committing aggression, it seems clear that his rejection of the balance of power must simply have been a rhetorical device designed to make the participation of the United States in world politics palatable to the American people.

The capacity of the United States either to withdraw from world politics or to become involved in a global crusade was seen to be highly destabilizing now that the country had a dominant position in the international hierarchy. In contrast to Churchill's attempt to disguise balance of power thinking, however, realists such as Morgenthau worked to institutionalize the concept. He dismissed the conventional view that the American Founding Fathers had wished to eschew a balance of power approach to foreign policy;[19] they were, he argued, extremely sensitive to its dictates, recognizing that the security of the United States depended upon the European balance of power.[20] Morgenthau wished to see a return to this orientation.

Realists recognized that in addition to the ideological cleavage between the great powers there were other difficulties about restoring the balance of power. Conditions which had sustained the balance in earlier centuries no longer seemed to obtain and the new conditions confronting the nascent superpowers posed further obstacles to the implementation of realist solutions. There were, now, only two superpowers left to reformulate a global balance of power. But traditionally realists had believed that a stable equilibrium required at least four or five equally powerful states, competing in the international arena, and importance had, in addition, been attached, to a balancer state, willing to change alliances in order to maintain an equilibrium.[21]

Realists also began to re-examine how the balance of power had traditionally operated. Dehio, for instance, asserted that the balance of power had survived in the past not by manipulating power relations within Europe, but rather by drawing in assistance from beyond the boundaries of Europe. So, in the sixteenth century when Charles I of Spain had threatened European stability, the French had restored an equilibrium within Europe by forming an alliance with the Turks.[22] Now that security was defined at the global level, there could be no external parties to rectify any imbalance between the superpowers.[23]

Nuclear weapons also seemed to undermine the operation of the balance of power. In the past, while war was considered, on occasion, necessary to maintain the balance, realists never recommended that it be employed indiscriminately; Clausewitz's assessment of war as the extension of politics by other means was unconditionally accepted. The costs of war had to be kept commensurate with the potential political gains.[24] Atomic weapons eliminated any possibility of maintaining this equation. As Morgenthau notes:

> The total war of our age has fundamentally altered this traditional relationship between political ends and military means. War in the atomic age, fought by both sides with all the instruments of modern technology, has become the *reductio ad absurdum* of policy itself. Today war has become an instrument of universal destruction, an instrument that destroys the victor with the vanquished.[25]

In the same vein, a few far-sighted strategists saw at a very early stage that nuclear weapons had transformed the nature of strategic thinking. Brodie argued, in 1946: 'Thus far the chief purpose of our military establishment has been to win wars. From now on its chief purpose must be to avert them. It can have almost no other useful purpose.'[26] The significance of this argument was initially lost in the first few years of the nuclear age and nuclear weapons were simply integrated into plans for conventional warfare.[27] But with the successful development of the H-bomb, representing another qualitative leap in the destructive power of weapons, the significance of Brodie's proposition was reasserted; but it also reinforced the realists' conviction that the balance of power had become redundant. Herz, for example, indicated that an equilibrium could only be established if power was a relative phenomenon. The principle of equilibrium becomes obsolete in an era of 'absolute power'; even if more world powers developed, the situation would remain utterly different from the conditions in eighteenth- and nineteenth-century Europe.[28] An alliance could not bolster any state which already possesses 'absolute' power.

The uncertainty precipitated by these new developments made it imperative, from the realists' vantage point, to reach an accommodation with the Soviet Union. In 1948, Churchill argued that it was essential to negotiate with the Soviets. He indicated that it is idle to reason or argue with the communists. It is, however, possible to deal with them on a fair, realistic basis, and, in my experience, they will keep their bargains as long as it is in their interests to do so, which might, in this grave matter, be a long time, once things are settled.[29]

But the efforts made by the realists to encourage the West to reach an accommodation with the Soviets failed. The realists were unable to turn the tide of opinion demanding a search for absolute security. As Lippmann, the influential American commentator, indicated in the late 1940s, he felt like someone 'trying to swim up Niagara Falls'.[30] In the early 1950s, Morgenthau, another outspoken critic, accused the American administration of deception and insisted that it had 'falsified the real issue between the United States and the Soviet Union into a holy crusade to stamp out Bolshevism everywhere on earth'.[31] At the same time, realists were unsurprised by their failure. Although they believed that an opportunity had been missed, they recognized that this was not the first time that great powers had failed to reconcile their differences. They were not, by the same token, inclined to blame either the Americans or the Soviets for the outbreak of the cold war. As Butterfield indicated, international relations can always deteriorate even if we assume parties are equally 'righteous and well-disposed' because we are still left with what he sees as the 'tragic human predicament' which arises when parties begin to distrust each other.[32] For the realist, then, the United States and the Soviet Union were caught in a security dilemma. As each party struggled to maintain security, it carried out moves which increased the insecurity of the other, thereby precipitating a vicious downward spiral. Such a downward spiral is inevitable when states fail to aim for relative security.

During the early 1950s, realists continued to push for a negotiated settlement with the Soviets and Lippmann was disturbed by the assertion that it was not possible to make a deal with the communists. As his biographer notes

> his approach was simple: power would be balanced against power to achieve an acceptable accommodation. Ideology played no part in his calculus. The Russians, he told Professor Quincy Wright, 'will expand the revolution if the balance of power is such that they can; if it's such that they cannot, they will make the best settlement they can make for Russia'.[33]

An attempt had to be made to reach an agreement which was mutually acceptable to East and West. Once established, there would then be a reciprocal interest in upholding and defending the agreement. Morgenthau persistently railed against what he saw as the mindless resort to military strength. He believed that because of a failure of leadership the West was 'incapable of recognizing, either in thought or action, the two fundamental propositions that diplomacy without strength is futile and that strength without diplomacy is provocative'.[34] It was vital, moreover, to achieve a settlement while the West still had superiority in nuclear weapons. As Soviet strength increased, the West's bargaining position could only deteriorate.

But as the Soviets improved their strategic position, realists began to realize that the quantum leaps in military technology since 1945 had had a positive, although inadvertent consequence. As Morgenthau came to recognize: 'It is no exaggeration to state that both the United States and the Soviet Union have ruled out the use of nuclear force as an instrument of their national policies . . .'.[35] This posture reflected the emergence of mutual deterrence as a strategic doctrine. Once the Soviets and the Americans possessed lethal amounts of nuclear weapons, then both parties had no alternative but to accept the 'dynamic of reciprocal self-restraint'.[36] Paradoxically, the mutual drive for absolute security had precipitated a condition of relative security, since it was equally clear to both sides that neither could resort to war. Hinsley provided a characteristic response:

> The weapons are the logical culmination of that growth of technological deterrents against irresponsible policy, hasty decisions and war which has been so rapid since the beginning of the century. They are so in the sense that they constitute for the first time a true deterrent, one that will never have to be activated so long as it exists — and this is likely to be for ever.[37]

Hinsley went on to argue that as yet people had not fully appreciated the significance of this development:

> Fearful of the dangers that have flowed from the preponderance of one power, they have overlooked the fact that Russia and the United States have each become Powers on such a colossal scale that, whatever the number of its allies, neither can hope to defeat the other, and thus constitute an all pervasive and ineluctable check upon each other.[38]

The system of bipolar deterrence not only conditions the behaviour of the two superpowers, it also provides a dominant framework which circumscribes and influences the security activity of every member of the international arena.[39] So the emergence of bipolarity and deterrence did not constitute a negation of the balance of power, but rather a continuation of the balance system, in an 'altered form' and elevated on to the global stage.[40]

In the early 1960s, many realists agreed that, ironically, nuclear weapons and bipolarity had produced a more stable and peaceful world than had ever existed in the past. Nowhere was this more evident than in Europe. With the collapse of the European balance, the division of Europe into two spheres of influence had been seen as a necessary step towards establishing a stable and secure global balance of power. Before the end of the Second World War, Lippmann noted that it was 'not only unavoidable but eminently proper that each great power does have a sphere of influence in which its influence and responsibility are primary'.[41] Such spheres provide buffer zones between the great powers and can help to play an important role in producing stability.[42] As Steel has argued, 'a true balance of power must be based on spheres of influence which grant to the Great Powers certain rights in areas that they deem essential to their own security'.[43]

Although the division of Europe was not consciously designed, realists have consistently acknowledged the advantages of the inadvertant arrangement. In De Porte's judgement:

> It is not easy to make a convincing case that some other outcome *which could have been achieved* would have been more stable or even would have served the interests of those states better. This judgement does not overlook the most conspicuous victims of European stability in this form, the nations of Eastern Europe, left in forced dependence on the Soviet Union. It does not exalt stability as a value over self-determination. But analytically it is true that the European system came to be what it is because, to paraphrase Thiers, it divided least those with power to affect it.[44]

Realists were confident that as the balance of power came to be reconceptualized in terms of deterrence, their approach was once more going to prevail. But their hopes were soon to be dashed. Security problems have persisted, and been exacerbated by policies pursued, in particular, by the superpowers — those states traditionally responsible for establishing a stable security environment. Problems persist, realists argue, because neither of the superpowers have given up what is often identified as 'globalism', associated with attempts by the United States and the Soviet Union to propagate their own view of the world. Globalism precipitates an overextension of commitments and an inflated conception of national security interests, discouraging the Soviets and Americans from establishing policies based on balance and reciprocity. Problems have persisted in three major areas. First, globalism has exacerbated the task of maintaining security in the Third World; second, it has complicated the major alliance relationships with the two superpowers; finally, it has tended to undermine strategic deterrence which realists see as the bedrock of contemporary security relations.

The Third World became a major security problem after the process of decolonization began. Before the Second World War much of the Third World was still controlled from Europe. Although the original process of colonization precipitated some conflict amongst the metropolitan states, in practice the balance of power had encouraged the Europeans to regulate the process and prevent the colonized territories from playing one state against another.[45] With the collapse of Europe and the rise of the two superpowers, each threatening a globalist strategy, it seemed only a matter of time before the Third World would become a major arena of conflict.

The first signs of Western globalism became apparent in 1947 when Truman offered help to any state engaged in the struggle between democracy and totalitarianism. Morgenthau noted, that

> in so far as the Truman Doctrine defines its objectives and methods in terms of a world-embracing moral principle, it vitiates its consideration of the national interest and compels a foreign policy derived from it, as the results have shown, to be half-hearted and contradictory in operation and threatened with failure at every turn.[46]

Nearly two decades after the Truman Doctrine was formulated, as the Vietnam War persisted, Lippmann remained deeply concerned about this dimension of American policy.

> Since in this generation we have become a great power, I am in favour of learning to behave like a great power, of getting rid of the globalism which would not only entangle us everywhere but is based on the totally vain notion that if we do not set the world in order, no matter what the price, we cannot live in the world safely . . . in the real world we shall have to learn to live as a great power which defends itself and makes its way among other great powers.[47]

Realists have maintained this line of argument from the moment Truman established his doctrine. Globalism precipitated what were seen to be 'unnatural alliances' with weak states. These alliances do not add to the strength of the United States, and merely serve to draw the United States into unnecessary conflicts which would alienate America's 'natural' allies in NATO. Lippmann complained in 1947 that containment meant that the Americans must

> stake our own security and the peace of the world upon satellites, puppets, clients, agents about whom we can know very little. Frequently they will act for their own reasons, and on their own judgements, presenting us with accomplished facts that we did not intend, and with crises for which we are unready.[48]

The attachment to globalism, therefore, has been seen to increase the power of minor states, presenting them with the capacity to manipulate American policy. Morgenthau has observed that the American commitment to anti-Communism has encouraged allies to adopt a similar stance, whereas, in fact, such a policy is 'at best incidental to concrete national objectives and at worst irrelevant to them, being a mere device to secure and keep American support'.[49] Realists have also been concerned about the danger of both superpowers being sucked into conflict. Attention has been paid to the series of crises before the First World War where the great powers were drawn into potential conflict because of events on their periphery.[50] A commitment to globalism inevitably reduces the willingness to engage in reciprocal restraints and increases the possibility of the two superpowers unintentionally being drawn into conflict.

At the other extreme, realists have also noted that the commitment to globalism can have the effect of encouraging a great power to develop a hypocritical line of policy, masking its actions with justifictions which fail to ring true. Steel has claimed that

> where injustice is combined with an absence of a communist problem, as in Haiti or Rhodesia, we have been indifferent to the call of our moral imperatives. Where a communist problem exists, as in Vietnam, we have found the defense of freedom to be an unshirkable obligation, even if performed on behalf of a regime which may be as indifferent to freedom as the communist one it opposes.[51]

Far from aiding its moral position, such an approach can only serve to undermine America's credibility. Commenting on the inconsistent way

Americans have defended the principle of self-determination, Rovere notes:

> There is a sound but rarely acknowledged reason for this: a commitment to fight for self-determination everywhere and at all times, would, if honoured, involve us in unending military combat on several continents, and even, conceivably, within our own boundary. The selective application of the principle is no doubt prudent, but we have talked as though we had undertaken and were determined to fulfil a universal mission, and thus we face situations in which we can do nothing but talk and, in talking, expose our pretensions.[52]

Globalism, therefore, has prompted a vacilating and dangerous policy of intervention into Third World conflicts. Intervention can only be justified, realists argue, when national interests are directly under threat. These strictures, although mainly discussed in the context of the United States, are applicable to any great power. Certainly realists are in no doubt that the Soviets are also culpable for the deteriorating security conditions in the Third World.

The second problem area involves the relationship between the two superpowers and their major European allies. Realists have obviously never been, in principle, opposed to alliances.[53] As already indicated, European realists originally favoured NATO because of the need to demonstrate that the United States was committed to maintaining a balance of power in Europe. But realists in the United States have been much more sceptical about the value of NATO and initially strongly opposed the form which the alliance took and the tone in which it was justified. This sceptical position was adopted by Kennan, who argued that if the idea of a North Atlantic Treaty was pushed it would mean that

> Germany must divide into Eastern and Western governments and Western Europe must move toward a tight military alliance with this country which can only complicate the eventual integration of the satellites into a European community. From such a trend of developments, it would be hard — harder than it is now — to find 'the road back' to a United and Free Europe.[54]

The formation of NATO was also seen to make the establishment of a global balance of power more difficult because Kennan believed that such a balance was 'unthinkable so long as Germany and Japan remain power vacuums'.[55] Kennan further believed that NATO would divert attention from the major factors for ensuring European security: 'the struggle for economic recovery and internal political stability'.[56]

Kennan agreed, however, that there was a subjective European need for reassurance, and realists in general accepted the formation of NATO in the same way that the dominant role of the Soviet Union was tolerated in Eastern Europe. Nevertheless, they were strongly opposed to the European commitment being expressed in terms of a struggle between freedom and communism and justifying NATO in terms of containment. It was argued that the aim should be

> not to stop Communist revolutions all over the world, but to demonstrate in practice that the Communist form of government is not necessarily identical with subservience to the objectives of Russian imperialism, that a national leader can be a good Communist ideologically and still be opposed to Russia as a great power.[57]

There was also strong opposition to extending the alliance to embrace countries like Greece and Turkey, Lipmann noting that 'an alliance is like a chain, It is not made stronger by adding weak links to it.'[58]

Realist scepticism about NATO has persisted. At the end of the 1950s, for example, Morgenthau argued that 'Nato has never developed a convincing philosophy of purpose'.[59] By the mid-1960s, for some realists, NATO was proving to be a self-perpetuating and dangerous exercise. As Steel noted:

> Having accepted the responsibility for the defense of Europe at a time when the Europeans were obviously too weak to defend themselves, we came to assume that both the Soviet menace and European weakness were permanent fixtures of the postwar world. NATO — which was designed as an extraordinary commitment for a specific situation, a commitment that involved great dangers for the United States — became an ingrained dogma of American foreign policy.[60]

The dangers attached to this policy have steadily increased with time as the Soviets and the Americans have moved into a position of nuclear parity.

> While the atomic equilibrium has provided a balance of terror between the United States and the Soviet Union, it has also had a corrosive effect on the old concept of alliances . . . the terrible destructiveness of nuclear weapons had undermined the old idea that national interests could be

defended through war. In an age of thermonuclear bombs and intercontinental missile defense alliances appear to involve more risk than they do security. No nation can be expected to accept its own incineration to help out a friend.[61]

Attempts to deal with this strategic dilemma have compounded without in any way resolving the problem. As Morgenthau has noted, 'the paradox remains unresolved, and the modes of thought which the nuclear powers have brought to bear upon it can at best do no more than delay its destructive effects'.[62] In the first place, the dilemma has been handled primarily in military terms using the strategy of flexible response. The effects of this policy, were it ever to be implemented, would result in a catastrophic European war. It has, moreover, had the effect of turning Europe into an armed camp. A group of retired NATO generals have noted how this policy has been extremely divisive, since it is primarily the Europeans who would have to bear the brunt of any future conflict. It is argued that NATO's strategy has become subordinated to the interests of the United States:

> American military policy and, above all, American nuclear strategic thinking, clearly tends towards a unilateralism which is centred exclusively on American interests . . . This complete subjugation of NATO's strategy to the needs and interests of the United States, illustrated in the transition from 'massive retaliation' to 'flexible response', is at the root of serious doubts about the credibility of NATO's European nuclear strategy.[63]

For the realists, such a development must inevitably jeopardize the alliance, because membership of an alliance must be determined by national security. The situation is exacerbated by the fact that the Europeans have no effective control over NATO's nuclear strategy. The generals go on to argue that 'too much policy domination by the United States has emasculated the control that its Western European allies have over their individual as well as their collective security'.[64]

The depiction of the Atlantic alliance as a dumb-bell, with the United States balancing the European partners, constitutes a serious misrepresentation.[65] The United States has always been the dominant partner because it has supplied the nuclear umbrella. Apart from the dangers attached to the present strategy, realists assert that there are no good reasons for allowing the situation to persist. As Bull has argued, there is no material reason why Western Europe cannot provide the resources for its own security without depending on others; the reasons why it has failed to do so are not material but spiritual or psychological. It may be honorable for small and weak nations to look to outside powers to provide security for them . . . But it is demeaning that the rich and prosperous democracies of Western Europe in the 1980s . . . should fail to provide the resources for their own security and prefer to live as parasites on a transatlantic protector increasingly restless in this role.[66]

Realists, who were not happy with the military response to the Soviet threat, in the first instance, have in recent years become increasingly convinced that the perennial crises which overtake NATO about the roles played by the Europeans and Americans cannot be resolved within existing framework. By the same token, the problems confronting the Soviet Union have also grown as their European allies have become increasingly restive. NATO contingency plans to exploit this disaffection in Eastern Europe are seen to be dangerous and counter productive.[67]

The third problem area relates to the strategic relations between the United States and the Soviet Union. Realists, as already indicated, have acknowledged that, with the creation of mutual deterrence, the relationship between the two superpowers was considered to have been stabilized. Realists continue to accept that deterrence is, in practice, extremely resilient. As Marshal Shulman observes,

> the scale of nuclear weapons is so great that the nuclear-military balance is not a delicate one. Even if the disparities in one nuclear category or another were greater than they are, neither side could attack the other without suicidal effect. The fact is that we have a sturdy balance of mutual deterrence.[68]

The emergence of stable mutual deterrence has transformed the nature of strategy. It has meant that it is no longer rational to contemplate using nuclear weapons to wage war. Realists have been persistently disturbed, therefore, by developments in nuclear weapons and planning which identify a failure to accept the logic of nuclear deterrence. Morgenthau argues that

> we have been trying to apply conventional modes of thought and action to the nuclear sphere. Instead of emphasizing the distinctiveness of nuclear weapons, we have been trying to assimilate them to

conventional ones. Instead of maintaining and strengthening the separation of the two spheres, we have endeavoured to integrate nuclear weapons into our conventional armoury.[69]

Initially, these attempts at integration were restricted to the development of tactical nuclear weapons. It was observed in the early 1960s that 'the issue of counterforce strategy has fortunately remained in the realm of theoretical planning'.[70] But this restraint was not maintained. Soon after the emergence of mutual deterrence, plans for a counteforce strategy emerged with important consequences for the arms race. The NATO generals for peace argue that 'the production of nuclear weapons was increased. They were no longer considered political weapons of mutual deterrence but once again were seen as a means of waging war.'[71]

Realists have listed a large number of objections to this development. It could lower the nuclear threshold; it supports the illusion that the escalation of nuclear war can be controlled; and it encourages an unlimited strategic arms race.[72] The development of a counterforce strategy has been seen as part of a general drive for superiority with the superpowers switching from a strategy of deterrence which presupposes reciprocity and balance to a strategy of defence. Realists argue that such a strategy is unrealistic since it ignores the durability of the deterrence as well as being self-defeating, since it is bound to encourage retaliation. The American search for supremacy also ignores the fact that, in military terms, the Soviet Union is in a position to maintain parity. As Caldwell notes:

> The Soviet Union is a global military superpower. Its economy is strong enough to maintain overall military parity with the United States. It probably can achieve that apparent objective while still providing a steady, if unspectacular, improvement in the standard of living enjoyed by the Soviet people . . . To achieve military superiority, or even to attempt it, would require defence expenditure on a scale that would threaten the entire fabric of American democracy.[73]

The ex-NATO generals argue that

> Any policy of strength interferes with the legitimate interests of other states. It will be perceived as a threat and will inevitably result in counter-measures. Provoking an arms race will not only result in the failure of military and political objectives; it will also undermine any chance of finding political solutions to conflicts and thus will pave the way for extremely dangerous, preventive defence strategies.[74]

The search for security in purely military terms is seen, therefore, to be self-defeating. But it is also seen by realists to be exceedingly dangerous. Kennan identifies a significant risk that 'the momentum of this tremendous and infinitely dangerous weapons race will get out of hand, will become wholly uncontrollable, and will, either through proliferation or by accident carry us all to destruction'.[75]

Once the political dimension is eschewed, moreover, militarism is encouraged. There is now a military industrial complex in the United States and the prevailing sense of insecurity is used to justify the steady supply of funding to the Pentagon. As a result 'what are ostensibly the requirements of national defense has become something much more than a feature of defense policy — it has become a species of national-economic addiction — a habit which we could not easily or rapidly break'.[76]

This addiction has encouraged a 'terrible militarization of thinking', and created 'the kind of obsession which compels all who have fallen prey to it to direct their entire attention to the 'hopeless eventalities of military conflict and, at the same time, to ignore the hopeful chances of talking to each other to achieve a balance'.[77] Globalist tendencies in the Soviet Union and the United States have undermined the desire for balance and reciprocity which are seen by realists to be the only practical means of dealing with the security dilemma.

Solutions

Realists believe that in the absence of an international society, states experience chronic insecurity. Their solutions to specific security problems, therefore, are all designed to strengthen the international society. All sense of insecurity is not thereby eliminated, but realists do believe that solutions cast in this form can promote a condition of relative security. For such a condition to prevail, security relationships must be sustained on the basis of reciprocity and a balance of power. Realists acknowledge that their solutions must, in the first instance, take account of the power hierarchy which characterizes the international society. In the contemporary international arena, this involves bipolarity since all problems can, potentially, be influenced by the Soviet–American relationship. As Caldwell has noted

> although American and Soviet power seems reduced, global military power, in fact, remains fundamentally bipolar . . . and the failure to understand that, or to keep it sharply in mind, constitutes one of the greatest dangers of the coming decade. The Soviet Union and the

United States retain military power on a scale greatly disproportionate to that of all other actors in the international system, and most other 'significant' military powers are in some critical way militarily dependent on one or the other of them.[78]

It follows that a failure to find solutions to security problems which are mutually acceptable to both the United States and the Soviet Union are unlikely to have long-term success. Realist solutions, therefore, have been couched in terms of *détente*.

Turning, first, to security problems in the Third World, realists are resigned to the fact that there will, in the near future, continue to be outbursts of violence in these regions. Although nothing can be done to prevent these outbursts, it is essential to constrain and limit their effects. Steel, for example, argues that

> there will be revolution in Latin America, upheaval throughout Asia and the Middle East, and violence in Africa, no matter what we or the communists do or refrain from doing. The most we can hope for is to try to restrain that violence and isolate it before it involves the great powers.[79]

This policy of restraint, may, on occasions, result in communist regimes coming to power in the Third World. But it is argued that such a development should not be a source of concern. It does not pose a threat to the security of the West, any more than a right-wing revolution in the Third World poses a threat to the Soviet bloc:

> What is important is not the label a region chooses to pin on itself, but the policies it follows. Small communist nations in the Southern hemisphere are no threat to the United States. Nor, as we should now have learned from experience, are they likely to remain the satellites of Russia or China for very long. The kind of government they choose to live under is their affair not ours.[80]

A strict policy of non-intervention, however, is only likely to be successful if it is observed by both of the superpowers. Realists accept that unilateral intervention could add to the existing instability. As Zagoria argues:

> The danger is not so much that Moscow will achieve hegemony in the Third World. That is unlikely for many reasons. The danger is rather

that the spread of communism and Soviet power will upset regional balances of power, lead to intensified regional instabilities, and make even more difficult the settlement of a variety of regional clashes that could lead to war.[81]

The two powers would benefit by a mutual policy of non-intervention and they should engage in mutual attempts to prevent the escalation of conflict in Third World countries.[82] Realists, therefore, were encouraged by the attempts of Kissinger and Nixon to persuade the Soviets to think in terms of crisis prevention rather than simply crisis management and also to consider a joint American–Soviet approach to the settlement of regional disputes.[83] Legvold has argued that the United States and the Soviet Union must make a

> far more strenuous effort to reduce the risks and moderate the effects of our rivalry in areas of instability. To this end no initiative is more desperately needed than a restored search for 'rules' helping to regulate the role of the two countries in areas of instability. By rules of the game, I do not mean negotiated principles but patterns of restraint, usually tacit, perhaps merely insinuated, but seriously pursued.[84]

Such rules must not only cover direct intervention, but also extend to the supply of arms to unstable areas. There is a need, therefore, for bilateral dialogue in the context of arms transfers between the superpowers which would identify 'mutually acceptable patterns of behaviour' and lead to 'diplomatic undertakings tailored to specific areas'.[85] The growth of *détente* between the United States and the Soviet Union will not eliminate conflict in the Third World. But it could have a considerable restraining influence on these conflicts.

The second problem area is associated with the relationship between the two superpowers and their European allies. It is argued that current NATO strategy serves American rather than European interests. The realist fear that the formation of NATO would remove the European incentive to develop their own security arrangements has materialized. The realist solution, therefore, has remained unchanged. Morgenthau argued in the late 1950s that the Europeans 'can stand on their own feet again and look beyond the wall of containment for new outlets for their energies and products'.[86] In the 1980s, Howard argued in the same vein:

> What is needed is a reversal of that process whereby European

governments have sought greater security by demanding an even greater intensification of the American nuclear commitment; demands that are as divisive within their own countries as they are irritating for the people of the United States. Instead we should be doing all that we can to reduce our dependence on American nuclear weapons by enhancing, so far as is militarily, socially and economically possible, our capacity to defend ourselves.[87]

The way forward is seen to lie on two fronts. First, Western links with the Soviet Union and Eastern Europe must be strengthened. As Bull has indicated, however, this approach must be 'on the basis of a willingness to live with the Soviet dominated bloc and not an attempt to subvert it'.[88] The recurrent upheavals in Eastern Europe have always posed a threat to stability, and realists acknowledge the wisdom of not calling into question the legitimacy of Soviet security interests in Eastern Europe. Although there has been tacit cooperation between the United States and the Soviet Union to prevent an escalation of local conflict in Eastern Europe, there can be no assurance that such restraint will continue indefinitely. Both countries need to adopt more imaginative methods to defuse future crises in Eastern Europe. Valenta has argued that 'the United States must concentrate on preventing spasms of violence on the Soviet periphery that can at the very least seriously damage East–West relations and possibly spark wider military conflict.'[89] Realists believe that these spasms will only be eliminated if the Soviet Union allows the East European states greater independence. Such a development can be facilitated if the West guarantees not to interfere or take advantage of the situation when the Soviet Union makes the necessary readjustments. The aim must be, therefore, to continue to normalize frontiers and encourage political coexistence — a trend initiated with the neutralization of Austria in 1955 and furthered by the 1975 Helsinki Conference on Security and Cooperation in Europe (CSCE).

Second, the Europeans must reorientate NATO strategy and develop a conventional deterrent. It must be recognized that 'not only is it possible to give up the nuclear defence component in Central Europe without loss of security, but that it is absolutely imperative for our survival that we do so'.[90] The call for a conventional deterrent has come from many different quarters; but all believe that the idea of 'escalation dominance' associated with the strategy of flexible response has lost its credibility and is exceedingly dangerous.[91] As a strategy it no longer provides reassurance. An alternative strategy, realists insist, must take account of 'the fact that security in the nuclear age can be achieved only if the policy intended for the prevention of war takes into consideration both one's own security interests and those of the potential opponent'.[92] Realists argue that a conventional deterrent can achieve this end. They have been attracted, for example, to the strategy of deep defence involving large numbers of small mobile units armed with weapons which can destroy invading tanks.[93] The advantage of this strategy is that it can be implemented by the Europeans and is purely defensive in orientation. It therefore overcomes the disadvantage of the existing conventional forces. As Garrett notes:

> NATO has persisted in creating armies in much the same mould as those it faces — heavily mechanized forces backed by massive fire power, best suited for fluid, aggressive battles. By aping the Pact model — that of World War II armies in the European theatre — the Alliance's style favors the attacker.[94]

A policy of deep defence is intended, therefore, to deter a conventional attack by the Soviet Union. The deterrence rests on a strategy of denial, rather than retaliation or punishment. It is not provocative and it could be effected by the Europeans.

Although realists believe that the Europeans could substantially enhance their security prospects by developing an independent conventional deterrent, ultimately, their security relies upon the relations between the superpowers. Global security can only be satisfactorily achieved if adequate solutions are found for the third problem area, which involves the arms race between the Soviet Union and the United States. Realists were initially very encouraged by the attempts made by the two superpowers after the Cuban missile crisis in 1962 to promote *détente*. The establishment of a direct communication link between the two superpowers, and the Partial Test Ban agreement of 1963, provided hopeful signs of a more constructive approach to the relationship. These developments persisted during the 1960s and culminated in the Basic Principles Agreement (BPA) signed by Nixon and Brezhnev in 1972, designed, in part, to prevent the outbreak of future crises. But despite these optimistic signs of a desire to reach a super power accord, relations during the 1970s and 1980s steadily deteriorated.

Realists consider that there is only one way to improve the present situation and that is by adopting a more positive approach to the task of arms control. There is, however, considerable scepticism about the strategic arms talks which have taken place since the late 1960s. To the extent that they were carried out in good faith, they have invariably been overtaken by technological developments. But realists also believe that the negotiators in these talks have not been seriously interested in halting the arms race.

Progress requires both sides to accept that parity and deterrence, in the sense of mutual destruction, are permanent features of the strategic environment. These two factors, therefore, need to be taken as given. Next, it must be accepted that both parties have legitimate security interests. Realists acknowledge that the Americans and Soviets have very different perspectives on the strategic position: 'It is important that we interpret these respective perspectives properly for they influence the perceptions which we have of the "enemy". It is time we stood in each other's shoes and took a long, hard look at how the one sees the other.'[95] Finally, it is argued that the two sides must stop trying to make political capital from the process of arms conrol and must stop presenting to the public assessments of the arms race which are obviously erroneous. Some of these assessments it is argued are of 'such intrinsic unsoundness, and so highly misleading,that one is surprised to see them emanating from responsible circles'.[96]

Realists start from the premise that if the arms race could be reversed, international society, in general, as well as the security of the two major participants, would increase substantially. During the 1970s, when it appeared that there was a measure of agreement between the two superpowers on the need to control the arms race, realists were favourably inclined towards a joint search for solutions. The process of negotiations was seen to encourage the parties to appreciate each other's security needs and thereby reduce tension and promote confidence. As confidence grew so the task of reaching agreements should have got steadily easier.

In practice, however, the talks have degenerated into 'contests to see how much the one could contrive to keep, in the way of nuclear weaponry, and how much the other could be brought to give up, as though the entire purpose of the exercise was simply to get the other party at a maximum disadvantage'.[97] When there is a considerable distrust between the parties, formal negotiations can actually get in the way of arms control. As Osgood notes, 'this is because both sides bring to the negotiation table precisely those attitudes and beliefs about the other which generated the arms race in the first place'.[98] Realists, therefore, have returned to their earlier preference for unilateral measures. Both the Soviets and the Americans have independently, in the past, enhanced deterrence, for example, by using locking devices on nuclear missiles to prevent the danger of unauthorized firing. It was argued in the early 1960s that these measures had gone a long way towards reducing the danger of nuclear war. After an assessment of arms control, at that time, Halperin concluded that unilateral measures could be very successful. He went on: 'This is not to say that formal arms-control measures would have also contributed to these objectives, but rather that tacit understandings and informal arrangements may accomplish many of the objectives pursued through arms control.'[99]

Since the arms race developed on the basis of a series of independent but reciprocated moves, realists believe that it could be easier simply to reverse this process, rather than try to aim at a negotiated reduction. The importance of balance and reciprocity in the arms race is caught in an analogy used by Osgood:

> John and Ivan stood facing each other near the middle, but on opposite sides, of a long, rigid, neatly balanced seesaw. This seesaw is balanced on a point that juts out over a bottomless abyss. As either of these husky men takes a step outward on his side away from the center, the other must quickly compensate with an equal step outward on his side, or the balance will be destroyed.[100]

Osgood comes to the conclusion that there is no reason, in principle, why this process should not be reversed, since it is in the interests of both parties to do so. The initial desire for a unilateral approach to arms control was later swamped by the enthusiasm for strategic arms talks, but as the difficulties of attaining agreements have been exposed, realists are returning once again to the idea of unilateral but reciprocated steps as a way forward to arms control.

At the heart of this solution is the belief that the nuclear balance is, in practice, much more stable than Osgood's analogy would suggest. Realists argue that there is scope for unilateral reductions in the level of nuclear weapons without in any way affecting the existing nuclear balance. Provided that these moves are then reciprocated by the other side, there should then be scope for further reductions. According to this view,

> it does not matter which side has more weapons. In the past, having a larger army than one's neighbour allowed one to conquer it and protect one's own population. Having a larger nuclear stockpile yields no such gains. Deterrence comes from having enough weapons to destroy the other's cities; this capability is an absolute, not a relative.[101]

It follows that, for the realists, arms control 'signifies stopping one's nuclear armaments at the point where they provide an invulnerble, effective deterrent and cutting them back to that point in so far as they have exceeded it'.[102] Cutting back can take place on a unilateral basis and, as a consequence, the cuts can take place initially in the areas where an established superiority already exists. Such a strategy, therefore, overcomes the difficulty generated by the asymmetrical force structure possessed by the United States and the Soviet Union.[103] These asymmetries have proved to be a major stumbling block in negotiated settlements.

The realist approach to security has been discussed here in terms of a set of discrete problems and solutions. In practice, realists believe that these issues are interrelated; security must be considered in holistic terms.[104] Realists accept that for practical reasons it is necessary to deal with problems separately, but they also acknowledge that a failure to proceed on all fronts will prove ultimately self-defeating. Nevertheless, realists are confident that if the principles of balance and reciprocity are observed there is in fact, scope for substantially enhancing international security.

Notes

1. A.W. De Porte, *Europe Between the Superpowers: The Enduring Balance*, New Haven, Yale University Press, 1979, p. 2.
2. R.L. Rothstein, 'On the Costs of Realism', *Political Science Quarterly*, **87**, 1972, 347–62.
3. R.E. Osgood, *Ideals and Self Interest in American Foreign Relations*, Chicago, Chicago University Press, 1942, p. 443.
4. H. Kissinger, *A World Restored*, London, Gollancz, 1973, pp. 144–5
5. M. Howard, 'Military Power and International Order', *International Affairs*, **40**, 1964, 397–408, p. 405.
6. Kissinger, op. cit., pp. 144–5.
7. H. Butterfield, *History and Human Relations*, London, Collins, 1971, p. 20.
8. H. Butterfield, *Christianity and History*, London, Bell, 1939, p. 39.
9. J.H. Herz, *International Politics in the Atomic Age*, New York, Columbia University Press, 1959, p. 239.
10. L. Woodward, 'A British View of Mr Wilson's Foreign Policy' in E.H. Beuhrig (ed.), *Wilson's Foreign Policy in Perspective*, Bloomington, Indiana University Press, 1957, p. 155.
11. De Tocqueville developed this argument in the nineteenth century. By the beginning of the twentieth century, Americans were arguing that the United States would shortly take over from Britain as the balancer in the global balance of power. See H. Beale, *Theodore Roosevelt and the Rise of America to World Power*, Baltimore, John Hopkins Press, 1956, p. 256.
12. The collapse was, however, seen very clearly after the war by European historians. See L. Dehio, *The Precarious Balance: The Politics of Power in Europe 1499–1945*, London, Chatto and Windus, 1962; and H. Holborn, *The Political Collapse of Europe*, New York, A.A. Knopf, 1964.

13. Cited in M.W. Graham, *American Diplomacy in the International Community*, Baltimore, John Hopkin Press, 1948, p. 271.
14. See A. Resis, 'Spheres of Influence in Soviet Wartime Diplomacy', *Journal of Modern History*, **53**, 1981, 417–39; and Resis, 'The Churchill–Stalin Secret "Percentages" Agreement on the Balkans, Moscow, October 1944', *American Historical Review*, **83**, 1978, 368–87. See also discussion by L.C. Gardner, *A Covenant with Power: America and World Order*, London, Macmillan, 1984, Chapter 3.
15. For an account of this failure, see L.E. Davis, *The Cold War Begins: Soviet–American Conflict over Eastern Europe*, Princeton, Princeton University Press, 1974.
16. See N.H. Wessell, 'Soviet Views of Multipolarity and the Emerging Balance of Power' *Orbis*, **23**, 1979, 785–813.
17. H.J. Morgenthau, *Politics Among Nations*, 5th edn, New York, A.A. Knopf, 1973, p. 339.
18. Cited in J.M. Siracusa (ed.), *The American Diplomatic Revolution: A Documentary History of the Cold War 1941–47*, Milton Keynes, Open University Press, 1978, p. 209.
19. See H.J. Morgenthau, *American Foreign Policy: A Critical Examination*, London, Methuen, 1951 (Published in the United States under the title *In Defense of National Interest*).
20. See the discussion in F. Gilbert, *To the Farewell Address: Ideas of Early American Foreign Policy*, Princeton, Princeton University Press, 1961; and J.H. Hutson, *John Adams and the Diplomacy of the American Revolution*, Lexington, University of Kentucky Press, 1980.
21. See E.V. Gulick, *Europe's Classical Balance of Power*, Ithaca, Cornell University Press, 1955, pp. 65–7, and M.A. Kaplan, *System and Process in International Politics*, New York, John Wiley and Sons, 1964, p. 116. Brook Adams, whose views influenced President Roosevelt at the turn of the century, believed that the United States would eventually become the balancer in a global balance of power. See note 11.
22. See the discussion in Dehio, op. cit.
23. Some historians trace the collapse of the European balance of power back to 1918. G. Barraclough, for example, argues that the effect of the First World War was to 'destroy for all time the basis of the European balance of power': see Barraclough, *An Introduction to Contemporary History*, London, C.A. Watts, 1964, p. 112.
24. Realists, therefore, had always adhered to the idea that war must be kept limited. For a discussion of the argument that this convention was built upon reciprocity, see I. Clark, *Limited Nuclear War: Political Theory and War Conventions*, Oxford, Martin Robertson, 1982.
25. See Morgenthau, *American Foreign Policy*, p. 58.
26. Cited in C.S. Gray, *Strategic Studies and Public Policy*, Lexington, University of Kentucky Press, 1982, pp. 31–2.
27. See D.A. Rosenberg 'American Atomic Strategy and the Hydrogen Bomb Decision', *Journal of American History*, **66**, 1979–80, 62–87.
28. See Herz, op. cit., p. 35.
29. Quoted in Morgenthau, *American Foreign Policy*, p. 157.
30. See R. Steel, *Walter Lippmann and the American Century*, London, Bodley Head, 1980, p. 488. It is worth noting that Lippmann was a convert to realism. In the inter-war years he was a compensatory liberal.

31. Morgenthau, *American Foreign Policy*, p. 240.
32. Butterfield, *History and Human Relations*, p. 14.
33. Steel, op. cit., p. 499.
34. Morgenthau, *American Foreign Policy*, p. 200.
35. Morgenthau, *A New Foreign Policy for the United States*, New York, F.A. Praeger, 1969, p. 209.
36. ibid., p. 210.
37. F.H. Hinsley, *Power and the Pursuit of Peace*, Cambridge, Cambridge University Press, 1963, p. 347. See also the discussion by C.M. Woodhouse, *British Foreign Policy Since the Second World War*, London, Hutchinson, 1961, pp. 237–40.
38. Hinsley, op. cit., p. 353. But note that Hinsley also places tremendous emphasis on the impact of bipolarity.
39. See, for example, A. De Porte, op. cit.
40. See, for example, I. Clark, *Reform and Resistance in the International Order*, Cambridge, Cambridge University Press, 1980, p. 168.
41. See Steel, op. cit., p. 408–9.
42. For a discussion of spheres of influence in traditional realist thinking, see P.G. Lauren, 'Crisis Prevention in Nineteenth-Century Diplomacy' in A.L. George (ed.), *Managing U.S.–Soviet Rivalry: Problems of Crisis Prevention*, Boulder, Westview Press, 1983.
43. R. Steel, 'A Spheres of Influence Policy' *Foreign Policy*, **5**, 1971–2, 107–18, p. 111.
44. A. De Porte, op. cit., p. 165.
45. See H. Bull, 'European States and African Political Communities' in H. Bull and A. Watson, *The Expansion of International Society*, Oxford, Clarendon Press, 1984.
46. Morgenthau, *American Foreign Policy*, op. cit., p. 117.
47. Quoted in Steel, *Walter Lippmann*, pp. 565–6.
48. W. Lippmann, *The Cold War*, New York, Harper & Bros, 1947, p. 23.
49. H.J. Morgenthau, *Truth and Power*, New York, Praeger, 1970. pp. 330–1.
50. See, for example M. Kohler, 'Rumors of War: the 1914 Analogy' *Foreign Affairs*, **58**, 1979–80, 374–96.
51. R. Steel, *Pax Americana*, New York, Viking Press, 1967, pp. 318–9.
52. Quoted in ibid., p. 320.
53. See H.J. Morgenthau's chapter on alliances in *Politics in the Twentieth Century*, abridged edn, Chicago, University of Chicago Press, 1971.
54. See T.H. Etzold and J.L. Gaddis, *Containment: Documents on American Policy and Strategy 1945–50*, New York, Columbia University Press, 1978, p. 138.
55. J.L. Gaddis *Strategies of Containment: A Critical Appraisal of Postwar American National Security Policy*, Oxford, Oxford University Press, 1982, p. 39.
56. See Etzold and Gaddis, op. cit., p. 154.
57. Morgenthau, *American Foreign Policy*, p. 124.
58. See, for example, Steel, *Walter Lippmann*, p. 408–9.
59. Morgenthau, 'Alliances' in *Politics in the Twentieth Century*, op. cit., p. 378.
60. R. Steel, *The End of Alliances: America and the Future of Europe*, André Deutsch, 1964, p. 13.
61. Ibid., p. 35.
62. H.J. Morgenthau, *New Foreign Policy*, p. 238.
63. Generals for Peace and Disarmament, *The Arms Race to Armageddon: A Challenge to US/NATO Strategy*, Leamington Spa, Berg Publishers Ltd., 1984, pp. 63, 74.

64. Ibid., p. 5.
65. See, for example, J.W. Holmes, 'The Dumbbell Won't Do', *Foreign Policy*, **50**, 1983, 3–22.
66. H. Bull, 'European Self-Reliance and the Reform of NATO', *Foreign Affairs*, **61**, 1982–3, 874–92, p. 877.
67. Generals for Peace, op. cit., pp. 51–7.
68. Interview given in 1982, quoted in Generals for Peace, op. cit., p. 43.
69. Morgenthau, *New Foreign Policy*, p. 208.
70. Morgenthau, *Truth and Power*, p. 155.
71. Generals for Peace, op. cit., p. 60.
72. Ibid., pp. 67–8.
73. L.T. Caldwell and W. Diebold, *Soviet–American Relations in the 1980s*, New York, McGraw Hill, 1981, p. 35.
74. Generals for Peace, op. cit., p. 69. These have, of course, subsequently materialized in the shape of the Strategic Defence Initiative. Realists insist that the drive for a defence system is an illusion. See W.E. Borrows, 'Ballistic Missile Defense: The Illusion of Security', *Foreign Affairs*, **62**, 1984, 843–56.
75. G.F. Kennan, *The Cloud of Danger*, London, Hutchinson, 1978, p. 202.
76. Ibid., p. 11.
77. Kennan, cited in Generals for Peace, op. cit., p. 31–2.
78. Caldwell and Diebold, op. cit., p. 24.
79. Steel, *Pax Americana*, p. 332.
80. Ibid., p. 322.
81. D. Zagoria, 'New Soviet Alliances in the Third World', *Foreign Affairs*, **57**, 1977, 733–54, p. 741.
82. See, for example, A. Etzioni, *Winning Without War*, Garden City, N.Y., Anchor Books, 1965, who talks of 'remote deterrence'.
83. See D. Caldwell, *American Soviet Relations: From 1947 to the Nixon & Kissinger Grand Design*, Westport, Greenwood Press, 1981, and A.L. George (ed.), *Managing U.S.–Soviet Rivalry*. It is not clear, however, how sincere these efforts were. Kissinger reveals in his memoirs, for example, that '[t]o some extent my interest in détente was tactical as a device to maximize Soviet dilemmas and reduce Soviet influence in the Middle East' (H. Kissinger, *White House Years*, Boston, Little, Brown & Co., 1979, p. 1255).
84. R. Legvold, 'The Super Rivals: Conflict in the Third World', *Foreign Affairs*, **57**, 1979, 755–78, p. 775.
85. B.M. Blechman *et al.*, 'Pushing Arms', *Foreign Policy*, **46**, 1982, 138–55, p. 151.
86. Morgenthau, *Politics in the Twentieth Century*, p. 371.
87. M. Howard, 'Reassurance and Deterrence: Western Defence in the 1980s' *Foreign Affairs*, **61**, 1982, 309–24.
88. Bull, 'European Self Reliance', p. 390.
89. J. Valenta 'The Explosive Soviet Periphery', *Foreign Policy*, **51**, 1983, 84–100, p. 96.
90. Generals for Peace, op. cit., p. 109.
91. See M. Howard, 'Reassurance and Deterrence'; and L. Freedman 'NATO Myths', *Foreign Policy*, **45**, 1981–2, 48–68.
92. Generals for Peace, op. cit., p. 107.
93. For a comparison of 'defence in depth' with its major conventional alternative 'deep

attack', see H. Strachan, 'Conventional Defence in Europe', *International Affairs*, **61**, 1984–5, 27–43. For an endorsement of 'defence in depth', see J.M. Garrett, 'Conventional Force Deterrence in the Pressure of Theatre Nuclear Weapons', *Armed Forces and Society*, **11**, 1984, 59–84.

94. Ibid., p. 61.
95. Generals for Peace, op. cit., p. 4.
96. Kennan, *Cloud of Danger*, p. 159.
97. Ibid., p. 203.
98. C.E. Osgood, *An Alternative to War or Surrender*, Urbana, University of Illinois Press, 1962, p. 76.
99. M.H. Halperin, *Contemporary Military Strategy*, Boston, Little, Brown & Co., 1967, p. 152.
100. Osgood, op. cit., p. 86.
101. See R. Jervis, 'Why Nuclear Superiority Doesn't Matter' *Political Science Quarterly*, **94**, 1979–80, 617–33.
102. Morgenthau, *New Foreign Policy*, p. 232.
103. This line of argument has been made in a number of proposals to get talks moving after the breakdown of the START talks. See, for example, A. Frye, 'Strategic Build-Down: A Context for Restraint' *Foreign Affairs*, **62**, 1983, 293–317; and H. Brown and L. Davies, 'Nuclear Arms Control Where Do We Stand?', *Foreign Affairs*, **62**, 1984, 1145–60.
104. For an excellent discussion of a holistic approach to security, see B. Buzan, *People, States and Fear: The National Security Problems in International Relations*, Brighton, Wheatsheaf, 1983.

PART V: CONCLUSION

11 Reflections on world order

This book began by contesting the commonly held belief that there is a set of extant global problems which, if solved, would permit the emergence of world order. Instead we have argued that an examination of the literature in the fields of international economics and security reveals that there is a kaleidoscopic and bewildering array of assessments about what constitutes a global problem and its solution. Economic aid, military intervention, tariffs and nuclear deterrence, for example, are advanced by some as global problems and by others as solutions. What we have tried to do is to reveal the configuration which underpins this confusing body of literature.

The key to the configuration is the conception of order. In its most general sense, order can be equated with a pattern; and any attempt to discover a pattern, therefore, can be identified as a search for order. For instance, to the extent that natural science is associated with efforts to find behavioural regularities, the scientific enterprise can be characterized as an exercise in the creation of order. For social scientists, however, there is a second dimension to order. It arises because social behaviour is purposeful and goal-orientated. In contrast to the mindless movement of molecules in a gas chamber, human behaviour is meaningful and reflects intent. Before we can define the nature of an action we need to understand the motivation. If a person is killed falling from a window, the motivation underlying the action determines whether it should be described as murder, accident or suicide.

In social situations, however, actions must be collectively or socially defined in the context of the overall goal of the group. The audience and actors in a theatre, for example, tacitly, but collectively, acknowledge that entertainment is the central goal. If a member of the audience begins to heckle the actors, then this behaviour is considered disordered because it impinges upon the collectively defined goal. It generates a problem which can only be solved, and order restored, when the recalcitrant is silenced or removed. However, if the playwright places an actor in the audience who is required to heckle — as a dramatic device — then the same action must be redefined as ordered, because it conforms to the established goal-orientated pattern of behaviour.

This example demonstrates, therefore, that disorder is associated with the existence of problems which emerge when the satisfaction of a goal is being impeded. The heckler hinders the ability of the actors to entertain the audience. It is also apparent from the example that a resolution of the problem requires an understanding of the stuctural arrangement which ensures that a goal is achieved. In the case of the theatre, the structural arrangement presupposes an uninterrupted line of communication between the audience and the actors on stage. The heckler endangers this structural arrangement and it can only be restored when the heckling has stopped. By the same token, the actor as heckler is actually maintaining the structural arrangement and thereby assisting the fulfilment of the goal. Our conceptualization of order, therefore, is defined in terms of a goal, a structural arrangement and a set of beliefs which support the goal and account for the structural arrangement.

The theatre obviously requires a collectively defined goal to be able to function effectively. In many settings, however, there is an absence of any collectively agreed goals. As a consequence, order must be seen in contested or ideological terms because there are competing ideas about the goals which should be pursued. This leads to the emergence of rival views of order. Even the theatre example can be re-expressed in terms of competing conceptions of order. Provided that the heckler is operating from rational intentions it would be erroneous to suggest that the disturbance is not designed to achieve order. If, for example, the play had an anti-Semitic theme, and the heckler wished to live in a society free from racial prejudice, then the heckling can be seen to be goal-orientated action designed to promote a new type of society. From the perspective of the heckler, it would be offensive to equate an anti-Semitic play with entertainment and so the agreed goal of the theatre would not be achieved by performing such a play. The heckling, therefore, would not be disorderly behaviour but a political act designed to change the ideological orientation of the actors, along with the rest of the audience, and to promote a new form of order.

The conceptualization of order developed here, is designed to accommodate rival views and it embraces, therefore, although perhaps in unusually formal terms, a conception of ideology. Eccleshall provides the following description of ideology:

Ideologies share two principal characteristics: an image of society and a political programme. The image renders society intelligible from a particular viewpoint. Aspects of the social world are accentuated and contrasted to illustrate both how the whole *actually* operates and *ideally* should be organized. The specific social image forms the core of each ideology. From it radiates a programme of action: prescriptions of what ought to be done to ensure that social ideal and actual reality coincide.[1]

We argue that every ideology generates a distinctive view of order and has its own identifiable conception of problems and solutions which can be understood in terms of a desired goal and its related structural arrangement which permits the satisfaction of the goal.

From our formal and abstract conceptualization of order we developed three models of world order having very different substantive content while sharing the same abstract conceptualization of order. The subsequent application of these models to the identification of global problems and solutions leads us now to establish four main conclusions.

The first of these argues that the models serve as problem-defining, explicating and creating devices. Problems only become apparent once deviations from a stipulated goal are identified. Problem definition is contingent, therefore, on prior goal specification. The liberal, socialist and realist models each identify problems in terms of deviation from their goals. As such, the models are problem-defining devices.

It is not uncommon to see this process, the movement from goal to problem definition, being short-circuited. Statements, such as 'the main problematic of international relations is the management of the security dilemma between states', frequently imply a fixed set of problems. This problematic is unequivocally not a fixed problem but a problem as defined by the realist model. Problems do not exist in the abstract but in the context of goals and are, therefore, a systematic function of goals. Whenever people assert that there is a fixed list of problems, they are working from and within only one particular goal or collection of goals.

One of the main utilities of Parts III and IV has been to make a systematic exposition of the very different problems defined by the three models. By working from different goals the models automatically and of necessity define different problems. Equally, of course, defining problems entails also defining non-problem areas. When socialists define inequalities as problems, they are defining non-problems for the pure liberal. Or again, when pure liberals define the new mercantilism as a problem they are defining what to the realists is a non-problem.

It is therefore quite erroneous to think that the three models represent different strategies for confronting a common and fixed set of problems. Problems can only become apparent in the context of goals and problems are not defined for but defined by the models.

The models do not simply define but also explicate problems. The key to an understanding of this point is the appreciation that the models do not merely profile goals. A hallmark of each of the three models of world order is that they also profile a structural arrangement by which the apporprite goal can be pursued. It is on the basis of the structural arrangement, following the argument of Chapter One, that the explanation of problems is developed.

Although the models do define very different problems by virtue of being attuned to different goals, it may appear somewhat anomalous that they often confront a common array of issues. Thus, in Parts III and IV we often see each of the models confronting such common topics as multinational corporations or aid programmes or the arms race and so on. This might seem to contradict the point that the models define different problems. There is, however, no contradiction here.

One of the reasons we see some commonality in topics covered is simply that each of the models is extremely comprehensive. The fact that it is rather difficult to find any issue on which any one model is totally mute does not mean that the models look at all issues in the same manner. Rather it is simply testimony to the extraordinarily macro nature of the models.

The critical point is that when the models do confront the same issue, the explication of that issue is radically different across the different models. For instance the multinational corporation for the pure liberal is an agency ideally suited to the promotion of an integrated open world economy. In their capacity to move capital and expertise and in their ability to foster global efficiency through enhanced comparative advantage, the multinationals are a force for progress. The only problems to which the pure liberals will look are restrictions on global efficiency that may be produced by excessive monopolization. The socialists on the other hand process multinational corporations in terms of the increasing centralization and concentration of imperialist monopoly capital. The problems to which they look as a consequence are the enhanced inequities stimulated by the expansion and diffusion of capitalism. The realist will likely express neither any principled support for nor objection to multinationals. As long as such corporations are controlled and monitored by national governments then they are acceptable. The problems to which the realist would look are any threats to governmental sovereignty that might be posed by multinationals. The point then is that even when the models look to the same topics, the general framework within which the topic is processed leads to systematic variation in problem explication.

As a final point in this discussion of problem explication, a further variation across the models should be noted. While it is true that many topics are represented in all the models, it is also the case that any one model may confront a given issue area much more extensively than others. For example, all three models have something to say on the issue of tariffs. Thus, it would be erroneous to think that only one model either notices or processes tariffs. On the other hand, it is unquestionably the case that there is a substantially larger liberal literature on tariffs than there is socialist or realist and the basic reason for this is that tariffs constitute a greater problem, other things being equal, to the liberal model than to either of the others.

In addition to problem definition and explication, the models are also problem creating. We use the expression of problem creating in this particular context to refer to cross-model problems. The combination of both goals and structural arrangements means that each model, as seen extensively in Parts III and IV, can profile solutions to problems. In this respect the models represent macro forms of social engineering. What we mean in this context by problem creating is that as any one model begins to engineer solutions to its perceived problems, it will in all likelihood create a problem for another model.

For example, when realists advocate the use of tariffs as a solution to some threat to the autonomy of a national economy, they will create a problem for pure liberals. When liberals advocate free exchange controls to promote muiltinational investment, they will create a problem for socialists. When socialists advocate a planned economy geared to satisfying mass needs, they are proposing a fundamental threat to a pure liberal system and thereby creating a problem for the liberals.

This capacity for solutions to one model to appear as problems to another is a further factor that explains a feature, noted above, that the models often confront a common range of issues. Thus in addition to their comprehensive nature, a further reason for this commonality is that the models do respond to each other. There is, for instance, a pure liberal literature on Third World inequality. This is not an area which is, as it were, naturally defined for the pure liberal, for whom inequality is not *ipso facto* a major problem. The pure liberal is in fact often reacting to socialist literature which advocates the eradication of inequality and it is this eradication which constitutes a problem to the pure liberal.

In seeking to establish very different worlds, the models define different problems, explicate problems differently, and create problems for each other. They hold very different views of world order, they profile different degrees and forms of disorder, and they advocate different resolutions to their perceived disorder. As such the models are not merely different blueprints but engender different conceptions of social reality. They do not simply wish to create different worlds but process the current world in different ways.

Our second main conclusion relates our two abstract conceptualizations of order. It argues that we can order, as pattern, the complex array of competing views of global problems and solutions by deploying the pattern ordering device of the conceptualization of order as goal satisfaction, elaborated in the form of the substantive models of world order. We can thereby understand and explain the controversy and conflict in the debate over world order. This, as indicated in the Preface, is the single most important objective of this study.

The core idea underlying the conceptualization of order as pattern is that a pattern can only be said to exist when otherwise disparate information is arrayed in a coherent manner according to some rule. Pattern-creating is that process whereby coherence and structure are provided in an area that would otherwise simply represent a confusion or disarray. In the simple illustration of the Fibonacci sequence, order as pattern in the sequence of numbers is provided by the rule that any number is the sum of the two preceding ones. Once this rule is known then an otherwise confusing set of numbers is arrayed in a clear pattern or order.

In the context of international studies our point of departure was confusion. Deterrence to some is a strategy for peace, while to others it is a means of perpetuating conflict and tension; the New International Economic Order (NIEO) package to some represented a way of resolving some enduring problems, while to others it would create problems; the World Bank to some has the potential for contributing to the alleviation of Third World development problems, to others it is an agency for promoting underdevelopment. Such illustrations, which are myriad, profile a confusion or disarray.

The rule we have developed to order this disarray or disorder, the rule we have developed to create a pattern, is provided initially by the second conceptualization of order as goal satisfaction. From this conceptualization we then developed the three substantive models. These models constitute the rule of coherence whereby we can order as pattern the otherwise confusing array of different threats to and solutions for world order.

Deterrence is a strategy for peace to the realist but not to the socialist.

The NIEO package is broadly acceptable to the compensatory but not the pure liberal. The World Bank is a useful organization for the compensatory liberal but not for the socialist. More systematically, following the argument above, the reason we find different problem definition, different problem explication, and problem creation, all of which culminate in different views of social reality, is that there exist competing models. Different perceptions of world problems and solutions are a systematic function of different models being deployed. By recognizing and using these models we can explain the conflicting profiles of world problems and solutions. It is in this respect that we would argue that we have ordered the disorder (deploying models as the rule of coherence to create a pattern) in the analysis of world order.

While we can understand and order as pattern the conflict over world order, our third main conclusion argues that this conflict cannot be resolved.

In general terms, resolution could be achieved in either of two different ways. One of these is through amalgamation, which would require that the three models be fused into a new, all-embracing model. Such fusion, however, presupposes like elements. Since the models profile goals, structural arrangements and belief systems that for the most part are diametrically opposed, then it is inconceivable that amalgamation can take place.

Our analysis does in fact contain an interesting illustration of the very severe limits on amalgamation. The compensatory liberal model has developed to some extent as an explicit attempt to fuse liberalism and socialism. It does indeed contain some consideration of negative freedom together with some concern for equality. But this does not constitute an amalgamation of liberalism and socialism. The preoccupation with equality is different from that of the socialist, and this in turn detracts from the salience attached to negative freedom. The result is not amalgamation but a partial fusion, which even though lying more firmly in the liberal rather than socialist tradition often places the compensatory liberal at serious odds with the pure one.

The second and very different form of resolution involves rejecting two of the models. With only one model there would be no conflict. Resolution through rejection presupposes some form of comparatively valid evaluation procedure, entailing some decision rule which would stipulate which model was to be retained. We suggest that there is only one comparatively valid evaluation procedure. Before indicating it we may note some illustrations of invalid procedures.

One possibility may be thought to hinge on an investigation of which model best characterizes global problems. Such a procedure is invalid in that it violates one of the principal contentions of this study that there is no fixed agenda of global problems. Since problems are a function of goals and vary across the models as their goals differ, then there is simply no set of common problems for which we could comparatively evaluate competing explanations.

To ask which model offers the best solution is equally invalid. Solutions are premised on problem identification and explanation, and since this varies systematically from model to model then so too will solutions. Whether realists, socialists or liberals have the best solutions to security problems depends very critically on how security problems are defined, and these, as we have seen, differ substantially. Realist, liberal and socialist solutions are truly non-comparable in the sense of which are the best as they are solutions to different problems.

The only comparatively valid test procedure is to inquire whether each model is internally consistent. If it could be shown that there are inconsistencies in say the liberal belief system or in the connections between the belief system and the structural arrangement and goal, then this would seem to us to provide a major flaw in the liberal model which could lead to rejection. What is significant in the context is that the same evaluation procedure could be applied to each model. In our view, while the models profile very different goals, structural arrangements and belief systems, they all manifest extremely impressive degrees of internal coherence and consistency.

While conflict among the models cannot be resolved either through amalgamation or rejection based on any comparatively valid evaluation procedure, this does not mean that in practice resolution will not be achieved. This could happen either through conversion or imposition, where imposition is simply forceful conversion. Conversion would entail an explicit rejection of one set of values for another, which would require change of a very substantial magnitude and which could only be made on purely normative grounds. In the absence of conversion or imposition, we must continue to live in a problem-ridden world. In the relatively unlikely event of wholesale conversion or imposition, either to one of these models or to some entirely new one, then a problem-free world would be created, though this problem-free environment would endure only as long as the global consensus on the particular model was sustained.

Except in the unlikely event of global conversion, conflict over global problems and world order cannot be resolved. Our fourth and final conclusion argues that there is a relatively widespread failure to appreciate this fully.

The first of three common failings in this context is the relatively common propensity for any one model to reject others by using its own values as the criteria of evaluation. Socialists, for instance, attack liberals and realists for failing to achieve equality, or liberals criticize socialists and realists for undermining freedom. Such attacks are invalid. What in effect is happening is that a model is being evaluated from the values and perspectives of another and being accused of failing to produce outcomes to which it is not committed.

A second common failing is the propensity of each model to distort the others. At a 'theory' level, realism to the non-realist becomes the blind pursuit of national interest; liberalism to the non-liberal becomes the promotion of the interests of the haves at the expense of the have-nots; while socialism to non-socialists becomes enforced and stultifying homogenization. What is happening here is a form of caricaturing whereby a critical feature of a model is translated into pejorative terms and exaggerated. In this context we expect that readers will be more critical of our presentation of the model to which they are adherents than of the other two models. This expectation is based on the suspicion that readers will perceive that many nuances and subtleties of their own model have been ignored, but that this charge will not be levelled at the models to which they are not adherents.

At a 'practice' level this same distortion commonly leads critics of any one model to see various features of social organization as being in conformity with the dictates of other models even though this may be adamantly denied by the protagonists of the other model. Thus, to non-socialists the Soviet Union is seen to be a manifestation of socialism and consequently critiques of the Soviet Union (which to make matters worse are often, following our first failing above, made from non-socialist criteria) constitute a vindication for the rejection of the socialist model. Similarly, international intervention, especially of a military form, becomes equated with realism. Or, the current international status quo, especially in the international economic system, becomes synonymous with liberalism. That socialists have delivered strident critiques of the Soviet Union, that realists are staunch opponents of many interventions, or that liberals perceive many problems in the international economic system, commonly do not daunt protagonists of any one model in their critiques of other models.

A final common failing relates to ideology, where two principal corruptions take place. In the first instance, there is a propensity in criticizing other models to ignore the widely used definition of ideology, as sets of values and programmes for action, and to use ideology as a pejorative term indicating a distorted image based on false values without any empirical or scientific validity. Thus protagonists of any one model commonly dismiss the others as mere ideologies, implying thereby that the other models are somehow spurious. It is this type of thinking that could lead some liberals, rejoicing in the perceived victory of liberalism, to declare the 'end of ideology' and thereby the end of false and spurious views of reality. The same form of thinking again led some liberals to charge in the face of UNCTAD and similar demands that the international economic system was becoming 'politicized'. It had of course always been 'politicized' — all that was happening was that certain liberal values were being challenged.

A second corruption is the converse of this point. Even when ideology is conceptualized in a more positive manner, there is a widespread failure for advocates of any model to forget their own ideological foundations or, in the terminology of our analysis, their own belief system. These underlying beliefs are conveniently forgotten so that analysis of problems and presentation of solutions are taken as purely empirical tasks. So the liberal, though the point is equally true against others, will often forget the ideological roots of the complex of values that make up the belief system, which actually structures and give coherence to the liberal model. Liberal analysis, then, does not begin in values but in more tangible features such as graphs of supply and demand or laws and theorems of international factor movements. Identification of problems suddenly therefore appears free of values while solutions become pragmatic proposals rather than sets of prescriptions for evaluatively defined problems. What this does in effect, therefore, is to seduce protagonists of any model into endowing their model with a spurious empirical or scientific validity, which is made all the more striking in contrast to the mere 'ideology' offered by other models.

A major consequence of this failing is that inter-model debate is often of a very low calibre or more precisely is conducted from systematically biased positions. The validity of one protagonist's model is reified against a simultaneous distortion of the juxtaposed model.

Returning to the points made in our third conclusion, we would argue that the scope for constructive inter-model debate and dialogue is extremely limited. We can of course compare the models in the sense of looking simultaneously at them through common dimensions. Furthermore, we would argue that it is only through such comparative analysis that the true nature of any one model can be fully appreciated. None the less, the sophistication and internal coherence of each model, combined with their very different goals, structural arrangements and belief systems, make meaningful inter-model debate well nigh impossible. The models produce, as we have shown, very different sets of problems and solutions and in this respect engender very different views of reality. As such the models pass like ships in the night. Compromise and constructive debate can largely only be conducted within the confines and parameters of a single model.

Note

1. R. Eccleshall, 'Introduction: The World of Ideology' in R. Eccleshall *et al.*, *Political Ideologies*, London, Hutchinson & Co., 1984, p.7.

Index

(NOTE: *passim* means that the subject so annotated is referred to in scattered passages throughout these pages of text. 'f' indicates a figure. The letter 'n' indicates the reference is in the form of a note.)

ABM (antiballistic missile) agreement 197
Acheson, Dean 192
Act, Prevention of Terrorism 213
adjustment assistance 107–8
Afghanistan, 135, 145n
aid, foreign 2
aim, fundamental, of world community 40
Ajami, F. 159
Akroyd, C. 212, 213
Albrecht, U. and Kaldor, M. 219
Althusser, Louis 221
Amin, S. 139, 146n
analysis of world order 21–3
anarchical system 73
anarchic arena, 86, 87
anarchic hierarchy 74
anarchism 25
anarchist tradition 70n
Andean Common Market 161
Andean Pact 112
Anderson, P. 208, 214, 228
arms, 1, 135, 166, 175, 181, 183–4, 188, 195, 199, 217–18, 220, 250, 253, 255–6, 257
Aron, R. 80
array 10
Austria 175, 176, 254

Bahro, R. 57, 60, 61, 68n, 135, 139, 140, 145n
ballistic missile defence system (BMD) 195
Bandung 166

bank(s)
American
borrowing from 98, 162
deposits with 98
international 155
loans from 98, 155
merged with industrial capital 126
Baran, P. and Sweezy, P.M. 138, 143n, 210, 217–18
basic
constituency 45
elements of the power of the state 75
unit of pure liberalism 35–6
Basic Principles Agreement (BPA) 255
Behrman, J.N. 38
belief system 22, 41–8, 63–7, 270, 272
beliefs 82–7
Bell, D. 125
benefits
desirable 37–8
of multinational corporations 97
Bergsten, C.F. 166
Berki, R.N. 83
Berlin I. 24, 26, 27, 28, 48n, 49n, 56, 69–70n
Bernstein, E. 63
Betts, R.K. 196
bipolarity 160, 242–3
blacks 213
Bolsheviks 78 *see also* revolutions, Soviet Union
books 15–16
Bottomore, T. 69n
Brandt Report 104, 137–8, 140, 145n, 199

Brandt, Willy 202n
Brazil 227
Bressand, A. 160
Bretton Woods 91, 93, 94, 102, 109, 116n, 128, 130-1, 139, 152-3, 155, 156, 160, 162
Brezhnev Doctrine 190
Brezhnev, Leonid 255
Bright, John 176
Britain 91, 115n, 152, 213, 217, 238
British
  Cabinet 78
  colonial markets 128
  Foreign Office 78
Brown, Barratt 143n
Bull, H. 71, 78-9, 80, 81, 240-50, 254
Bunyan, T. 209, 212, 213
bureaucracy 61
Butterfield, H. 236, 241

Caldwell, L.T. 167, 228, 250, 251
Calleo, D.P. 155, 157
Callinicos, A. 221
Campaign for Nuclear Disarmament (CND) 222
CAP *see* Common Agricultural Policy
capacity to buy 28
capital 21
  accumulation 221-2
  centralization of 126
  finance 126
  fusion of 131
  international concentration on 127, 217
  and labour 57
  movement of 32-3, 93, 97, 111
  and multinationals 97, 131
  theoretic model 61
capitalism 61, 63-4, 65, 122-4, 129-30, 134-43 *passim*, 205, 208, 210-12, 217, 223, 227, 266
  analysis of 36-7, 132
  competitive 126
  European 131
  Japanese 131
  and science 68n
capitalist
  core 131

countries 143n
  foreign 128
  mode of production 61, 124
  monopoly 126
  sphere 128
  state 61, 123, 221
  world system 131, 133-4, 220
cars
  as a mechanical system 17-19
  problems with 23
Castells, M. 213
causal
  relationship 65
  regress 17, 20
centre-periphery *see* core, periphery
change
  drastic 111-12
  in exchange rates 94, 103
  external 134
  and innovation, 42, 98, 100, 225
  universal 86
Charles I, King of Spain 239
Charter of Algiers 116n
Chile 154
China 184
choice and opportnity 27
Chomsky, N. and Herman, E.S. 210
Churchill, Winston S. 237-9, 240-1
Clark, I. 2
Clausewitz, K. von 240
class
  advantages of 55
  bourgeois, 122, 124, 127, 133, 206-7
  privileged 55
  purchasing power of different 58
  rule 59
  ruling 210
  struggle, 205, 206, 220, 223
  working 136, 140, 141, 206-7, 209, 214, 218, 223, 225
Clemenceau, G. 186
clues 12-13
Cobden, Richard 175
Cockburn, C. 205
COCOM *see* Committee on Export Controls
Code of Subsidies and Countervailing Duties 108

coercion
  instruments of 73, 123, 156, 212
  liberal abhorrence of 41, 46, 52n
  protection from 30
coercive
  instrument 123
  machinery of state 72
  powers 212
collaboration 144n
collective ownership of the means of production 57, 58, 59, 61, 66
colonialism 125, 127, 213, 226
COMECON see Council for Mutual Economic Aid
Committee on Export Controls (COCOM) 109–10, 120n
Common Agricultural Policy (CAP) 102, 108, 129, 158 see also European Economic Community, Euromarket
common sense 80
communication, facilitation of 12
communism 151, 156, 166, 173, 174, 176–80, 182–5, 188–9, 192, 194, 204, 206, 241, 247, 252 see also COMECON, Soviet Union
community
  domestic 62
  liberal 45, 47
  obligations of 47
  socialist 66
  university 141
comparative advantage
  definition of 32
  as liberal principle 42, 45, 105, 110
  in the market place 37
  and the movement of capital 32–3
  realist view of 149
compensatory variant 45, 49n, see also liberalism
competition
  belief in 124
  interactions through 29–30, 43
  lack of 31
  liberal view of 44
  and multinational corporations 97
  perfect 30–1
  socialist view of 65–6

competitive growth state 110, 121n
concept
  characteristics of 12
  expansion of 28
  formation of 12
  of independence of states 76
  of order as goal attainment 21
conceptions
  of equality 56
  of harmony 53n
  liberal 31
  of national interest 85
  of order 263
  of problems and solutions 265
  socialist, of development 134
conceptualization
  of democracy 50n
  developmental 40
  of order 264, 268
  of progress 44, 47
  protective 40
  of Third World development issues 131
  of welfare 47, 48
conclusion 263–73
Conference on Security and Cooperation in Europe (CSCE) 181, 198
conflict
  between the masses and the elite 134
  between Third World States 206, 231n
  between United States and Soviet Union 218–19, 245
  capital and 127
  East–West 93, 218–19
  generation of 85
  local 216
  military 251
  overcoming 66
  social 141, 164
  violent 204, 205
conscious
  area of 140
  false 125
  raising 140
consensus, the 110
conservatism 5
Conservative 5

constitutional government 35
constitutional provision 34, 50n
consumer
  as an individual 42
  incentives for 1
  individual liberal 36
  interaction with procedures 29–30
  trends 97
containment 92–3, 174, 179, 187, 190, 192–3, 197, 200–1n, 245
contract 72
Contradora Group 112
controversey, sources of 127
convergence, process of 37
Cooper, R.N. 148
cooperation 65–6, 74, 76, 83, 108, 112, 114
core (of capitalist economy) 132–3, 138, 154, 218 *see also* periphery
Corn Laws, repeal of 91
Council for Mutual Economic Assistance (COMECON) 103–4, 106
Cox, O.C. 205
Creativity, spontaneous 44
critique
  of compensatory liberals 46, 52n
  empirical 37, 49n
  of the inequalities of capitalism 63, 65–6
  of pure liberals 116n
  socialist 145n, 218
  of Soviet Union 271
Crocker, L. 26–7, 49n
Cuban missile crisis 187, 189, 255
cultural bias 12
currency 94, 104 *see also* exchange, foreign and United States, dollars
Czechoslovakia 145n, 190, 226

Dahl, R.A. 50n
Darwin, C. 63
Davignon Steel Plan 102
Davis, M. 218, 219, 220, 226
decision-making 38, 47, 54, 60, 166
decolonization 208, 244
Dehio, L. 239
demand and supply 29
demilitarization 197
democracy
  ethos of 40
  liberal 60
  meanings of 59
  multiplicity of definitions 50n
  parliamentary 208, 244
  protective 34–5
  socialist conception of 60
  unlimited 50n, 222
dependence (of Third world countries) 132–2, 144n
De Porte, A.W. 234, 243
d'Estaing, Giscard 163
destiny, man can control his own 52n
detective story 12–13
détente 160, 181–2, 194, 255, 261n
deterrence 242–3, 250, 255, 256, 257, 268
Deutscher, T. 226
developing countries *see* North–South dichotomy, Third World
development strategy 104, 110, 112, 145n, 153
deviant regime 92
deviation *see* divergence
devices, problem-solving 265
dilemma, security 85
disarmament 197–8, 223, 236
disorder 3, 4, 8–9
  in books 15, 16
  as deviation 10
  international 89n
  NIEO demands signpost to 95
  symptoms of 18
divergence
  from the compensatory perspective 29, 106
  of emphasis 45–6
  offsetting 39
  from perfect competition 30–1
  from socialism 61, 134–5
divine right of kings 51n
doctrine
  of an international system 77
  of progress 65
  of salvation 64–5, 69–70n
  socialist 66, 69n
domination
  by alien power 144

and inequality 64, 137
  perpetuation of 56
Dominican Republic 190
Draper, T. 189
Dulles, John Foster 176
Dwokin, R. 27, 28, 49n
dynamic of reciprocal self-restraint 242
dynamism, inequality in 52n

Eastern bloc countries 103, 115, 193, 226, 252, 254
East–West confrontation 93
East–West economic relations 103–4, 109, 254
Eccleshall, R. 264–5
echo-effect 190
Eco, Umberto 13
economic
  arena, 30, 147, 168
  base 57, 65
  decisions 42
  development 98, 105, 153
  exchange 103–4
  growth 104
  inequality 55
  management, international 41
  nationalism 92
  negative 191
  order *see* New International Economic Order (NIEO)
  orthodoxy 39
  planning 36, 57
  policy 148
  power 149
  relations, world 125, 167
  system 30, 91, 92, 96–8, 100, 106, 116n, 151, 153, 158, 271, 272
  theory, liberal 44
  see also freedom, planning
economy
  command 37, 93
  free 37
  governed by plan 58
  international 115, 165
  liberal 93
  market 39
  national 97, 123, 132, 161, 267
  and popular democratization 59

private 102, 110
  of third World countries 105
  world 32, 33, 38, 94, 97, 110, 111, 152, 162, 187, 211–12, 215, 217–18, 226
  see also market
education 60, 66
efficiency, liberal view of 43, 47
egalitarianism, new 166
elections 34, 60
electoral requirements 35
employees 30, 31
energy consumption 117n
Engels, Friedrich 63, 205–6, 228n
Enlightenment, the 64
epistemology 13, 15
equality
  demand for 82
  liberal view of 28, 36, 45–6, 49n, 108
  promotion of 122
  of opportunity 67n
  socialist view of 28, 54, 55, 59, 63, 67n, 134
  sovereign 75
equilibrity 80
equilibrium 81, 240, 247
Eurobanks 118n
Eurocentric system 92, 151, 160
Eurocurrency market 108–9, 155, 162
Eurodollar 98, 117–18n
Euromarket 98, 100, 102, 103, 117n, 118n
Europe 118n, 176
European
  allies 253
  balance of power 236–43, 244, 246, 259
  currency unit (ECU) 163
  Economic Community (EEC) 101, 129, 158, 161 *see also* CAP and Euromarket
  government 254
  integration 143n
  Monetary System (EMS) 158, 163, 165
  recovery 92–3
  stability 239–40, 247
  state system 234, 236–7

280 *Index*

evolution, geological 14
exchange rate 93, 94, 97, 98, 102–3, 108, 155, 163
exploitation 135
export
  credits 37, 108
  subsidies 102
exports *see* goods
factor-endowment theory 32
factor movement 33
Fascism 173, 176
Fibonacci sequence 10, 11, 12, 268
flexible response strategy 194
forces, non-market 37
foreign
  exchange 118n
  investment 155, 161
  policy 147
  reserves 117n
'fortress neurosis' 135
framework
  conceptual 4
  constitutional 128, 198
  determinants of 148
  government 25–6
  for international economic cooperation 92
  for international order 35
  of international society 71
  liberal constitutional 91
  political 170n
Frank, T.M. and Weisband, E. 190
free
  association 62
  enterprise 110
  trade systems 91, 98, 149, 164
  world 193, 197
freedom
  capacity to buy 28
  compatibility with equality 56
  counter-extractive 49n
  defence of 245
  developmental 49n
  economic 29
  of the individual 42, 81, 85, 192
  in liberal discussion 48n, 177
  loss of 26
  negative 24–9 *passim* 30, 34, 48n, 54, 69–70n, 269
  positive 25–9, 48n, 49n, 56, 67n, 69–70n
  sense of 27
  of trade 32
  see also liberty
Freidman, M. 25, 30, 33
Friedrich, C.J. 204, 206
Fromkin, D. 73, 83

Galbraith, J.K. 36–7, 49n, 51n
Galileo 15
Galtung, J. 145n, 255
Garrett, J.M. 255
GATT *see* General Agreement on Trade and Tariffs
General Agreement on Trade and Tariffs (GATT) 91, 92, 98–9, 101, 107, 108–9, 111, 153, 164
Generalized System of Preferences 106, 166
German Democratic Party 69n
German monetary authorities 115n
Germany 3, 246
Gilpin, R. 147, 148, 151, 168–9
global
  definition of 6n
  economic problems and solutions 91–171, 191
  position of the United States 194
  problems 1, 4, 5, 263
  security problems and solutions 172–262
  solutions 1
globalism 244–6, 251
goal
  affinity in 24
  of armament 183
  compensatory liberal 49n
  discussion of 70n, 264–5
  of equality 57
  of the group 263
  incompatibility 19
  liberal 94
  modification of 21
  of negative freedom 36
  organizing 24
  -orientation 4, 15

political 157
pursuit of 22
of realism 71, 74
satisfaction 15–21, 268
of socialist model 54–7, 122
specification 17, 18
terms of 4, 16, 44
gold 93–4, 102, 115n, 156, 170n
goods
export of 32, 110, 111, 120n
import of 32, 96
range of 58, 105
trade in 37
government
constitutional 33, 35, 42
duties of 33, 38–9, 73, 150, 172, 185
'housekeeping' function of 33, 39
intercourse between 175
intervention 102, 110, 158, 162
legitimacy of 73
liberal view of 40
policies 39, 154, 173
power, limits to 25, 33–4, 50n
representative 47
as a state attribute 74
unrestrained 50n
Gramsci, A. 123, 212, 224
Gray, C.S. 181, 184
Greece 83
Green, P. 45
Gross National Product (GNP) 123, 148
Group of 77, 116n
growth 44, 47, 124
guerrilla warfare 226–7
Guevara, Ernesto 'Che' 227

Halliday, F. 219
Halperin, M.H. 256–7
Hampshire, S. 69n
Handlin, O. 181, 185
Haq, M. U1, 112, 113, 121n
Haq, Thusul 104
Hardie, Kier 207
Hayek, F.A. 24–5, 26, 29–30, 31, 34, 35, 48–9n, 50n, 52n
Hayter, T. 137
Heckscher, A. 32
hegemony

American 127–9 *passim*, 130–1, 153, 155, 160–1, 208, 217
development of 139
repression of 61
state 80, 100, 123–4, 212, 236, 252
Helsinki, Conference on Security and Cooperation in Europe (CSCE) 254
Herz, J.H. 83, 236, 240
Hilferding, R. 63, 126
Hill, Cordell 186
Hinsley, F.H. 74, 204, 242, 260n
Hinton, J. 223–4
Hirsch, F. 107
historical materialism 64–5
Hitler, Adolf 3
Hobbes, Thomas 71
Hobhouse, L.T. 45, 52n, 53n, 185
Hoffmann, S. 165, 168n
Hofstadter, R. 186
Howard, M. 253
human
behaviour *see* social behaviour
interaction 64
interference, absence of 24
intervention 15, 16, 48n
organizations 64
Hunter, R.E. 149, 158
Huntington, S.P. 173, 192, 196, 222
hypothesis 11
hypothesis-generation 11, 13

IDA *see* International Development Association
idealist 84
ideological struggle 190
ideologies 4–5, 124–5, 151, 173–4, 176, 265, 271–2 *see also* idealist, liberalism, Marxism, pluralism, realism, socialism
IBRD *see* International Bank for Reconstruction and Development
ideological foreign policy 90n
IFC *see* International Finance Corporation
IMF *see* International Monetary Fund
illiberal regimes 176
imperialism 63, 82, 122, 125, 126, 128,

imperialism (*continued*)
    130, 133, 138, 141, 142n, 144n, 211, 217, 218, 220
imports *see* goods
income, 38, 59, 62, 95
incrementalism 145n
independence
    of practices 123
    promotion of 128
    of states 71, 73–4, 76, 78, 79, 81
Independent Commission on Disarmament and Security Issues 202n *see also* Palme Report
individual
    commitment to the 41–2, 53n
    conceptualization of 45, 199
    freedom of 57
    initiative 43
    socialism and 66
    and society 52n
    spontaneous creativity of 44
industrialization 92, 132
inequality
    attacking 56
    between core and periphery 132
    eradication of 267
    freezing of 46
    growing 104
    liberal view of 43, 46
    promotion of 54
    realist view of 150
    socialist view of 64, 122
inflation 94, 96, 155–6
information sources 60
innovation 42, 43, 46
institutions 64, 71, 77, 84, 153, 192, 205
instrumentalism 123, 143n
intelligence tests 11–12
interdependence of economies 132, 167, 192, 200n
interest(s)
    accommodation of 150
    common 87, 112
    conflict of 124
    core 85, 89n
    identifying 86
    peripheral 85, 89n
    rates 20, 21, 120n

inter-governmental organizations 100
inter-imperialist competition 131
inter-model debate 272–3
international
    arena 74, 75, 84, 85, 176, 208
    banking market 98
    definitions 6n, 200n
    economic intercourse 97, 149
    economic relations 149
    government agencies 41
    institutions 86
    monetary system 93, 94, 100, 102, 103, 161
    opposition 85–6
    order 149
    power hierarchy 86
    relations 1–2, 5, 62, 175, 206, 235, 241
    society 74, 77–8, 83, 87
    system 87, 157, 206, 210, 236
    welfare system 113, 114
International
    Bank for Reconstruction and Development (IBRD) 91, 92, 93, 98, 99, 118n, 129, 153, 162
    Central Bank 109, 113
    Development Association (IDA) 99–101, 118n
    Development Fund (IDF) 113
    Energy Agency (IEA) 163
    Finance Corporation (IFC) 99–101, 118n
    Monetary Fund (IMF) 91–5 *passim*, 98, 99, 109, 113, 118n, 119n, 129, 153, 162, 166, 170n
    Second 229
    Trade Organization 113
interventionist programme 106, 253
investment
    attracting 43, 46
    finance 91
    funds 97
    private 99, 100
    sphere of 126
    world 130
invisible hand
    analogy 30, 31, 160
    management system 38, 39

'Iron Curtain' 238
isolationism 152, 173, 216
issues 22

Japan 100, 153, 158, 161, 193
Jaurès, Jean 207
Jay, P. 166
Jessop, B. 124
Jews, extermination of 3
Johnson Doctrine 190
Johnson, H.G. 101, 102, 117n, 121n
Jones, Ernest 206

Kaldor, M.H. 227
Kautsky, K. 207-8, 221, 224
Kennan, G. 74, 178, 200n, 246-7, 251
Kennedy, John F. 98
Kennedy, Robert 187
Kennedy Round (of negotiations) 98
Keynes, J.M. 39, 109
Keynesian conception 39
Keynesian revolution 39
Kirkpatrick, J.J. 195-6
Kissinger, Henry 219, 235, 253, 261n
Kleinen, J. 228
knowledge
  acceptable 15
  definition of 13
  of individuals 31
  poorer 21
Kolko, G. 187
Krauss, M.B. 110, 119n
Kremlin 177-80

labour
  and capitalism 154
  division of 42, 45, 58, 60, 99, 110, 132
  'does not move' 37
  force 133
  free movement of 33
Laclau, E. and Mouffee, C. 224
Lasch, Christopher 221
Laski, H.J. 72
Latin America 227
laws
  definition of term 14
  of development 75

domestic 77
  enforcement of 26
  international 76-7, 81
  of nations 81
  of value 58
lawyers 87n
LDCs (Less Developed Countries) 110-11
League of Nations 186-7
legislation 50n
legitimacy 139, 166, 197, 222, 225
Legvold, R. 253
Lend-Lease Agreement 128 *see also* Marshall Plan
Lenin, V.I. 63, 125, 126-7, 140, 211
liberalism 5, 24-53
  compensatory 24, 27-9. 36-41, 44-8, 52n, 54, 65, 102, 103-14 *passim*, 119n, 145n, 172, 174, 269
  compensatory, statement of 52n
  evolution of 41-8
  and government 50n, 192
  and international security 172
  parallel with socialism 204
  pure 24, 28, 29-36 *passim*, 37, 40, 43, 45-8, 52n, 68n, 101, 103-14, *passim*, 120n, 145n, 172, 174-5, 265, 269
  six corollaries of 46
  variants of 28, 29
liberal(s) 5, 24-53, 56, 136, 170n
  construction 76
  economic international problems and solutions 91-121
  international security problems and solutions 172-203
  literature 267
  model 22, 24-53
  origination of term 41
  orthodoxy 45
  programme 121n
  and socialist thought 222
  world order 192
  writers 51n
liberty 26
  government's duty towards 33, 192
  as independence 27
  negative 50n
  positive 56, 70n

284 *Index*

liberty (*continued*)
  see also freedom
Lichtheim, G. 204–5
Liebknecht, K. 63
Lippmann, Walter 241, 243, 244–5, 247, 259n
literature, academic 1, 2
living, standard of 105, 126
Lloyd George, D. 186
Locke, John 41, 51n
Lomé Convention 102, 106
Luxemburg, R. 63

MacCallum, G. 49n
Machlup, F. 26, 27
Machiavelli 82–3, 87, 147
McKenna Duties 115
Macpherson, C.B. 34–5, 40, 49n, 59
Malmgren, H.B. 102
management
  consultancy 20
  device 39
  economic 161, 231n
  of international economic system 114, 167
  non-intrusive 107
  system 115, 153
Mandel, E. 124, 131, 135, 139, 207, 214, 217, 223, 225, 228
market
  access to 157
  appeal of to liberals 42
  COMECON 103
  compensatory liberal view of 36
  convertibility 94
  credit 98
  disruption of 96
  divided 130
  domestic 110
  economy 39
  expansion of 18–19
  forces 46
  free 29–32, 35, 37, 38, 42–3, 47, 105, 114
  international 33, 102, 127, 161
  intervention 65
  labour 132
  mixed 36–7
  place 97, 102
  open 93
  reliance on 113
  share 19
  spontaneity of 52n
  transformation of 49n
  unrestrained 38
  vagaries of 58
  world 35, 37, 106, 110, 111 *see also* economy, world
  see also Euromarket
Markovic, M. 204, 209–10
Marshall Plan 92, 128, 129, 153
Marx, Karl 56–7, 63–4, 69n, 122, 125, 138, 143n, 147, 204, 205–6, 228n
Marxism 127, 140
Marxist 63–5, 69n, 124, 139, 140, 146n, 181, 219, 238
Meany, G. 181
mechanism(s)
  effective 107, 219
  of emancipation 140
  ideological 215
  market as a 38, 104, 108
  price 29
  primitive 79
  of progressive taxation 40
  realist 75
  of reciprocity 76
  trade-diverting 101
  transmission 133
  of war 228n
  see also containment
Medvedev, Roy 225, 226
Meinecke, F. 72
mercantilism, new 101, 102, 103, 107, 118n, 131–2, 142n, 147, 152, 158, 164, 265
mercantilist imperialism 133
meritocratic
  inequality 65
  principles 46
  pusuit 56
Merleau-Ponty, M. 209
Milibrand, R. 122
military
  expenditure 191
  intervention 189–90

security 191, 252
technology 174
Mill, John Stuart 45, 176
Milton, John 41
minimalist 42
MNCs *see* multinational corporations
models
  capital theoretic 61
  of the centre and periphery 134, 144–5n
  competitive state 111
  dimensions of 22, 263–73
  free market 36
  Pact 255
  Soviet 93
  transnational class 209, 211
  of world order 4–6, 24–90 *passim*, 136, 265–7; conservative 5; liberal 5, 24–53 *passim*; realist 5, 71–90 *passim*, 265; socialist 5, 54–70 *passim*, 124, 138
monetary system, regional 163
monopoly(ies)
  capital 266
  of capitalism 125, 129
  control 113
  desirability of 49n
  on instruments of coercion 73
  and lack of competition 31
  local 97
  nuclear 174
  of power 74
  state 142n
monopolists 130
Montague, R. 45
Morgenthau, H.J. 75, 238–42 *passim*, 244, 247–9, 253
Morse, E.L. 115
Moscow 183, 194, 252
multilateral
  approach 62, 129
  foundation 131
  monopoly imperialism 127
  negotiations 107
multilateralism 127, 130, 131
multinational corporations
  activity of 97–8, 100
  dominate international production 37
  growth of 97, 117n, 130, 161

  problems caused by 154, 162, 266
  transfer of technology by 111
multipolarity 160
Muslow, B. 228
myths of perfect competition 30

nationalism 66
national boundaries 98
national interest 150, 151, 156
nationalization 156 *see also* collective ownership of the means of production
NATO *see* North Atlantic Treaty Organization
nation state 41, 45, 48, 62, 67, 68n, 72, 74, 75, 77, 84, 106, 154 *see also* state
nature, state of 71, 79, 82
New International Economic Order (NIEO) 90n, 94–6, 101, 113, 116n, 117n, 134, 159, 268–9
Niebuhr, R 81
NIEO *see* New International Economic Order
Nixon, R. 213, 153, 255
nomothetic
  concept 6, 9
  contents 122
  definition 10
Non-Aligned Movement 95, 112, 116n, 159
non-intervention 75, 252–3
non-tariff barriers (NTBs) 99, 101, 102, 108
norms 75, 135, 236
normative attack/choice 37–8
North–South dichotomy 95, 104, 106, 111, 119–20, 143–4n, 155 *see also* Third World
North Atlantic Treaty Organization (NATO) 93, 128, 129, 180–1, 193, 245, 246–9, 250, 253, 254–5
Northedge, F.S. 71, 73
Northern Ireland 212–13
NSC68 177–8, 180
NTBs *see* non-tariff barriers
nuclear weapons 1, 180, 187, 203n, 223, 240, 242, 247–8, 249–50, 256
OECD (Organization for Economic

OECD (*continued*)
   Cooperation and Development) 104, 106, 107, 110, 114, 115, 117n, 158, 160, 164–6
Ohlin, B. 32
oil 95, 96, 117n, 155, 156–7, 163, 170n *see also* Organization of Petroleum Exporting Countries
oligopolies 31, 49n
'Open Door' policy 129
OPEC *see* Organization of Petroleum Exporting Countries
Oppenheim, H. 80–1
Oppenheimer, M. 221
order
   conceptualization of 8–23
   as goal satisfaction 15–21
   international 35
   as pattern 10–15
   world 1–3, 6n, 21–3, 263–73
organization
   ethnocentric 97
   geocentric 97
   global 87
Organization
   for African Unity 199
   of Petroleum Exporting Countries (OPEC) 95, 96–7, 117n, 156, 157, 163 169n
Osgood, C.E. 256, 257
Osgood, R.E. 235

Paine, Tom 173, 175
Palme Report 188, 190, 198
Parkin, F. 55, 58–9
Parekh, B. 174–5
Paris club 162
Paris commune 206
Partial Test Ban 255
patern(s) 10–15, 21, 268 *see also* trade
Pax Americana 152, 153, 157, 168
payments
   balance of 91
   deficit 93
   system of post-war trade and 115n
Payne, K.B. 182
peace 205, 210, 223–4, 236
Pentagon, the 251

periphery (of the capitalist economy) 132–3, 138–9, 146n, 154, 211, 216, 218, 245, 254 *see also* core
perspective
   American 256
   divergence from 29
   goal 16
   liberal 98, 151, 175, 188
   realist 77, 148
   socialist 219, 221, 228
   Soviet 256
petro-dollars 96
petrol, consumption in cars 17–19
planning
   by central government 32, 42–3
   for change 31
   ethic of 60
   'new' 51n
   role of 58
   techniques 104
   theoretical 250
pluralism
   and diffusion of power 100, 106
   in liberalism 44, 55, 58, 70n, 114
Podhoretz, N. 181
police 213
policy making 155
politicians 8
politics, power 73
political
   arena 38
   and economic arrangement 29
   liberty 24
   organization 84–5
   system 33, 55, 75, 148
   theory 49n
   transformation 148
popular democratization 59–60
population 74, 84, 190, 225
power
   American 130, 158
   balance of 54, 75, 78–82 *passim*, 88n, 89n, 148, 176–8, 201n, 234, 236, 238–9, 253, 258
   capabilities 88n
   coercive 31
   commodity 95
   division of 34

exercise of 168n
Great 81
hierarchy 74, 150, 167, 251
industrial 92
political 34, 84, 126
socialist 215
of the state 26, 61, 71–2, 134, 216–7
structure 100, 159
Prague 135, 145n
price
changes 163–4
control of 37, 110
fixing 31
food 113
mechanism 29–30
reduction in 44
rises, effects of 96, 117n
setting of 31
problem(s)
explication of 267
global security 172–91
international 91–107, 122–36
in realism 147–61
security 204–20, 234–51
in social systems 19–20, 136
solving 20–1, 266
and solutions 273
source of 20
producer(s)
alienation of 57
and central authority 60
incentives for 31
as an individual 42
individual liberal 36
interaction with consumers 29–30
overseas 102
production
alternative 31
food 110
improved 44
increased 96
international apparatus of 128
and market demand 43
plan 112, 136
sectors 140
specialist 32, 130
see also systems
profit-making 18

programmes, stabilization 118n
progress, liberal view of 44, 47
proletariat 214, 216, 217, 220, 222
protectionism, new 101, 102, 107, 108, 164

raison d'état, 73, 205
realism 5, 82, 147, 150, 152, 156, 234, 271
radicalism 140, 141, 145n, 222
realist(s) 54, 56, 62, 68n, 136, 145n, 172–3, 190, 234–62 *passim*, 267, 271
international economic problems and solutions 147–71
model 22, 71–90
Rapid Deployment Force 164
reciprocity 75–8, 81–2, 98, 150, 163, 164, 169n, 236, 244, 251
Realpolitik 82–7 *passim*, 147
recognition as a state attribute 74
reconstruction, post-war 127, 129
redivision 129
reformist 224
reforms 111–12, 137, 232
relative autonomy 123
reflections on world order 263–73
Renaissance, the 64
repression 213–14, 221–2
reserves, foreign 102
resources 31
allocation of 43, 108
distribution of 50n
economic 152
productive 47
protection of national 157
security 249
world 98
restrictionism 108
revisionist movement 63
Revolution
Bolshevik (Russian) 63, 92, 158, 208, 214
commitment to world 67, 70n
French 63
Industrial 63
proletarian 140
and reform 220
socialist 69n, 139, 141
world 226

Ricardo, D. 32, 91
right(s)
  to equal treatment 28
  to self-realization 57
  to treatment as an equal 28
  universal 66
Romans 83
Roosevelt, F.D. 151, 186
Rousseau, H. 63
Ruggie, J.G. 155
rule
  of diplomatic immunity 76–7
  GATT 101
  half-the-square 10–11
  of law 111
  of the liberal system 114
  methodological 15
  negative 25
  or order in patterns 11, 12
  shaping of 86

SALT *see* Strategic Arms Limitation Talks
Sanchez, N.O. 185
Sayre, Francis 237
Schelling, T.C. 148
Schuman, F.L. 79
Schurmann, F. 205
Schmidt, Helmut 109, 165
Schwarzenberger, G. 76–7
scientific
  inquiry 13–14
  knowledge 13
  method 13
scientists, natural 3–4, 6n, 7n *see also* social scientists
SDRs (Special Drawing Rights) 109, 113
security
  cover 129
  definition of 199
  dilemma 85, 89n, 235f, 236
  international 172, 234–62 *passim*
  national 86, 193, 215
  personal 216–17
  policy 148, 174, 188, 234
  problems 5, 6, 185, 204–33 *passim*, 270
  provision 31, 195
  relative 235

rationale 103
self-reliance among developing countries 112
semiology 13
Senghaas, D. 216
services, range of 58
Schonfield, A. 36, 39, 51n
Shulman, Marshall 249
Siberian Gas Pipeline 109
Sidney, Sir Philip 41
Simes, D.K. 194
Smith, Adam 30, 91, 147
Smith, D. and Smith R. 217
social
  behaviour 4, 15, 21, 263
  group 56
  life 54, 56, 60
  order 4, 8, 16, 124
  organization 54–5, 61, 66, 72
  preconditions 124
  privilege 81
  sciences 3
  systems 16, 18, 22, 177
Social Democrats 55, 105, 207
social scientists 4, 88n, 263
socialism, 5, 24
  achievement of 224
  global 138, 139
  humanistic 38
  opposition 129
  parliamentary 229
  problem 190
  promotion of 64–5, 68n, 69–70n, 122, 137, 141
  and social order 56
  true 134
  variants of 28
socialist(s) 5
  economy 58, 269
  ethics 63, 64
  international economic problems and solutions 122–46
  and international issues 68n, 265
  international security problems and solutions 204–33
  model 22, 54–70
  parties in Third World countries 93
  tradition 63

view of free market 36
writings 67n, 69n, 206
socialization of the means of production *see* collective ownership of the means of production
society
  absorbed by the state 61
  bourgeois 140
  civil 123
  closed 205
  democratic 40
  egalitarian 212
  forms of 35, 205
  and the individual 42, 209
  international 72, 74, 76, 80, 251, 256
  limits to freedom 56
  open 25, 52n
  organization 141
  of sovereign states 71, 74
  structure of 5, 27, 56
  views of 52n
socio-economic
  preconditions 55
  structures 223
Solo, R.A. 39, 50n
solutions 13, 18, 21, 22, 107–15, 128, 136–41, 161–71, 192–9, 220–8, 251–8, 263, 270
Sonnenfeldt, H. 193
sovereignty
  consumer 37
  discussion of 87n
  economic 150
  external 73
  has no place in constitutional government 34, 49n
  internal 73, 74
  and international security 71–2
  popular 35, 40, 50n
  state 74, 149, 157, 266–7
  threats to 148
Soviet Union
  bureaucracy 228
  command economy of 96
  'crimes' of 145n
  defence programme 181
  development of socialism in 139
  and Eastern Europe 237–8
  economic isolation of 103
  economy 119n
  establishment of 208
  and Euromarket 118n
  exclusion from Western Europe 93
  foreign policy of 152, 177–9
  imperialism 134–5, 247
  military performance of 92, 174, 188–9, 250
  planning and control in 37
  repression of 214, 225
  after Second World War 92
  and security policy 160
  socialist critique of 61–2
  and the United States 74–5, 128, 143n, 166–7, 182, 237, 241–2, 251–8
soviet aid 93
Soviet bloc *see* Eastern bloc
Spanier, J.W. and Nogee, J.L. 183, 195
speculation in money market 94
sphere of influence 243, 259n, 260n
Stalin, J. 92, 208, 214, 237
START talks 262n
state
  apparatus 226
  as an autonomous entity 209
  authority of 74
  bourgeois 139, 209
  capitalist 210
  city 82
  development 126, 141
  and imperialism 122
  increased management role of 167–8
  insecurity of 251
  intervention, argument for increase in 45
  legitimacy of 74, 223
  militarized 216
  and multinationals 130
  and nation 89n
  organization of 150
  policies 86
  power base of 73
  'proto-socialist' 208, 211, 216, 230n
  role of 123, 205
  socialist 230
  society of 149
  sovereign 71

state (continued)
  system 176, 236
  theory of
  trading boards 110
  world 85
Steel, R. 151, 157, 158, 159, 166, 245, 247
Strategic Arms Limitation Talks (SALT) 184, 197, 255, 257
Strategic Defence Initiative 261n
strategic studies 204
strategy 194, 216, 221
stratification 61, 68n, 134
Strausz-Hupé, R. 174, 180, 193
strikes 207
structural
  arrangement 22, 26, 29–41, 42, 57–63, 65, 74–82, 134, 136, 145n, 159, 264, 266–7, 270
  change 65, 106, 139
  influence 133
  organizations 122
  violence 209–10
Superpower 1, 3, 135, 151, 160, 166, 188, 196, 242–3, 244, 253, 255, 256
superstructure 65, 140
supra-imperialism 131
surplus value 125
symbiotic relation 29, 126
systems
  authority 61
  belief 22, 41–8
  decentralized 163
  Eurocentric 92, 151, 160
  governmental 34
  incentive 43
  international 157, 252
  international monetary arangement 93
  liberal 54, 98, 153
  mechanical 16–18, 19–21
  of mutual deterrence 194
  open 158
  power 72
  problem-solving 100
  production 37
  social 16, 19–20, 21, 65
  socialist 57
  of states 76

  two-track 160
  world financial 109

Taber, R. 226–7
Tawney, R.H. 67n
tariff 102, 267
tariff reductions 98–9
tax
  liberal view of 46–7, 199
  on rich countries 113
Taylor, General Maxwell 194
Taylor, R., and Pritchard, C. 222
technical rationalism 124
technocrat 129
technology
  advances in 241
  importance of 36
  impact of 51n, 119n, 212
technostructure 36, 51n
tendency, universalizing, of liberalism 44, 45
territory as a state of attribute 74
terrorism 210
Thatcherism 223
theories
  as combination of patterns 14
  of evolution of human society 63
  factor-endowment 32
  plate 14
  power-political 79
  of the state 61
Tinbergen, J. 38, 40
Third World
  countries 137, 139, 153, 159, 166, 184, 211, 215–16, 218, 226, 253
  dependence on capitalism 132–3, 143n
  development 104–5, 106, 110, 111, 112, 116n, 131, 268
  East–West confrontation in 93
  equality 267
  imperialism 219
  liberal view of 114, 120n
  loans to 155, 162
  markets 110
  militarism 216
  neo-colonial states in 129
  political organization in 95
  security in 244, 252

socialist revolution in 69n
Soviet influence in 246
terminology 119n
Thompson, K.W. 77
Tokyo Round (of negotiations) 98–9, 108
totalitarianism 244
Touraine, A. 140
trade
  agreements, preferential 108
  arms 219, 222
  barriers to 127 see also tariffs
  COMECON 103–4
  embargoes on 119n
  exchange 156
  foreign 155
  free flow of 93, 186
  growth in 97, 119n
  importance of 148
  international 119n
  non-tariff 107
  North–South 111
  patterns of 32
  payments on 103
  prediction of 37
  preventives for restrictions to 91
  realist view of 164
  strategy 167
  vulnerabilities 163
  wars 91, 115n
  world 132
transnational corporations see multinational corporations
transport as a goal 17, 18
Treaty of Westphalia 236
Triffin, R. 99, 165, 170n
Trojan Horse strategy 167
Trotsky, L. 207–8, 228
Truman, H.S. 151, 244
Tucker, R. 79, 159, 164–5, 170n
Tyler, G. 169n

ultra-imperialism 131
unemployment 39
United Nations (UN)
  Charter 198–9
  Economic and Social Council Resolution of 157
  needs restructuring 113
  role of 198
  Secretary-General of 96, 117n
UNCTAD (United Nations Commission for Trade and Development) 95, 116n, 159, 272
United States
  and Britain 237–9
  capital 128
  constitution of 50n
  corporate interests of 222–3
  diplomacy 157
  dollars 93–4, 98, 102, 109, 115–16n, 118n, 153, 156, 161–2, 165, 170n
  foreign policy 190, 247
  government 143n, 151
  and imperialism 217
  isolationism of 173
  military policy of 160, 174, 189, 219–20, 248, 251
  multinational corportions 130
  planning and control in 37
  Policy Planning Staff 178
  power of 152–3, 15
  primus inter pares role for 114
  public sector in 100
  role of 158
  Secretary for Defense 119n
  and the Soviet Union 74–5, 135, 166–7, 182, 237, 241–2, 251–8
  tariff barriers 91
  Trade Expansion Act 98
  Treasury 109
  and Vietnam War 94
  and Western Europe 92, 127 see also lend-lease, Marshall Plan
Universal Postal Union 77
universalizing doctrine 47
Urry, J. 123, 142
use value 58

Valenta, J. 254
Versailles Peace Conference 237
vertical
  escalation 194
  integration 31
violence as disorder 8, 9
Voltaire (François Marie Arouet) 63

wage
  labour 62
  rates 43, 46
War
  Cold 151–2, 167, 169n, 185, 187, 208, 218–20 *passim*, 226, 232n
  fear of 183
  First World 84, 91, 127, 128, 152, 186, 187, 204, 207, 209, 237, 245
  Hobbesian 95
  as instrument of universal destruction 240
  nuclear 187–95 *passim*, 250
  prevention of 255
  Second World 84, 91, 92, 93, 100, 127, 128, 135, 173, 174, 178, 181, 184, 187, 189, 208, 209, 211, 217, 220, 234, 237, 243, 244
  Thirty Years' 236
  Vietnam 94, 156, 189, 219
  world without 85
Watson, A. 71, 76
welfare
  community 44
  domestic 148
  imperialism 152
  liberal view of 47, 52n
  orientation 108
  provision 39–40
  state 69n, 102, 111, 117n, 119n
Western Europe
  economic recovery in 100
  economic relations of 169n
  exclusion of Soviet Union from 93, 181
  and former colonies 184
  reconstruction of 92, 96, 127–8
  security 248–9
  and the United States 128
West–South relations 104
White, G. 216
Whitman, M.N. 157
Williams, R. 218
Wilson, Woodrow, 186, 187, 237
Wolfe, A. 220
work-force 21
World Bank 99, 100, 109, 113, 118n, 137, 166, 268–9
World Development Authority 113
World Economic Conference 115n
World, First 211, 213–4, 218, 221, 224
World Food Organization (WFO) 113
world order 1–3
  concept of 3
  definition of 6n
  government 89n
World, Second 211, 214–15, 218, 224, 226
Wright, Professor Quincy 241

Yankee Trader strategy 167

Zagoria, D. 252–3
zero-sum
  redistribution method 105
  terms 87
Zysman, J. and Cohen, S.S. 161, 162